Community Development in Perspective

Community Development in Perspective

EDITED BY

JAMES A. CHRISTENSON & JERRY W. ROBINSON, JR.

 Iowa State University Press / Ames

James A. Christenson is professor and chair of the Department of Sociology at the University of Kentucky.

Jerry W. Robinson is professor of sociology and rural sociology at the University of Illinois, Urbana-Champaign.

©1989 Iowa State University Press, Ames, Iowa   50010

Composed by Iowa State University Press
Printed in the United States of America

First edition, 1989

Library of Congress Cataloging-in-Publication Data

Community development in perspective / edited by James A. Christenson & Jerry W. Robinson, Jr. –
    1st ed.
        p.   cm.
    Includes index.
    ISBN 0–8138–1474–X
    ISBN 0–8138–1473–1 (pbk.)
    1. Community development.   I. Christenson, James A., 1944-   .   II. Robinson, Jerry
W., 1932-
HN49.C6C644   1989
307.1′4–dc19   88–37954
                                                                                CIP

Dedicated to

| Patricia Lyle
Christenson | Barbara Jean
Robinson |

We cannot tell the precise moment when friendship is formed.
As in filling a vessel drop by drop, there is a last drop
which makes it run over; so in a series of kindnesses there
is at last one which makes the heart run over.

—SAMUEL JOHNSON
Boswell's Life of Johnson

Contents

Preface

THE practice of community development is an art, grounded in experience, guided by theory, honed by research, and dispensed with normative implications. Community development is profound and simple, difficult to define but clearly recognizable, a moral mandate and a social responsibility. Community development has been and will continue to be a major means of problem solving. The idea of community focuses on people and their opportunity for proactive or reactive approaches to changing conditions throughout the world and in their own backyards. The idea of development implies improvement, growth, and change. However, change which improves the lot for some does not necessarily improve the lot for all. Change is not neutral. And people approach change depending on their place in the social structure, their access to resources, and their organizational skills.

Nearly ten years ago we published a book to address some of these ideas. Because community development is both interdisciplinary and not tied to a single theoretical paradigm, we invited some of the best scholars from a wide range of perspectives in the Community Development Society of America to write chapters for the book *Community Development in America*. The discussion in the book was limited to domestic efforts in community development. The book met with considerable success, went through several printings, and served as a text for a wide range of classes both in America and throughout the world. But, the world has changed dramatically in the last decade. Community development today is not the same as it was ten years ago. We now live in a global society and we need global perspectives. Yet, most change that directly affects an individual occurs in one's locality or place. Thus, we need global perspectives that relate to place.

The world economic system has changed considerably during the last decade. Communities and neighborhoods are more closely tied to state, national, and world conditions. As a result, community development cannot be effectively viewed from a national perspective. Over the past ten years there have been major changes in community development efforts and in the profession itself. In contrast to the high expectation for community development in the 1970s, there was a dismantling of programs, resources, and support for community development in the United States in the 1980s. In the international arena, this dismantling had begun a decade earlier. However, the increased evidence of deteriorating conditions in the inner cities, in the rural hinterland of America, and in countries throughout the world has stimulated a resurgence of interest and reconsideration of community development efforts. Initiatives from national and state governments and resources from private and public sources are becoming available. In the 1990s we forsee a rebirth, a revitalization of community development throughout the world. Therefore, this book attempts to stimulate the reader to reconsider his or her perceptions of community development and to inform him or her of the relevance of community development for today's problems.

Overview.   This book begins with a discussion of the major concepts that surround community development and then provides a working definition of community development, describes the relevance of community to the changing conditions in the world today, charts the ebb and flow of the community development profession, and finally speculates on the future of community development in the 1990s. The second chapter provides a content analysis of the literature that has been published on community development over the last two decades. It highlights some guiding themes (self-help, technical assistance, and conflict), major research issues (needs assessment, community growth, services, and evaluation), professional roles (teaching, training, and evaluating), and related issues that are apparent in the *Journal of the Community Development Society.*

     The next three chapters critique three specific approaches to community development. In Chapter 3, Littrell and Hobbs review the most commonly espoused theme of community development: nondirective or self-help. They discuss how self-help can be a viable mode of intervention to improve people's situations. They also point out the difficulty of achieving significant change using this approach in today's complex world. This chapter focuses on the importance of people learning the process of helping themselves. In Chapter 4, Fear, Gamm, and Fisher describe how the technical intervention approach to community development has evolved into major governmental intervention programs. For many years, federal government and university programs have provided technical assistance to community groups, cities, and towns in the form of grants, education, and information to improve the quality of life in neighborhoods and communities. The role of government in community development has far-reaching implications for the future of the profession, as discussed later by Voth and Brewster in the chapter on international community development. Fear, Gamm, and Fisher raise the question of whether directed task development is community development, whether technical assistance without public involvement enhances capacity building. In Chapter 5 on the conflict approach, Robinson indicates that the self-help approach to community development may be irrelevant to those groups without adequate resources. He argues that people outside the political process, particularly the poor and minority groups, have little influence on the direction of self-help or technical assistance programs and derive few benefits from them. As a result, they must resort to confrontation. Meaningful change cannot be achieved without the redistribution of some benefits and resources. And redistribution is not likely to occur without conflict. Techniques and tactics for using, preventing, and managing community conflict are discussed.

Roles for professionals and practitioners, techniques and tactics for the practice of community development, and concepts for the teaching of community development make up the next part of the book. In Chapter 6, Warner presents a framework for interpreting the work and roles of community development professionals, including their traits, their tasks, and their relationships to clientele as well as the institutional settings in which they carry out their roles. In the next chapter (Chapter 7) Fischer provides a wealth of practical examples and ideas for putting community development into practice. These how-to-do-it hints provide experiential insights for practical application. In Chapter 8, Cary outlines some fundamental concepts that should be taught in a community development curriculum. By building on a historical analysis of the evolution of institutional programs and curricula, he provides a framework for training practitioners.

In Chapters 9, 10, and 11, economic and social research implications for community development are presented and implications for evaluation are discussed. Shaffer and Summers (Chapter 9) present economic models for development, an assessment of what is known about a variety of strategies to stimulate economic development, some dead ends, and some future strategies for small towns, cities, neighborhoods, and urban areas. Creativity, marketing, entrepreneurship, and an understanding of the world economy are key ingredients for success. Garkovich (Chapter 10) looks at some of the social implications of community development from an organizational and leadership perspective. The future success of community development may well lie with the ability to identify, train, and nurture indigenous leaders. Voth (Chapter 11) discusses the difficult problem of evaluating community development efforts. He concludes that community development work often is done in a process framework, helping people to achieve community improvement through their own efforts. Such process efforts are difficult to evaluate. Some suggestions for evaluating both process and task achievements in community development programs are provided.

The next two chapters present perspectives on the history of community development, one focusing on America and the other on international community development. Phifer, List, and Faulkner (Chapter 12) describe the rise of community development in America as the logical outgrowth of the founding fathers' view of participatory democracy. They emphasize the self-help philosophy behind early community development efforts and behind the development of academic departments in the United States and Canada. Voth and Brewster (Chapter 13), on the other hand, point out some of the disappointments of international efforts because people-oriented programs originated as or became government programs and were perceived as mechanisms of control rather than processes for improving social and economic environments. Community development programs were initially successful because they were able to harness excess labor available in most underdeveloped countries. But the expectations were high and the results were slow to evolve, particularly in economic terms. Helping people to help themselves also created situations where people challenged governments. The authors talk about the opportunities for community development today and what can be learned from past efforts.

The final two chapters focus on the future of the community development enterprise. The authors present two quite different views. Blakely (Chapter 14) assumes that conditions determine both theory as it relates to community development and the likely consequences of community development efforts. He questions whether community as a spatial entity is a viable idea as we move into a global society. Networks of common interests for multiple purposes set the stage for planned intervention strategies. The future for community development as historically envisioned, with people working together in a locality, may become more a myth to be fondly remembered than a reality in modern society. Wilkinson (Chapter 15), on the other hand, emphasizes that no matter how complex and interdependent the world becomes, the viability of human interaction will be spatially focused and that the heart of humanistic aspirations for improvement of conditions will be grounded in people participating in common endeavors. Both authors present thoughtful and well-articulated visions of the future.

Study questions for each chapter and case studies for some chapters are provided at the end of the book. The questions and case studies strive to stimulate discussion, reactions, and integration of the material not only for the chapter under study, but for the diversity of perspectives presented throughout the book.

Acknowledgments. We would like to express our appreciation of Nancy Strang in the Department of Sociology at the University of Kentucky for proofreading, rewriting, and overall copyediting of this material. In addition, we are grateful to Bill Silag, Gretchen Van Houten, and Judy Stevens Brown of Iowa State University Press for their assistance. Finally, we appreciate the encouragement and support of the Community Development Society. The costs of production for this book were born by the authors and the universities in which they work. We feel strongly that the society needs more books focusing on the profession, and, to this end, all royalties generated from this book will go to the Community Development Society of America to be used to encourage and support future endeavors.

Community Development in Perspective

1

Community Development

JAMES A. CHRISTENSON
KIM FENDLEY
JERRY W. ROBINSON, JR.

C HANGE is a pervasive condition of our times. People have the opportunity to effect change or be affected by it. The growing complexity of societies and the interdependence of the smallest community with the world economy makes it almost impossible for an individual working alone to initiate, conduct, and sustain change. But with a little bit of help from others, a group of people working together can initiate, conduct, and sustain efforts to improve their situation, to improve their social and economic well-being.

The primary goal of community development is to help people improve their social and economic situations. The underlying philosophy is to help people become subjects instead of objects, acting on their situation instead of simply reacting to it. Community development is concerned with public policies, governmental actions, economic activities, institution building, and other types of actions that not only affect people but can be affected by people. It primarily is concerned with people as stimulators of social action processes. It focuses on the humanistic elements involved in change and how such change contributes to social and economic well-being.

Community development will be more important in the 1990s than it was in the 1970s or 1980s because of the growing complexity of societies and the increased interdependence of the world economic system. It is becoming more difficult to depend on the government for policies, programs, and monies to deal with local problems. Government leaders can initiate programs that impact localities, but these

3

programs seldom result from requests by specific localities. Community development can impact localities because it can (1) stimulate local initiative by involving people in the process of social and economic change; (2) build channels of communication that promote solidarity; and (3) improve the social, economic, and cultural well-being of community residents. Community development can provide government with a rationale for working in partnership with community leaders and citizens to solve local problems, and it can serve as the rationale for individuals to get together and initiate a social action process with or without the help of government. In short, community development is people coming together and implementing the process to improve their situation.

Purpose and Scope.   The purpose of this book is to provide a critique of various perspectives about, practical application of, research involved in, and possible futures for community development. When we wrote the first chapter for *Community Development in America* in 1980, we limited our discussion to what was occurring in the United States and Canada. These countries now are much more interdependent with the rest of the world, and thus community development must be seen in a world context if we are to understand what is going on in our own community. One example is that conflict in the Middle East can raise gas prices at the local pump. Another is that the value of the dollar in Japan directly influences the price of stocks, real estate, and merchandise.

We titled this book *Community Development in Perspective* because there is no single view of community development. As we will discuss later, the two words *community* and *development* may be a contradiction in terms. Building community solidarity and improving the social and economic situation of the community (or neighborhood) as a whole or improving the situation for a particular group in the community may or may not be related to development efforts such as deregulating banks; deindustrializing an area; building a highway, bridge, or downtown shopping center; organizing cottage industries; or holding a town forum. Sometimes social and economic development go together; sometimes they do not. Clearly, economic development without people development is not community development.

What follows is a range of perspectives on issues related to community development. We try to put some conceptual and organizational structure into this enterprise by having four interrelated parts in this book. The first part of the book focuses on the themes of community development. In the second part of the book, we discuss roles for community development professionals and practitioners, the "how to do it" aspects of community development, and what to include when one teaches community development. The third part of the book looks at research issues related to economic development and social development along with considerations of how to evaluate the impact of development. The final part of the book provides an overview of community development history both in the United States and throughout parts of the world and then looks at the current and future role of community development. Thus, many perspectives confront the reader. We hope that these points of view will stimulate, arouse (or provoke), and inform the reader about community development. From this, the reader can assimilate and formulate his or her own perspective of and orientation toward community development.

Major Concepts. Concepts help us define our perceptions of reality. They exist in our minds as the result of organized or systematic experiences of our senses. As basic elements of theory, concepts define and guide intellectual research efforts. Community development encompasses a loosely tied group of concepts based on the experiences of community development practitioners. Few will argue with Dunham's (1972, p. 37) conclusion that in the United States the term *community development* is used loosely, ambiguously, and with various meanings. We believe that clarification of the meanings of *community, development, social change, community development,* and related concepts is in order before a review of the approaches, roles, history, and perspectives of community development is presented.

COMMUNITY. The word *community* means "fellowship" in the Greek language. Reflecting on the meaning of the word, Aristotle asserted that people came together in a community setting for the enjoyment of mutual association, to fulfill basic needs, and to find meaning in life. The philosopher Thomas Hobbes, on the other hand, saw community as the natural process of people coming together to maximize their self-interest. Hobbes felt that self-interest could be best satisfied in a group setting. Community allowed individuals to abandon the many

diversified and labor-demanding activities required in subsistence living. By coming together in a community setting, one individual could
be a farmer, another a baker, a third a merchant, a fourth a blacksmith
or a teacher, and so on. Men and women could pursue, within certain
limits as defined by customs and mores, the activities suited to their
abilities and/or likings.

In ancient societies, communities were relatively easy to identify.
They were groups of people living close to one another and isolated
from other groups of people. In early American rural society, it was
easy to identify the boundaries of communities by observing the way
wagon ruts from a farmstead turned when they entered the main road.
Communities were small and geographically dispersed. For example,
in 1790 there was no city in the United States larger than 50,000. By
1840, there were only five cities of this size (New York, Boston, Philadelphia, Baltimore, St. Louis). But a century later there were over two
hundred cities of 50,000 or more.

Today it is more difficult to see and define a community geographically. Dirt has given way to asphalt, and self-sufficiency of groups has
given way to mutual interdependence. The rural-urban cultural and
social gaps have narrowed. With growth in population and rapid means
of transportation, patterns of social interaction have become much
more complicated. Places of work, of commerce, of recreation, and of
sleep are often miles apart, perhaps communities apart. Yet no matter
how complex communities have become, the need to understand and
to be able to define community is still of critical importance for community development. Most of our meaningful interaction takes place in
a defined spatial area. Most of us live; work; attend church; send our
children to school; drive on the same roads; complain about the same
traffic problems; and buy groceries, gas, and clothing in a general
locality, neighborhood, or community. Before we can discuss change or
development, we have to come to a common understanding of what a
community is.

Hillery (1955) and Willis (1977) have summarized much of the
literature and suggest four main components for defining the concept
of community. First and foremost a community involves *people.* There
is little debate over this element. Also, few authors deny that *place* or
territory should be an element of community (Hillery 1955). However,
not all writers include territory, land, or geographical boundaries in
their definitions of community. Wilkinson (1986) argues that people
live together in local ecologies with blurred territorial boundaries.
However, he notes that the blurring of boundaries is irrelevant if one is
searching for the core characteristics of a community or neighborhood

rather than for the outer limits. One can recognize the horizontal and vertical linkages between local activities and those of the larger society without dismissing local activities as irrelevant. Earlier, Warren (1978) labeled local communities the "nubs" of society in that they are a microcosm for the larger society, dependent on the larger society, but a separate arena of social interaction. In short, a community or neighborhood can exist with close linkage to the larger society and still retain its identity and viability because it provides a basis for the local population to engage in community actions (Christenson 1982). On the other hand, Blakely (Chapter 14 of this book) argues that place is becoming less relevant, that it is being replaced by networks. People can form their own community of interest independent of spatial boundaries. And more and more of people's activities are involved in specialized networks. He describes community as an open system or network and suggests areas of interest and action without territorial implications. Wilkinson (Chapter 15), however, notes that community development is not place, but a process that occurs in a place or locality. The editors of this book think that spatial boundaries are an integral part of community and that most socially meaningful interaction takes place within defined and proximate spatial limits. Consequently, place or territory is considered a second component of our definition.

Social interaction is another component of community (Kaufman 1959; Wilkinson 1972, 1979, 1986). Social interaction has slightly different meanings to writers and researchers of different perspectives. Most suggest that people within a defined geographical area in some way relate to or are interdependent on one another. According to Hillery (1955) and Willis (1977), this social interaction suggests a collection of organizations such as businesses, schools, police and fire departments, industries, banks, hospitals, and units of local government with which people relate and on which people depend. Kaufman (1959) writes that these associational networks suggest the possession of some common norms, customs, and means for obtaining desired ends. Social interaction as a process usually occurs when unusual events threaten local residents. Wilkinson (1986) observes that amid all the diversity of perspectives, it is clear that the potential for community action persists and can come into play at crucial moments when people act or react to conditions to enhance their threatened situation.

The fourth element of community is the idea of common attachment of or psychological *identification* with a community. Most people are able to give you the name of the community in which they live. People become dependent on a particular locality for the purchase of goods and services, for public services, for recreation, for employment, and for socializing. This locality is what most people identify with as community. People may also identify with and have strong ties to a neighborhood, a particular subdivision in a city, or some other geographical referent. However, the pervasive, all-embracing community identity and solidarity, which some writers recall from earlier times, are not likely to be found today, and likely were more myth than reality in the past (see Bender 1978). As noted above, when people's situations are threatened, people can come together, find solidarity, identify with locality, and effect change (Wilkinson 1986).

In this book we do not normally consider neighborhoods, subdivisions, or similar entities as communities. While people may have strong ties to their subdivisions, such entities are, by definition, dependent on the larger community for institutional and public services and for governance. Yet in urban settings, "neighborhoods" often signify communities. They can be self-sufficient little worlds within the larger context of the city. They can, and often do, contain the necessities for life: fire and police stations, grocery stores, lawyers, physicians, parks, banks, laundries, restaurants, retail stores, drugstores, perhaps a farmers market, and a local government. Although most rural communities are separate entities having their own facilities (water, sewage) and electing their own officials, more and more rural communities are sharing facilities and governance. Urban neighborhoods have traditionally shared facilities like water or sewage, yet an increasing number are functioning as separate entities with independent facilities, services, and amenities, including electing their own officials. Many cities have a form of municipal government that requires ward elections or a combination of ward and at-large elections. And the people vote in neighborhood-based (i.e., ward-based) elections to select counselors to represent them in the city government.

An urban neighborhood in a large city generally meets our definition of a community. Adams-Morgan, in Washington, D.C., is an example of a neighborhood community. It is an ethnically diverse neighborhood with a national–chain food market (Safeway) down the street from a Hispanic market, which in turn is next door to a whole foods market. The restaurants are equally as diverse, specializing in foods from El Salvador, Cuba, Japan, New Orleans, Ethiopia, Nigeria, and the Middle East. On warm evenings people "stoop set" and chat with passers-by. The open outdoor cafes offer an alternative to stoop setting. Many evenings the cafes are full of locals who have stopped by after work to discuss the happenings of the day with their neighbors. Adams-Morgan has a farmers market on the Perpetual Building's front sidewalk, numerous parks and playgrounds, ward-based elections, and even a yearly festival – "Adams-Morgan Day." If residents of this neighborhood were asked where they live by a fellow Washingtonian, they would reply Adams-Morgan. It is a recognizable neighborhood (community), both to the residents and to those living outside the locality.

In summary, to facilitate discussion of community development one must be able to define a community, understand how it functions, and perceive elements stimulating consensus or common interest, while at the same time identify elements that might divide or polarize a community. From our perspective a *community* is defined as "people that live within a geographically bounded area who are involved in social interaction and have one or more psychological ties with each other and with the place in which they live."

DEVELOPMENT. "Perhaps no single word has been more widely and frequently used by such a large number of people in so many countries of the world today than the term development" (Kim 1973, p. 462). *Development* implies improvement, growth, and change. It is concerned historically with the transition of cultures, countries, and communities from less advanced to more advanced social stages. Such terms as *industrialization, modernization,* and *urbanization* have been used interchangeably with the broader concept of development. We imply these changes when we contrast developed and underdeveloped countries. Let us analyze development in terms of improvement, growth, and change.

Development when treated as a normative concept is synonymous with improvement. In this context, development means social transformation in the direction of more egalitarian distribution of social goods such as education, health services, housing, participation in political decision making, and other dimensions of people's life chances. It is improvement from the perspective of those to be affected by change. Obviously, improvement for some may mean less for others.

While development as improvement tends to focus more on the social and psychological transformations in societies and communities, development as growth involves technological and economic transformation. Development as growth focuses on economic prosperity. It includes the institutional transformation of structures to facilitate technological advancement and improvement in the production and distribution of goods and services. For example, Portes (1976) employed the gross national product (per capita) as an indicator of national growth and found a rapidly enlarging gap between the developed and the less developed nations of the world.

Development as change involves a broader perspective. Development has come to be regarded as a type of social change (Kim 1973). While social change can be considered a concept that charts the transformation of societies, states, and communities, development is seen as planned or directed social change. Development does not just happen but entails some deliberate policies that are sustained by those in power (Portes 1976). Development as social change is putting a particular ideological orientation into action to restructure the social normative and economic order for desired ends. Development is based on and grounded in a societal vision. Such a societal vision is not shared by all. For one person the planned transformation of a society or a city would be development; for another person it would be social or economic deprivation (Ilvento, Fendley, Christenson 1988). The desire to change the social order is a biased perspective of the person or group desiring such change. No major restructuring of benefits in a society, country, or community occurs without some cost to a segment of that society, country, or community.

INTERVENTION.   Development as a form of social change can be seen more easily by presenting two visions of the social order. First is the vision of those who adhere to the law of nonintervention. This perspective has evolved from the natural-law and "invisible-hand" ideology of the laissez-faire doctrine under which Western nations, such as the United States, expanded during the eighteenth and nineteenth centuries. It is based partially on economic analysis and partially on the ideological belief that tampering with the natural environment and/or the social order would upset the harmonic forces at work within the universe. It holds that if *homeostatic* forces are left to evolve by themselves, they will bring about the maximum good for both the physical and the social universe. In short, don't fool with the system; let things happen as they will. In other words, don't plan for change.

The idea of development stems from another vision of society, one that emphasizes planned intervention, which stresses the utilization of knowledge, human capital, and technology to help solve the problems of individuals and groups. It is based on the philosophical idea that in applying systematic and appropriate knowledge to the problems confronting the social system, we can facilitate purposefully directed change for the betterment of some, or ideally, for all members of society. The idea of intervention finds many of its philosophical roots in the early works of Adam Smith, Max Weber, Karl Marx, Emile Durkheim, Ferdinand Toennies, Fredrick Olmstead and Alfred Bettman, to mention but a few. Each of these men has a unique view of intervention. Some look more to government and leaders, others look to people and their mandates.

To facilitate an understanding of classical and contemporary views of development as intervention, three types of planned community change processes are presented in Chapters 3, 4, and 5: the self-help, the technical assistance, and the conflict approaches. An arbitrary and therefore artificial boundary has been established in limiting this discussion to these three basic areas of analysis. In reality these three themes or perspectives overlap and can complement one another.

Other writers have developed models of change. Rothman (1974) formulated three models of practice that include locality development, social planning, and social action. Crowfoot and Chesler (1974) formulated the counter-cultural, the professional-technical, and the political models. Chin and Benne (1976) have developed the rational-empirical, the normative–re-educative, and the power-coercive models. The three approaches presented in Chapters 3 through 5 are more closely related to those presented by Chin and Benne than to those by either Rothman or Crowfoot and Chesler, and draw heavily upon the previous writings of Christenson and Robinson (1980).

COMMUNITY DEVELOPMENT. A wide variety of definitions of community development is available in the literature, especially in the *Journal of the Community Development Society* and the international *Community Development Journal.* To provide an overview, we reviewed these journals and collected a variety of definitions. *Community development* is, according to

Cawley (1984, p. 16): "a deliberate, democratic, developmental activity; focusing on an existing social and geographical grouping of people; who participate in the solution of common problems for the common good."

Darby and Morris (1975, p. 43): "an educational approach which would raise levels of local awareness and increase the confidence and ability of community groups to identify and tackle their own problems."

Dunbar (1972, p. 43): "a series of community improvements which take place over time as a result of the common efforts of various groups of people. Each successive improvement is a discrete unit of community development. It meets a human want or need."

Huie (1976, pp. 14–15): "the process of local decision-making and the development of programs designed to make their community a better place to live and work."

Long (1975, p. 29): "an educational process designed to help adults in a community solve their problems by group decision making and group action. Most community development models include broad citizen involvement and training in problem solving."

Oberle, Darby, and Stowers (1975, p. 64): "a process in which increasingly more members of a given area or environment make and implement socially responsible decisions, the probable consequence of which is an increase in the life chances of some people without a decrease in the life chances of others."

Ploch (1976, p. 8): "the active voluntary involvement in a process to improve some identifiable aspect of community life; normally such action leads to the strengthening of the community's pattern of human and institutional interrelationships."

Ravitz (1982, p. 2): "the active involvement of people at the level of the local community in resisting or supporting some cause or issue or program that interests them."

Voth (1975, p. 148): "a situation in which some groups, usually locality based such as a neighborhood or local community . . . attempt to improve [their] social and economic situation through [their] own efforts . . . using professional assistance and perhaps also financial assistance from the outside . . . and involving all sectors of the community or group to a maximum."

Wilkinson (1979, p. 10): "acts by people that open and maintain channels of communication and cooperation among local groups."

Other often-used definitions or typologies that have appeared in major books include those of Roland Warren, Irwin Sanders, and the United Nations. Warren (1978, p. 20) defines community development as "a process of helping community people analyze their problems, to exercise as large a measure of autonomy as is possible and feasible, and to promote a greater identification of the individual citizen and the individual organization with the community as a whole." Sanders (1958) presents a fourfold typology of community development: (1) process, (2) method, (3) program, and (4) movement (see Table 1.1).

Table 1.1. Four Ways of Viewing Community Development

I. A PROCESS	II. A METHOD (Process and Objective)
CD as a process moves by stages from one condition or state to the next. It involves a progression of changes in terms of specified criteria. It is a neutral, scientific term, subject to fairly precise definition and measurement expressed chiefly in social relations; e.g., change from state where one or two people or a small elite within or without local community make decisions for rest of the people to state where people *themselves* make these decisions about matters of common concern; from state of minimum to one of maximum co-operation; from state where few participate to one where many participate; from state where all resources and specialists come from outside to one where local people make most use of their own resources, etc. Emphasis is upon what happens to *people,* socially and psychologically.	CD is a means to an end; a way of working so that some goal is attained. Other methods (such as change by decree or fiat; change by use of differential rewards; change by education) may be supplementary to the CD method which seeks to carry through the stages suggested under *process* in order that the will of those using this method (national government, private welfare agency, or local people themselves) may be carried out. The process is guided for a particular purpose, which may prove "harmful" or "helpful" to the local community, depending upon the goal in view and the criteria of the one passing judgment. Emphasis is upon some *end.*

III. A PROGRAM (Method and Content)	IV. A MOVEMENT (Program and Emotional Dynamics)
The method is stated as a set of procedures and the content as a list of activities. By carrying out the procedures, the activities are supposedly accomplished. When the program is highly formalized, as in many Five-Year Plans, the focus tends to be upon the program rather than upon what is happening to the people involved in the program. It is as a *program* that CD comes into contact with subject-matter specialties such as health, welfare, agriculture, industry, recreation, etc. Emphasis is upon *activities.*	CD is a crusade, a cause to which people become committed. It is not neutral (like process) but carries an emotional charge; one is either for it or against it. It is dedicated to *progress,* as a philosophic and not a scientific concept, since progress must be viewed with reference to values and goals which differ under different political and social systems. CD as a movement tends to become institutionalized, building up its own organizational structure, accepted procedures, and professional practitioners. It stresses and promotes the *idea* of community development as interpreted by its devotees.

Source: I. T. Sanders (1958). Used by permission of *Rural Sociology.*

The United Nations' definition of community development has also served as a basis for community development work. Community development is

> the process by which the efforts of the people themselves are united with those of governmental authorities to improve the economic, social, and cultural conditions of communities, to integrate these communities into the life of the nation, and to enable them to contribute fully to national

progress. This complex of processes is, therefore, made up of two essential elements: the participation by the people themselves in efforts to
improve their level of living, with as much reliance as possible on their
own initiative; and the provision of technical and other services in ways
which encourage initiative, self-help and mutual help and make these
more effective. It is expressed in programmes designed to achieve a
wide variety of specific improvements. (1963, p. 4)

Based on an analysis of key aspects in these diverse definitions,
we have come to define *community development* as "a group of people in
a locality initiating a social action process (i.e., planned intervention) to
change their economic, social, cultural, and/or environmental situation." This definition seems to encompass and synthesize many elements from the definitions presented. We prefer this definition over
Warren's definition because we do not feel that promotion of autonomy
and community attachment are central elements in defining community development. Sanders's typology provides a more historical and
philosophical background for defining community development, and
we see his model as a useful elaboration of our definition. Finally, we
chose not to adopt the United Nations' definition because of its emphasis on government control, national progress, and self-help. It excludes
any consideration of conflict or dissension. Use of the concept of community development in subsequent chapters of this book draws upon
this definition and other definitions as appropriate. Can community
development occur without change? While it is philosophically appealing to talk about community development as improving the life
chances for all people in a community, in reality change usually involves a redistribution of goods and resources. No change occurs
without some costs, as Littrell and Hobbs discuss in Chapter 3. Does
community development have to be grounded in the decisions made by
people in a community? Fear, Gamm, and Fisher in Chapter 4 describe
how most technical assistance programs, particularly those initiated by
government, are unilateral in the decision-making process. Is community conflict a sign of a viable community development effort? This
issue is discussed by Robinson in Chapter 5. In short, definitions of
community development are not clear-cut, and how one interprets
community development affects one's orientation when initiating a development program. Such issues are complex and require more space
than is accorded for this brief overview. In subsequent chapters each
of these themes in light of the aforementioned definitions of community development will be presented.

COMMUNITY DEVELOPMENT IN A WORLD ECONOMY. People specu-
lated that we might live in a postindustrial society that would be driven
not by competition and deprivation but by cooperation and affluence.
This dream has been shaken in the past two decades as living standards have stagnated and as people have realized the social and environmental consequences of large-scale industrialization. Where then are
we today? Peter Drucker (1986) has presented his snapshot of the
world economy and in the process identified three critical worldwide
changes occurring around us.

First, the primary-products economy has come uncoupled from
the industrial economy. Growth in industrial production no longer indicates growth in the production of raw materials. In other words, raw
materials are no longer a major element in most new products. Thus,
as the demand for raw materials has decreased, the production in extractive industries (worldwide) has increased, leaving an oversupply of
raw materials. One possible conclusion from this scenario is that the
extractive industries are on a long-term decline and likely will never
again assume their influence and power of earlier times. In the short
run, except in situations of critical need and shortages stimulated by
unusual situations such as wars, markets, or cartels, the decline in
extraction industries likely will cause professionals working in the area
of community development to look to other parts of the economy for
planned intervention efforts.

Second, industrial production has become uncoupled from industrial employment. The proportion of traditional blue-collar workers in
the labor force of developed countries has been declining for over fifty
years. In recent years, the rate of decline has increased. This trend has
occurred simultaneously with the increase in industrial production. La-
borers in manufacturing firms are being replaced with new technologies and capital (e.g., robotization). There is also a shift from labor-
intensive companies to knowledge-intensive companies. Another
development is the trend toward smaller, more easily managed organizations. Each of these changes has served to separate industrial production from industrial employment. Change opens new opportunities
for creative change agents to tap into the world economy and helps
communities find their niche in this economy. It also portends times of
change for most small communities throughout the world, with some
prospering from the opportunities and others dealing with the negative
consequences.

Third, capital movements rather than trade in goods and services have become the driving force of the world economy. This change refers to the shift from an economy solely based on the flow of capital and goods to one based on both the flow of capital and goods and the flow of intangibles – capital movements, exchange rates, and credit flows. World trade in goods and services amounts to around three trillion dollars a year. By comparison, twenty-five times this amount is handled by the London Eurodollar market.

It is doubtful that communities can join in world competition in credit flows and capital movements. However, communities will have to find their niche in the state, national, and world economies if they are to survive and prosper. Therefore, it is time for communities and neighborhoods to stop thinking in grand, expansive terms (e.g., attracting huge factories) and to start thinking in terms of supporting economic enterprises that maximize resources unique to the area. Then they need to develop a market in the world economy. Communities need to recognize this world economic situation in order to identify both which structures in their area need to be preserved and which can be changed.

Social Science Perspectives on Development.

Each of the social sciences has a slightly different perspective toward development and a unique interpretation of social change. Portes (1976, p. 63), in his review of the sociology of development, summarized the concept's historical evolution as the gradual qualitative passage from less to more differentiated social forms. This transformation occurs through processes of ever more complex specialization and functional interdependence. Through such specialization and differentiation, Portes contends, social roles are transformed to approach modern standards of universalism, specificity, and achievement. Portes (1976) suggests that as societal development proceeds, certain adaptive features that increase the capacity of the system to survive in its environment are incorporated. The money economy, formal rationality, administration of justice, and finally the democratic association are among such structural features.

A considerable amount of sociological investigation has focused on the polarization of types of development (Inkeles and Smith 1974). Such polarization can be seen in Ferdinand Toennies's transformation of societies from *Gemeinschaft* to *Gesellschaft*, Emile Durkheim's change from mechanical solidarity to organic solidarity, and Robert

Redfield's evolution from folk to urban (Christenson 1984). One of the main problems sociologists have confronted is the adaptation of societies and communities to the increased complexity of the developing situation.

Anthropologists view development primarily from cultural and social perspectives. They build cultural models of society and view the world through the eyes of the members of that society. Anthropologists view social change from open-minded induction and try not to be prejudiced by a priori theory. In contrast to the anthropological phenomenological approach, economists view the study of social change and development with a priori theories of changes in technology, production, and distribution of goods and services. Economists are particularly concerned about value utilities and the changes that transform cultures, nations, and communities to new levels of productivity.

Historians view development from a social evolutionary perspective. They have aided studies of development by charting and interpreting the stages of industrialization and urbanization of modern societies. However, considerable question has been raised as to whether contemporary less developed societies and communities go through the same processes today as did the less developed nations, societies, and communities that have been historically documented. For example, Kim (1973, p. 465) argues that psychological attributes such as achievement, entrepreneurship, and individualism (which were preconditions for development in Western societies) may not be necessary preconditions for modernization of non-Western, less developed societies.

The most empirical approach to development today seems to be in the hands of planners. Since Frederick Law Olmstead and Alfred Bettman developed the first master plan of a city in the early 1930s, community planners have worked extensively to meet the needs of governmental decision makers. The master form of planning originally entailed architectural and geographical designs of model cities. Today, planning has expanded to include social, economic, and environmental considerations as well. Although criticisms of the planning ethic have been raised and many evaluative studies have shown comprehensive planning to be rather unsuccessful, the ideas contained in the planning approach offer considerable food for thought (Friedmann 1976, pp. 274–77). In summary, these social science disciplines, along with political science, philosophy, geography, psychology, and related disciplines, have different but viable insights when approaching community development. They have influenced the profession and therefore the way community development is practiced.

The Profession.   The term *community development* came
into popular use after World War II (Clinard 1970). It has supplanted
terms such as *mass education, village improvement, rural development,
community self-help,* and *community organization.* Most of these labels
reflected planned intervention strategies through public participation
and outside technical assistance to encourage and/or stimulate local
community efforts.

The term community development has acquired a certain band-
wagon status, and it has been used for anything from local self-help
efforts to building tracts of low-income homes. This does not mean that
attempts have not been made to conceptualize what community development is and to outline, in a theoretical perspective, the ideas of
community development. For example, authors from two major
journals and authors of a broad range of books have discussed,
described, criticized, proposed, and outlined community development.
However, many of these definitions and descriptions are conflicting.

Sanders (1958) has pointed out that community development
evolved from major forces. On the one hand is *economic development*
from which it takes its surname, and on the other hand is *community
organization* from which it takes its first name. Economic development
has been chiefly concerned with increasing productivity and efficiency,
spreading forms of economic organizations that multiply and distribute
material resources more broadly, and planning exercises to improve
the economic situation of a locality. This type of development may be
seen as development *in* the community (see Chapters 9 and 10 of this
book). From the community organization perspective which emphasizes public participation and social planning, community development
evolved out of the early works of the community chest movement,
United Community Services, and the United Fund. It is operationalized
through associational and group work, community councils, programs
in public health education, and community surveys directed at the
desires and needs of community residents. Such programs seek to
improve the decision-making process of the community as well as the
quality of local life and may be seen as development *of* community.

Community development as a discipline within an institutional
structure in the United States probably began with the work of William
Biddle at Earlham College, Richmond, Indiana, in 1947. Cary (Chapter
8) discusses how community development programs have developed in
many other academic institutions during the last thirty years. Today
over eighty universities and colleges offer courses in community development, and many have master's programs with a community development option.

The Community Development Society was established in 1970. In the first ten years it grew to over one thousand members. Thereafter membership declined slightly and stabilized. The *Journal of the Community Development Society* celebrates two decades of service in 1990. Approximately four hundred articles and notes have been published. The *Community Development Journal,* published by Oxford University Press and located at Newcastle-upon-Tyne in England, will celebrate its twenty-fifth anniversary in 1990. These journals along with other related journals and professional societies have brought the discipline of community development to its present state; that is, although still in search of theoretical underpinnings, it is an established force in the professional literature.

The Future. Is the idea and practice of community development relevant to and practical for dealing with social and economic issues today? Can the idea of people working together to solve problems and improve their situation be implemented in our complex society and in light of the changing world economy? The dream of isolated places with concerned citizens coming together to assert their autonomy and manifest their attachment to place, independent of the larger state, national, and worldwide forces, has faded. The tendency is to view people as objects rather than subjects. On the other hand, people are better educated today. The idea of volunteerism has not died with the rapid growth of dual career families. And the concern to resolve local problems is as apparent today as ever. What may be missing is skilled leadership. However, we do not want to leave the impression that society is too complex and that world forces are too overwhelming and inhibiting to initiate community development. A few examples of local initiatives and state programs in the United States and other countries may provide some ideas for the future of community development.

The U.S. Cooperative Extension Service inititative called "Revitalizing Rural America" has been one recent program to get things going at the local level. The initiatives for this program include (1) economic development to maintain rural jobs and income, (2) institution building to meet expanding rural needs, and (3) cultural change to adapt to external national and international influences. Examples of such efforts are a Wisconsin farmer raising ginseng for export to the Orient, an Oregon sawmill operator installing state-of-the-art equipment in order to ship lumber to Japan, a Minnesota farmer experimenting with white corn that he sells to a Chicago company for making Mexican tortillas and tacos, and Louisiana officials attracting two Italian tanneries to the Louisiana swamps to tan alligator hides (Extension Committee on Organization and Policy 1986, p. 6).

Another idea for community development has been called "rural reflation" (Fendley and Christenson 1987). This concept assumes that many towns have never been "vital." The focus here is to restructure the inflated (e.g., boomtown) or deflated economy to a desired or sustainable level. The terms *inflated* and *deflated* are not used here in the strictly economic sense of a rise or a fall in prices, but are meant to designate the use of expansion or control to obtain a working, livable economy. The assumption of previous vitality is unimportant. Therefore, the methods used in reflating a small town's or neighborhood's economy must be structured for the characteristics of that small town or neighborhood. Rural or urban reflation is a relative concept as well as a program aimed toward survival in a changing world. The keys to success are (1) having informed leaders with access to outside sources, (2) understanding the current economic system of the community in light of the changing world economy, (3) having public participation, (4) finding what is unique to a community (i.e., finding its niche in the local, state, and world economy), (5) being willing to be innovative, to accept alternatives, and finally, (6) organizing and maximizing human and financial capital. Some examples of development in a world economy are included below. In the following chapters many other examples will be given, particularly in Chapter 9 on economic development and in Chapter 10 on social development.

An example of organizational assistance to stimulate development is the Mountain Association for Community Economic Development (MACED) in the United States. This is a regional organization which combines research and policy analysis with technical assistance and financial investments to stimulate development that benefits low-income households in central Appalachia. Since 1977, MACED has worked with community groups and local leadership on community development projects and has invested directly in small businesses. This is a good example of the self-help and technical assistance approaches working together. Over the past three years, the program has concentrated on "sectoral intervention," in an attempt to stimulate incremental change in an important industry for the benefit of poor people and poor places. And this part of the United States has some of the poorest people and some of the most inaccessible places. Currently MACED has projects or investments in the following industries: housing, finance, banking, hardwood lumber, water system management, and coal. The staff works on research, technical assistance, investment, or policy analysis as the issue requires. The key to MACED success is effective and creative leadership. This example suggests how dedicated leaders can make a significant difference in one of the poorest sections of America in a short period of time.

The hardwood lumber industry was the first sector MACED became involved with because it employs so many low-income people in the most rural parts of eastern Kentucky. After assisting and financing a number of lumber ventures, MACED established a sawmill and marketing company to help the area's numerous small mills reach the national and world markets and get reasonable prices for their lumber.

The lack of affordable mortgages appeared to be a major obstacle to housing development in the area, so MACED staff worked with ninety-four lenders. They helped the lenders make better mortgage loans and negotiated with national secondary market institutions to make their programs more usable in rural areas like eastern Kentucky. With a consortium of these lenders, MACED has issued tax-exempt mortgage revenue bonds to provide more mortgage funds for low-income households in the region.

The Jackson County Development Association, in Kentucky, was formed as a citizens' group in 1984 to promote tourism and recreation in their county. Thus far, they have been successful in attracting Mid-South Industries, in establishing an Industrial Authority which will attempt to attract more industries, and in promoting a county festival. They presently are planning a nursing home (Ilvento 1987).

Hardin County, Kentucky, is an example of a rapidly expanding area working to maintain control of its growth. This area received several major highway junctions in the 1950s and 1960s. Development followed. To maintain control of the rapid growth, the Development Guidance System (DGS) was formed. Rather than using zoning laws, the DGS assesses each proposed development project in light of the county's goals of "reinforcing the capital investments already made by local government agencies and protecting the county's prime agricultural land" (Gordon 1986, p. 18).

For those communities with companies just beginning to move out, one possible solution that hinges on participation by the people is to develop community-owned businesses. This is an old but rarely used solution to job losses. The Pacific Northwest Plywood Cooperatives, which has been in business for twenty-five to thirty years, is an example of such a company (Greenberg 1986). Perhaps it is time to actively recognize worker ownership or community ownership of companies as a viable alternative to private ownership.

The main points we want to make here are that we should not give up on the people in poor areas and that dedicated informed leaders can make a difference. We need to facilitate ways for new informed leadership to build on pragmatic ideas for development while at the same time help those who need retraining, retooling, or even relocation. We need to reflate the local economy and must have confidence that it can be done.

In summary, the prescribed methods (e.g., bring in a major plant) of revitalizing an economy are no longer sufficient to reestablish solvency. Not only is a county's dependence on one industry for economic survival a mistake considering the international mobility of companies, but finding and acquiring an industry is becoming less and less feasible for even vital communities and certainly for depressed areas. Rural reflation, in terms of expanding a depressed economy, sidesteps the difficulty of relying on just one industry. Rural reflation depends on citizens' participation in the community, on internal leadership, and usually on some help from outside the community to develop a unique community identity. The term *rural* or *urban reflation,* though, should bring to mind solutions attempted on a human scale, with the goal of expanding or controlling an economy to a working, livable level.

Rural revitalization and rural reflation are only two current efforts in the United States. Throughout the world, new initiatives are springing forth. For example, Muintir na Tire in Ireland celebrated in 1987 its fiftieth anniversary of local community development projects, such as the development of community information centers; the promotion of the establishment of credit unions; the initiation of the community alert program, in association with Garda Siochana, for the protection of elderly people living in isolated areas; and the promotion of social service and community care committees. Antur Aelhaearn in Wales celebrated its tenth anniversary as a village community cooperative association in 1984. The Center for Employment Initiatives in England has been promoting the concept of community business, which stresses the values of community ownership and control along with goals that are not exclusively commercial. Throughout Africa, local cooperatives and community organizations are being born. While major government-controlled community development efforts in Third World countries are in decline (see Chapter 13), many locally initiated efforts are evolving.

In conclusion, the future of community development may lie in an old problem from the past. Where do we find the creative leadership to make things happen? Or how do we train individuals to become leaders so that people's life chances can be improved? Our hope is that this book can serve as a stimulus to develop skilled and creative leaders, as well as a source for ideas to implement coordinated social action processes for improving the world about us. It is much easier to describe how to do something than to find the people to do it. It is our belief that community development is a viable process for dealing with today's problems. It is our hope that this book and the ideas, suggestions, and caveats contained herein will further this process.

References

Bender, T. 1978. *Community and Social Change.* New Brunswick, N.J.: Rutgers University Press.

Cawley, R. 1984. Exploring the dimensions of democracy in community development. *Journal of the Community Development Society* 15(1):15–26.

Chin, R., and K. Benne. 1976. General strategies for effecting change in human systems. In *The Planning of Change,* 3d ed., W. Bennis, K. Benne, R. Chin, and K. Corey, eds., pp. 13–21. New York: Holt, Rinehart and Winston.

Christenson, J. A. 1982. Community development. In *Rural Society: Research Issues for the 1980s,* D. Dillman and D. Hobbes, eds., pp. 264–72. Boulder, Colo.: Westview Press.

_____. 1984. Gemeinschaft and Gesellschaft: Testing the spacial and communal hypotheses. *Social Forces* 63(1):160–68.

Christenson, J. A., and J. W. Robinson, Jr., eds. 1980. *Community Development in America.* Ames: Iowa State University Press.

Clinard, M. B. 1970. *Slims and Community Development.* New York: Free Press.

Crowfoot, J. E., and M. A. Chesler. 1974. Contemporary perspectives on planned social change: A comparison. *Journal of Applied Behavioral Science* 10(3):278–303.

Darby, J. P., and G. Morris. 1975. Community groups and research in Northern Ireland. *Community Development Journal* 10(2):113–19.

Dunbar, J. O. 1972. The bedrock of community development. *Journal of the Community Development Society* 3(2):42–53.

Dunham, A. 1972. Community development in North America. *Community Development Journal* 7(1):10–40.

Drucker, P. F. 1986. The changed world economy. *Foreign Affairs* 6(4):768–91.

Extension Committee on Organization and Policy. 1986. *Revitalizing Rural America.* Madison, Wis.: Cooperative Extension Service.

Fendley, K., and J. A. Christenson. 1987. Rural reflation. Paper presented at the annual meeting of the Rural Sociology Society, Madison, Wis.

Friedmann, J. 1976. The future of comprehensive urban planning. In *Readings in Community Organization Practive,* 2d ed., R. Kramer and H. Specht, eds., pp. 275–88. Englewood Cliffs, N.J.: Prentice-Hall.

Gordon, D. A. 1986. How Kentucky's Hardin County deals with growth. *Rural Development Perspectives* 2(2):17–19.

Greenberg, E. S. 1986. *Workplace Democracy.* Ithaca, N.Y.: Cornell University Press.

Hillery, G. A. 1955. Definitions of community – Areas of agreement. *Rural Sociology* 20(2):111–23.

Huie, J. M. 1976. What do we do about it? – A challenge to the community development professional. *Journal of the Community Development Society* 6(2):14–21.

Ilvento, T. W. 1987. The Jackson County Development Association wins award. *Community Development News* 6(4):2.

Ilvento, T. W., K. Fendley, and J. A. Christenson. 1988. Political definitions of rurality and their impact on federal grant distribution. *Journal of the Community Development Society.* 19(1):1–20.

Inkeles, A., and D. H. Smith. 1974. *Becoming Modern: Individual Changes in Six Developing Countries.* Cambridge: Harvard University Press.

Kaufman, H. 1959. Toward an interactional conception of community. *Social Forces* 39(Oct.):8–17.

Kim, K. 1973. Toward a sociological theory of development: A structural perspective. *Rural Sociology* 38(4):462–76.

Long, H. B. 1975. State government: A challenge for community developers. *Journal of the Community Development Society* 6(1):27–36.

Oberle, W., J. P. Darby, and K. R. Stowers. 1975. Implications for development: Social participation of the poor in the Ozarks. *Journal of the Community Development Society* 6(2):64–78.

Ploch, L. A. 1976. Community development in action: A case study. *Journal of the Community Development Society* 7(1):5–16.

Portes, A. 1976. On the sociology of national development: Theories and issues. *American Journal of Sociology* 8(1):55–85.

Ravitz, M. 1982. Community development. *Journal of the Community Development Society* 13(1):1–10.

Rothman, J. 1974. Three models of community organization practice. In *Strategies of Community Organization,* 2d ed., F. Cos, J. Erlich, J. Rothman, and J. Tropman, eds., pp. 22–39. Itasca, Ill.: Peacock.

Sanders, I. T. 1958. Theories of community development. *Rural Sociology* 23(1):1–12.

United Nations Ad Hoc Group of Experts on Community Development. 1963. *Community Development and National Development.* New York.

Voth, D. E. 1975. Problems in evaluating community development. *Journal of the Community Development Society* 6(1):147–62.

Warren, R. 1978. *The Community in America,* 3d ed. Chicago: Rand McNally.

Wilkinson, K. 1972. A field theory perspective for community development research. *Rural Sociology* 37(1):3–52.

_____. 1979. Social well-being and community. *Journal of the Community Development Society* 10(1):4–13.

_____. 1986. In search of the community in a changing countryside. *Rural Sociology* 51(4):1–17.

Willis, C. W. 1977. Definitions of community II: An examination of definitions of community since 1950. *Southern Sociologist* 9(1):14–19.

2

Themes of Community Development

JAMES A. CHRISTENSON

W HAT should be included in a book on community development? In preparation for this endeavor, I reviewed a substantial number of journal articles and a few books to identify some common themes and to point out some of the evolving issues facing professionals working in the area of community development in the 1990s. Since the *Journal of the Community Development Society* is the major forum for issues related to community development, this chapter presents a content analysis of this journal. References to other journals and books will be included as appropriate within the space constraints of this chapter. Many other excellent sources such as the classic writings on local initiatives by Poston (1950), Batten (1957), and Biddle and Biddle (1965); the insightful community organization conflict approach of Alinsky (1969); the adult education approach of Roberts (1979); the broad collection of material by Chekki (1979); the historical work of Bender (1978); and the wide range of edited works such as that of Cary (1973) and Blakely (1979) will be presented in other chapters. Many of these authors have contributed articles to the *Journal* and their views will be discussed accordingly.

I should note at the outset that the practice of community development may be somewhat different from that which is reflected in any one journal. The fact that some issues have received more attention than others may be a function of both the interests of editors/reviewers and the subject matter on which professionals choose to write. However, for nearly two decades the *Journal* has documented the what, where, and why of the discipline. Its articles manifest the philosophies, strategies, roles, models, research findings, practical insights, and ideological debates of those involved in this field of work. In short, the *Journal* reflects the intellectual, research, and practical concerns of the professional community called the Community Development Society.

This chapter reviews more than three hundred articles that have appeared in the *Journal.* Each article was independently read and classified by two persons, discrepancies were discussed, and consensus was reached on the classification of each article. More than 95 percent of the reviewed articles are listed in Table 2.1. Some articles were difficult to classify because they were welcoming addresses at professional meetings, keynote addresses that did not deal with community development, or short essays on subjects impossible to classify.

Table 2.1. *Contributors to the* Journal of the Community Development Society *Categorized by Thematic Areas of Contribution*[a]

Thematic Areas	Contributors
	Major Themes of Community Development
Self-Help	Long, 1972; Poston, 1972; Dunbar, 1972; Biddle, 1973; Poston, 1973; Batten, 1973; Lewis, 1974; Ternette, 1974; Oberle, Stowers, and Darby, 1974; Koneya, 1975; Kaufman, 1975; Warren, 1975; Huie, 1975; Ploch, 1976; Moschenros, 1976; Cary, 1976; Schaller, 1978; Bevins, 1978; Wilkinson, 1979; Frazier, 1979; Cary, 1979; Greisman, 1980; McMurtry, 1980; Beatty, 1981; Ravitz, 1982; Dressel and Nix, 1982; Richards, 1984; Gillis and Schaffer, 1985; Weir, 1986; Israel and Wilkinson, 1987; Lackey, Burke, and Peterson, 1987; Jones and Harris, 1987
Technical Assistance	Leadley, 1971; Jones, 1971; Melvin, 1972; Foster, 1972; Pell, 1972; Beach, 1972; Gustafson, O'Hanlon, and Smythe, 1972; Bonner, 1972; Sargent, 1973; Boesch and Heagler, 1973; Stockdale and Clippinger, 1973; Clavel and Goldsmith, 1973; Blase, Green, and Matson, 1973; McNeill, 1974; Moyer, 1974; Long, 1975; Kleinsasser and Slipy, 1975; Shocket and Smith, 1975; Ritchie, 1975; Schnabel and Simoni, 1975; Deberton and Huie, 1975; Bonner, 1975; Fisher and White, 1976; Blakely and Zons, 1976; Meyer and Gamm, 1976; Paulson and Folkman, 1976; Danner and St. Clair, 1976; Kellams, 1976; Bevins, 1976; Cotton and Linder, 1977; Mushkatel and Slipy, 1977; Nelson, 1977; Robertson, 1978; Hahn, 1978; Daley and Labit, 1979; Nelson, 1979; Mathews and Fawcett, 1979; Sorter and Simpkinson, 1979; Deseran, 1980; Honadle, 1982; Preston, 1983; Woods and Doeksen, 1984; Barkley and Cory, 1985; Elgie and Montgomery, 1985; Bakker, 1985; Fisher, 1985; Summers

Table 2.1. (Continued)

Thematic Areas	Contributors
	and Hirschl, 1985; Meyer, Shane, and Radtke, 1986; Booth and Favero, 1986; Wilson and Netting, 1986; Fitzgerald and Meyer, 1986; Napier and Camboni, 1987
Conflict	Hunt, 1972; Robinson, 1972; Hynam, 1973; Blizek and Cederblom, 1973; Steuart, 1974; Blizek and Cederblom, 1974; Schilit, 1974; Walker and Hanson, 1976; Sabke, 1980; Gondolf, 1980; Reitzes and Reitzes, 1980; Daley and Kettner, 1981; Wellman and Marans, 1983; Gondolf, 1983; Gondolf, 1986; Daley and Kettner, 1986; Favero, 1987

Citizen Participation

Citizen Involvement or Action	McClusky, 1970; Wireman, 1970; Hahn, 1970; Anderson, 1970; Brooks, 1971; McMurtry, 1972; Hammock, 1973; Scharlach, 1974; Robertson, 1974; Parko, 1975; Cook, 1975; Stam and Stinson, 1976; Christenson, 1976; Saunders, 1976; Collins and Downes, 1976; Sorensen and Pfau, 1976; Nix and Dressel, 1978; Koneya, 1978; Meiller and Broom, 1979; MacNair, 1981; Crompton, Lamb, and Schul, 1981; Marsh, 1982; Compton, 1982; Stoneall, 1983; Freudenburg and Olsen, 1983; Korte, 1984; Moxley, 1985; Martin and Wilkinson, 1985; Moxley and Hannah, 1986; Ryan, 1986; Donnermeyer and Mullen, 1987

Research Related to Community Development

Needs Assessment	Basson, 1970; Gibson and Mulvihill, 1970; Kurzman, 1970; Kilbourn, 1970; Franklin, 1971; Walker, 1971; Long, 1971; Hauswald, 1971; Sofranko and Bridgeland, 1972; Hobgood and Christenson, 1973; Nix, Singh, and Cheatham, 1974; Christenson, 1975; Arnot, 1975; Oberle, Stowers, and Darby, 1975; Blake and Ryan, 1976; Darabi, 1976; Nix, Brooks, and Courtney, 1976; Dillman, 1977; Goudy and Wepprecht, 1977; Cohen, Sills, and Schwebel, 1977; Allen, 1977; Gessaman, Janssen, and Morris, 1977; Blake, Kalb, and Ryan, 1977; Schwebel et al., 1978; Gordon and Mulkey, 1978; Ball and Heumann, 1979; Meyer, 1979; Goudy and Tait, 1979; Preston and Guseman, 1979; Garkovich, 1979; Luloff and Ilvento, 1981; Ryan and Lorenz, 1981; Luloff, Greenwood, and Ilvento, 1981; van Es and Schneider, 1983; Wokutch and Verdu, 1983; Singh, 1983; Camboni and Napier, 1985; Sommer and Nelson, 1985; Truman et al., 1985; Seroka, 1986; Sorter, 1987; Fisher and Woods, 1987; Dalecki, Ilvento, and Moore, 1988
Growth	Erickson and Johnson, 1971; Wyckoff, 1973; Brinkman, 1973; Pulver, 1974; Francis, 1974; Shaffer and Tweeten, 1974; Napier and Wright, 1974; Booth, 1975; Davis, Sorenson, and Walters, 1975; Darling, 1976; Rogers, Goudy, and Richards, 1976; Lonsdale, Kinworthy, and Doering, 1976; Kale, 1976; Smith and Tweeten, 1976; Summers, 1977; Williams, Sofranko, and Root, 1977; Cockerman and Blevins, 1977; Stanfield and Heffernan, 1977; Klay, 1978; Smith, 1978; Patton and Stabler, 1979; Kuehn, Braschler, and Shonkwiler, 1979; Napier, Maurer and Bryant, 1980; Chicoine, Scott, and Jones, 1980; Voss, 1980; Smith,

Table 2.1. (Continued)

Thematic Areas	Contributors
	Deaton, and Kelch, 1980; Sofranko and Fliegel, 1980; Webb, Krannich, and Clemente, 1980; Smith and Pulver, 1981; Napier and Mast, 1981; Hines and Napier, 1982; Christenson and Crouch, 1982; Albrecht and Geertsen, 1982; Hoy, 1983; Weigel and Busch-Rossnagel, 1984; Bender and Stinson, 1984; Brown, 1984; Greider and Krannick, 1985; Albrecht, 1986; Heumann and Marlatt, 1986; Smith and Barkley, 1988; McGrath, 1988; Blevins and Bradley, 1988
Evaluation	Thomas, 1970; McNeill and Miller, 1971; Ritchie, 1971; Vaughn, 1972; Cebotarev and Brown, 1972; Voth, 1975; Cohen, 1976; Goudy, 1976; Mackeracher, Davie, and Patterson, 1976; Maesen, 1976; Bannon, 1977; Burton, 1978; Daley and Winter, 1978; Giles, 1980; Lackey, Peterson, and Pine, 1981; Cawley, 1981; Voth, Miller, and Flaherty, 1982; Hickey, 1982; Howie, Phillips, and Underwood, 1982; Henderson and Bialeschki, 1982; Chase and Pulver, 1983; Davie, 1983; Grimes, DeVille, and Leonard, 1984; Goodwin and Doeksen, 1984; Cook, Howell, and Weir, 1985; Verma, 1986; Ilvento, Fendley, and Christenson, 1988
Services	Napier, 1972; Ching, Frick, and Tonks, 1973; Lyon, 1977; Shaffer, 1978; Keith, 1978; Warner and Monk, 1979; Murdock and Schriner, 1979; Hamilton, 1980; Rogers, Pendleton, and Goudy, 1981; Goudy, 1983; Luloff et al., 1984; Smith, 1984; Cook and Poremba, 1985; Glaser, 1986; Murdock et al., 1987; Doeksen, 1987; Allen and Gibson, 1987; Beaulieu and Luloff, 1987; Pankau and Sander, 1988

The Profession

Roles	Ratchford, 1970; Warren, 1970; Fanning, 1970; Wadsworth, 1970; Pulver, 1970; Abshier, 1970; Cary, 1970; Biddle, 1970; von Lazar and Hammock, 1970; Beal, Coward, and Brooks, 1971; Spiegel, 1971; Evans, 1971; Vlasin, 1971; Edwards, 1971; Wortman, 1971; Nix and Seerley, 1971; Anderson, 1972; Cary, 1972; Bennett, 1973; Abshier, 1973; Sargent, 1973; Winterton and Rossiter, 1973; Melvin, 1974; Child, 1974; Frederickson, 1975; Willis, 1975; Vaughn, 1976; Nicastro, 1976; Sebring, 1977; Pulver, 1977; Arnot, 1977; Gibson, 1977; Parsons, 1978; Lionberger and Wong, 1980; Tobin, 1982; Blakely and Bradshaw, 1982; Linneman, 1983; Kuehn, Nelson, and McGill, 1983; Jimmerson, 1984; Lackey and Burke, 1984; Seroka, 1984; Jones, 1988; Roszak, 1988
Training	Lotz, 1970; Santopolo and Johnson, 1970; Weaver, 1971; Hanson, 1972; Richmond, 1972; Klimoski and Krile, 1973; Cary, 1973; Saunders, 1974; Miles, 1974; Williams, 1974; Suzuki, 1975; Persell, 1976; Napier and Maurer, 1978; Smith, 1978; DePuydt and Persell, 1978; Yoak, 1979; Checkoway, 1979; Dodge, 1980; Williams, 1981; Harris, 1982; Fanslow, 1982; Sisson, 1983; Cawley, 1984; Gibson and Worden, 1984; Rossing and Heasley, 1987

[a]The articles listed in this table but not included in the list of references for Chapter 2 appear in various issues of the *Journal of the Community Development Society*. Only those references cited in the text are in the list of references.

The following procedure was used in coding each article. First, the general approach or theme was classified as *self-help, technical assistance,* or *conflict.* Most articles presented an overall theme, or at least recognizable strategies, philosophies, techniques, and procedures for conceptualizing or practicing community development. Few of these articles presented any data or data analysis. Second, there was a group of articles that focused more on *citizen participation, public involvement,* or *community action* than on any of the three aforementioned themes. Often these citizen participation articles involved more than one theme or approach, so I developed a separate category for such articles. This might be considered a fourth theme. But if we were forced to eliminate this classification, most of these articles would end up in the self-help list. In short, we felt that we gained more by including these articles in a separate listing. Third, a broad range of *research* articles were codified. The four major research themes are presented in Table 2.1. Fourth, for all articles, the content was inspected for the inclusion of concepts and/or propositions that were tested or discussed in a theoretical context. If the article contained such, it was labeled a *theory* article. No list of these is provided in the table because of the small number of articles that fit these parameters. Finally, the *background of the author(s)* was documented as to academic, extension, government, or private sector affiliation. The purpose of this chapter is not to present a catalogue or annotated index of the articles for the last two decades, but rather to synthesize the content. While I have tried to be faithful to what has been published in the *Journal,* essentially this is my interpretation of major issues, themes, and content areas in community development. It is the history of the *Journal* through my eyes.

First Impressions.   One is impressed with the variety

of articles that have appeared in the *Journal of the Community Development Society* during the past twenty years. A journal is usually limited to a specific academic area such as economics, sociology, or political science, or to a substantive area such as administration or urban affairs. The *Journal,* however, seems to embrace most social science disciplines and to include a wide range of subject matter. This variety of articles is reflected in the diversity of its contributors. Although sociology, community development, and economics (in that order) have been the major academic backgrounds of the contributors, a wide range of articles have appeared from writers in areas such as adult education, geography, urban affairs, political science, law, philosophy, psychology, and home economics. The majority of the contributors to the *Journal* (close to 90 percent) are housed in academic institutions (including those with extension appointments); the remainder come from the private sector and the government. More than 30 percent of the contributors are affiliated with the Agricultural Cooperative Extension Service. This may be a conservative estimate since titles do not always include extension ties. The only trend found in this two-decade review is a slight decrease in the number of practitioners (extension, private sector, and government) contributing to the *Journal.*

The early years of the *Journal* were dominated with articles on philosophies of community development, strategies for doing community development, exhortations about the value of the community development enterprise, and success stories of community development in action. Whether the theme was self-help, technical assistance, or conflict, the articles attempted to present a perspective on how to "do" community development. Articles published in recent years on such issues tend to be presidential addresses or keynote presentations. This abundance of articles concerning philosophy and strategies of community development reflected the themes of the early national meetings and the decision by the Community Development Society's Board of Directors to publish all major papers presented at the annual meetings. It also reflected the continuing intellectual struggle to identify what community development is, what it should be, and how it should be done. At times, I found it difficult to determine whether an article should be listed as a theme article or a research article. For the early years, the decisions were fairly easy since few of the theme articles contained any data or data analysis. However in more recent years, particularly in relation to the technical assistance theme, the distinction becomes more judgmental since many of these articles advocate a philosophy or strategy of community development at the same time they are presenting data to support the merit of their arguments.

In recent years, research articles have dominated the pages of the *Journal.* During the first five years of the *Journal*'s existence (1970–1974), few articles could be classified as research. In fact, only about 8 percent of these articles contained data and provided any kind of data analysis. Beginning in the 1980s, the number of research articles grew to represent over half of all manuscripts. While most of these research articles alluded to community development, many seemed to be discipline oriented (i.e., sociology, economics). Some of these appeared to be watered-down efforts which likely were prepared for other disciplinary journals. In more recent years, greater effort appears to be made to directly address community development questions. In short, recent articles appear to be conceptualized and written for the *Journal.* This is a clear sign of growth within the discipline.

Major Themes of
Community Development.
At the most general level, almost all of the articles in the *Journal* have an underlying theme relating to what Batten (1973, p. 35) calls the "betterment of people." While considerable divergence exists on terminology and definitions, as noted in Chapter 1, most articles imply that community development is people initiating a social action process to improve their situation. People achieve this "betterment" of their situation through a variety of methods such as self-help, technical assistance, and conflict. Most readers readily agree that people should initiate action to improve their situation in their locality, but how to do it generates considerable debate.

In reviewing two decades of the *Journal,* I found three major themes which seemed to differentiate and categorize the many articles. They can be labeled (1) the self-help, nondirective, or cooperative theme; (2) the technical intervention, planning, or assistance theme; and (3) the conflict or confrontation theme. Such categorization of themes artificially creates some divergence where there is considerable overlap. As will be argued in various chapters throughout this book, the most successful community development efforts use a little bit of each theme.

SELF-HELP. Self-help is a major theme in the *Journal.* Inspection of Table 2.1 may not indicate a long of list of articles, but this is partly an artifact of my organizational procedure. Citizen participation or action was designated a separate category both because it is a major interest area for authors and because it can include elements of all three themes. However, if this theme had not been broken out, most of the articles would have been classified under self-help. A similar argument could be made about the community development profession category.

The assumption of the cooperative or self-help theme is that by working together, people can improve their situation. Many of these self-help articles are descriptive studies of community development in practice. They focus on people and could be classified as more process oriented than task oriented. Cebotarev and Brown (1972) describe process as the approach whereby people arrive at group decisions and take actions to enhance the social and economic well-being of their community. The reason the process aspect of the self-help approach is emphasized over the task aspect is that the subject matter is not as important as is the process through which people go to achieve a goal. Essentially, the self-help theme assists people in learning how to handle their own problems. During the process people may achieve a task or objective, but this is incidental to the long-range implications of teaching people how to improve their situation. For example, Ploch (1976) presented a detailed analysis showing how a small number of volunteers who were interested in improving the level of health-care delivery in their community evolved from an informal group into a board of directors of an incorporated, community-based health center. The creation of the center is an excellent example of the voluntary, nondirective involvement of community residents to improve their situation. He noted that the process that people went through was more important than the establishment of the health center. The process appeared to strengthen the community's patterns of human and institutional relationships.

The role of the change agent in the cooperative or self-help approach is educational and organizational (see Table 2.2; see also Table 4.2). While the change agent may advocate the self-help process, he or she should not advocate a particular course of action. Rather, self-help change agents help people explore alternatives and organize for action. Batten (1973) argues strongly against advocacy of goals or manipulation of people toward specific ends in the self-help approach. He points out that such manipulation often leads people to undertake tasks which they do not have the skills, the desires, or the resources to achieve. Advocating specific goals or objectives may hinder a person's ability to learn the action process by lessening his or her ability to confront

Table 2.2. Comparison of Three Themes of Community Development

Themes	Roles of Change Agent	Task/Process Orientation	Typical Clientele	Speed of Change	Sustainability of Change
Self-Help	Facilitator, educator	Process	Middle-class	Slow	Excellent
Technical Assistance	Advisor, consultant	Task	Leaders, administrators	Moderate	Good
Conflict	Organizer, advocate	Process and task	Poor, minorities	Fast	Weak

future problems. The role of the change agent is to provide people with the skills and knowledge to facilitate their decision-making process and the accomplishment of their specific objectives. Frequently, an agent will contribute to the organizational aspect by helping people learn how groups function and by helping people to work together. But here again, the agent is serving in an advisory capacity and as an unbiased consultant.

The advantage of using the self-help approach is that the people themselves determine what is to be done; in the process they learn both how to achieve a specific task and how to accomplish future goals. Self-help has been criticized as not achieving any meaningful change. Warren (1975) argues that no meaningful change can occur without some conflict. He points out that if everyone is satisfied, nothing changes.

Self-help is not a theory. It can be considered a strategy, a philosophy, a mission of the Cooperative Extension Service, but not a theory based on research-tested procedures. After two decades of articles published by community development professionals, the discipline is not any closer to a theory related to self-help than are the classic ideas presented by Batten (1957), Biddle and Biddle (1969), Cary (1973) and others. In Chapter 14 of this book, Blakely attempts to explain why and where theory might be found. A few articles from the *Journal* might be included as having theoretical implications related to self-help (Lewis 1974; Kaufman 1975; Warren 1975; Wilkinson 1979). Several other articles list concepts (Santopolo and Johnson 1970; Sofranko and Bridgeland 1972; Stanfield and Heffernan 1977) or schemes, such as Long's (1972) heuristic development matrix. And a few have attempted to link theories like exchange theory (Napier and Maurer 1978) or the human resource development model (Napier and Camboni 1987) to community development. But after comprehensively reviewing all these articles in the *Journal* as well as articles in related journals (Hobbs 1980; Wilkinson 1986), I feel relatively safe in asserting that few self-help articles were related to or based on theory during the last two decades.

In the 1990s, the self-help theme needs to move from a philosophy and approach to research-tested, theoretically related ideas. The questions that have to be resolved from a scientific standpoint are whether this procedure works, why it works, and when it is most successful. For example, is the self-help orientation most appropriate for middle-class neighborhoods and communities? Will it work with low-income neighborhoods and areas of limited resources? The most frustrating aspect of this approach is that after two decades of the *Journal,* we still have little factual information to support or to disprove the self-help theme.

TECHNICAL ASSISTANCE. Technical intervention or planning encompasses a broad range of articles that have appeared in the *Journal* over the last two decades. The philosophy behind the technical assistance or planning theme is that structure determines behavior. In most cases, advocates of this theme work for people rather than with them. While planners and technical assistance change agents may argue against this characterization, it is fairly well documented that the technical intervention or planning orientation has largely ignored public input or participation (Melvin 1972; Koneya 1975, p. 8). However, this is not to say that the technical intervention or planning orientation has not been successful. It likely has had more lasting impact than the combined efforts of the other two themes. However, for technical assistance to be considered community development, people have to be involved in the process (see Chapter 4).

Technical assistance emphasizes accomplishing a task such as building a bridge, stimulating economic development, establishing a new health center, or developing planning and zoning ordinances for a particular area. For example, Brinkman (1973) and Rogers, Goudy, and Richards (1976) discuss community development from the perspective of attracting and establishing new industries as well as the impact of such industries on communities. Boesch and Heagler (1973) write about the establishment of a sanitary landfill. Webb, Krannich, and Clemente (1980) study the impact of power plants. Chase and Pulver (1983) write about downtown shopping centers. Others (Bonner 1972; Napier 1972; Blase, Green, and Matson 1973; Goodwin and Doeksen 1984) write about regional health centers, regional planning, and planning models.

The role of the technical expert or the planner is to assess the situation in a locality and, based on the best technical information, to suggest the most economically feasible and socially responsible approaches for improving the situation. Usually this involves some sort of physical intervention such as building a convention center, establishing a comprehensive plan, or developing zoning ordinances. Technical assistants and planners are technicians with specialized professional skills for designing and developing projects. In recent years, the federal government has required greater effort to include public input to such efforts. However, Koneya (1975) notes that little more than token involvement of the public is manifest in this approach to community development.

Technical assistance appears to be the main theme in more recent years as is manifest in the articles published in the *Journal*. I include articles in the table that reflect the planning of change with public involvement and without public involvement. It is the editors' opinion that public involvement is necessary if technical assistance is to be labeled *community development*. Inspection of the publication dates of the articles listed in Table 2.1 suggests that this approach seems to be overshadowing the other themes. Specifically, if one were to list the research categories under the various themes, almost all would be classified as technical assistance. This may be a reflection of the research emphasis in the *Journal* in more recent years. Today, articles are more likely to be grounded in research. Research seems to be organized more easily around the technical assistance approach than either the self-help or the conflict approaches. An excellent example of research grounded in theory is the article on industrialization by Summers (1977) which summarizes the theoretical implications of the issues involved in industrialization for community development. Other good examples of specific models or typologies are apparent in the works of Shaffer and Tweeten (1974) and Darling (1976).

Obviously, a new bridge, a new industry, a mobile service center, or a comprehensive plan will have a major impact on a neighborhood or a community. The questions become, Who benefits? and Who are the clientele? Again, theory is a gaping hole in this area of investigation. We have theories that relate to economic development and theories that relate to spatial location of businesses and services (e.g., central place theory). But such theories do not directly address community development. Wilkinson (1979, p. 14) comments that "economic development without community development can increase the gap between social classes and reduce the expression of natural human tendencies toward interpersonal warmth, cooperativeness, tolerance, and respect." Community development as a purposive activity is needed to realize the human side of social action and to reap the benefits of the economic side of development. In short, we need to know how the structural imposition of change on communities and on segments of communities contribute to community development as well as how the technical assistance approach contributes to community development, how it works to better the social and economic environment, and how it might interrelate with the self-help and the conflict approaches.

CONFLICT. Over the past two decades, a consistent number of articles on the conflict or confrontation theme have appeared yearly. Most of these articles comment on Alinsky (1969) rather than present ideas of their own or show how conflict actually works in community development efforts. The philosophy behind the conflict theme is a normative emphasis on justice (Blizek and Cederblom 1973, 1974; Sabre 1980). It stresses that there should be more equal distribution of resources in society and usually focuses on those with limited resources and power (e.g., poor, minorities).

The operational procedure prescribed in the conflict approach is similar to that of the self-help approach. The procedure is to get people together to articulate their needs and problems, to develop indigenous leadership, and to help organize viable action groups. While the self-help theme emphasizes people working together to achieve their goal, the conflict theme emphasizes polarization of groups based on salient issues and stimulates confrontation between opposing sides. Conflict does not mean violence. Alinsky was a master of nonviolent confrontation. Reitzes and Reitzes (1980) provide an excellent summary of Alinsky's philosophy and methods. They point out how the use of nonviolent conflict as a means of unifying diverse local interests along with collective bargaining with extra-community agents can facilitate sustainable social change.

Confrontation usually is employed to achieve a particular normative goal such as justice or equality and, in the process, to achieve specific objectives such as the alleviation of forms of job discrimination or the development of new job opportunities for specific groups. Although the conflict theme is interesting to discuss, when it comes down to using the approach it seems that most authors who write for the *Journal* do not become involved in or do not become participant observers of the conflict approach. Instead, they write about Saul Alinsky.

The role of the change agent in the confrontation approach is to get people together, to show them that they have power in numbers and that an organized, focused voice spoken by an active minority can influence what is done within a neighborhood or community. The role of the conflict agent is not to lead, but to help organize. Those using the Alinsky model strive to polarize the need into a well-defined issue and then to help a group of people organize to change the situation.

The advantage of the conflict theme is that it can achieve change in a very short period of time. The problem is whether this change can be sustained. The development of a permanent structure to sustain change is essential. There is considerable concern in the conflict theme about backlash. The backlash of those challenged, particularly the rich and powerful, may place poor people in a situation worse than their initial circumstances. While some detailed studies of the conflict approach exist, there is little systematic analysis that shows when, how, why, and with what success conflict can be used. This normative theme usually is advocated for those outside the power structure but may be equally applicable to middle- and upper-class groups.

Citizen Participation.

The betterment of people, the involvement of people in a democratic society, and the participation of people in community are ideas that underlie much of what is written for community development. The key debate is the difference between working for people and working with people, that is, helping people or enabling people to help themselves. The assumption is that people can help themselves, that all they need is a little educational or organizational help from the outside (i.e., the community development professional) and their situation will be improved. This assumption is the ideal for all three themes. Only the way it is played out differs.

In the 1980s, we saw a decrease in citizens' expectations for government to deal effectively with local problems. Much of the rhetoric from national leaders was to stimulate local problem solving (without national support). The growing complexity of regulations in obtaining governmental support for local services and projects, the continued increase in the cost of local services combined with a decreasing ability of communities to generate supporting tax dollars, and a disenchantment with the role of government in neighborhood and community affairs has led to an increase in citizen activities and involvement in local decision making. These ideas have been reflected in recent articles in the *Journal.*

There is an increased demand for people to initiate group efforts such as food cooperatives, community gardens, and volunteerism (e.g., volunteer fire departments). Likewise, there is a greater need for acquiring both traditional and new skills of participation (e.g., litigation, grantsmanship, advocacy). The *Journal* provides a wide range of articles that address traditional concerns and evolving opportunities for participation. In some recent examples, Luloff and his associates (1984) discuss local volunteerism and what it means for the future; Korte (1984) discusses the determinants of social support in urban settings; Moxley and Hannah (1986) study individual participation patterns in social action; and Ryan (1986) writes about surveys and public interests.

Citizen participation is a persistent theme in all articles that have appeared in the *Journal* during the past two decades. It is always an issue whether by inclusion or exclusion. Community development is grounded in the idea that people should be subjects rather than objects, that people should be proactive rather than reactive. This humanistic thrust is the most common element of all community development elements in the *Journal* articles.

Research. Needs assessment research contributes to all three themes. It focuses on ways to assess the needs, concerns, and goals of citizens; techniques for collecting data such as mail and telephone surveys (Christenson 1975; Dillman 1977); and how public input through needs assessment can contribute to community development. For example, applying Dillman's (1977) synchronized survey model, Garkovich (1979) shows how a countywide citizen survey designed by a county planning commission can stimulate problem identification by both citizens and officials, and can generate a formal action agenda through an interactive decision-making process. Most of the needs assessment research attempts to show how public input can be quantified, organized, and brought to bear on the decision-making process. In short, it shows how research can stimulate and reflect public participation.

The 1970s and 1980s were times of growth for many communities. Natural resource extraction in the western United States created boomtowns and industrial expansion and relocation to the Sunbelt; it also created new problems for communities involving the provision of services and amenities. Many of the articles in the *Journal* attempted to measure the consequences of rapid growth on social pathologies such as crime rates, demand for services, quality of life, and jobs (Webb, Krannich, and Clemente 1980; Albrecht and Geertsen 1982; Greider and Krannich 1985; Albrecht 1986). Others provided economic assessments of the consequences of growth (Pulver 1974; Chicoine, Scott, and Jones 1980; Bender and Stinson 1984).

Evaluation is another identifiable area of concern of writers during these two decades. Evaluation is more an issue for discussion and exhortation than it is an area of documentation and study. However, a few provocative models have been suggested (e.g., SHAPES by Mackeracher et al. 1976) and tested (Cawley 1981). Miller, Voth, and Chapman (1984) provided a controversial quantitative model of community development programs in the journal *Rural Sociology*. And in Chapter 11 of this book, Voth provides a programmatic and research perspective on evaluation. While quite a few articles on the subject are listed in Table 2.1, many in more recent years (e.g., Freudenburg and Olsen 1983; Gibson and Worden 1984), most of these are not evaluation studies per se. But clearly, the discipline seems to be moving in this direction and I would imagine that some real progress in this area will be seen in the next decade.

Services, both the provision of and the need for, are integral in the development of infrastructure for communities. The *Journal* provides a variety of articles on citizen perception of need for services (Warner and Monk 1979; Allen and Gibson 1987), services and the ideal community (Goudy 1983), services for specific groups such as the poor (Glaser 1986), and other aspects of service provision and delivery. Many of the articles focus on a specific service such as a health-care facility, a volunteer fire department, an emergency medical service, and so forth. They provide excellent how-to-do-it case studies and present the likely consequences of such endeavors.

The Profession.

As can be seen in Table 2.1, a range of articles focus on roles for community development. Some of the commonly identified roles include teacher, facilitator, consultant, enabler, motivator, integrator, critic, and resource channel. In a related context, some articles have struggled with the issue of professional certification (Gibson 1977; Parsons 1978). A companion series of articles was written on training, educating, and evaluating community development workers or relevant clientele. These articles include academic program outlines, content area schemes, and performance evaluation measures. Three subsequent chapters in this book will therefore focus on roles, practice, and teaching.

Another group of articles that should be acknowledged, but were difficult both to list and to organize, focused on specific countries, cases, or success stories. Several of these involved community development in foreign countries such as the Dominican Republic, Panama, Turkey, Ecuador, or Sri Lanka (von Lazer and Hammock 1970; Franklin 1971; Suzuki 1975; Daley and Winter 1978; Daley and Labit

1979; Compton 1982); case studies of programs such as OEO (Pell 1972), VISTA (Walker 1971), and HUD (Kellams 1976; Ball and Heumann 1979); neighborhood studies in large cities (Kurzman 1970); and how-to-do-it case studies. These efforts show community development in action but are limited in use because of the specific nature of such studies. In short, they are most interesting to read, but difficult to generalize from.

Implications. The absence of articles soundly based in a theoretical perspective is particularly apparent. Many schemes, models, taxonomies, and other organizing procedures can be found, but most of them deal with a particular substantive area rather than with concepts or the interrelationships of concepts in a theoretical context. While the *Journal* is not nor should be devoted to theory, editors and authors should make a special effort to ensure that theory is addressed in the years ahead. We need to organize our insights to see where, when, and why different social action models work. Blakely, in Chapter 14, elaborates on this issue.

The discipline devoted to community development seems to be caught in a treadmill of descriptive studies and needs assessments. While descriptive studies manifest different types of community development and are very much needed, we also need some systematic attempts to assess why development occurs, what its effects are, who benefits and who pays, and who determines who bears the burden of the downside in developmental efforts. Special attention should be given to linking theory and practice. We need to discuss general theories such as exchange theory, systems theory, field theory, and central place theory, along with theoretical strategies such as cost-benefit analysis, social risk assessment, and social impact assessment; and then we need to document and test their contributions to community development. We need to draw from the best insights of each discipline and adapt it to the practice of community development. Kurt Lewin's oft-quoted phrase sums it up well: "A good theory is practical." Or putting it another way, what seems to work practically should have theoretical implications. We are a discipline still in search of theory. Or if you think that this is inappropriate because of the interdisciplinary foundation of the society, then we are a discipline still in search of guidelines and examples for applying discipline-related theories to community development.

One more area of concern is identifying the roles of those working in community development. While there are many articles on roles and training in the *Journal,* few deal with the institutionalization of jobs within government and universities. Has such institutionalization of roles placed practitioners in the position of supporting only the status quo rather than pursuing change-oriented, and perhaps conflict-generating, courses of action? Robinson provides a perspective on this issue in Chapter 5.

Another area that needs attention is the teaching and training of community development. What should be included in a graduate pro-gram? What should be included in the training of citizens? In an earlier book (Christenson and Robinson 1980), a wide range of professional roles were described (e.g., the planner, the consultant, the extension agent, the community psychologist, the activist, the government spe-cialist). We need an overview of the parameters of the profession, of what skills and information should be taught, of what role models should be presented, of what theories should be learned, and of how one blends theory and practice. Warner in Chapter 6 on roles, Fischer in Chapter 7 on practice, and Cary in Chapter 8 on teaching provide perspectives and suggestions related to these issues.

Evaluation has received some emphasis throughout the two dec-ades of the *Journal's* existence. Some systematic efforts have been made to determine the impact of community development programs and projects (see Chapter 11). This concern for evaluation needs to be amplified in the 1990s. While the *Journal* has reported a large number of success stories, these are limited in advancing the discipline. Touched-up pictures of success stories tend to play down limitations of various approaches and to hide potential problems. We need more sto-ries that show the failures and limitations of developmental efforts. We need to know where and how we have not succeeded so that we might do a better job in the future. One of the few articles that has pointed out what can be learned through failure is the excellent article by Cohen (1976). Evaluation must move from descriptive success stories to quantitative documentation. This shift should be of particular con-cern to practitioners in this time of increased emphasis on accountabil-ity. It raises a new challenge to those in community development and will be an issue not easily solved during the next decade, but one that we must squarely face.

This review is my assessment of the trends and issues in the *Journal of the Community Development Society.* It is limited by my biases, organization, and analysis. However, I do feel that the areas outlined and the themes described capture the different lines of thought winding through the *Journal* these past two decades. I have tried to stimulate a rethinking of who we are, where we are going, and what we need to do to get there. In the following chapters, some of the best scholars in the profession treat these issues, themes, and problems in greater detail and with provocative insight.

References

Albrecht, D. E. 1986. Agricultural dependence and the population turn-around: Evidence from the Great Plains. *Journal of the Community Development Society* 17(1):1–15.

Albrecht, D. E., and H. R. Geertsen. 1982. Population growth in rural communities: Residents' perceptions of its consequences. *Journal of the Community Development Society* 13(2):75–90.

Alinsky, S. 1969. *Reveille for Radicals.* New York: Random House.

Allen, L. R., and R. Gibson. 1987. Perceptions of community life and services: A comparison between leaders and community residents. *Journal of the Community Development Society* 18(1):89–103.

Ball, T. E., and L. F. Heumann. 1979. An analysis of the HUD nonmetropolitan community development program. *Journal of the Community Development Society* 10(1):49–56.

Batten, T. R. 1957. *Communities and Their Development.* London: Oxford University Press.

_____. 1973. The major issues and future direction of community development. *Journal of the Community Development Society* 4(2):34–44.

Bender, L. A., and T. F. Stinson. 1984. Migrating impacts of rapid growth on local government. *Journal of the Community Development Society* 15(1):59–73.

Bender, T. 1978. *Community and Social Change in America.* New Brunswick: Rutgers University Press.

Biddle, W. W., and L. J. Biddle. 1965. *The Community Development Process.* New York: Holt, Rinehart and Winston.

Blakely, E. J., ed. 1979. *Community Development Research.* New York: Human Sciences Press.

Blase, M. G., P. R. Green, and A. Matson. 1973. Selected impacts of public water supply districts on firms, households, and communities. *Journal of the Community Development Society* 4(2):94–101.

Blizek, W. L., and J. Cederblom. 1973. Community development and social justice. *Journal of the Community Development Society* 4(2):45–52.

_____. 1974. Revolution and justice. *Journal of the Community Development Society* 5(1):35–39.

Boesch, D. M., and J. B. Heagler. 1973. St. Francis sanitary landfill. *Journal of the Community Development Society* 4(1):40–47.

Bonner, W. S. 1972. Role of regional planning in community development. *Journal of the Community Development Society* 3(2):70–76.

Brinkman, G. 1973. Effects of industrializing small towns. *Journal of the Community Development Society* 4(1):69–80.

Cary, L. J., ed. 1973. *Community Development as a Process.* Columbia: University of Missouri Press.

Cawley, R. 1981. Testing a predictive model of the community development process. *Journal of the Community Development Society* 12(2):47–62.

Cebotarev, E. A., and E. J. Brown. 1972. Community resource development – An analytical view of work strategies. *Journal of the Community Development Society* 3(1):40–55.

Chase, R. A., and G. C. Pulver. 1983. The impact of shopping center development on downtowns of small nonmetropolitan communities. *Journal of the Community Development Society* 14(2):51–66.

Chekki, D. A., ed. 1979. *Community Development.* New Delhi: Vikas.

Chicoine, D., J. T. Scott, Jr., and T. W. Jones. 1980. The application of goal programming in rural land use policy. *Journal of the Community Development Society* 11(1):77–94.

Christenson, J. A. 1975. A procedure for conducting mail surveys with the general public. *Journal of the Community Development Society* 6(1):135–46.

Christenson, J. A., and J. W. Robinson, Jr., eds. 1980. *Community Development in America.* Ames: Iowa State University Press.

Cohen, M. W. 1976. A look at process: The often ignored component of program evaluation. *Journal of the Community Development Society* 7(1):17–23.

Compton, J. L. 1982. Sri Lanka's Sarvodaya Shramdana Movement. *Journal of the Community Development Society* 13(1):83–104.

Daley, J. M., and C. Labit. 1979. Factors influencing the success of intercultural community development. *Journal of the Community Development Society* 10(1):67–82.

Daley, J. M., and T. Winter. 1978. An evaluation: Intercultural use of community development. *Journal of the Community Development Society* 9(2):62–75.

Darling, D. L. 1976. Fiscal impact of new residential development on communities. *Journal of the Community Development Society* 7(1):40–47.

Dillman, D. A. 1977. Preference surveys and policy decisions: Our new tools need not be used the same old way. *Journal of the Community Development Society* 8(1):30–43.

Franklin, R. 1971. Diary of an action research journey. *Journal of the Community Development Society* 2(1):13–32.

Freudenburg, W. R., and D. Olsen. 1983. Public interest and political abuse: Public participation in social impact assessment. *Journal of the Community Development Society* 14(2):67–82.

Garkovich, L. 1979. What comes after the survey? A practical adaptation of the synchronized survey model in community development. *Journal of the Community Development Society* 10(1):29–38.

Gibson, D. L. 1977. Professional certification for community development personnel. *Journal of the Community Development Society* 8(1):30–38.

Gibson, L. J., and M. A. Worden. 1984. A citizen's handbook for evaluating community impacts: An experiment in community education. *Journal of the Community Development Society* 15(1):27–42.

Glaser, M. A. 1986. Redefinition of the service delivery function of community based organizations. *Journal of the Community Development Society* 17(1):89–109.

Goodwin, H. L., Jr., and G. A. Doeksen. 1984. Consolidation: A viable option for improving operational and financial stability of rural water systems. *Journal of the Community Development Society* 15(2):59–71.

Goudy, W. J. 1983. Desired and actual communities: Perceptions of 27 Iowa towns. *Journal of the Community Development Society* 14(1):39–49.

Greider, T. R., and R. S. Krannich. 1985. Perceptions of problems in rapid growth and stable communities: A comparative analysis. *Journal of the Community Development Society* 16(2):80–96.

Hobbs, D. 1980. Rural development: Intentions and consequences. *Rural Sociology* 45(1):7–25.

Kaufman, H. F. 1975. Community influentials: Power figures or leaders? *Journal of the Community Development Society* 6(1):71–80.

Kellams, D. R. 1976. HUD block grants in Illinois. *Journal of the Community Development Society* 7(2):154–59.

Koneya, M. 1975. Toward an essential definition of community development. *Journal of the Community Development Society* 6(1):4–12.

Korte, C. 1984. Individual and social determinants of social support in an urban setting. *Journal of the Community Development Society* 15(2):31–45.

Kurzman, P. A. 1970. The neighborhood conservation program in New York City: An administrative view. *Journal of the Community Development Society* 1(2):113–24.

Lewis, G. F. 1974. Sociological studies of communities. *Journal of the Community Development Society* 5(1):10–18.

Long, H. B. 1972. Observed community development patterns: 1950–1970. *Journal of the Community Development Society* 3(1):112–20.

Luloff, A. E., W. H. Chittendon, E. Kriss, S. Weeks, and L. Brushett. 1984. Local voluntarism in New Hampshire: Who, why, and at what benefit. *Journal of the Community Development Society* 15(2):17–30.

Mackeracher, D., L. Davie, and T. Patterson. 1976. Community development: evaluation and development: Shapes approach. *Journal of the Community Development Society* 7(2):4–17.

Melvin, E. E. 1972. The planner and citizen participation. *Journal of the Community Development Society* 5(1):40–48.

Miller, M. K., D. E. Voth, and D. D. Chapman. 1984. Estimating the effects of community resource development efforts on county quality of life. *Rural Sociology* 49(1):37–66.

Moxley, R. L., and T. S. Hannah. 1986. Individual participation patterns in community social action. *Journal of the Community Development Society* 17(2):1–23.

Napier, T. L. 1972. Mobile service centers: A potential mechanism for small rural community development. *Journal of the Community Development Society* 3(1):56–63.

Napier, T. L., and S. M. Camboni. 1987. A comparison of human resources characteristics of employed and unemployed primary income earners in Ohio. *Journal of the Community Development Society* 18(1):50–63.

Napier, T. L., and R. C. Maurer. 1978. Correlates of commitment to development efforts. *Journal of the Community Development Society* 9(1):12–27.

Parsons, T. 1978. Professional certification for practitioners of community development. *Journal of the Community Development Society* 9(1):4–11.

Pell, K. 1972. The role of OEO in community development. *Journal of the Community Development Society* 3(2):54–61.

Ploch, L. 1976. Community development in action: A case study. *Journal of the Community Development Society* 7(1):5–16.

Poston, R. 1950. *Small Town Renaissance.* New York: Harper and Row.

Pulver, G. C. 1974. Conflicting goals in growth. *Journal of the Community Development Society* 5(1):53–60.

Reitzes, D. C., and D. C. Reitzes. 1980. Saul D. Alinsky's contribution to community development. *Journal of the Community Development Society* 11(2):39–52.

Roberts, H. 1979. *Community Development: Learning and Action.* Toronto: University of Toronto Press.

Rogers, D. L., W. Goudy, and R. O. Richards. 1976. Impacts of industrialization on employment and occupational structures. *Journal of the Community Development Society* 7(1):48–62.

Ryan, V. D. 1986. Citizen surveys, democracy, and public interests: Words of caution and words of advice. *Journal of the Community Development Society* 17(2):39–53.

Sabre, R. M. 1980. An ethical principle for social justice in community development practice. *Journal of the Community Development Society* 11(1):15–22.

Santopolo, F. A., and R. J. Johnson. 1970. Sociological concepts relevant to training extension workers. *Journal of the Community Development Society* 1(2):104–17.

Shaffer, P. A., and L. Tweeten. 1974. Estimating net economic impact of industrial expansion. *Journal of the Community Development Society* 5(2):79–89.

Sofranko, A. J., and W. M. Bridgeland. 1972. A community structure approach to data collection and recommendations for use of data bank. *Journal of the Community Development Society* 3(2):110–28.

Stanfield, G. G., and W. D. Heffernan. 1977. Critique of theorizing studies of manufacturing expansion in rural areas. *Journal of the Community Development Society* 8(2):50–60.

Summers, G. F. 1977. Industrial development of rural America: A quarter century of experience. *Journal of the Community Development Society* 8(1):6–18.

Suzuki, P. T. 1975. Community development in an urban setting. *Journal of the Community Development Society* 6(1):102–10.

von Lazer, A., and J. C. Hammock. 1970. Community development in the Dominican Republic: Summary reflections on four case studies. *Journal of the Community Development Society* 1(2):89–99.

Walker, M. T. 1971. Two Vista programs among poor whites in a southern Illinois community. *Journal of the Community Development Society* 2(1):33–38.

Warner, P. D., and P. M. Monk. 1979. The formulation and testing of a process model for community development. *Journal of the Community Development Society* 10(1):17–28.

Warren, R. L. 1975. External forces affecting local communities – Bad news and good news. *Journal of the Community Development Society* 6(2):5–13.

Webb, S., R. Krannich, and F. Clemente. 1980. Power plants in rural area communities: Their size, type and perceived impacts. *Journal of the Community Development Society* 11(2):81–95.

Wilkinson, K. P. 1979. Social well-being and community. *Journal of the Community Development Society* 10(1):5–16.

_____. 1986. In search of the community in the changing countryside. *Rural Sociology* 51(1):1–17.

3

The Self-Help Approach

DONALD W. LITTRELL
DARYL HOBBS

The Self-Help Concept.   The idea of self-help is one
of several distinguishing features of community development theory,
practice, and ideology (Bilinski 1969). Self-help is based on the premise
that people can, will, and should collaborate to solve community problems. In addition to the practical problem-solving utility of this perspective, self-help builds a stronger sense of community and a foundation for future collaboration. It embodies the notion that a community
can achieve greater self-determination within constraints imposed by
the larger political economy in which it is embedded.

Without a commitment to self-help, a community may exist as a
place, an organization, or an interest group but be lacking the capacity
to effectively act on its own behalf. In brief, self-help is a community
building strategy. It is a style of planning, decision making, and problem solving which is endemic to the very idea of community—especially that of the small, face-to-face community (Christenson and Robinson 1980). A commitment to self-help is part of a normative specification of what community life should be, and as such is firmly
embedded in a Western democratic and pluralistic ideology. There is
an accompanying presumption, backed in many cases by national policies, that communities committed to self-help are an integral feature of
a broader notion of social development (Bender 1986). Self-help is the
centerpiece of national social and economic development strategies in
many Third World countries such as Tanzania (Ujamaa) and Kenya
(Harambi).

The idea of self-help—not just as an endemic feature of life in many small communities, but as a practice to be instigated in conjunction with broader regional and national development plans and ideologies—will be the focus of this chapter. Self-help is emphasized not only as a goal to be achieved in and of itself, but also as a strategy for the accomplishment of broader development objectives (Bilinski 1969).

INSTIGATING SELF-HELP: A FOUNDATION OF A PROFESSION. Helping communities achieve a capacity for self-help is fundamental to both the theory and practice of community development. If a spirit of self-help doesn't exist within a community as an extension of the members' dedication to common goals and mutual respect, then, from the perspective of community development or empowerment, a capacity for self-help may be instigated with the assistance of an outside community development practitioner or organization. It is this idea of intervention to produce a greater capacity for self-help among a group, or residents of a place, that is a cornerstone of the community development profession. In community development practice it is rudimentary that the solution to community problems is sought first within the community and its resource capabilities. While the community development approach does not assume that all important social, economic, or political problems of communities can be resolved by a community's own efforts, the idea of mobilizing broad community participation is prescribed as a goal of any community development effort. Most definitions of community development include reference to self-help (see Chapter 1).

DEVELOPMENT *in* VERSUS DEVELOPMENT *of* THE COMMUNITY. Self-help embodies two interrelated features: (1) it is expected to produce improvements of people's living conditions, facilities, and/or services, and (2) it emphasizes that the process by which these improvements are achieved is essential to development *of* the community. The "developed community" is both improved and empowered as a result. Of these two features, the self-help perspective emphasizes that the process is more important in the long run than the improvements, because the collaboration that derives from a strong sense of community can be the means to continuing improvement of community services and quality of life (Summers 1986; Wilkinson 1986). By contrast, if community services, facilities, or improvements are contributed by an outside agency or organization with little or no community involvement, such "improvements" are likely to be transitory, to increase community dependency, to contribute little to a greater sense of community, and to diminish the community's future capacity to act on its own behalf. Thus a self-help approach not only emphasizes *what* a community achieves, but more importantly, *how* it achieves it. Another way of stating this is to distinguish between development *in* the community (the improvements) and development *of* the community (how these improvements are achieved) (Summers 1986).

Self-Help *as a* Development Strategy.

Community development's emphasis on self-help emerged as a component of a modernization strategy aimed at improving living conditions while at the same time advocating a democratic version of empowerment, but within a framework of maintaining political stability. Writers such as Biddle and Biddle (1965) and Batten (1957) conceptualized many of what have come to be widely accepted self-help principles from the experiences gained through these efforts. The roots of self-help were both pragmatic and idealistic—pragmatic in that they sought to improve material conditions of life for people of poverty and low productivity, and idealistic in that they sought to establish democratic procedures of participation in an attempt to produce these improvements. Organizations such as the United Nations, the U.S. Agency for International Development, and the U.S. Cooperative Extension Service were among the most active in experimenting with the methods and procedures of self-help. To an important degree these organizations viewed self-help as a feature of national development, not as a stand-alone strategy. Self-help was to be first instigated through intervention of an agent and subsequently guided. These organizations emphasized that various forms of external financial and technical assistance should be combined with village-level, self-help efforts to compress time and hasten improvements in both material and social quality of life.

EMERGENCE OF THE COMMUNITY DEVELOPMENT WORKER. The instrument at the disposal of governments and development agencies to promote the self-help strategy became the community development worker. These workers were typically assigned to groups of villages to mobilize effort toward accomplishment of development objectives.

Workers were charged to work with communities as opposed to working with individuals; agricultural extension work was based on the latter. This assignment was predicated on the notion of the worker being able to mobilize collective effort toward accomplishment of both individual and collective goals. It was generally believed that a community was large enough to be an efficient basis for providing many services, yet small enough to be characterized by face-to-face associations and the cooperative effort that could evolve from the associations.

In many places where a self-help strategy was initiated, planners perceived that a strong sense of fatalism existed and that by simply implanting the idea that ordinary people could intervene in shaping their own destiny, substantial creative energy would be unleashed. Frustration was encountered as often as success, but these experiences contributed to refinement of self-help procedures employed by community development workers.

Channeling development resources through the community development worker often unintentionally converted that worker into a gatekeeper—a position of considerable power. Access to outside resources was often enhanced if the people's desires and the agency's goals matched—the community development worker could not give that which was not his or hers to give. With resources being made available through the community development worker, it was often easy for the worker to become an official rather than a facilitator. Workers were frequently charged with the responsibility of being helpful and "producing results," but they usually had little training in the intricacies and subtleties of instituting a self-help approach. Consequently community improvements often occurred, but were not necessarily accompanied by the community's increased capacity to more effectively organize itself to specify and achieve future goals. These faltering experiences of early workers made important contributions to the development and refinement of ideas about what skills and abilities were needed.

CONFLICT BETWEEN LOCAL AND NATIONAL GOALS. In these early efforts attention was seldom devoted to the prospects for mismatch between national development goals and community plans and aspirations. Where a mismatch occurred it became the task of the community development worker to iron out the difficulty and overcome the resistance. Resistance was often interpreted as an indication of failure. It began to be realized, however, that a way of overcoming such resistance was to involve community members in identifying their needs and attempting to respond to them. But even those plans that were a product of a comprehensive, self-help community development process frequently ran aground when economic and political forces beyond community control were encountered. The philosophy emphasized a greater degree of community autonomy, which often was perceived as threatening to sponsoring central governments. Central governments were generally interested in producing "improvements" for which they could claim credit, but were much less interested in letting loose the reins of political control. Thus the gatekeeper role of community development workers was often emphasized to the detriment of the process role.

SELF-HELP IN INDUSTRIALIZED NATIONS. While self-help approaches were being widely and variously employed in many Third World countries, different perspectives on community, self-help, and development were emerging in industrialized nations. As Russell-Erlich and Rivera (1987) recall, the rallying slogans of many groups and communities in the United States during the 1960s and 1970s were "self-determination," "community control," and "power to the people." Social development was not perceived as an accompaniment of economic growth and technological sophistication. As observed by Goulet (1978, pp. 31–33), "In the face of increasing bureaucratization of life in 'developed countries' there is growing readiness to entertain the possiblity at least that rich countries are emotionally, esthetically, communally and spirtually underdeveloped. . . . Probes into the deeper meaning of the economic and technical backwardness of the Third World have led developed peoples to suspect that they too are 'underdeveloped' in certain basic human dimensions."

While the self-help perspective emphasizes a spirit of cooperation and mutual enhancement of effort among community members, it also recognizes that many of the political, economic, and technological features of the modern world have been destructive of those kinds of relationships. Typically, communities have become incorporated into larger national, or even international, economic, political, and/or service delivery systems. Transportation and communication technology have expanded the boundaries of people's social, political, and economic interaction. In short, communities have become increasingly dependent on external markets or political forces over which they have little control (Wilkinson 1986). In the face of such changes, the locality declines in importance as the locus for people's economic or social needs (Warren 1975). Residents' attention to local needs and opportunities becomes more outwardly than inwardly oriented. As participation in a larger system increases, participation in the locality diminishes. To an extent the locality *dis*integrates.

But as these circumstances have transpired, many social analysts (e.g., Warren 1975) have noted that many people mourn the loss of a sense of community that has attended these changes. That loss is more than abstract. In a recent survey of rural Missouri leaders, 94 percent agreed that restoration of a sense of community was important to the future of rural Missouri (University of Missouri 1985). Thus the modern world has contributed conditions that have produced economic growth (although unevenly) and has extended the coverage of professional health, education, and other services while simultaneously eroding some of a locality's capacity for self-help, cooperation, collaboration, and, therefore, self-determination. It is this set of conditions that is fueling further reflection on the place of self-help and its relevance to restoring or retaining a sense of community. These conditions also serve as a reminder that patterns of self-help are a product of the social history and social conditions prevailing in different societies (Bender, Bargal, and Gidron 1986).

CURRENT REFLECTIONS ON SELF-HELP. The promise and limits of self-help as a strategy of empowerment and improvement have stimulated critiques of its ideological and practical foundations. Such reflections contribute to improved understanding of the role it can play in the service of a broader concept of social development. As suggested by Freire (1972, p. 41), "Action without reflection is performance within ideology, not participation in exposing and recreating it."

In 1986 the *Journal of Voluntary Action Research* devoted a special issue to a comparative analysis of the present status of the self-help idea. In their epilogue to that issue, the editors begin, "Self-help in the middle of the 1980's is no longer an isolated or marginal phenomenon. Involving millions of people in a wide geographic distribution around the world, it has become a force which conceivably qualifies as an ubiquitous social movement" (Bender, Bargal, and Gidron 1986, p. 85). The authors cite as evidence the fact that self-help has had a cumulative impact on major institutions (e.g., the health-care industry, the social services delivery system, the media, the church, and adult education).

But despite the claim of broad contemporary impact, another analyst, Kotze (1987), asserts that the principle of "self-help" in CD [community development] remains vague. It was certainly originally not formulated as an anti-dependency device. It was more likely intended as encouragement for poverty-stricken communities to use what local resources they had. Was this to be development on the cheap? Recognizing this difficulty as well as that no community could live and develop in isolation, and that no community could claim to be independent of other, CD protagonists contradict their own "principle" and say that a measure of external assistance is allowed, but warn that external assistance should be in the form of goods or manpower or knowledge. (P. 32)

Kotze goes on to emphasize that such outside assistance does not come without strings attached and that continued dependence is as great a prospect as self-determination, if not greater.

SELF-HELP AS IDEOLOGY.   Other writers emphasize that it is important to realize that self-help is itself an ideology, for example, "that which is manifested in practices, both formal and institutional" (Sayer 1986, p. 296). Therefore self-help practitioners are likely to benefit from realizing "that by our very existence at the boundary between informal and institutional practices we are involved in ideological development whether we like it or not" (Sayer 1986, p. 296). Sayer's observation gives cause for reflection to those practitioners who regard their community work as ideologically neutral. Whether recognized or not, there are values involved in "objective" community diagnosis and even in facilitating self-help for accomplishment of the community's own perceived needs.

In addition to a utilitarian, problem-solving perspective of self-help, there are other perspectives that have implications for community workers. To an important degree, the community worker's role as gatekeeper or program intermediary is that of a change agent in the sense of promoting the diffusion of expert knowledge and innovations through centralized or packaged programs (Dillon 1984). But as the focus of development has begun to add social development (i.e., development of people themselves) to economic growth and technological change, the role of the community worker has changed substantially. This change in development perspective might be rephrased to reflect that emphasis given to empowerment as a development objective now equals or surpasses emphasis given to adding community facilities and services.

Dillon (1984, p. 247) observes that, in order for the community worker to contribute to social development, "there is general agreement amongst field workers that the change agent's role is basically twofold: that of a catalyst to set ideas into motion, and that of facilitator to help structure the development process as and when people require." Bender (1986, p. 81) also emphasizes that self-help groups can make important contributions to a member's sense of identity, stating that "self-help groups can provide an arena for individuals to consolidate an identity, develop a feeling of belonging, and develop coping and action skills. . . . [They] thus strengthen the individual and give the individual both permission and power to act on his or her own behalf as well as on behalf of the group. Feelings of helplessness are supplanted by feelings of power and control over one's destiny."

Many discussions of self-help occur at an idealistic level as if people generally were free to organize and pursue their interests in the most effective way. Self-help rests to a large extent on the assumption that freedom of association exists and consequently that voluntary associations can play a major role in development. However, Kotze (1987) reminds us that it is questionable whether such freedom does exist in all societies. The potential benefits of self-help may be significantly limited by the constraints different societies place on freedom of association and collective action.

Implications for Contemporary Self-Help Practice.

After years of experience and practice, a question emerges as to whether self-help, originally formulated in simple settings concerned with primary needs, can be effective in today's complex world. Many practioners, citizens, and organizations pledge allegiance to a self-help philosophy, but an ideology of democratic self-help appears to be easier to describe than to practice.

As our review indicates, the centrality of a norm of self-help as a key element of quality community life remains in place; the conditions to achieve it have changed markedly. We now review some of these conditions and suggest implications for practice.

PARTICIPATION AND DEMOCRATIC DECISION MAKING. The self-help literature continues to stress that bringing people together to discuss their various concerns will lead to agreements being reached and to plans of action being made and implemented. Implicit is the notion that people are interested, motivated, and want to be involved if there are no structural impediments to their participation. But experience of community workers suggests that those conditions seldom prevail. This is partly because of the complexity and external dependence of modern communities described above. In addition, public involvement and democratic procedures are seldom efficient in the sense of arriving at direct decisions quickly—that is, involving people in the decision-making process typically increases the complexity of decisions and is very time-consuming.

Current conditions of community life, especially in the United States and other industrial nations, have caused many community problems and decisions to become translated into technical questions requiring some degree of technical understanding or expertise as a condition for solution. Such technical questions often emerge as a result of communities' dependence on state and federal agencies for some funding support and tend to encompass technical specifications, regulations, legal issues, etc. The more community issues and problems become translated into technical questions, the more they discourage self-help and broad participation. However technical questions need not remain technical. They can be translated into broader policy options which are understandable and encourage rather than discourage participation. In addition, it does not negate the ideology of self-help for communities to contract for needed technical assistance.

Because community problems often become technical problems, community leaders and officials find it easier and more "efficient" to make decisions and take actions without much community input, unless there is organized opposition. This pattern of official decision making is frequently vindicated by an apparent lack of public interest, but such a lack of public involvement is often attributable to a self-fulfilling prophecy. Participation, involvement, and perceptions of collaborative opportunities have to be perceived as making a difference if they are to be practiced. It is this question of a connection between participation and perceived outcomes of participation that has become an issue. For example, voting participation has continued to decline in the United States even though information about candidates and issues has become voluminous. It is reasonable to assume that voting is perceived by many as not making much of a difference. People tend to weigh the costs of their participation against the perceived benefits.

This contemporary circumstance creates several challenges for the community development worker or anyone wishing to garner broader participation in self-help efforts. It cannot be assumed that people will perceive their participation as making a difference; the potential benefit will most likely need to be made explicit to both citizens and the community. People will need to perceive that options are within their grasp, and that self-help efforts are feasible and appropriate for the task. This involves implementing what Bennis, Benne, and Chin (1969) refer to as a *normative–re-educative* strategy.

But there are two sides to stimulating broader participation in self-help efforts. One issue is to ensure that citizens understand that their participation can make a difference. The other equally important issue is to initiate discussion of self-help options to ensure that they are practical, feasible, and likely to make a difference.

COMMUNITY OR GROUP AUTONOMY. Most communities have become implicated in and dependent on economic, social, and political interactions that are not only regional but also national and international in scope. These interactions have, on the one hand, greatly expanded the "boundaries" of communities, but on the other hand, have made communities dependent for their services and economic survival on market forces over which they have little control. Thus, the political economy within which individual communities are embedded serves to constrain local options and place real and perceived limits on self-help initiatives.

An implication of declining community autonomy is that there is a growing need for communities to become aware of the external influences that constrain their options so that these can be taken into account. Self-help initiatives, if they are to be effective, must be based on informed selection so that they may be reasonably expected to have an impact. Many U.S. agricultural communities, for example, have suffered both economically and socially as a result of low farm prices and heavy debt loads. A growing number of family farm foreclosures and bankruptcies are consequences. These have been caused by a set of circumstances originating largely outside the community—that is, the prices farmers receive for their products are influenced largely by national and international market forces over which the community has little control. This situation has precipitated a desire among agricultural communities to *do* something. Such an effort might begin with identifying needs that have emerged as a result of this crisis, and then identifying what options the community might have at its disposal to address those needs. The role of the community worker in such a situation might include a heavy emphasis on education about the problem and its sources. This would be an important step in a community's efforts to do something about the problem. In the absence of such an educational effort, communities often conclude there is nothing that can be done and thereby miss opportunities to pursue those possiblities for making a difference that might be open to them.

SELF-HELP AS A PROCESS WITHIN THE COMMUNITY. The self-help model has often been presented as a self-contained process; that is, self-help initiatives are limited to problems that can be resolved by employing only those resources found within the community. As suggested by Kotze (1987, p. 34), ideally "CD [community development] is essentially a micro-level process mobilizing community resources which are by definition small, meagre and localized, using simple technology." Thus, there is a contradiction to self-help's core ideology when a community becomes dependent on outside sources for technical assistance, for support of local institutions, and even for its economic base. That external dependence has become a fact of modern life throughout much of the world. The question is whether it negates the idea and philosophy of self-help. It has been argued both ways. It cannot be denied that dependence on such external sources diminishes community autonomy and control. On the other hand, given this reality, the question becomes whether or not a community can maintain a modicum of control, judiciously employing outside resources to accomplish the community's purposes instead of bending community aspirations to match the resources available.

Another consideration is that modern political economies have tended to drain smaller communities of many of their resources. This is especially true of human resources, given the prevalent tendency for well-trained people from small communities to migrate to larger centers of employment. In effect, smaller communities have tended to subsidize national and predominantly urban economic growth and development. Therefore, on equity grounds it is argued that it is not only appropriate but it is necessary that development resources be channeled back to smaller communities. Wilkinson (1986) contends that the federal government must play a role in rural community development. He argues that it is unrealistic, given the diminished resource base, for rural communities to achieve an equitable quality of life by their own self-help bootstraps.

But whether community development occurs as a result of using outside resources reduces to a question of whose initiative is responsible for the kind and amount of outside resources needed. This of course begins with the notion of community as having devoted collaborative efforts to establishing its own priorities and to identifying those goals that require external support for accomplishment. If external support is sought, implications for local control, both in the short and long run, should be a prominent consideration. Do the resources contribute to the kind of community that members have decided they want to achieve?

Community "self-help" efforts are increasingly oriented toward obtaining needed resources from outside agencies and organizations. Self-help efforts may therefore be directed more toward grant writing and/or exercising external political influence than toward finding the resources within the community. Employing external support, therefore, carries with it the caveat that communities need to be effectively organized to pursue sources of outside support. Martin and Wilkinson (1984) have found that those communities whose leaders were most actively involved outside the community (representing the community interests) were most successful in obtaining federal assistance to support local initiatives. A ramification is that community workers need to be able to educate and inform communities of outside sources of support and be able to initiate discussions of the probable intended and unintended consequences.

There is clearly a narrow line between sustaining a norm of self-help and becoming largely dependent on external resources. Dependence can extinguish a spirit of self-help. In most countries economic development has been too uneven—both socially and spatially—for communities to achieve an equitable quality of life exclusively with their own resources. The issue has therefore become how to blend these resources in such a way that community aspirations remain the paramount consideration.

HOMOGENEOUS AND CONSENSUS-BASED COMMUNITIES. Communities have become more heterogeneous both socioeconomically and in terms of interests. In modern societies, contiguous geographic residence provides little assurance that people have shared interests, values, or beliefs. As populations have become more mobile and interests more diverse, a concomitant growth of special interest organizations has occurred even within small communities.

Semipublic interest groups, such as those concerned with industrial development, environmental protection, and farm prices, affect not only what occurs in their domain but what occurs in the at-large community as well. In addition, different elements of local government and public agencies have become increasingly specialized and connected with external sources of funding and regulation, and therefore have become special interest groups. For example, schools, volunteer fire departments, and special ambulance districts can each serve as a basis for a relatively well-defined special interest group. Therefore "communities" based on interest rather than on geography are increasingly becoming the basis for many people's community participation. A consequence is that a geographic community may be composed of many, relatively well-organized, special interest groups, with each having well-developed connections beyond local community borders. The commitment of members' time and support to these special interests can be a source of conflict when the initiatives pertain to the geographic community.

The local planning and decision-making process has therefore become more complicated, to a great extent because the various special interest groups, including those based on various governmental services, tend to have relatively little interaction with each other and tend to devote their participation to their particular interests rather than to those pertaining to their common place of residence. Consequently, self-help initiatives may be more frequently instigated in communities of interest than in communities of residence. In addition, this circumstance suggests self-help initiatives pertaining to the community of residence will likely require the formation of coalitions (i.e., bringing about interorganizational collaboration and cooperation).

Implications for the community development worker interested in promoting community self-help efforts are numerous. Initial self-help efforts may need to be explicitly addressed to determine what, if any, shared interests exist in a locality. Making such a determination may need to begin with meetings involving representatives of different special interest groups. It cannot be assumed that these different interest groups meet together very often to explore their common interests. Equally important is determining what conflicts of interest exist among these groups, since such conflicts would adversely affect the potential for collaboration toward achieving larger community goals. Flora and Darling (1986), in discussing methods for increasing communities' capacity for self-help, emphasize the importance of creating an umbrella organization of the different interests as a mechanism for identifying and working on the common interests of the larger community.

Another ramification for the community development worker is to understand the basis for conflicts of interest and how these conflicts can be resolved. It is important to understand the difference between those conflicts that are real and those that are apparent. Given the increasingly fragmented nature of community life, the existence of conflict between interest groups may be assumed rather than being a product of direct interaction. As an outsider, the community worker has an advantage in being able to bring together different factions to determine how real and profound the conflicts of interest might be.

SKILLS AND ABILITIES NEEDED FOR PARTICIPATION. Strategies abound based on the assumption that if people are aware of the opportunity, they will add their effort to designing and implementing community improvement projects. In most communities it is possible to find a small percentage of the residents who are intensely active in community projects, planning, and decision making. An often-encountered problem, however, is that these are the only community residents playing an active role. And of course through their involvement they continue to refine their skills in community organization. A problem most communities face is how to broaden the base of participation. Some who choose not to be involved may not care, preferring to leave community matters in the hands of the "leaders." But there is an equal or greater possiblity that these residents may feel excluded, that their input is not needed or wanted, or that they feel they lack the skills to participate.

It is important for the community worker to be sensitive to reasons why some people choose not to participate. Sometimes increasing participation may be as simple as asking people to join some activity or to take some responsibility. Few persons are likely to volunteer, particularly if they have the feeling that things are going well without them or that the leaders are not interested in their participation.

A charge of apathy is often leveled at people because of their failure to participate. It is important to recognize that people may be aware of situations needing attention, but they may have come to the conclusion that they cannot affect the situation or that their ideas are not appropriate. The modern world with its sophisticated media and worldwide coverage can contribute to a reduced inclination to participate. We live in a world where people have an opportunity to become better and better informed about things over which they perceive they have less and less control. A predictable response for many people is apathy – Why bother becoming informed or participating if it is perceived as making little difference? That perspective can extend down to the locality, especially if the belief persists that the locality can do little to achieve greater self-determination.

In many cases a basic tenet – *to start where the people are* – may be applied to helping people understand how they can make a difference. Practitioners should acquire skills in areas such as problem analysis and action research through which people can visualize how they can take effective action. Enlisting people to become involved in activities such as community surveys or other forms of needs assessments can be a good way of achieving small beginnings. Close attention should be given to developing avenues for participation where nonparticipants can feel comfortable and where they are not threatened. Many community development practitioners have worked with people who expressed interest or willingness to become involved but were fearful or apprehensive that they might have to assume a leadership role. Lack of interest may frequently serve as an excuse to cover fear of failure based on one's perceived lack of knowledge, skill, or confidence. If there is a desire to involve those who traditionally have not participated, it is important that these people be encouraged to participate in smaller neighborhood, organization, or committee activities where their participation is recognized and they have an opportunity to overcome some of their hesitancies, experience some success, and begin acquiring participation skills.

For self-help to become operational, it may be necessary for community workers to concentrate on helping people learn to participate in different arenas, using procedures and skills previously unfamiliar to them. Effective participation is necessary for self-help to occur, since it is the participation of people learning to do for themselves that distinguishes self-help from directive approaches. Participation is an acquired skill, and practice is one of the best methods of acquiring it.

OPEN OPPORTUNITY TO PARTICIPATE. A basic value and belief of self-help is that "people have the right to participate in decisions which have an effect upon their well-being" (Littrell 1971, p. 4; 1987). It is not safe to assume that all people and communities share this value. Communities where important decisions and activities are concentrated in the hands of a few appear to outnumber those where there is a history of broad-based citizen involvement. In some communities, those who have "been in charge" may not only view additional citizen involvement as unnecessarily time consuming, but may also perceive it as threatening, because they may have to modify their control over some issues and directions. In addition, community leaders accustomed to making plans for others may sincerely feel that they have a finger on the pulse of the community and know what is best for the community as a whole. A result is that some of the community's active participation sectors that will be affected by the decisions and the actions will be excluded. Very often patterns of exclusion follow lines that have been a basis for past discrimination, including sex, race, age, social class, and/or level of income. Although some of these bases for discrimination may have been quite intentional (such as race or social class), others (such as age) may result from oversight. Whatever the basis for discrimination or exclusion, communities deprive themselves of the most important self-help resource – the effort and talent of residents – if participation of any segment of the community is systematically excluded.

Keeping a decision-making system open is not easy, and people must perceive it to be open if it is, in fact, to be open. Over the long run a norm of self-help is more likely to be realized in a setting where all points of view can be expressed than in one where views are systematically excluded or suppressed. Open discussions may seem to slow the process, but unless diverse perspectives are considered, presumed conflict can impede collaborative action. One of the community worker's roles should be to raise questions about who will be affected, and how, in order to ensure that different points of view are taken into account. While such a role may generate conflict in the short run, especially if exclusion has been intentional, it is important to realize that creating a stronger sense of community and achieving collaboration toward common goals is unlikely to occur without an open opportunity for participation. However, besides ideological reasons for open participation there are strong pragmatic reasons. The ideology of self-help includes the principle that people will support what they have helped create. But the opposite also tends to be true: if people have not had an opportunity to have a role in defining an issue, they will have a higher probability of nonsupport and may even oppose what has been developed.

ADDITIONAL CONSIDERATIONS FOR THE COMMUNITY WORKER. Community development workers often find themselves mediating between three different sets of expectations: (1) a philosophy of community development emphasizing an ideal of broad participation and a norm of self-help; (2) expectations of the worker's employer, whether that employer is a government, university, foundation, or the community itself; and (3) expectations of the community or some segments of the community. Obviously the ideal situation is when all three sets of expectations coincide, but community workers need to be prepared for the greater likelihood that they will not.

The people's only goal (especially early in the process) may be the completion of a specific project or activity (they want action more than process), while the community development worker has been trained in a process and wants people to learn how to accomplish objectives in an effective, collaborative, democratic manner and to transfer that experience to future situations so that they can become more independent. This dilemma is more elaborately described by Batten (1967):

> Community workers work for the betterment of people. But "betterment" is a very vague and general term which every person will interpret for himself according to his own ideas of what is good. Thus what the worker regards as betterment for the people with whom he works they may not regard as betterment for themselves. If this should happen, what then should the worker do? Should he try to direct, lead, guide, or persuade people to accept his judgment of what is good? If he does, how can he be sure that he is right? Or should he try to help them think out for themselves what they want? If so, and if the people decide on something that conflicts with his own ideas of what is good, what then becomes of his purpose of promoting betterment for them? (P. 3)

An additional dilemma may confront the community development worker in that his or her employing agency or organization is likely to be more interested in the hard evidence of tangible accomplishments and projects completed than in the "softer" evidence of *how* those projects were completed. Funds for agencies tend to be allocated more on the basis of accomplishments than on the methods employed. The community worker may realize that more projects will be accomplished in the long run if a self-help participatory process is established, but again funding allocations tend to be made on short-run accomplishments.

While there is no simple solution to these dilemmas, for the community development worker each project represents an opportunity to further broaden a base of participation and to emphasize and inculcate additional principles of self-help. Thus, through a series of projects a community may gain greater practice and appreciation of the value of self-help principles. As we have emphasized, in contemporary communities there are many factors which have been destructive of shared values and have become impediments to the practice of participatory self-help. Overcoming these impediments and establishing a norm of collaboration is not likely to be accomplished quickly, or through the experience of one project. Repetition and demonstration of the practical value of self-help to both the community and employing agency are likely to be crucial to acceptance of the process as an integral part of community improvement.

It is often stated that self-help efforts should start where the people are. This statement is true, but starting where the people are does not mean agreeing with whatever people say they want to do. The people may desire a new community center or an industrial plant, but it is not the sole purpose of the community development worker to help them obtain these specifics. Additionally the worker has an analytical and educational role to play in helping people think through why they want what they want, the short- and long-run effects, and whether the thing they want will produce the intended results. Bennett (1969, p. 10) points out that "community development education is not simply education for action, but education in action." Williamson (1979) emphasizes a similar point, stressing that education should be viewed less as a commodity and more as a program of action. To a great extent the community development worker's role is that of educator—teaching others not only the evaluation of alternatives but also the practice of participation.

POLICY DEVELOPMENT AS SELF-HELP. Self-help approaches are often linked to the accomplishment of specific projects or activities that respond to specific community needs. We suggest, however, that many contemporary communities are in need of general policies as well as specific improvements. Policy establishes the general direction in which a community wants to go. In the absence of general policies, it is quite likely that communities will proceed with piecemeal and ad hoc projects and issues with no clear expectation of where they may be leading the community. Many of these will be in response to opportunities to support certain initiatives or programs that originate with funding agencies outside the community. Such opportunism may, or may not, contribute to a community achieving its aspiration of being the kind of community it would like to be. Thus we suggest that there is a need for broad community policies and that formulating these policies provides a golden opportunity to employ the principles of participation and self-help.

Input into policy formation has great potential as part of the self-help approach for the future. Policy formation can place people and their communities into an initiating rather than a responding stance. Policy formation by local, area, state, and national governments is not new, but the idea that people can learn to interact with various units of government to form policy at all levels is a somewhat new, exciting, and largely unexplored aspect of self-help. It is a step toward the greater degree of self-determination that is integral to the community development philosophy.

Policy formation is often treated as a role of government officials and agencies and large private firms rather than as a function of citizens interacting with various units of government or other organizations. What has been overlooked is that people can be influential in setting overall guidelines for various units of government to utilize in day-to-day functioning. Through the political process they can create policy and then monitor and enforce the policy's implementation. For example, many towns, rural areas, and cities are rethinking their growth policy. In many such cases citizens' groups have played major roles in determining whether the area will actively seek growth, no growth, or some point in between. Likewise, in many urban areas school systems have been forced to change operational procedures and allocations as a result of organized citizen input. In most such cases, the special interest groups described above have taken an active role in policy formation, modification, and monitoring. These groups have proven to be effective at all levels of government.

However, we are suggesting that there is a need for policy discussion and formulation that goes beyond special interests or even different units of government. There is a need for different groups and interests to come together to address broad community goals and priorities. One method many communities have employed to accomplish this is to collaborate in conducting a comprehensive community survey that spans all issue areas and provides an opportunity for all citizens to express their preferences. The results of such a practical exercise in self-help and participation can serve as the foundation for a coherent set of community goals and priorities (policy).

Conclusion.   The self-help approach to community development is a simple concept: People have the basic right – and will be well served if they exercise that right – to collaborate in setting common goals, in organizing themselves, and in mobilizing the resources necessary to achieve those goals. But despite its simplicity, many more communities pledge allegiance to that philosophy than actually practice it. The chapter specifies a number of reasons why, in an increasingly interdependent world, the practice of self-help often becomes a casualty. But because of the greater interdependency, it also means that many communities are increasingly influenced by social, economic, technological, and political forces over which they have little control. Consequently, it is possibly more important than ever for communities to orient themselves toward achieving a greater degree of self-determination and adopting the self-help procedures and principles that will allow the idea of community to retain its meaning in coming years.

References

Batten, T. R. 1957. *Communities and Their Development: An Introductory Study with Special Reference to the Tropics.* London: Oxford University Press.

_____. 1967. *The Non-Directive Approach in Group and Community Work.* London: Oxford University Press.

Bender, E. I. 1986. The self-help movement seen in the context of social development. *Journal of Voluntary Action Research* 15(2):77–84.

Bender, E. I., D. Bargal, and B. Gidron. 1986. Epilogue. *Journal of Voluntary Action Research* 15(2):85–90.

Bennett, A. E. 1969. Reflections on community development education. Bulletin 576. Orono: University of Maine, Northeast Regional Extension Public Affairs Committee.

Bennis, W. G., K. D. Benne, and R. Chin. 1969. *The Planning of Change.* New York: Holt, Rinehart and Winston.

Biddle, W., and L. Biddle. 1965. *The Community Development Process: The Rediscovery of Local Initiative.* New York: Holt, Rinehart and Winston.

Bilinski, R. 1969. A description and assessment of community development. In *Selected Perspectives for Community Resource Development,* L. T. Wallace et al., eds. Raleigh: North Carolina State University, Agricultural Policy Institute.

Christenson, J. A., and J. W. Robinson, Jr., eds. 1980. *Community Development in America.* Ames: Iowa State University Press.

Dillon, B. 1984. The change agent: A radical perspective. *Community Development Journal* 19(4):246–51.

Flora, C., and D. Darling. 1986. Community capacity building to take advantage of opportunities for agricultural and rural development. In *Interdependencies of Agriculture and Rural Communities in the Twenty-First Century,* P. Korsching and J. Gildner, eds. Ames, Ia.: The North Central Regional Center for Rural Development.

Freire, P. 1972. *Pedagogy of the Oppressed.* London: Penguin Books.

Goulet, D. 1978. *The Cruel Choice: A New Concept in the Theory of Development.* New York: Atheneum.

Kotze, D. A. 1987. Contradictions and assumptions in CD. *Community Development Journal* 22(1):31–35.

Littrell, D. W. 1971. Theory and practice of community development. MP 184. Columbia: University of Missouri, Extension Division Publication.

_____. 1987. Civic governance: A role for community development? Paper presented at the annual meeting of the Community Development Society. Morgantown, W.Va.

Martin, K., and K. P. Wilkinson. 1984. Local participation in the federal grant system: Effects of community action. *Rural Sociology* 49(3):376–88.

Russell-Erlich, J. L., and F. G. Rivera. 1987. Community empowerment as a non-problem. *Community Development Journal* 22(1):2–10.

Sayer, J. 1986. Ideology: The bridge between theory and practice. *Community Development Journal* 21(4):294–303.

Summers, G. F. 1986. Rural community development. In *New Dimensions in Rural Policy: Building upon Our Heritage,* D. Jahr, J. W. Johnson, and R. C. Wimberly, eds. Washington, D.C.: Joint Economic Committee of Congress.

University of Missouri. 1985. Rural Missouri 1995: Challenges and issues. Special Report 335. Columbia: University of Missouri, College of Agriculture.

Warren, R. 1975. External forces affecting local communities – Bad news and good news. *Journal of the Community Development Society* 6(2):5–13.

Wilkinson, K. 1986. Communities left behind – Again. In *New Dimensions in Rural Policy: Building upon Our Heritage,* D. Jahr, J. W. Johnson, and R. C. Wimberly, eds. Washington, D.C.: Joint Economic Committee of Congress.

Williamson, B. 1979. *Education, Social Structure and Development.* New York: Holmes and Meier Publishers, Inc.

4

The Technical Assistance Approach

FRANK A. FEAR
LARRY GAMM
FREDERICK FISHER

TECHNICAL ASSISTANCE has deep historical roots; the act of seeking advice from others is as old as humanity itself. Moses, for example, established a network of village advisors (technical assistants) based on advice received from his father-in-law. Technical assistance is intended to help communities define their problems, needs, and potential solutions and may allow for some degree of community autonomy, or "ownership," of problem definition and solution. Technical assistance might be broadly defined as the provision of "programs, activities, and services . . . to strengthen the capacity of recipients to improve their performance with respect to an inherent or assigned function" (Wright 1978, p. 343). A key ingredient in this definition is the application of expertise to aid the recipient in these efforts (Poats 1972).

Technical Assistance as an Approach to Planned Change.
For analytic purposes, it is possible to profile the professional practice of technical assistance. In this approach, society is viewed as a complex system

with functionally specialized structures that are managed by legitimate authority figures. Change is inevitable, but its purpose should be to improve current structures rather than to replace them with new structures. Bureaucratic authority is well respected and conflict is considered a dysfunctional process.

From a technical assistance position, the scientific method is highly valued, advances in technology are considered signs of progress, and rational planning in the decision-making process is viewed as a corollary of the scientific method. Indeed, planning is a prized process, and the collection and analysis of data are important elements in that process. It is assumed that all situations can be objectively analyzed and that bad decisions are frequently the result of poor planning.

In the technical assistance mindset, technical know-how is assumed to be good because efficiency is a valued end. New technology may be uncritically accepted as a better way of doing things. Technology transfer is often defined as the process of effectively communicating or marketing the technology's benefits to potential users. However, full attention may not be given to the technology's fit to the sociocultural context and the dysfunctional consequences that may come about because of its introduction.

The official power structure is often the employer or sponsor of technical assistance work. Economic growth or improvement of the physical infrastructure is typically the focus of attention; advancing community-based capacity may not be a central concern. Local resources – physical and human – may or may not be drawn upon during the assistance episode.

COMPARISONS OF SELF-HELP AND CONFLICT APPROACHES. The three major themes of community development advanced in Chapter 2 – self-help, technical assistance, and conflict – generally parallel the approaches to planned change as treated in the broader literature. For example, in comparing schools of thought about planned change, Crowfoot and Chesler (1976) discuss the counter-cultural (self-help) perspective, the professional-technical (technical assistance) perspective, and the political (conflict) perspective. In a discussion of the primary areas of community organization in social work, Rothman (1974*b*) identifies three approaches: locality development (self-help), social planning (technical assistance), and social action (conflict). And, Chin and Benne (1976) consider three strategies of planned change: the normative–re-educative (self-help), the empirical-rational (technical assistance), and the power-coercive (conflict).

A unifying theme in these treatments is that the approaches (or perspectives) differ in a number of fundamental areas. Crowfoot and Chesler, for instance, emphasize ideological distinctions by showing how the approaches vary in their response to very basic, value-laden questions: (1) What are their general images of society? (2) What are their general images of the individual? (3) What are their diagnoses of contemporary society? and (4) What are their priorities with regard to change? Rothman focuses on selected practice variables, including salient practitioner roles, differential conception of the client's role, tactics and techniques used, and orientation toward the community power structure. A comparative analysis of the approaches is presented in Table 4.1 (see also Chapter 2, Table 2.2).

The differences described by these authors are most worthy of note, especially for students and practitioners of technical assistance. For our purposes, a useful distinction may be drawn between self-help and conflict, on the one hand, and technical assistance, on the other hand. Both the self-help and conflict approaches fix attention on human and collective development; community residents are expected to come together, identify problems through mutual agreement, mobilize resources, and attack problems collectively. However, the *process* of change that is fundamental to technical assistance is just as important—perhaps more important—than the products derived from the change episode. That is, the process of collective action represents a literal learning laboratory where persons can expand their repertoires of community change skills. Self-help and conflict practitioners are successful (other things being equal) to the extent that they possess well-developed process skills—something emphasized in the literature on practice roles (Bennett 1973).

Indeed, the differences between the technical assistance approach and the self-help and conflict approaches are more than superficial. For example, because the power structure is the employer or sponsor of technical assistance efforts, citizens are frequently defined by the technical assistance approach as consumers or end users. In contrast, the concept of community residents as consumers or clients is frequently eschewed, if not pejoratively viewed, in the self-help approach. In the conflict literature, residents are often described as the victims of social inequities and injustices. Similarly, members of the local power structure are collaborators, at best, and "blockers," at worst, in the self-help approach; they are oppressors to those who espouse the conflict approach.

Table 4.1. *Comparison of Self-Help, Technical Assistance, and Conflict as Planned Change Approaches*

Factor	Planned Change Approach		
	Self-Help	Technical Assistance	Conflict
Image of society	Dehumanized, mechanical	Bureaucratic organizations with authority figures	Groups constantly struggle to maintain or add to their power base
Image of the individual	Inherently good, but goodness suppressed	System-defined player of roles	Oppressed
Assumption example	People have the right and ability to identify and solve collective problems	Science provides a means to solve problems	Power is the most basic of all resources
Core problem to be addressed	Capacity of people to take collective action	Capacity to harness science to solve human problems	Concentration of power in the hands of few persons
Action goal example	Community capacity building	Technical problem solving	Redistribution of power

Sources: Adapted from Rothman (1974*b*), Chin and Benne (1969), and Crowfoot and Chesler (1974).

Types of Technical Assistance. Is it possible

to classify technical assistance by type? We believe it is, and two classifications will be discussed here: (1) classification by auspices and impetuses, and (2) more importantly, classification by developmental activity.

TECHNICAL ASSISTANCE BY AUSPICES AND IMPETUSES. Technical assistance relationships, and decisions to enter into them, may vary according to the auspices under which they are organized and the impetuses for undertaking technical assistance. The *auspices* under which technical assistance is provided can be categorized as (1) legislative – having the powers to create, legislate, and appropriate; (2) administrative – having the power to manipulate resources, knowledge, and information; (3) educative – having the knowledge, skills, and processes of a specialized nature associated largely with educational and research institutions; (4) collaborative – creating mechanisms, often mutually, for the specified purpose of providing or enhancing technical assistance in the recipient's domain; and (5) consultative – generally, performing specific tasks by private consultants.

The *impetus* for offering technical assistance – how it finds its way into a recipient's domain – can be categorized in the following ways: (1) imposed – thrust on the recipient unilaterally from the outside; (2) negotiated – reached by mutual consent; and (3) community-initiated – invited by those who perceive that they have such a need. Examples of the substance or form that technical assistance might take according to auspices and impetuses are outlined in Table 4.2.

NONDEVELOPMENTAL AND DEVELOPMENTAL TECHNICAL ASSISTANCE. Although technical assistance essentially involves the acquisition of problem-solving resources, the rationale for the resource exchange and the nature of the relationship between the provider and the recipient are critically important issues if we are to view technical assistance as a theme of community development. Contemporary technical assistance efforts are predominantly associated with the desire of the provider to enable recipients to do what they are incapable of doing or unwilling to do on their own. That is, the provider is committed to some goal that, if it is to be attained, requires an adoption of particular skills or technologies by the recipient. Additionally, the provider is unwilling to wait for "natural" (communication, travel) means of trans-

Table 4.2. Forms of Technical Assistance Categorized according to Auspices and Impetuses

Impetus for Technical Assistance	Legislative (e.g., Congress, state legislature)	Administrative (e.g., national or state agencies)	Educative (e.g., universities, research institutes)	Collaborative (e.g., national or state professional organizations)	Consultative (e.g., private consultants)
Imposed	Policies Laws Programs Funds Structural changes	Evaluation Management criteria Guidelines			
Negotiated	Funds Personnel	Programs Hardware Software Information Training Personnel exchange and training Management systems	Knowledge Skills Research Information Personnel training	Standards Information Research Personnel training	
Community-initiated				With other communities: Personnel exchange Task forces Knowledge exchange Joint data systems	Grant writing Data systems Management systems

Source: Gamm and Fisher (1980).

fer to reach the recipient and is unwilling or unable to directly take over the recipient's responsibilities.

These points are essentially captured in the basic assumptions of technical assistance:

1. Someone knows about something that another does not.
2. Someone decides that the potential recipient needs assistance.
3. A provider-recipient relationship can be established.
4. The provider provides and the receiver receives.

Given this backdrop, it can be argued that technical assistance, although an important approach to planned change, may or may not be an approach (or theme) of community development. Technical assistance as a nondevelopmental approach to change is generally described by Batten (1975) in his discussion of the directive approach to group and community work as follows:

> The directive approach means that the agency . . . decides . . . whatever it thinks people need or ought to value or ought to do for their own good, and sometimes how they ought to behave. These decisions become the agency's goals for people. The agency will then provide whatever staff, equipment, premises, and programmes it thinks are needed to meet the needs or interests of the people it wishes to help, in the hope that they will avail themselves of the services or activities it provides. This will bring them into contact with the agency's workers who will then try to influence people in relation to the agency's ideas of betterment for them. . . . The agency and its workers think, decide, plan, organize, administer, and provide for people. Always the main initiative, and the final say, remain with them. (P. 5)

On the other hand, Christenson and Robinson's (1980) widely quoted definition describes community development as the *shared decision by community residents to initiate a planned change process.* When conceptualized through this filter, technical assistance involves the residents' desire to accept assistance because of its fundamental importance for improving the locale's social, economic, and/or physical environment. Outside assistance is therefore necessary and appropriate. In addition, legitimate representatives of the community collaborate with external change agents (i.e., those providing the assistance) as well as with inside change agents on a "planned change team." That collaboration is based on a mutually agreeable set of role relationships.

If these elements are in place, then it is possible for technical assistance to be compatible with the Oberle, Stowers, and Darby

(1974, p. 61) definition of development as the "process in which increasingly more members of a given area or environment make and implement socially responsible decisions." This approach to technical assistance can be classified as the *developmental* approach.

Perhaps the basic difference between technical assistance as a nondevelopmental and developmental approach to planned change rests in the question of values. In reviewing the definition and assumptions associated with technical assistance, a development ethician such as Goulet (1977) might pose the question: *Who* decides *what* assistance will be provided *to whom, how,* and *when?* It is in this realm that value-oriented questions may be raised—questions that surround the issues of goal selection, problem definition, means selection, and the assessment of consequences (Kelman and Warwick 1978):

1. Whose values are to be served by the intervention?
2. To what extent do the recipients have an opportunity to participate in the choice of goals?
3. To what extent does the process enhance the power of the target population to solve problems?
4. To what extent is the provider engaging in a self-serving activity?
5. Whose problem(s) is (are) being primarily addressed in the technical assistance episode: the provider's or the recipient's?
6. Are a reasonable set of alternatives available to the recipient? Does the recipient have the power of choice? Even if so, does the provider assist the recipient in making informed choices?
7. Is incomplete or distorted information presented about the effects of assistance? Or, are only the probable benefits emphasized? Indeed, does the provider know, understand, and communicate the probable sociocultural, economic, environmental, and psychological impacts?
8. Will the assistance create a dependency relationship between the donor and receiver?

For example, if the assistance is knowledge-induced (knowledge in search of an application) or profit-induced (knowledge primarily or exclusively transferred with a profit motive in mind), then development is not likely to be served. To the extent that the recipient fully participates—indeed, is at least a co-owner—of the assistance process, developmental technical assistance is possible. (For a discussion of values as they relate to practice, see Chapter 6.)

The fundamental importance of these questions and the contouring of the process leading to the answers need to be emphasized because technology transfer characterizes much of what we know as technical assistance. *Technology transfer,* according to Glaser, Abelson, and Garrison (1983), *is the application of available knowledge or technology by a new user.*

From our perspective, technology transfer may or may not be a means of development. Technology of itself is equivocal, according to Glaser and his colleagues. The reasons for its application, the process surrounding its application, and the consequences of its use, typically define the relative goodness and badness of the transfer in development terms. That is why different evaluators can advance very different—sometimes incompatible—criteria to evaluate the process and its effects. Glaser, Abelson, and Garrison (1983) emphasize the need to consider the impacts from a developmental point of view:

> Technology is defined as more than technique—that is, more than science and engineering. It encompasses the totality of specialized means, including those of management, administration, and public policy, used to develop goods or services for human sustenance and comfort. Technology also has a deeper anthropological meaning. It is a key element of culture; it determines the relationship of a community with its natural environment and is the most concrete expression of values (Wenk 1979). Sooner or later, each society that strives to upgrade its technical capability discovers that it is both unfeasible and socially counterproductive simply to paste a veneer of technology onto indigenous culture. Hence, transfers of technology require a high sensitivity to match technical resources congenially not only with social goals but also with infrastructural, or cultural/social, foundations. (P. 383)

Technical Assistance as Community Development: Areas of Interest.

Given this background, we believe that technical assistance exists at both ends of a continuum: it exists as both nondevelopmental and developmental modes of planned change. At one extreme, technical assistance involves imposing assistance, technology, information, or ways of thinking *on* a community. Community involvement exists, at best, for appearances or legitimation; at worst, it serves the purpose of co-optation. As a developmental mode, on the other hand, it is a vital and necessary approach to community development: recipients need assistance, donors are able and willing to provide it, and recipients regulate the assistance process in self-protective ways. The challenge to community development scholars and practitioners rests not in debating whether technical assistance is community development; our argument is that it is *and* it is not. In our opinion, the field is better served by uncovering (1) *when* technical assistance is an appropriate approach to community development, and (2) *how* the community developer may effectively implement the developmental mode of technical assistance.

Technical Assistance as an Appropriate Approach to Community Development.   The concept of appropriateness occupies a central place in the vocabulary of community development. It is difficult, and probably wasteful, to discuss literally any aspect of community development by pointing to the one, best, or right way of doing things. The successful practice of community development requires that practitioners selectively draw from their tool kit of skills, strategies, and tactics. Indeed, being able to analyze a situation and to determine how to appropriately proceed are essential community development skills.

What this means is that technical assistance has its place as an approach to community development. Where? The concept of reliance on local resources and indigenous capacity is stressed again and again in community development literature. However, the notion of complementing these resources, when necessary, with outside resources and assistance is also emphasized. It would be myopic to believe that all the resources necessary for all successful community actions are available within the local setting. Community leaders often need resources (e.g., money, technology, advice, personpower) that exist outside the locale.

TECHNICAL ASSISTANCE AS COMMUNITY DEVELOPMENT.   The developmental question that looms large is this: How is it possible to acquire, direct, and control outside resources in ways that are consistent with local values and preferences? The tail-wagging-the-dog scenario in technical assistance comes to pass when the cost of external resource mobilization is such that it subverts the residents' ability to capacity build. The challenge to technical assistance as community development is that it take place within a *process* whereby local people have an opportunity to enhance their individual and collective problem-solving abilities. This is the same challenge facing self-help and conflict as community development. The basic difference is that both of these latter approaches are inherently oriented toward capacity building—an orientation that is inherently absent in the technical assistance approach but which must be added to the approach if community development is to occur.

The collective capacity-building notion is equivalent to the opportunity to enhance the sense of community in the locale. Frequently in community development we naively assume—sometimes with disasterous consequences—that sufficient levels of communityness exist, in the psychological and sociological sense, so that all practitioners need to do is focus attention on the substantive problem(s) at hand. In the developmental sense, levels of communityness vary with the extent to which people psychologically identify with the locale and aspire to strengthen its capacity to solve problems (Cottrell 1977).

In self-help community development, the fundamental task of people wanting to come together to deal with common problems assumes that sufficient levels of communityness exist. We know from experience that people often do not participate in self-help opportunities because of their belief that an alternative means of action (e.g., participation in the social welfare system) can provide needed resources more quickly and effectively (Rothman 1974*a*; Rothman, Erlich, and Teresa 1976). Similarly, lower levels of communityness may exist in precisely those environments where community organizing (the conflict approach) would seem most appropriate. That may be primarily because feelings of collective powerlessness—frequently expressed as fatalism and apathy—are often ubiquitous in disadvantaged environments. Much of Alinsky's work focused on describing *tactics* that organizers can use to effectively bring people together—that is, to enhance the sense of communityness for the purpose of taking collective action (Alinsky 1971). This often involved using local institutions (e.g., the church) as a medium to broaden the sense of community.

Nondevelopmental technical assistance does not require the existence of high levels of communityness. Outside change agents can "do for" the community because community capacity building is not a goal. At times, community members even request such a structure. External assistance, in this case, is not viewed as a means to capacity building, but as an end in itself. This is precisely when technical assistance is not community development but simply an approach to planned change.

In technical assistance as community development, practitioners must resist playing a service delivery role only. Recognition of the existing sociocultural environment, the leadership structure, and an understanding of the consequences of extending assistance is imperative (Truman et al. 1985). For example, are the potential dysfunctions of the technical assistance considered prior to the initiation of the assistance process? To what extent will the leadership structure be affected by the assistance process?

To further enhance technical assistance as community development, we recommend that greater attention be given to (1) increasing the instances where technical assistance is subsumed under one of the other approaches to community development, and (2) considering how technical assistance can be serially joined with other approaches.

In the first case, this would mean delivering technical assistance as part of a larger self-help or conflict process. Opportunities exist to accomplish this goal, although they are often missed. On the other hand, the political realities of agency agendas may preclude this, especially with respect to linking technical assistance with conflict. A recent experience of the senior author comes to mind. Research services (to be offered by a publicly funded university) were requested by a community group to document the supposed unjust and arbitrary decision by a local school district to close its neighborhood elementary school. The researcher providing the assistance quickly found himself in several confrontational sessions with representatives of the city power structure, most notably the superintendent of schools.

The serial linking of technical assistance with other approaches to community development appears to be a more politically reasonable option, especially for organizations involved in longer-term development efforts within specific community settings. The experience of nongovernmental organizations that provide assistance in the developing world is that they constantly struggle with choices between relief and development. Church-related organizations are ideologically drawn to the self-help notion of community development as a medium for holistic development, but also search for ways to break out of the seemingly vicious cycle of providing relief without development even though technical assistance is very much needed. This suggests that technical assistance is being viewed only as a nondevelopmental approach. The temporal sequencing of developmental technical assistance (first) with self-help (later) would seem to be a strategy for providing emergency services within a long-term developmental thrust.

Alliband (1983, p. 3), a developmental writer, argues that both nondevelopmental *and* developmental technical assistance are needed in the developing world because "each one works to solve different problems and to address the problems of different socio-economic groups." On the one hand, when considering Third World rural development, he believes that many larger farmers stand ready to adopt new production technology imported from Europe and the United States. On the other hand, he feels that the purpose of the developmental approach is "to generate community-based, community-wide, problem-solving capacity" (Alliband 1983, p. 5). The relevance of this approach is to encourage the cooperative pooling of internal resources (mental, material, and financial) so that optimal change can occur when these resources are comingled with scarce outside assistance.

Effective Implementation of Technical Assistance.

In developmental technical assistance, the *process* with which the assistance is carried out is as important as the content of the assistance. Increasing concern is being directed toward including nonproduct and process criteria in the determination of development effectiveness. Consider these effectiveness criteria advanced by the U.S. Agency for International Development (USAID) in 1973 for leaders of technical assistance teams. Note that the criteria pertain to issues of competence (items 1, 2, 3), morality (items 4, 5, 6), and developmental orientation (items 7, 8):

1. Are the technical assistance givers technically qualified?
2. Can they administer what will probably be a complex task?
3. Will they be perceptive and politically astute in picking up undercurrents and tensions in interpersonal and interagency relations?
4. Do they exhibit decency, sensibility, and interpersonal skills?
5. Will they understand and accept their responsibility for the attainment of stated objectives?
6. Will they be able to defend convictions under stress?
7. Can they be relaxed about their own status in the community and be willing to share credit for success openly and freely?
8. Will they accept the challenge of development and institution building as primary tools so as to leave behind local skills and resources to carry on?

Perhaps the most impressive movement designed to bring developmental thinking to technical assistance involves what has come to be

known as *appropriate technology.* Appropriate technology may be defined as

> a way of thinking about technological change, recognizing that tools and
> techniques can evolve along different paths and toward different ends. It
> includes the belief that human communities can have a hand in deciding
> what their future will be like, and that the choice of tools and techniques
> is an important part of this. It also includes the recognition that technolo-
> gies can embody cultural biases and sometimes have political and distri-
> butional effects that go far beyond a strictly economic evaluation. Ap-
> propriate technology therefore involves a search for technologies that
> have, for example, beneficial effects on income distribution, human de-
> velopment, environmental quality, and the distribution of political
> power—in the context of particular communities and nations. (Darrow,
> Keller, and Pam 1981, p. 326)

The paradigm statement associated with the appropriate technology movement was published in 1973 by Schumacher in *Small Is
Beautiful: Economics as if People Mattered.* Schumacher extolled the
virtues of "small scaleness" as a development alternative and emphasized the importance of such concepts as local autonomy, consumer
participation in decision making, and the optimal use of local resources
in the problem-solving process (Alliband 1979, p. 136). Development
does not start with goods, "it starts with people and their education,
organization, and discipline" (Schumacher 1973, p. 159).

> If you want to go places, start from where you are. If you are poor, start
> with something cheap. If you are uneducated, start with something rela-
> tively simple. If you live in a poor environment, and poverty makes
> markets small, start with something small. If you are unemployed, start
> using your labour power because any productive use of it is better than
> letting it lie idle. In other words, we must learn to recognize our bounda-
> ries. A project that does not fit, educationally and organizationally into
> an environment, will be an economic failure and a cause of disruption.
> (As quoted in Dunn 1979, p. 1)

Dunn (1979) conceptualizes appropriate technology as technology
that is community-based, small to moderate in scale, and includes the
following characteristics: (1) is labor-intensive, (2) is amenable to
management by its users, (3) encourages local innovativeness, (4) is
compatible with local values and customs, (5) helps meet local needs,
(6) contributes to local self-sufficiency, and (7) relies on local human
and natural resources.

Even those who would eschew appropriate technology as an approach to technical assistance might agree that the more we attempt to

impose technical assistance from the outside, the more we come to realize it does not work as often or as well as those involved had hoped it would. The World Bank (see Cernea 1985) and other international development assistance groups are finding this to be the case and are realizing the importance of defining projects from the points of view of the clients rather than from the points of view of the technical assistance teams who assess the situations. The international experiences are equally germane to the United States.

This suggests, and indeed there is evidence, that developmental thinking is creeping into the writing and practice of those who would classify neither themselves as community developers nor their work as community development. The reason is that experience has revealed that developmental thinking is vitally important for "effective" (i.e., putting into place) technical assistance whether it be embodied (artifact-based) or disembodied (conceptual) in nature (cf. Egea 1975).

Along this line, it is interesting to review the considerable research that has been conducted on the factors that are associated with planned change effectiveness. Zaltman (1983), for one, believes that consensus is beginning to emerge from this research and that the successful practice of planned change can be described in a compact set of concepts and guidelines. A convergent validity seems to exist, according to Zaltman, because the work in diverse disciplines seems to be pointing to the same, general conclusions about what works in the field.

Among the numerous attempts to summarize what is known about the successful practice of change is the well-known and frequently cited work of Davis (1971) and Davis and Salasin (1975). Based on their work in the mental health field, these authors have developed an eight-factor framework, arranged in the mnemonic form, A V-I-C-T-O-R-Y. Each letter represents a factor that change agents should consider when designing and implementing planned change projects. Note that literally every element in the framework addresses one or more of the developmental aspects discussed in this chapter.

Ability:	The ability of members of the target system to understand and evaluate the assistance being offered.
Values:	The "degree of fit" between the assistance party's and target system's philosophy and operating style.
Information:	The adequacy of the target system's knowledge and understanding of the assistance process to be used.
Circumstances:	The extent to which those offering the assistance understand the target system's sociocultural context.

Timing:	The ability of the party offering assistance to consider the optimal timing for structuring the change process.
Obligation:	The need for the assistance party to consider the change from the target system's point of view, particularly in terms of whether or not the change relates to one or more of their felt needs.
Resistance:	The assistance party should understand and appreciate the myriad of forces – cultural, social, organizational, and psychological – that may lead to change resistance.
Yield:	What are the benefits and payoffs to the end user(s) if the change is put into place?

Zaltman (1983) has extended the utility of the framework by deducing a set of principles and propositions that fine tunes the requirements associated with successful planned change. With respect to ability, for example, planners are advised that it is important for them to distinguish between client inabilities that can be altered and those that are relatively fixed and to which they must adapt. The more unalterable a client's inability is, Zaltman counsels, the more change agents should focus on innovation-related alterations and the less on client-related alterations.

One concrete example of how developmental thinking has been applied to planned change efforts is the work associated with "farming systems research" (FSR). This approach to agricultural development has gained widespread popularity within the international agricultural community. Gilbert, Norman, and Winch (1980) describe FSR this way:

> Increasing empirical evidence shows that the needs of small farmers often have not been adequately addressed in development programs in the Third World over the past twenty years. Many development projects have been introduced without sufficient understanding of the environment in which small farmers operate. The chequered pattern of success is traceable in part to the way research has been organized and undertaken in low-income countries. Public investment of agricultural research has not always been spent with the needs of small farmers – who should be the major customers of the results of such research – in mind. Instead, allocation of funds often has been based on (1) expressed needs of the more influential farmers, (2) research that will appeal to professional "peer groups" of the researchers, and (3) types of technology that have been developed in high-income countries. (P. 1)

Casey and Barker (1982) do not see FSR as a new research technique but, rather, as a new concept of research—a concept that emphasizes the need for professional agriculturalists to respect farmers' current practices and to collaborate with them during the agricultural development process. One of the fundamental premises of community development—starting where the people are—has become a basic tenet of FSR. Technology transfer then becomes an adaptive process that takes place within the overall effort "to understand what, how, and why farmers do what they do; what intangible and tangible factors enter into the farmer's system; what value can be ascribed to the different components of the system; and what effect change would have on that system" (Casey and Barker 1982, p. 13).

One of the core elements in FSR is the recognition that, to be truly effective, agricultural development efforts must be couched within an understanding of how other systems—family, community, region, nation, and world—link to the individual farm unit. As Axinn and Axinn (1987) contend, what is the purpose of developing a rice variety that outproduces current varieties if the demand in nearby markets is for a rice with different cooking and eating characteristics? In their estimation, greater profitability will likely result from producing and marketing the current variety unless researchers can develop a higher-yielding variety that also fits local preferences.

Concluding Observations. We have argued that technical assistance is the only theme or approach to community development that is not inherently developmental in nature. In the past, technical assistance has been inappropriately used in the name of community development. To be community development, technical assistance activities must conform to the underlying tenets expressed earlier in this chapter and volume, namely, that it take place within a larger process where community residents make a shared decision to initiate a planned change process—a process that is based on a mutually agreeable set of role relationships between community members and outside providers.

Contemporary emphasis on the "people component" of development, as reflected in current literature and practice (e.g., Korten and Klauss 1984; Cernea 1985), suggests the timeliness of the developmental approach to technical assistance. To take advantage of this situation, community development must use its value-oriented, normative base as the foundation for "sciencing" the technical assistance process. This means carefully documenting processes and results as well as testing process alternatives.

What this all signifies, at least to us, is that community development must prove itself as a worthy colleague in the development arena. Its potential has already been recognized; the community development way of thinking is being increasingly viewed as relevant, appropriate, and necessary. Now, the challenge becomes one of "delivering the goods," that is, producing efficient and effective results. Brokensha's (1968) assertions of twenty years ago—that community development is known for its "knowledge-freeness, murky banalities, and half-truths"—must be invalidated. The very future of the field, especially as a scholarly enterprise, hinges on disproving them.

References

Alinsky, S. D. 1971. *Rules for Radicals.* New York: Random House.

Alliband, T. 1979. Community development and the search for appropriate change: A book review essay. *Journal of the Community Development Society* 10(1):135–39.

———. 1983. *Catalysts of Development: Voluntary Agencies in India.* West Hartford, Conn.: Kumarian Press.

Axinn, G. H., and N. W. Axinn. 1987. Farming systems research in its macro policy dimensions. Paper presented at Farming Systems Research and Extension Symposium, University of Arkansas.

Batten, T. R., with M. Batten. 1975. *The Non-Directive Approach in Group and Community Work.* London: Oxford University Press.

Bennett, A. 1973. Professional staff member's contributions to CD. *Journal of the Community Development Society* 4(1):58–68.

Brokensha, D. 1968. Comments. *Human Organization* 27:78.

Casey, F., and R. Barker. 1982. A course in farming systems research: The Cornell experience. Ithaca, N.Y.: Cornell University, Department of Agricultural Economics.

Cernea, M. M., ed. 1985. *Putting People First: Sociological Variables in Rural Development.* New York: Oxford University Press (for the World Bank).

Chin, R., and K. D. Benne. 1976. General strategies for effective changes in human systems. In *The Planning of Change,* W. G. Bennis, K. D. Benne, R. Chin, and K. E. Corey, eds., pp. 22–45. New York: Holt, Rinehart and Winston.

Christenson, J. A., and J. W. Robinson, Jr. 1980. In search of community development. In *Community Development in America,* J. A. Christenson and J. W. Robinson, Jr., eds., pp. 3–17. Ames: Iowa State University Press.

Cottrell, L. S., Jr. 1977. The competent community. In *New Perspectives on the American Community: A Book of Readings,* R. L. Warren, ed., pp. 546–60. Chicago: Rand McNally.

Crowfoot, J. E., and M. A. Chesler. 1976. Contemporary perspectives on planned social change: A comparison. In *The Planning of Change,* W. G. Bennis, K. D. Benne, R. Chin, and K. E. Corey, eds., pp. 188–204. New York: Holt, Rinehart and Winston.

Darrow, K., K. Keller, and R. Pam. 1981. *Appropriate Technology Sourcebook,* Vol. 2. Stanford, Calif.: Volunteers in Asia, Inc.

Davis, H. R. 1971. A checklist for change. In *A Manual for Research Utilization.* Washington, D.C.: U.S. Government Printing Office, National Institute of Mental Health.

Davis, H. R., and S. E. Salasin. 1975. The utilization of evaluation. In *Handbook of Evaluation Research,* Vol. 1, H. R. Davis and M. Guttentag, eds. Beverly Hills, Calif.: Sage.

Dunn, P. D. 1979. *Appropriate Technology: Technology with a Human Face.* New York: Schocken Books.

Egea, A. N. 1975. Multinational corporations in the operation and ideology of international transfer of technology. *Studies in Comparative International Development* 10:11–29.

Gamm, L., and F. Fisher. 1980. The technical assistance approach. In *Community Development in America,* J. A. Christenson and J. W. Robinson, Jr., eds., pp. 48–63. Ames: Iowa State University Press.

Gilbert, E. H., D. W. Norman, and F. E. Winch. 1980. Farming systems research: A critical appraisal. East Lansing: Michigan State University, Department of Agricultural Economics, Rural Development Paper, No. 6.

Glaser, E. M., H. H. Abelson, and K. N. Garrison. 1983. *Putting Knowledge to Use.* San Francisco: Jossey-Bass.

Goulet, D. 1977. *The Uncertain Promise: Value Conflicts in Technology Transfer.* North America, N.Y.: IDOC, in cooperation with the Overseas Development Council, Washington, D.C.

Kelman, H. C., and D. P. Warwick. 1978. The ethics of social intervention: Goals, means, and consequences. In *The Ethics of Social Intervention,* G. Bermant, H. C. Kelman, and D. P. Warwick, eds., pp. 3–33. Washington, D.C.: Wiley.

Korten, D. C., and R. Klauss, eds. 1984. *People-centered Development: Contributions Toward Theory and Planning Frameworks.* West Hartford, Conn.: Kumarian Press.

Oberle, W. H., K. R. Stowers, and J. P. Darby. 1974. A definition of development. *Journal of the Community Development Society* 5(1):61–71.

Poats, R. M. 1972. *Technology for Developing Nations.* Washington, D.C.: Brookings Institute.

Rothman, J. 1974*a. Planning and Organizing for Social Change.* New York: Columbia University Press.

———. 1974*b.* Three models of community organization practice. In *Strategies of Community Organization,* F. M. Cox, J. L. Erlich, J. Rothman, and J. E. Tropman, eds., pp. 22–39. Itasca, Ill.: Peacock.

Rothman, J., J. L. Erlich, and J. G. Teresa. 1976. Fostering participation. In *Promoting Innovation and Change in Organizations and Communities: A Planning Manual,* J. Rothman, J. L. Erlich, and J. G. Teresa, pp. 96–133. New York: Wiley.

Schumacher, E. F. 1973. *Small Is Beautiful: Economics as if People Mattered.* New York: Harper Colophon Books.

Truman, B., C. H. Grether, L. Vandenberg, and F. A. Fear, with J. J. Madden, L. Joesting, and W. J. Kimball. 1985. When the tire hits the pavement: A case study of the dilemmas associated with conducting action research. *Journal of the Community Development Society* 16(1):105–16.

U.S. Agency for International Development. 1973. *Selecting Effective Leaders of Technical Assistance Teams.* Washington, D.C.: Bureau of Technical Assistance.

Wenk, E., Jr. 1979. *Margins for Survival: Overcoming Political Limits in Steering Technology.* Oxford: Pergamon.

Wright, D. S. 1978. *Understanding Intergovernmental Relations.* North Scituate, Mass.: Duxbury.

Zaltman, G. 1983. Theory in use among change agents. In *Handbook of Social Intervention,* E. Seidman, ed., pp. 289–312. Beverly Hills, Calif.: Sage.

5

The Conflict Approach

JERRY W. ROBINSON, JR.

WHY should a chapter on the conflict approach be included in a book on community development? While most community development work may be viewed as planned social change, it often involves or leads to conflict. Not all planned community change is led by self-help or technical assistance agents. Some professionals advocate the use of conflict as purposeful social intervention (Alinsky 1969, 1972*b*).

Conflict seems to be increasing in our modern world. It is international and inevitable (Hornstein et al. 1971). Countries that espouse free enterprise, freedom of the press, freedom of speech, freedom of assembly, and the right to dissent shall certainly continue to have conflict (Kriesberg 1973). Democracies are built on the foundation of an adversary system, and conflict is seen as doing more good than evil (Coser 1971). Also, a widening economic gap between the developed and developing nations and a scarcity of resources leads to conflict. Therefore, a chapter on the conflict approach to community development seems most appropriate.

Definition of Social Conflict.   Social conflict is

a behavior threat by one party directed at the territory–rights, interests, or privileges–of another party. The threat is usually directed toward limiting or eliminating one party's access to some resource or goal (Robinson 1972). The goals of conflicting parties are incompatible. Group and individual behavior in conflict situations is threatening because one party seeks to attain its goals or to achieve its interest with enough behavioral intensity to limit the goal attainment of the other party. It takes two or more parties to have a "good" fight.

Policies, goals, and values define rights, interests, and privileges in our society. All groups and individuals do not share commitments to common policies, goals, or values. One group may favor the development of a nuclear power plant and another may oppose it. One group may favor zoning, daylight saving time, strip mining for coal, or organic farming; and another group may oppose one or all of these issues. Because their goals and values are incompatible and their feelings are strong, the respective groups are likely to encounter conflict.

While values are always important in conflict situations, the essence of a conflict is the behavior threat. Behavior threats are prompted by values and goals and are directed toward policy change. Williams (in Robinson and Clifford 1977, p. 220) writes that conflict can be studied as a "process of concrete events occurring in real time and space—not as a set of cultural patterns." A situation does not become a conflict until someone does something. This approach is highly operational in conflict management-resolution scenes. One cannot manage the feelings, frustrations, values, and goals of others; but one may be able to redirect or exert some control over the behavior of others in conflict (Rubin and Brown 1975). If one is able to redirect behavior, one can begin to reshape the course of a conflict (see Figure 5.1).

CONFLICT AND TERRITORY. Often, the conflict process can be organized into tangible segments, and then analyzed and simplified in terms of behavior directed at territory. Almost everyone is familiar with traditional conflicts over land use, civil rights, and religious beliefs. How do these relate to territory? The explanation lies in viewing territory as more than physical or spatial. Humans need space, but why do they define the space called home with such sentiment? (Ardrey 1971). One explanation can be found in a wider interpretation of territoriality.

Territory has a psychological dimension (Robinson and Clifford 1977). Psychological territory is based on personal values and beliefs, on individual privileges, or even on the myths that one believes. One's beliefs do not have to be "correct" to be real. Myths by definition are not true, but belief in them is real. People own beliefs just as they can own an idea, a city lot, or a piece of furniture. Examples of psychologi-

Figure 5.1. An Operational Model of Social Conflict

cal territory are beliefs that one nation or one race is superior, that abortion is murder, or that one religion is better than another. Trying to change or destroy beliefs or take them away from people can cause much conflict.

Conflict also occurs because of threats to social territory – society's role expectations or an organization's job descriptions, for example. If these "territories" are threatened, conflict develops. For instance, certain places are naturally reserved for "special" people at the dinner table, at church, in the parking lot, in the office, and even in the job market (although such discrimination in the job market is illegal). Recently many examples of social conflict have occurred in communities where women have moved into roles formerly reserved for men. To invade another person's space is regarded as socially inappropriate and it may be the precipitating event to a confrontation.

Psychological, sociopsychological, and physical territory are not mutually exclusive. Values, goals, and policies influence people's perceptions of symbols in our society (Sherif et al. 1961). Territoriality is an example of how values, goals, and policies are intertwined in conflict situations, and how conflict can be analyzed in terms of tangible behavior or intangible beliefs. Analyzing a community conflict in terms of territoriality helps one deal with it more effectively. Territoriality explains some of the emotional and rational issues in a conflict and helps in understanding what the problem is and who is causing it. For example, burning biology textbooks at a local high school can be analyzed in terms of strong commitment to social and psychological territories, conflicts over roles of the family and the school, and who has the right to teach certain information to children. Sometimes the values, goals, and policies underlying a conflict are objective and rational; other times conflicts are charged with emotions and irrational behavior.

In brief, community conflict involves two or more parties with incompatible goals that relate to specific value attachments. The behavior of one party is threatening to the goals and territory of the other party, and the two parties compete with varying levels of interest and power. The relative power of the opposing parties is the key issue. The alternatives for resolution vary. Because of strong value attachments, few resolutions please all persons associated with both sides of a conflict.

Conflict and Values.

The value orientation of those who support a conflict strategy is quite contrary to the normative neutrality espoused by the professional using the self-help or nondirective community development approach. Normative principles are essential for advocates of social conflict. In many cases it is impossible to be neutral (Blizek and Cederblom 1973; Laue and Cormick 1978). Community conflict involves planned and unplanned strategies and awakens both emotional and rational responses (Alinsky 1972*b*). Persons causing or using conflict do not pretend to be value-free (Leas and Kittlaus 1973). The desired change is thought to be as good as or better than the status quo. Advocates using a conflict strategy are goal directed, as are agents of planned social change. They see conflict as good for the community or for themselves.

FUNCTIONS OF CONFLICT: POSITIVE AND NEGATIVE. Perhaps we can begin to understand conflict better by listing several of its functions. Coser (1971), in his classic work, summarized six functions of conflict in society.

1. Conflict permits internal dissension and dissatisfaction to rise to the surface and enables a group to restructure itself or to deal with dissatisfactions.

2. Conflict provides for the emergence of new norms of appropriate behavior by surfacing shortcomings.

3. Conflict provides a means of ascertaining the strength of current power structures.

4. Conflict may work to strengthen boundaries between groups – a sharper distinction between the groups appears.

5. Conflict creates bonds between loosely structured groups – unifying dissident and unrelated elements.

6. Conflict works as a stimulus to reduce stagnation. Conflict may alter society.

Conflict has positive and negative effects on organizational groups and individuals. A summary of these effects is seen in Figure 5.2.

The basic premise of conflicts is usually distribution of benefits in society, with one group seeking to maximize its potential. Advocates of conflict believe that people should not be subjugated to the status quo. Conflict – contrary to some movements in a community – usually involves the powerless versus the powerful. However, the powerless may not be deeply enough involved or skillful enough to proclaim their needs. They may not have the time, skill, or motivation to implement

A. HOW CONFLICT AFFECTS GROUPS	
Positive	*Negative*
Defines issues	Increases bitterness
Leads to resolution of issues	Leads to destruction and
Increases group cohesion	bloodshed
Leads to alliances with other	Leads to intergroup tension
groups	Disrupts normal channels of
Keeps groups alert to members'	cooperation
interests	Diverts members' attention from
	group objective

B. HOW CONFLICT AFFECTS INDIVIDUALS	
Positive	*Negative*
Learning	Inactivity
Energy	Confusion
Creativity	Stress
Change	Violence
Growth	Diversion

Figure 5.2. Effects of Conflict

and maintain an effective program of conflict. One author writes that community development is often used as a pacifier, in the hopes of avoiding conflict and disagreeable agitation, and that most community development efforts avoid issues of the distribution of benefits (Erasmus 1968). Instead, they work for the continued efficient functioning of the status quo.

Most community developers are familiar with the science of change and although much is written about it, few people write about the science of conflict as a planned process. Perhaps the emotional value orientation and action stance of conflict deter people from using it. Community developers might benefit from studying the work of political scientists regarding community disputes and political change. Carefully studying the basic values of justice, freedom, and improvement might give community developers reason to use conflict constructively and to convince their clientele that conflicts are often justified, good, and even desirable before progress can occur.

Types of Conflict.   Community confrontations come in all sorts, shapes, and sizes (Coleman 1957). Most conflicts are struggles for power and are related to justice and freedom. Some confrontations involve external forces against internal community forces. Such conflicts may be induced by court struggles or other efforts that attempt to force a community to comply with the values or changes in society. Struggles over equal employment opportunities for minorities are classic examples of external versus internal community conflict.

Some conflicts arise from disputes within the community. Local individuals in key power positions may disagree on an important issue. If their feelings are strong and concessions are not made quickly, the conflict can quickly escalate into a community problem (Walton 1969). Deciding whether to restore or remove a decaying building that has a rich cultural heritage might be a problem. A powerful old-timer may wish to preserve the building, while a newcomer who is active in developing off-street parking in the downtown may lead a coalition of opposition.

Personal conflicts often lead to conflicts between and within organizations and/or special interest groups. In the above example, it is easy to see how a chapter of a local historical society or the Daughters of the American Revolution might become an advocate for preserving the old building, while a committee of business persons with a mission to develop off-street parking might lead a campaign to get rid of the "old eyesore." However, not all organizational conflicts involve different organizations. Some involve actors within one organization. For example, the business community may be divided on renovating the downtown versus developing a suburban shopping center.

Causes of Community Conflict.

In democratic societies, change facilitates competition and promotes the adversary system. Change is inevitable. The conflicts preceding or following it are related to reallocating resources or redistributing power, although other factors also contribute to conflict. Some communities tend to have more conflict than others. Why? What factors precipitate community conflicts?

Diversity in a community seems to foster conflict (Kriesberg 1973). Increased economic differentiation and population changes lead to heterogeneous values. These factors add to community diversity and increase the likelihood of disagreements over territoriality.

Existing splits in the community are another important cause of conflict (Miller and Preston 1973). Sometimes opposing power structures seem to seek out an issue over which to fight. In some communities a residue of past experiences can be brought forward on almost any issue. Dredging up the past is especially popular in political struggles.

Significant and unique events are often sources of conflict (Coleman 1957). If an event such as locating a new industry or retirement home touches enough people in a community, and if it affects different power groups in different ways, conflict is likely to occur.

Another factor contributing to conflict is the presence of a leadership group with enough skill and feeling to gain support from local groups for its point of view (Leas and Kittlaus 1973). If it can develop suspicion or fear, the conflict may become a widespread community issue.

A final factor leading to disputes is a feeling of dissatisfaction by members of a group large enough to initiate action (Alinsky 1972*a*). When the community's power structure ignores the interests of a minority, conflicts are likely to occur. Coleman (1957) writes that revolts against a power group tend to follow a pattern:

1. The administration in power becomes the defendant.

2. A few activists become continual oppositionists and opportunists.

3. A large, silent, inactive group exists that does not necessarily support the administration.

4. An active group supports the administration.

5. The large, passive group (silent majority) becomes active.

6. The active oppositionists use the hostile atmosphere to promote their ideology and gain their ends.

In essence, through this process community conflicts are escalated, opponents become enemies, and disagreement leads to antagonism. The escalation of conflicts can be described in terms of a conflict cycle.

Conflict Stages. Community conflicts usually follow predictable stages or steps (Kriesberg 1973). They begin with a threat, then progress to tension development, role dilemma, injustice collection, confrontation, and/or adjustment (Robinson 1978). (See Figure 5.3.)

The conflict process begins when one party feels strongly enough about an issue to make a *threat* directed at the territory—interests, rights, or privileges—of another party. If the threat is strong and the issues are clear, some community members may choose sides at this

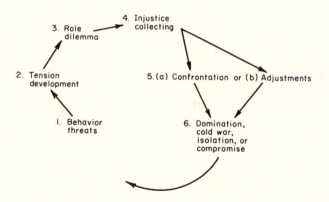

Figure 5.3. Steps in the Conflict Cycle

stage. Others may delay this decision until additional information is available or until pressure is applied. Sometimes threats are strong enough to cause fear or *tension development.* Peabody (1971) writes that the fear caused by a threat is worse than the conflict event itself.

Role dilemma follows tension development. Community residents and organizational leaders ask, "What is expected? With whom should we agree? Shall we take sides?" (Deutsch 1958). While asking such questions, people seek out information and expectations regarding changes in policy, goals, and values (Leas and Kittlaus 1973). If the issues are clear, positions and roles are taken. If the issues are unclear, the response may be to withdraw and test the situation. The parties may seek to determine what actions they can take and how far they can go without being associated with either side in the conflict. Everyone usually takes a side by the end of this stage. The community may become polarized, and new organizations with partisan positions may appear. Often, these new organizations spawn new leaders. Conflict often brings out latent skills in community residents.

Injustice collection follows role dilemma. All conflicts do not progress at the same rate, so collecting injustices may occur soon after threats are made or it may take some time for the conflict to gain enough momentum for strong feelings to be expressed. During injustice collection, adversaries become polarized further through a process of name-calling, making innuendoes, and taking public positions. Information and emotion are directed toward weakening the opponent's position. This information can be emotional or objective, rational or irrational; it may include accurate or inaccurate data. Some parties in a conflict seem to remember all previous negative experiences. They seek to weaken their adversary by itemizing or mentioning previous injustices that come to mind, by name-calling, and sometimes by revenge. When feelings are strong, they may be publicized in newspapers, on the radio, or on television.

Unfortunately, when one party uses injustices, the other party tends to reciprocate. Coleman (1957) writes about the tendencies for injustice collection to reinforce negative responses in community actors. This behavior leads to rigid polarization. In essence, collecting injustices intensifies a conflict, reinforces negative behavior, and encourages dysfunctional criticism in all parties. This led Sir Thomas Gresham to develop what he called the law of conflict: "The harmful and dangerous elements drive out those which would keep the conflict within bounds; reckless and unrestrained leaders head the attack; violent organizations arise to replace existing or moderate organizations; derogatory and inflammatory charges replace discussion; solving the issue becomes secondary to winning, to putting down the opponent" (Coleman 1957, p. 14).

Some conflicts move from injustice collection to *confrontation* (see Figure 5.3). Others move to a stage of adjustment. When adversaries in a conflict see each other as enemies, they are likely to resolve the conflict through a face-to-face confrontation. People do not force conflicts to confrontation unless they have very strong feelings regarding the issue of the fight and feel they will win through a confrontation. Severe outcomes are possible from any confrontation in which either party is extremely aggressive. Violent confrontations often lead to the destruction of property, to the usurpation of rights and interests of citizens of the community, and to permanent cleavages (Hornstein et al. 1971). Severe confrontations tend to reinforce the belief that conflict is always bad.

The final stage is the *adjustment process*. All conflicts do not develop into violent confrontations. Some conflicts may move quickly from the role dilemma stage to an adjustment stage. There are at least four adjustments to conflict: domination, cold war, withdrawal or isolation, and compromise (Robinson and Clifford 1977). While compromise may be regarded as a positive solution, domination, cold war, and isolation can have negative or positive effects depending on the opposing parties, the issue, and the feelings that the parties have toward the particular adjustment.

Domination occurs when the party with the most power imposes a solution. Because of its superior social, economic, or political strength, the stronger party can force the weaker party to give in. Domination tends to be a temporary adjustment. Since the weak party has no alternative but to comply, the conflict may reappear as soon as it gains strength.

Cold war is another adjustment, especially when the "solution" is not acceptable to either party (Kriesberg 1973). Cold war is a temporary adjustment. The contending parties continue to weaken each other through the innuendo and injustice collection stages. Cold war occurs when (1) the parties seem to be of equal power, (2) change would require both parties to surrender territory and power and lose face in the community, and (3) both parties see the change as a severe compromise. Cold war opponents may find themselves in a hot war at any minute.

Withdrawal or *isolation* occurs because some parties dislike disputes. The weaker party may temporarily withdraw to avoid losing face (psychological lynching). Isolation occurs when the weaker party finds the imposed "solution" to the conflict intolerable. It avoids the stronger party because the "solution" is worse than isolation. Isolation is not permanent. It may end when the weaker party gains strength in numbers, in economic power, or in confidence (Miller and Preston 1973).

Compromise is generally regarded as the healthy, functional adaptation to community conflict if issues are negotiable (Kriesberg 1973). However, compromise is not managed easily, because compromise requires new definitions of territories. It redefines policies, goals, and sometimes even values. Compromise is achieved through persuasion — direct and indirect — or through an inducement and reward system that involves negotiation and bargaining (Rubin and Brown 1975). For a compromise to occur, both parties must be committed to a dialogue process (Deutsch et al. 1967). They must possess enough trust in that process and in themselves to communicate openly about aspects that are important to them (Deutsch 1958). In some cases, a lot of time is required. A third party may be necessary to develop an acceptable compromise (Leas and Kittlaus 1973).

Factors Affecting Conflict.

Every conflict is unique. The structure of the community, skills of the leaders, attitudes of community residents, degree of discontent, possibility for solution, requests for assistance, presence of a mediator, and the problem itself are among the important factors that influence the conflict process (Coleman 1957; Deutsch 1973; Kriesberg 1973).

Community leaders shape controversies through their skills and attitudes. They may remain calm in the midst of the developing turbulence and carefully co-opt the leadership of the opposition in some situations. They may skillfully use their authority to suppress or direct the opposition. When power brokers are able to translate a conflict into tangible and specific terms that are relevant and understandable by community residents, they enhance their control. When leaders manifest confidence and act with deliberate purpose, they exhibit control that wins sentiment for their position.

The social structure of a community helps shape conflict (Warren 1974). The nature and strength of the predominant groups and the type of associational networks influence the outcome. The issue may not be important to the socioeconomic situation, or it may be extremely important. If the conflict is perceived as being initiated by outsiders (big government or big industry) who oppose grassroots leadership, the conflict is likely to have a strong local base. A local organizational structure is more likely to emerge to fight outsiders than to fight insiders.

When people are frustrated about something and discontentment is high, conflicts escalate. The frustration may be caused by social or economic injustice and is closely tied to ideology (Hornstein et al. 1971). Participation in conflicts is intense when the controversy touches the important territories of people in the community. Civil rights movements among blacks in the 1960s is one example. When the ideology of equal opportunity led to attacks on discrimination in jobs, voting, and housing, the civil rights movement gained momentum and local protests emerged with force.

Specific issues help generate support; solutions must be realistic and achievable. Some conflicts occur where injustice is felt and no solution is perceived. Unless resources are available in the community to help people obtain jobs, housing, etc., the discontentment is not likely to be channeled into planned action programs. When injustice is linked with realistic possibilities for change, success of a confrontation is enhanced.

Another factor affecting the course of a conflict is whether the leader of the group advocating change comes from within the community, is invited to the community, or comes unsponsored as an outside agitator. If change is to have a long-term effect, the desire and major leadership for it must come from the community group seeking the change (Alinsky 1972b). If change comes through an outside agitator, it will disappear when the outsider leaves.

Behavior Styles.

Probably the most important factor influencing a conflict is a participant's behavior style in the conflict situation. Each participant may be a dominator, a manipulator, a mediator, a compromiser, or an avoider. These behavior styles will be discussed in detail so that more can be learned about how to interpret the behavior of actors in conflict situations.

Each behavior style can be classified as flexible or rigid, and as indirect or direct (see Figure 5.4). Dominators are primarily direct and rigid, manipulators are direct and flexible, avoiders are indirect and rigid, and compromisers are indirect and flexible. But the mediator uses many behavior styles and can be direct and indirect as well as flexible and rigid depending on the situation. We will learn why and

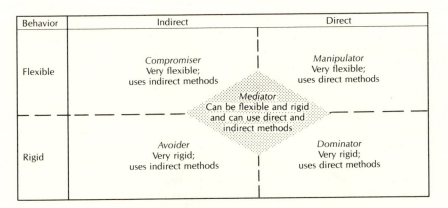

Behavior	Indirect	Direct
Flexible	*Compromiser* Very flexible; uses indirect methods	*Manipulator* Very flexible; uses direct methods
	Mediator Can be flexible and rigid and can use direct and indirect methods	
Rigid	*Avoider* Very rigid; uses indirect methods	*Dominator* Very rigid; uses direct methods

Figure 5.4. Behavior Styles of Actors in Conflict

how as we proceed. But first, let's look at each style of conflict management more carefully.

Dominator. The dominator confronts actors and situations head-on and uses direct persuasion. Dominators appear to know the best solution and use authority and power to impose it. Dominators do not like to be challenged. They are rigid and tell people what to do to resolve the conflict. Because dominators impose solutions, their solutions frequently do not last. When the suppressed group or individual gains courage or strength, the solution is challenged and conflict reappears. (Dominators can change their behavior, although it's difficult.)

Manipulator. The manipulator lacks the courage, strength, and power of dominators and thus appeals to actors' emotions by reminding them of their duty. Manipulators respect authority, but do not know how to use it except through guilt, pity, or a sense of ought or should. Manipulators are rigid, but can be active or passive, depending on the situation. Manipulators are always ready to blame actors in a conflict. The style of a manipulator is likely to offend people, just as the style of a dominator frequently does.

Mediator. The mediator uses a number of behavior styles necessary for effective communication and indirect persuasion. Primarily, a mediator will confront the communication process and the way people are acting. If necessary, the mediator uses authority and power. The mediator develops power from the trust he or she earns by being fair and objective with adversaries. The mediator navigates conversation to develop solutions to community conflicts (Daley and Kettner, 1981).

Mediators channel the conflict communication process, using active and passive behavior skills. Mediators explore and develop alternatives: they do not autocratically develop and impose them. Mediators use flexible behavior but can rigidly enforce fairness and rules of fair play as individuals discuss and decide on an issue. While the mediator takes primarily a third-party role, adversaries can use all of a mediator's behavior styles in a one-on-one situation.

If an irate citizen, concerned with potential ineligibility for government programs due to lack of compliance, confronts an elected official, the official can correctly shift the blame from himself or herself to that of policy. Venting a client's dissatisfaction against a written policy will sometimes enable him or her to blow off steam and also help to depersonalize an issue. If a mediator is requested by both parties in the dispute, his or her presence in and of itself generates pressure for dialogue and solution.

Compromiser. The compromiser would like to resolve conflicts in a favorable way, but may lack the patience, courage, and skills to do so. Thus, while the compromiser might argue a little, he or she avoids the judging and ridiculing behavior used by a dominator or a manipulator. However, the compromiser may try to buy solutions with rewards and bribes.

Compromisers also use pleasure to appeal to the actors' ego needs. Sometimes compromisers ignore the main issue in a conflict and attack another problem (e.g., planning a party). Compromisers are very permissive, flexible, and active. They are susceptible to dominators and manipulators.

Avoider. The least effective conflict actor is the avoider, who abhors conflict and avoids fights. The avoider gives up all responsibility and duty, creating a vacuum to subtly manipulate a situation. Other actors assume risks associated with the conflict. This delaying action creates a feeling of doom among group members. Avoider behavior is passive and indirect. An avoider submits to others' whims and wishes and is regarded as a very ineffective conflict manager.

FLEXIBILITY. What about your behavior in conflict situations? Does your style change? Are you direct, indirect, or both? Are you flexible and/or rigid? Can you be active and passive? If necessary, can you enforce rules or policy? Can you defend your values, even when powerful people disagree with you? Review the checklist in the Learning Exercise at the end of the book.

Ethics and Strategies in Community Conflict.

A community development agent may be asked to assist a special interest group (e.g., business persons) seeking information on how property values might change if mobile homes were allowed to locate near them. Developing answers to this question will take time, and zoning hearings may be necessary. Mobile homes may be the only housing option for some low-income people in the community. Some landowners may oppose mobile homes while others promote them. What should the agent's role be? What are the ethical considerations for the community development agent? Basic issues for the community development professional are raised by issues like this. Some argue that neutrality is a myth. The nondirective self-help approach appears to ignore many ethical issues, while the conflict approach uses ethical questions to formulate discontent and change (Alinsky 1969). In fact, a primary purpose of conflict may be to apply pressure on power centers to change the ideological position of those in power (Hornstein et al. 1971).

ETHICAL ISSUES. What ethical principles shall the change-conflict agent follow? Laue and Cormick (1978, pp. 217–18) suggest that the professional should ask, "Does the intervention contribute to the ability of relatively powerless individuals and groups in the situation to determine their own destinies to the greatest extent consistent with the common good?" They contend that humans are ends in themselves and ought to be treated as such. Involvement in community disputes is appropriate if it helps achieve three basic goals:

1. *Empowerment:* a requisite condition for individuals and groups to achieve the desired end-state of society – that is, justice.
2. *Justice:* a prerequisite to the maximum attainment of freedom by all individuals in the system.
3. *Freedom:* the condition that makes possible responsible choices from a number of options and the ability to live with the consequences of those decisions, thereby realizing the deepest form of meaning.

Freedom is essential for meaning. Justice is the ultimate social good, and empowerment for *all* is essential before groups and individuals can achieve freedom and justice (Laue and Cormick 1978, pp. 218–19). Laue and Cormick state that "empowerment, justice, and freedom are ends in themselves so long as all individuals and groups are equipped to advocate their interests to similar degrees."

STRATEGIES. The strategy used in conflict situations is determined by one's value orientation toward conflict as a viable process for change. If conflict is seen as a functional social process, one is likely to be committed to it as a useful tool to achieve the change desired. If it is perceived as a threat to the system or to the stability of the social and economic order, one is likely to oppose it and regard it as bad for the community. Thus, the basic strategies regarding conflict are to use it, prevent it, or manage and resolve it. Frameworks supporting the strategy for each orientation toward conflict follow.

USING CONFLICT: SOME BASIC RULES OF THUMB. Proponents of the conflict approach often strive to disrupt the social, economic, or political systems of a community. Advocates of conflict represent the disenfranchised elements—elements that lack economic or political power. Their position and cause represent that of a minority. Almost everyone involved in the political arena uses conflict. Conflict is viewed as the only effective way to cause change, so a strategy for agitation is planned.

One conflict approach that gained popularity during the 1950s and 1960s in the United States was associated with the leadership of Saul Alinsky and his Chicago-based "conflict school." This section draws heavily on his work (1969, 1972*b*) and on the works of Ross (1955), Kahn (1970), Coser (1971), Collins (1975), Coleman (1957), and Reitzes and Reitzes (1980). While the discussion does not directly follow the approach outlined by any one of these authors, it corresponds most closely to Alinsky's efforts.

Step 1. Appraise the local leadership. The first task of a conflict agent who is invited into a community is to appraise the indigenous leadership. Conflict leaders must have the ability to see the community as it is and as it could be. This vision must be both practical and communicable. Other characteristics beneficial to indigenous leaders are tact, courage, enthusiasm, and hard work.

The conflict agent must identify and involve individuals who can form an effective leadership team. Such effective power will not be found in one person but in a small group of persons who can work together. One individual will probably be the spokesperson for the group and must manifest tact, enthusiasm, and courage in confronting the power structure. Other individuals will organize the daily details.

Leaders must ensure that everything is done at the right time, in the right sequence, and with the necessary resources.

Step 2. Analyze the community power structure. The confrontation approach, to a greater extent than any other method of social action, focuses squarely on power. Power is the name of the game. It is defined as the capacity to mobilize resources for accomplishing intended effects (Clark 1968). Other approaches work from the perspective of legitimization—that is, they get approval of proposed projects or objectives before initiating them. The conflict approach is concerned with the redistribution of benefits. It implies a confrontation between those who have and those who have not. Power structures of local communities and the decision-making process within those communities vary widely. The power structure in a particular community is a function of the political life in that community (Goldolf 1983). The greater the number of elected positions and the greater the public participation in the electoral process, the greater the dispersion of power among various groups.

Step 3. Analyze the situation and territoriality. Before suggesting tactics or approaches to change, a conflict agent must understand the types of people and groups within the community and their past grievances, conflicts, and areas of consensus. The complex territorialities within the community, the social interaction of various community institutions, and the psychological ties that community members have to the community also must be appraised. Essentially four components must be taken into account: (1) people, (2) geographical boundaries, (3) organizational interdependence, and (4) psychological ties. Such community analysis can help the conflict agent understand where allies come from, which issues could be brought into the confrontation, which groups need to be neutralized, and which types of action would be most effective.

Step 4. Stimulate dissidents to voice grievances. A problem does not exist until people define it as such. Bringing people together to articulate their discontent motivates them to act and helps individuals become aware that their frustration may be shared by others. Such knowledge encourages them to realize shared consciousness in their plight. Power for the poor segment of society can be found only in numbers. As people join together to voice their discontent, their amplified frustration becomes an effective confrontation tool. The more people who share in the issue, the more likely it is that results will occur. It is difficult for even a highly motivated small group to achieve change unless their sentiments and objectives are shared by a large segment of the community.

Step 5. Define the problem. Social action, to be effective, must focus on a *single* issue. Such an issue may have many secondary implications, but all efforts focus on a single problem. It is particularly important at this time to address the heart of the problem, to focus on causes and not symptoms or solutions.

Step 6. Organize, organize, organize. Conflict agents usually work with clientele outside the power structure. They may work with poor people's organizations or low-income clientele. Thus, common organizational tactics have to be modified accordingly. Kahn (1970) comments that the key value in decision making within poor people's organizations is not efficiency but participation. He suggests that the time required to reach a decision is the amount of time it takes to educate all the members in the meaning of decision making and to involve them in the decision-making process.

A major problem in managing conflict is size. To be effective and to allow people to participate, the size of the working organizational structure must be relatively small. To accomplish this, it is often necessary to divide larger units into smaller localized subgroups. It is important to understand that low-income people tend to be skeptical of well-organized, formal meetings and organizations. While *Robert's Rules of Order* may help promote general participation in decision making, organizational meetings should be kept as informal and small as possible.

Step 7. Demonstrate the value of power. People outside the power structure are skeptical of their ability to move it. They have no power, money, property, or influence. But as Alinsky notes, they do have numbers. They have the power of people. Early in the planning process they must perceive the value of a large number of people working together. It is equally important that the first demonstration of power succeeds. This will help the clientele realize the power they do have, the possibility of using it, and the possibility of success in exercising their power in numbers. Alinsky (1972*b,* pp. 127–30) lists the following thirteen power tactics for confrontation in his book *Rules for Radicals:*

1. Power is not only what you have, but what the enemy thinks you have.
2. Never go outside the experience of your people.
3. Whenever possible, go outside the experience of the enemy.
4. Make the enemy live up to his or her own book of rules.
5. Ridicule is man's most potent weapon.
6. A good tactic is one your people enjoy.
7. A tactic that drags on too long becomes a drag.
8. Keep the pressure on.
9. A threat is usually more terrifying than the thing itself.

10. The major premise for tactics is the development of an operation that will maintain a constant pressure on the opposition.

11. If you push a negative hard and deep enough, it will break through into its counterside.

12. The price of a successful attack is a constructive alternative.

13. Pick your target, freeze it, personalize it, polarize it.

Step 8. Never confront the power structure directly. When people unite on a single issue they can present a rather impressive front of power. But it is by no means greater than the traditional exercise of power through money, property, and influence. In any battle, if a smaller army attacks a larger army head-on, the smaller army inevitably loses. In confrontation, as in military science, one tries to outflank the enemy. In the Back of the Yards movement in Chicago, Alinsky organized the meat-packing workers, not to confront the meat barons directly but to put pressure on the banks loaning money to the meat barons.

Step 9. Be realistic; compromise. It is very important that workers for change do not become stymied on minor issues or technicalities. The major issue must always be kept in perspective, and the goal of people as ends within themselves must be foremost. Minor issues and the means of achieving minor goals are secondary considerations. Alinsky (1972*b*, pp. 24–25) lists eleven principles relevant to his means-ends controversy:

1. Only people from a distance moralize about means-ends.

2. Judgment about means-ends depends on the political position of those sitting in judgment.

3. In war—the end justifies any means.

4. Judgment must be made in reference to the time, not independent of it.

5. Concern with ethics increases with the number of means available and vice versa.

6. The relative importance of the end affects ethics in choosing means.

7. Possibility of success or failure greatly affects ethical choices.

8. Morality of means depends on whether the means is being employed at a time of imminent defeat or imminent victory.

9. Any effective means is automatically judged by the opposition as being unethical.

10. You do what you can with "what you have" and clothe it with moral garments.

11. Goals must be paraphrased in honorifics.

The credibility of these principles must be weighed against the basic values of justice, freedom, and empowerment, as discussed earlier.

Step 10. Develop a permanent organizational structure. Various tactics are exercised to achieve the stated goal. Emphasis should be on establishing an organization which comprises all the various subgroups that can function effectively once the change agent leaves the community. This organization serves three purposes: (1) It to avoids backlash from the power structure once the change has been achieved. (2) It helps avoid Gresham's law of conflict by breaking down the change through radical unplanned efforts. (3) It provides for a group to carry on in the absence of the change agent.

Step 11. Begin again. Once the stated objective has been achieved, the clientele need an evaluation to determine what other changes they could realistically attempt in order to better their life situation. At this stage, the conflict agent will help the indigenous leaders assess their situation, assess what they have achieved, and assess where they might go from there. The agent's intentions of leaving the community should be reaffirmed. It is probably best if the agent phases out of the community picture as quietly as possible, leaving the administration and the recognition to the indigenous leaders. The experiences derived from the exercise of planning change through conflict should provide local community organizations with the confidence and ability to carry on in the future.

PREVENTING COMMUNITY CONFLICTS. Prevention strategies tend to be used primarily by the power structure, which has a vested interest in maintaining the status quo or in promoting a change that does not disrupt the status quo. Some of the strategies used by the conflict agent also may be used by the preventer (e.g., organization, planning). However, other tactics may be used by preventers who seek to work quietly and with great subtlety to keep an issue from becoming a conflict. This section presents some basic strategies that are used to prevent community conflicts. The reader must be cautioned about the success of prevention strategies. Community conflict is not easily stopped. It may be suppressed for a while or temporarily neutralized, but once a community conflict gains momentum it tends to run its course through the stages of the conflict cycle.

The basic problem with preventing conflict is timing. The sooner action is taken to prevent an issue from moving past the role dilemma stage of the conflict cycle, the better. Delaying action gives a dispute time to gain strength and support and provides opportunities for differing opinions to solidify. Efforts at preventing conflicts are almost always futile if an intervenor does not appear before the injustice phase of the conflict cycle.

What tactics prevent conflict? Rosemary Caffarella (in Robinson 1978, pp. RS 1–6) suggests the following: fragmentation, co-optation, outside expertise, education, and public relations. Each of these tactics requires resources and skills and may present ethical problems. They are operationalized in the following discussion.

Step 1. Fragment the conflict. Fragmentation involves reducing the proposed issue or project to a series of smaller components (Williams, in Robinson and Clifford 1977). These components may be introduced to the community in order of increasing significance. Piecemealing the relevant information reduces the shock; the smaller components may dissipate the explosive effect of one big issue. For example, instead of introducing a plan for massive urban renewal with great economic and social expense, the change agent might begin to talk about better housing for the poor, health hazards in the inner city, and how slums cost the city dollars in terms of tax revenue. The big issue in a conflict is fragmented into tangible and manageable problems. The issue is reduced to rational, concrete terms and experiences that citizens can understand.

Step 2. Co-opt the leadership. Co-optation involves redirecting the key leadership to another issue. Co-optation may have ethical connotations for the power structure that seeks to use it. The power structure asks the key person or organization beginning to create a conflict to serve on a study or planning committee to investigate the issue and to report back to the established planning committee. Since this new committee may be appointed by leaders in the power structure, the efforts of the opportunist can be redirected. When a report or suggestion for change occurs, it can be squelched or modified. It may seem that the establishment was the group that initiated the change, since they appointed the study committee.

Step 3. Employ outside experts who espouse established position. Experts who are critical consultants or national figures may be brought to a community to win over the opposition if these experts support your point of view and if the opposition holds the experts in high esteem. The power of the experts probably lies within the esteem held by the constituents rather than in knowledge or information. Heroes, such as movie stars and professional athletes, are used frequently in advertising and political campaigns. They may be used effectively in some community conflicts.

Step 4. Conduct an educational program. Education is a strategy often used by the establishment to prevent conflicts or to win over the opposition. Educational programs are more effective when they are directed at specific issues or at individual and organizational policies and goals instead of values. Values change slowly. Policies and goals change before values change. Thus, educational programs are most effective when they are developed in pragmatic terms around a particular issue and/or project. However, education may not be as helpful as some believe. Power usually whips truth in conflict situations, especially in community controversy.

An educational program used in preventing conflict must be rational, unbiased, and directed at the individuals and organizations who question an issue. Effective educators in conflict situations are knowledgeable, truthful, and fair. They must know the limitation of their information, be confident and tolerant in conflict situations, and communicate well.

Managing Community Conflict: Third-Party Role. Managing conflict is probably the most appropriate role for the community development professional. Since conflict is inevitable, coping with it creatively is essential. In recent years, numerous agencies and organizations have been established to help community groups manage conflicts. Some of these are the Community Relations Service, U.S. Department of Justice; Federal Mediation and Conciliation Service; Institute of Mediation and Conflict Resolution, New York; Community Disputes Services Division of the American Arbitration Association, New York; Community Conflict Resolution Program, University of Missouri, St. Louis; Center for Teaching and Research in Disputes Settlement, University of Wisconsin, Madison; Department of Law, Justice, and Community Relations, United Methodist Church, Washington, D.C.; Office of Environmental Mediation, University of Washington, Seattle.

How does one decide to become involved in a community dispute? The actions of the intervenor should help powerless groups and enable weaker parties to make their own best decisions. The rationale for an intervenor's decisions should be conscious, explicit, and public, without any claim to neutrality. Intervenors should not lend their skills to groups who do not hold the values of empowerment, freedom, and justice for all peoples, regardless of race, sex, religion, or national origin. In fact, an intervenor should place a high value on working *against* such groups (see Laue and Cormick 1978, pp. 220–22).

Conflict intervenors are more effective when they play third-party roles. As a third party, the mediator encourages rational discussion, asking open-ended, nonjudgmental questions that require adversaries to deal with their feelings and the issues in a conflict situation. Through this strategy the mediator helps adversaries explore alternative adjustments and issues. The mediator assures that open, two-way communication is used; helps to regulate the psychological and social cost of a conflict; and helps to create an atmosphere whereby an individual or group can make a graceful retreat, if desired, to change a position or withdraw. The mediator, at the onset of a conflict management dialogue, helps the adversaries develop ground rules and reinforces those norms. The mediator might help the adversaries secure additional resources (informative, economic, or physical) needed to manage a conflict.

A third party can manage conflict by using coercion, contingent reward, and indirect persuasion. A third party using *coercion* must possess the power to enforce an adjustment to the conflict. A county zoning board member who is impartial about where to locate new low-income housing may say to competing land developers and citizens, "If you people cannot agree on one location, I will not approve any request." However, a threat without power to implement it is meaningless.

The third party can use a *contingent reward* in some situations; for example, approval could be given to all efforts to accommodate both parties. We are familiar with the use of bribes and incentives by adversaries in a conflict. Big business or big government may offer attractive awards to a community to squelch a conflict or gain a favor. Incentives can be used by third parties who are seeking to manage a community conflict.

Incentives may encourage the adversaries to agree. For example, an impartial county board member acting as a third party may say, "If you will just stop fighting and agree on where to build the low-income housing, I will ask the county board to seek federal funds for low-interest loans that could be made available to people buying your houses." Incentives will appear to be bribes unless they are extended equally and fairly among all parties in a conflict.

The third party who uses coercion or contingent reward is likely to experience more difficulty in managing conflict than does the third party who uses *indirect persuasion*. Rather than enforcing or buying an adjustment, the third party facilitates developing mutual accommodation and enforces agreed-upon rules of fair play. Instead of advocating a specific solution, the indirect persuader advocates dialogue and encourages adversaries to develop and maintain a dialogue process. In essence, the indirect persuader is an intervenor, who advocates not for a particular party but for both parties, not for a particular outcome but for a process of discussion, negotiation, and adjustments. The goal of the indirect persuader is to mediate the conflict in such a way that both parties "win." A basic premise of indirect persuasion is that *community residents or adversaries are much more likely to support adjustments that they help create.* Indirect persuasion encourages adversaries to become involved in building solutions.

Six steps or strategies (Robinson 1978) are used by a third party in indirect persuasion. These steps and appropriate substeps are summarized in the following outline.

INDIRECT APPROACH TO CONFLICT MANAGEMENT

I. Initiate dialogue objectively
 A. Introduce subject of process to all parties
 B. Establish ground rules for everyone
 C. Channel communication (use feedback – dramatize if necessary)
II. Involve all parties
 A. Question, stimulate
 B. Listen actively
 C. Accept credibility of feelings (avoid being judgmental)
 D. Probe for causes of feelings
III. Assimilate feelings and information (record feelings and information for all to see).
 A. Record, structure, and organize feelings
 B. Record, structure, and organize facts
 C. Record, structure, and organize agreements
 D. Record, structure, and organize disagreements
IV. Reinforce agreements
 A. Participants have the right to agree or disagree
 B. Feelings and expressions are real
 C. Seek possible compromises
 D. Suggest and footnote solutions

      E. Personalize alternative solutions in relation to benefits
V. Negotiate differences
    A. Discover how each party feels about each issue and why (see Step III, A)
    B. Record, structure, and organize disagreements (see Step III, D)
    C. Prioritize differences (get consensus) and begin with the least important problem
    D. Seek adjustment on each issue
      1. Seek alternatives from each party
      2. Specify acceptable and unacceptable alternatives
      3. Review and pursue adjustments
    E. Process ground rules for third party at this step
      1. Avoid giving solutions
      2. Remember to use feedback, timing, and reinforcement
      3. Be sensitive to loss of face
      4. Avoid threats
VI. Solidify agreements (adjustments)
    A. Review compromises suggested
    B. Prepare contract summary
    C. Check for accuracy of perceptions
    D. Confirm areas of agreement and disagreement
      1. Give a handshake or hug
      2. Prepare and sign a written contract

Note that these steps are interdependent, not mutually exclusive, and that adversaries cannot proceed to Step V or VI until agreements are achieved on the first four steps.

Indirect persuasion places the major responsibility for developing solutions on the conflicting parties. Group consensus is more easily obtained through solution guiding than solution giving. Remember, people support adjustments they help create.

THIRD-PARTY QUALIFICATIONS. The mediator must understand the nature of conflict in order to help adversaries develop adjustments. The indirect persuader must be able to interpret conflict theoretically and operationally, understand group processes, and experience working with groups. Mediators must seek and accept feedback about the usefulness and effectiveness of their techniques and behavior. The ego of the third party must not be onstage in the outcome of conflict management dialogue. The role of the third party is regarded by some as similar to the role of a referee; the third party must be fair, alert, objective, skillful, decisive, insightful, and at times forceful.

Leas and Kittlaus espouse this position. In their insightful book, *Church Fights: Managing Conflict in the Local Church* (1973, pp. 65–67), they discuss the following as qualifications for an effective third-party mediator (referee): (1) has a high degree of tolerance for ambiguity, ambivalence, and frustration; (2) is confident in conflict management and refereeing; (3) advocates process, sometimes firmly; (4) does not take sides on an issue; (5) does not take substantive conflict personally; (6) gives credit to all parties; and (7) is able to express and accept strong feelings.

Leas and Kittlaus (1973, pp. 67–72) list the following as third party assumptions: (1) conflict is inevitable and resolvable, (2) conformity is not required, (3) few situations are hopeless, (4) one party affects another, (5) each side has a piece of the truth, (6) there is some similarity between opponents, (7) present problems are the ones to solve, (8) the process is of great importance, and (9) there is no right answer.

Summary.

Summary. This chapter presents an operational framework of the conflict approach to community development. Community conflict is given a behavioral definition; conflict usually involves a fight over social, psychological, or physical territory. Since conflict is not a value-free approach to community development, the chapter discusses its uniqueness, the types of cooperation that may occur, its functions and causes, the conflict cycle, and factors affecting the outcome of a conflict. Three basic strategies for dealing with conflict are to (1) use it, (2) prevent it, or (3) manage it in a how-to-do-it framework. The author leaves the selection of strategies to the readers—and the situations that exist in their communities—in their search for community development.

References

Alinsky, S. 1969. *Reveille for Radicals.* New York: Random House.
_____. 1972*a*. Playboy interview. *Playboy* 19(3):59.

_____. 1972*b*. *Rules for Radicals.* New York: Random House, Vintage Books.

Ardrey, R. 1971. *The Territorial Imperative.* New York: Dell, pp. 3–4, 232–33.

Blizek, W. L., and J. Cederblom. 1973. Community development and social justice. *Journal of the Community Development Society* 4(2):45–52.

Clark, T. N. 1968. Community structure, decision-making, budget expenditures, and urban renewal in 51 American communities. *American Sociological Review* 33(4):576–93.

Coleman, J. S. 1957. *Community Conflict.* Glencoe, Ill.: Free Press.

Collins, R. 1975. *Conflict Sociology.* New York: Academic Press.

Coser, L. A. 1971. *The Functions of Social Conflict.* Glencoe, Ill.: Free Press.

Daley, J. M., and P. Kettner. 1981. Bargaining in community development. *Journal of the Community Development Society* 12(2):25–38.

Deutsch, M. 1958. Trust and suspicion. *Journal of Conflict Resolution* 2:265–79.

_____. 1973. The *Resolution of Conflict.* New Haven, Conn.: Yale University Press.

Deutsch, M., Y. Epstein, D. Canavan, and P. Gumpert. 1967. Strategies for inducing cooperation: An experimental study. *Journal of Conflict Resolution* 11:345–60.

Erasmus, C. 1968. Community development and the encogido syndrome. *Human Organization* 27(1):65–74.

Goldolf, E. 1983. Institution/neighborhood interface: A case of divergent perspective. *Journal of the Community Development Society* 11(1):73–92.

Hornstein, H. A., B. Bunker, W. W., Burke, M. Gindes, and R. J. Lewicki. 1971. *Social Intervention: A Behavioral Science Approach.* New York: Free Press.

Kahn, S. 1970. *How People Get Power.* New York: McGraw-Hill.

Kriesberg, L. 1973. *The Sociology of Social Conflicts.* Englewood Cliffs, N.J.: Prentice-Hall.

Laue, J., and G. Cormick. 1978. The ethics of intervention in community disputes. In *The Ethics of Social Intervention,* G. Bermant, H. C. Kelman, and D. Warwick, eds., pp. 205–32. New York: Wiley.

Leas, S., and P. Kittlaus. 1973. *Church Fights: Managing Conflict in the Local Church.* Philadelphia: Westminster Press.

Miller, M. V., and J. D. Preston. 1973. Vertical ties and the redistribution of power in Crystal City. *Social Science Quarterly* 53(March):772–84.

Peabody, G. L. 1971. Power, Alinsky and other thoughts. In *Social Intervention: A Behavioral Science Approach,* Hornstein et al., eds., pp. 527–32. New York: Free Press.

Reitzes, D. C., and D. Reitzes. 1980. Saul Alinsky's contribution to community development. *Journal of the Community Development Society* 11(2):39–52.

Robinson, J. W., Jr. 1972. The management of conflict. *Journal of the Community Development Society* 3(2):100–205.

———. 1978. *A Conflict Management Training Program: A Leaders Guide for Extension Professionals*. Ithaca, N.Y.: Cornell University, Northeast Regional Center of Rural Development.

Robinson, J. W., Jr., and R. A. Clifford. 1977. Conflict management in community groups. Urbana: University of Illinois, Cooperative Extension Service.

Ross, M. G. 1955. *Community Organization: Theory and Principles*. New York: Harper and Brothers.

Rubin, J. Z., and B. R. Brown. 1975. *The Social Psychology of Bargaining and Negotiations*. New York: Academic Press.

Sherif, O. J., B. J. Harvey, W. R. Hood, and C. Sherif. 1961. *Intergroup Conflict and Cooperation*. Norman: University of Oklahoma Book Exchange.

Walton, R. E. 1969. *Interpersonal Peacemaking: Confrontations and Third-Party Consultation*. Reading, Mass.: Addison-Wesley.

Warren, Roland. 1974. *Community in America*. Chicago: Rand McNally.

6
Professional Community Development Roles

PAUL D. WARNER

PROFESSIONAL COMMUNITY DEVELOPMENT roles are as varied as the approaches used, the communities developed, and the backgrounds of the professional workers. In the mountains of Appalachia, the neighborhoods of the cities, the small towns of the plains, and the villages of Africa, there is community development taking place. And in the middle of the action can often be found a community development worker.

Community development is a distinct profession. The practice of community development is a blend of sociotechnical interventionary strategies that assist the community in achieving its goals. It is a field of endeavor that relies on a unique set of concepts, skills, and methods. Because of its broad nature, community development is a synthesis of various disciplines such as sociology, economics, geography, planning, social work, political science, and natural resources. But that is how it should be. Community development should not be bound by a single disciplinary perspective; rather, it should seek to draw from these different traditions.

This diversity has both positive and negative aspects. The positive aspect is that community issues are not viewed from the narrow perspective of only one discipline, but rather, the strengths of each are brought to bear on community problems. Local citizens don't care whether the information or approach comes from sociology, economics, or planning—they just want acceptable solutions to their problems. However, a negative aspect is that it is difficult to develop a sense of profession when there is no single, widely supported perspective on community development. Professional community development researchers and practitioners come from a variety of disciplinary orientations, each with its own traditions and approaches. In such an environment consensus is difficult to mold. Without a single disciplinary home, communication is more difficult, writings are scattered in the literature, and professionals possess many and varied loyalties.

Task Functions.   The perspective taken on development determines, to a great extent, expectations for the role of a community development professional. Early development efforts stressed economic advancement in rural communities. Accordingly, community betterment through the establishment of improved agriculture or basic services focused on the capacity of the professional to provide technical and planning assistance. Third World development focused on economic growth through the introduction of capital-intensive technology, the building of the infrastructure, and the education and training of the population.

Both domestic and international development programs have relied heavily on this task-oriented approach. Programs utilizing this strategy generally produce tangible goods as end products. The attention to outcomes places the community development practitioner in a role of emphasizing problem identification, fact-finding, analysis of alternatives, grantsmanship, and project implementation. Success is measured in terms of improvements in the institutional and physical environment, based on the assumption that a change in environmental conditions results in improved quality of life. Therefore, the successes of these community development workers is gauged by their skills in bringing about such changes.

At a somewhat later stage in community development history, there was a realization that the social, cultural, and political aspects of communities were just as important as the economic components. With this awareness, the attention shifted to the human being as a resource. This view focuses on the development of the person as an individual. This process approach emphasizes the ability of community members to participate and make meaningful contributions to community change. It is a technique for planned change, a means to an end, whereby the process becomes more important than the product. The development of persons into functioning individuals capable of making decisions and taking actions toward community improvements is the ultimate goal.

In the process approach, the community development professional has to be skilled in such areas as human relations, the social action process, small group behavior, and leadership development. The stress is on sociopsychological skills that assist and enable community residents to function successfully on their own behalf. The professional's objectives are then stated in terms of community members' capacity to progress through these steps of implementing change.

The task and process orientations represent the two most broadly defined, and probably most widely discussed, typologies of the community development role. However, in attempting to define the community development worker's role in terms of the tasks performed, one is struck by the wide range of diverse activities commonly associated with the community development professional. Just as there is no single approach to community development, there is no single role that describes all community development professionals even within these broad categories. Nor are all professionals who carry out community development activities called "community developers" — many are known as "planners," "community organizers," or "industrial developers."

Chin and Benne (1976) identified three types of strategies for effecting change. The first type is the *empirical-rational strategy* in which change agents are concerned with providing the person, group, or community with sufficient information so that a proposed change can be rationally justified. This follows the land-grant universities' research-extension model for disseminating research-based information. In this case, extension staff are seen as the bearers of glad tidings — information.

The second type of strategy is called *normative–re-educative*. According to this view, change occurs when people alter their basic norms. Change is effected by interventionary methods that seek to alter the very habits, values, and attitudes of individuals and communities. This perspective brings into question underlying human assumptions. The change agent attempts to stimulate a questioning, clarification, and reformulation of values.

The third type of strategy deals with the application of power. The *power-coercive* strategy focuses on the ability of one person or group to influence another. In the community context, we are generally concerned with the exercise of power over group decisions. Change agents utilize power-based methods when they work with community leaders; they may exert their own power, but they must also recognize that their attempts at empirical-rational and normative–re-educative change strategies can either be legitimized or destroyed by the power strategy of others.

In helping communities achieve their development goals, professionals perform many types of functions. They conduct needs assessments, encourage citizen participation, facilitate decision making, identify resources, educate others, present alternatives, analyze information, develop leaders, formulate plans, stimulate organizational efforts, and assist in the implementation of solutions.

Many of these specific functions of community development professionals have been delineated with reference to identifiable professional roles. From the social perspective, Gallaher and Santopolo (1967) identified four roles that link the change agent to the client system: analyst, advisor, advocator, and innovator. From this point of view, the community development worker is viewed as a specialist in process skills and a generalist in technical subject matter.

From a city and regional planning perspective, Meyerson (1956) outlines the following five task functions for a community development worker or planner: central intelligence, pulse taking, policy clarification, detailed development planning, and feedback review. The central-intelligence and pulse taking functions provide an analysis of the existing situation and begin to identify problems that need to be addressed. The policy clarification function is the statement and revision of community objectives, while the technical plan formulates alternative options. In addition, the evaluation of program consequences as a guide to future action is the feedback review.

The Cooperative Extension Service has defined six functions for the community development professional: (1) providing technical and analytical assistance, (2) helping identify community problems and development goals and objectives, (3) identifying consequences of development alternatives, (4) fostering liaison with outside individuals and groups, (5) stimulating community interaction, and (6) bringing diverse groups together (Extension Committee on Organization and Policy 1966).

Other efforts to define the role of the community development worker in terms of the tasks performed are variations on the basic concepts of the change agent, planning, and extension roles. For example, Morris (1970) specifies four work roles: field agent, advisor or consultant, advocate, and planner. A more general approach is suggested by Cary (1972), who uses the terms *educator* and *community organizer* to describe the roles.

In a cross-cultural comparison, Kelley, Balderrabano, and Briseno

(1986) identified twelve roles that are performed at different stages of the development process: (1) consultant, (2) researcher, (3) policy analyst, (4) enabler, (5) planner, (6) program developer, (7) organizer, (8) rehabilitator, (9) advocate, (10) coordinator, (11) educator, and (12) mediator. They found the planner and program developer roles to be the most commonly used in U.S. development, while the advocate and coordinator roles are most frequently used in Mexico. The educator role, however, is quite common to both countries. These findings suggest that the type of community development occurring as well as the functions performed by community development workers are somewhat different in developing countries than they are in developed nations.

In an attempt to synthesize the various listings of functions attributed to the community development role, Bennett (1973) developed a classification scheme based on five principal functions: process consultant, technical consultant, program advocate, organizer, and resource provider. The process consultant role focuses on the "hows" of problem solving, decision making, organizing, enabling, and implementing rather than on the particular group action outcomes; developing and implementing strategies for facilitating change are the process consultant's areas of expertise. The technical consultant, on the other hand, "provides information, know-how, and [an objective] perspective to the community in relation to specific programs of change" (Bennett 1973, p. 64). Supplying accurate technical information to a community is a vital part of development; therefore, information-giving and analysis concerning developmental alternatives are central to this role.

When community development workers propose a specific course of action, they are performing the advocate role. The professional analyzes the situation and decides what the best alternative is for the community. In this case, the professional goes beyond presenting the alternatives to the community for their action and recommends a specific alternative as the best solution for the problem.

The organizational role is concerned with the formation and renewal of an organizational structure that can deal with community problems. With this approach, the community development worker helps a community organize for action. This role has often been utilized in neighborhood settings through the use of the Alinsky approach. The organizer focuses on bringing individuals together in a group setting so they can have a voice in community affairs. The process consultant role is then involved in seeing that the organization continues to function effectively.

The fifth role presented by Bennett is that of resource provider.

He defines this function as the channeling of financial resources to the community. Ratchford (1970) and Ross (1967) also cited this role, although, contrary to Bennett, they did not limit the concept of resources to money. Rather, they focused on the role of the professional as identifying a community's need for outside help and determining how to go about securing it.

Although different categorical names are used by the various typologies, it is generally agreed that there is a logical order of succession—a set of sequential steps or stages—through which a community progresses. It is seen as a linear progression toward development. This process starts with a community defining its needs, taking stock of its resources, and helping its leadership emerge, as well as providing external assistance where necessary and carrying out action programs. A community development professional may be involved in one or more of these steps or in the entire process.

Relating to the Community.   Critical to the success of a community development practitioner is the relationship between the professional and the community members. Community development professionals work with a wide variety of clientele. The appropriate individual or group will be largely determined by what decisions are to be made, what actions are to be taken, and who will enter that process.

The assumption is that the professional brings to the community expertise that is not possessed by individuals within the community. Expertise includes technical skills (such as engineering, accounting, or marketing) and facilitating skills (such as grantsmanship, leadership development, or mediation)—both of which assist the community through the development process. From the community perspective the community development professional is the expert who has influence and credibility. However, the professional must be sensitive to the wishes of the community. As Morris (1970) concludes, the community development professional must believe that meaningful change will be change that the people themselves want and will participate in achieving. Not only do community members bring their own areas of technical expertise to the process, but more importantly, these persons and their families are the ones affected by the outcome. They care what happens because it is their community. Thus, decisions are expected to be governed not by the professionals' own self-interests but by their judgments of what would serve their clients' interests best.

Because the community development professional is an outsider to the community unique opportunities exist. An outsider can bring to a community a fresh perspective that is not bound by historical precedence, emotional attachments, social involvement, and political influences. By the same notion, these factors should not be overlooked. Completely ignoring these influences is a sure path to failure. Futhermore, the professional is in a position to establish linkages to the larger environment and to make the community aware of other information and resources that may be available. With the increase in influence being exerted by persons external to the community, this function is of vital importance.

Widespread participation is the hallmark of the democratic tradition. The most general level of clientele involvement is the public at large. Some developmental goals (for example, programs of general education and awareness) impact most or all citizens. However, most community development professionals tend to have regular, direct contact with a limited number of people. The community development professional generally works through these individuals or groups for the ultimate benefit of community residents. The nature of the professional assistance determines the setting, and the skills needed by the professional differ accordingly. For example, the worker may be responding to a very specific request of one person or helping a group through a decision-making process.

The clientele may be local lay leaders. Such persons are generally voluntary, unpaid individuals working for the good of the community. These persons possess a wide variety of education and experience and contribute a considerable amount of time to community development efforts. They are from the local community and may be self-appointed, designated, or elected; they may have a locally recognized status and following (Bilinski 1969). Working with voluntary lay leaders offers the professional an established linkage into the existing social structure of the community, although the volunteer leaders may be limited in community development training and experience and lack sufficient time. In this case the professional needs to offer these individuals informal support, training, and information within a very flexible time frame.

Local officials make up another important client group. They are usually elected or appointed and are charged with the responsibility of caring for specific governmental functions. Some are unpaid but most receive some compensation, either on a part- or full-time basis. They, like volunteer leaders, have knowledge, skills, and experiences that vary substantially. Also, their areas of responsibility and interests may be community-wide or very specialized. The success of the community development professional, to a great extent, lies in the professional's ability to support these officials without competing with them and thus threatening their power position in the community. The community development professional can provide general awareness education and assistance in problem solving and planning as well as specific factual information needed for carrying out a project or program. Planners are a prime example of professionals serving this client group; they provide assistance to governmental officials in the areas of problem identification, data collection and analysis, plan formulation and implementation, and feedback.

Civic and development organizations – through which many lay leaders work – are often directly or indirectly involved in carrying out or encouraging development. The goals of these groups may or may not be limited to development, or their involvement may be in a specific aspect of development (e.g., industry, health, education). Members of these organizations are volunteers, and their backgrounds and experiences are varied. Although sometimes the organizations' interests are very specific and the group processes may be slow, community development professionals have had and will continue to have an important impact on the development of communities because of their ability to draw on a wide range of skills and experiences of their members and to exert influence in order to mobilize resources.

Many developmental agencies and organizations have paid professional staff in communities. These professionals are supported from outside the community and usually work with a local advisory board or group. They are professionally trained in specialized subject areas and their status is derived principally from their professional position in the parent organization rather than from the community.

Individual Traits. Because community development is relatively new as a professional area, many persons employed in community development roles are trained in a variety of disciplinary fields. Nearly half (43 percent) of the 1986 Community Development Society's members reported their area of specialization as something other than community development; 57 percent claimed community development as their specialty. However, there is no one disciplinary home from which most members come; they are evenly distributed across the fields of sociology, economics, education, and planning. This is substantiated by Hamilton (1980), who found that of the community development professionals employed in the Cooperative Extension Service, 29 percent were trained in economics; 23 percent in sociology and other social sciences; 20 percent in education; and 28 percent in other areas including planning, recreation, and management.

It is evident that because of their diverse backgrounds, community development professionals hold different views and perspectives on community development. Those with economics training would more likely be involved in and knowledgeable of impact studies, industrial development, and community services, whereas professionals with a sociology background would more likely stress the social processes of group dynamics and leadership development. A community organizer needs an educational and experiential base in social organization, while a health planner needs to have technical knowledge of health services and the planning process.

The common thread for individuals with quite different disciplinary orientations is the application of their disciplinary-based expertise to the community setting. To a great extent, these community development workers have acquired their overall perspective on community development from professional improvement experiences, such as in-service training and conferences; from their association with colleagues at professional meetings, such as those of the Community Development Society or its state chapter meetings; and from on-the-job experiences. Furthermore, many of the general skill areas, such as working effectively with people, are transferable from other job roles and are developed by trial and error.

The formal training and experience a community development professional brings to the job are considered manifest traits. That is, they are the characteristics most evident and talked about—level of education, field of study, past positions held, skills, and knowledge. However, latent traits are also important, even though they are not so readily apparent. These are characteristics that underlie the qualities of the professional and serve to guide specific actions; they form the person's philosophy on development. As an integral part of the person's professional life, latent traits are that person's professional values and norms, the foundation of his or her efforts.

In addition to academic credentials, technical skills, and philosophical position, each professional also possesses a style and philosophy of work, personality traits, physical appearance, initiative, imagination, motivation, sensitivity, established relationships and contacts, a status position and reputation in the community, and a capacity for making decisions. Cohen (1980) concludes that the essential traits of a successful community developer are flexibility, tolerance of ambiguity, common sense, perserverance, and humility.

Many would say that it takes a special kind of person to be successful as a community development worker, perhaps one who can walk on water – or at least one who can fight off sharks! Personal traits that are desirable for a community development professional to possess are an even temper, a willingness to listen, and a knowledge of the art of negotiating and compromise (Huie and Crouch 1980). The person should also possess an ability to work with diverse audiences and be free from disciplinary dogma (Cohen 1980). Further, it is important for the professional to get along with people – to be sensitive, willing to listen, and willing to give encouragement to others.

Characteristics such as friendliness, enthusiasm, intelligence, decisiveness, persistence, and courage are desirable traits in successful professionals; however, as has been discovered in trait-oriented research on leadership, rarely do two persons agree as to which traits are essential (Stogdill 1974). Identifying individual factors is crucial for understanding the community development role, but there is no single set of traits that is best for all situations. Rather, a multitude of personal characteristics is important in defining the professional role.

Organizational Context. The community development role is influenced by the organizational context in which the professional is working. The nature of the organization influences the community development worker directly as well as indirectly. The organization has certain goals, purposes, and development philosophy, which in turn are generally subscribed to by their employees. For instance, the Cooperative Extension Service, as an example of a public agency, emphasizes the community development process in describing its approach. "The community development process involves collective and rational action on the part of people. Thus, it requires an education effort in which citizens carefully analyze their situation, study issues, and decide on ways of achieving community goals" (Phifer and List 1971, p. 4). In contrast, private sector development organizations are more concerned with the production of outcomes than with process. McCoy (1980, p. 105) states, "The private sector is concerned with doing rather than studying, with facts rather than options, and with product rather than process."

The goals and purposes of the organization may be specific or very general, and short term or of long duration (e.g., building a new park or improving the social and economic well-being of the people). Employees tend to pattern their roles according to the nature of the organization.

To function effectively, an organization requires some degree of shared beliefs and practices that unite the members, some agreement on important values. This normative system consists of the dos and don'ts that govern the actions and imply the sanctions and rewards for group members. An organization establishes patterns of interaction among its members and places them in various positions of authority in relationship to other members. Differing levels of responsibility and status are thus conferred by the organization. This status level, in turn, carries over into the community in the form of titles, prestige, and so forth. In addition to these relationships between individuals within the organization, the status attributed to the organization itself is also important. It may be a new and struggling consulting firm of three members or a century-old university of one thousand faculty.

Functional specialization within and among organizations has increased over the years. Developmental problems are generally complex in nature, requiring the input of many specialists. Most development efforts require, at a minimum, specialists in planning, financing, design, and organization. Increased specialization has made it necessary for the community development worker to interact across the boundaries of organizational subsystems and with other organizations and agencies. At the same time, large organizations have the capacity for employing many specialists on an on-call basis to address specific issues. One could conclude, therefore, that increased specialization has made the community development professional's role more complex, but it also has the potential for providing the community development worker with more specialized support.

The interorganizational climate in a community can impact the community development professional's role. Ecologists have generally distinguished between two basic types of relations: symbiosis and commensalism (Hawley 1950, pp. 36-39). The former refers to relations of mutual dependence and advantage, while the latter describes competition for the same scarce resources. Because developmental problems often require the input of many organizations, cooperation among agencies and agency representatives is crucial (symbiosis). Formal and informal linkages between organizations, in turn, set the framework in which the professionals work. If the organizations are competing for the same resources, recognition, or domain (commensalism), joint efforts of the workers will be severely hampered.

Contemporary Issues

CERTIFICATION AND ACCREDITATION.   For a number of years the Community Development Society's membership has struggled with the issues surrounding certification and accreditation. First of all, it should be made clear that these are two distinct issues. Certification is carried out at the individual level, while accreditation addresses the training program of an institution. In other words, people are certified and institutional programs are accredited.

Behind decisions on professional recognition are a number of assumptions. The reason most frequently given to justify a certification program is quality-assurance. In short, certification is to ensure that those persons professing to be civil engineers, surgeons, and planners do in fact have appropriate training and experience in order to perform competently in their professions. So first and foremost, a certification program is a quality-assurance program to protect the consumer against unqualified practitioners. This same reason carries over to accreditation. The training program is expected to meet certain minimum standards in order to protect students in the program and to protect the public when graduates apply their profession.

The second reason to justify a certification or accreditation program is to enhance the standing or prestige of the professional or institution as well as that of the certifying or accrediting body. Recognition of the individual or institution communicates to the public the message that a basic level of performance has been achieved. This act makes the individual or organization feel more professional. But in addition, it establishes the granting body as the keeper of the standard. Professional associations want to be seen as the groups that establish the standards. In fact, in some fields there may even be competition to secure the right to set standards.

A third purpose is to stimulate professionals and degree-granting institutions to continue to strive for excellence. The process of staying certified motivates professionals to acquire more skills and knowledge, thereby increasing their competency. Most certification programs require that professionals receive additional training. Just the fact that individuals are on the job does not ensure that they are current in their profession. Likewise, institutions are periodically required to show that they still meet the standards and have kept up with changes in the field.

After lengthy discussions and many drafts, the Community Development Society approved a list of Principles of Good Practice in July 1985. A community development professional should

1. promote active and representative citizen participation so that community members can meaningfully influence decisions that affect their lives.

2. engage community members in problem diagnosis so that those affected may adequately understand the causes of their situation.

3. help community members understand the economic, social, political, environmental, and psychological impacts associated with alternative solutions to the problem.

4. assist community members in designing and implementing a plan to solve agreed upon problems by emphasizing shared leadership and active citizen participation in that process.

5. disengage from any effort that is likely to adversely affect the disadvantaged segments of a community.

6. actively work to increase leadership capacity (skills, confidence, and aspirations) in the community development process.

In 1986 the Community Development Society further approved a voluntary accreditation program with appropriate mechanisms for implementation. But what is missing from that plan is a specific set of standards or criteria against which to judge a training program. This important element is left largely to the discretion of the review team members. The guidance they have is the list of these six general principles. Developing and implementing a certification and accreditation program from this list is very difficult because the list lacks sufficient specificity.

Why are the Principles of Good Practice so general? And why aren't they based on a more complete written body of the theory, principles, and techniques of community development? The problem is that the variability within the profession makes reaching a consensus on the content difficult. Inevitably some people feel that they, or their approaches, are not being adequately represented. Therefore, to accommodate all points of view, the statements become very general.

Some professionals feel that the Community Development Society needs to become active in the certification process, while others have opposed such action. In 1977, Gibson argued against professional certification as being contrary to the goals of community development in general and to the Community Development Society in particular. That article was followed by Parsons' response in 1978 with the case in favor of certification. His argument was basically that without certification, community development will be swallowed up by other academic fields. A 1987 candidate for president of the society argued that community development activities "ought to take place under the auspices of a responsible body such as the society" (Robertson 1987, p. 10) and further, that there was a need for the society to move ahead quickly before other groups seized the opportunity. Likewise, other candidates have registered their opposition.

If certification is to be implemented by the Community Development Society (or any other group), considerable effort would need to be put into the complex task of specifying and then reaching agreement on what constitutes a qualified community development professional. It is not adequate to talk in very general terms. Rather, there would have to be concurrence on what is community development's unique body of knowledge and how competency is measured. These assignments are not easy, but they are essential if the society expects to assure community leaders and the public that community development professionals are indeed qualified.

Closely tied to the certification issue is the subject of whether or not the profession, especially within the Community Development Society, encourages widespread participation and identification with community development. The variability within the society's current membership would suggest that over the years the profession has welcomed involvement of persons with quite diverse interests. It is generally held that the presence of different perspectives has been an invigorating force within the profession, a characteristic that has made the Community Development Society uniquely different from most other professional associations.

Currently the concern is this: Are we in danger of reducing the diversity of the members by recognizing only some as "legitimate" community development professionals? In effect, certification would be communicating the message that I am qualified and you are not. As such, certification could become an exclusionary measure, a gatekeeping device that withholds recognition from some and doles it out to others. Persons with a minority view might find it difficult to gain certification. Furthermore, certification could serve to limit entry to the profession. This could happen in a calculated, deliberate manner, or more likely in subtle ways by discouraging people from applying for certification. The mere presence of a potentially laborious and costly process could dissuade some.

Therefore, while trying to provide a measure of quality assurance and to enhance the prestige of professionals in the eyes of clientele, certification and accreditation programs can be divisive within the profession. If the program is to be meaningful, the society must be able to determine whether or not individuals qualify to be certified community developers and why.

CHANGING ROLE. Early development efforts occurred in small community settings where the people's total way of life was of primary concern. This holistic approach operated within an environment of shared interests and collective actions, and dealt with a wide range of problems over an extended period of time. Local residents were involved in the process from start to finish. They shared in the early conceptualization of the problem, in the consideration of alternative solutions, and in the program planning and implementation. However, with an increase in size and complexity of communities and the advent of funding programs from sources outside of the community, there has been pressure to abandon this holistic approach in favor of specific programs and projects (Cary 1973).

Blakely and Bradshaw (1982) indicate that the issues facing communities today require community development professionals to master a whole new set of skills. To ignore the substantial changes occurring in communities is to cause community development professionals "to be left behind" (p. 119). Some of the new skill areas they identify are input/output models, social indicators, structural analyses, and use of the media. They are very critical of current professional community development roles and go so far as to conclude that the individual and group social skills "are impractical and sometimes useless" in our modern complex society and that the "citizens can do little by themselves to alter their community's basic condition" (p. 118).

The role of the community development professional is being shaped by the very nature of community development itself. New technical skills are needed in dealing with an increasingly complex community. We have moved from an environment in which residents and leaders participated to the fullest in all community issues to one in which community decisions are compartmentalized by sectors (education, health care, economy), or even more specifically, by programs or projects. Furthermore, donor agencies from outside the community play a greater role in development decisions that affect the community at large. Local communities, thus, become implementors of programs conceptualized from outside. For example, employment programs designed at the federal and state levels may be implemented even though they may not relate to the most critical needs of an individual community. In addition, the sense of community as being territorially bounded is slipping away (see Chapter 14).

The role of the community development professional has been altered by these changes. The locally based generalist may very well be a dying breed. What is being lost is the ongoing presence of the community developer, who like a good coach convinces leaders and citizens that they can achieve a better life. The community development role includes hand-holding, giving encouragement, warding off and mediating conflicts, cutting through red tape, and writing proposals. Budgetary shortfalls have led to the consolidation and termination of many of these positions, with some of the functions being assumed by specialists. However, specialists generally contribute to only one portion of the development process. They may be consultants who design the facility or put together the financial package. That is, they contribute their expertise in a narrowly defined area which constitutes only a small part of the overall process. A specialist is no less a community development professional than is the generalist; but if generalists are phased out, who will bring all of these pieces together? Who will perform this integrative function?

The rationale behind eliminating the generalist role is that process skills are less important than technical skills, or in other words, that communities are capable of proceeding through the progression of steps without professional assistance. In reality, a series of problems result for the community. An externally designed program may not garner the necessary local commitment and support. Development efforts can become fragmented and piecemeal and can even be working at cross purposes with other efforts. It becomes more difficult to establish community-level priorities because neither sector leaders nor specialized professionals are capable of seeing the "big picture." Rather, they are focusing on only one component of the whole. In the end, the community can lose its sense of interrelatedness and coordination and cease to function as a community of shared interests.

THE REBIRTH OF COMMUNITY DEVELOPMENT. The community development profession is going through a transition period. The number of community development professionals has declined, as is reflected in a drop in Community Development Society membership. Although membership has now leveled off, there is some question as to whether it will decline further, possibly to the extent of threatening community development as a profession. Some of this decline can be attributed to a reduction in funding support for community development efforts. The U.S. government has cut back in domestic programs as well as in areas of foreign technical assistance.

Diminished resources have led to fewer professional positions and a reduction in project funds. At the same time, some agencies have reassigned or changed titles of roles that were formerly carried out by community development professionals. Some would argue that there has been a reduction in the number of professionals who call themselves community developers because others can perform the role as well, and perhaps more efficiently. Some critics have even suggested that it is time for community development to pack its bags and call it quits, that the functions can best be handled by integrating them into other agencies, and that many communities themselves can assume the role of community developers (Alldred 1979).

There has been a decline in the number of community development professionals, and there have been shifts in the roles performed by them. However, it seems that community development has recently experienced a rebirth. More than ever, agencies and communities have come to realize the importance of roles performed by community development professionals. At the national level, Congress is considering legislation that would substantially increase support for rural development efforts such as the provision of water and sewage systems, industrial development, and health care. The Cooperative Extension Service has identified rural revitalization as one of its seven national priority program emphases. And communities are asking for help as they attempt to take on an increased role in development. No longer can communities look to the state or federal government to provide the resources and expertise needed for local development projects. Therefore, agencies and communities are confirming a need for community development professionals.

Efforts to integrate community development functions into the roles of other professionals will lead to the loss of the community development perspective. It is not enough to conduct a feasibility study, design a water system, develop an accounting system, or provide other types of technical information to an impersonal client. The community development profession is much more than that. Community development professionals are capable of providing technical solutions to community problems, but they are also dedicated to helping individuals grow and develop into responsible citizens who function optimally within the community. In short, they communicate a vision of an improved lifestyle. The methods community development professionals use are rooted in democratic participation and stress the importance of different points of view—the agendas are community-driven. The community development profession is not just providing technical solutions, it is a way of thinking and a method of working.

Summary.   Because community development transcends national, state, and local boundaries, it is imperative that community development roles be responsive to the situational context, the cultural variations, the needs of the people, and the politics and economy of the area. Furthermore, community development professionals must have a mastery of disciplinary subject matter, an ability to apply knowledge and information to real-world problems, personal traits that enable them to relate effectively with people, and a flexibility to respond to changing conditions.

In attempting to describe professional community development roles, there is the temptation to draw grand-scale conclusions that contain universal prescriptions. However, in reality there is no one person, approach, or set of technical skills that will work in all situations. It is up to each community development professional to draw upon his or her resources and to shape a solution that satisfies the needs of each unique community setting.

References

Alldred, M. 1979. Community development: Problems and perspectives. *International Review of Community Development* 37(Summer):241–528.

Bennett, A. 1973. Professional staff members' contributions to community development. *Journal of the Community Development Society* 4(1):58–68.

Bilinski, R. 1969. A description and assessment of community development. In *Selected Perspectives for Community Resource Development,* L. T. Wallace, D. Hobbs, and R. D. Vlasin, eds., pp. 143–80. Raleigh: North Carolina State University, Agricultural Policy Institute.

Blakely, E. J., and T. K. Bradshaw. 1982. New roles for community developers in rural growth communities. *Journal of the Community Development Society* 13(2):101–20.

Cary, L. J. 1972. Roles of the professional community developer. *Journal of the Community Development Society* 3(2):36–41.

_____. 1973. The community approach. In *Approaches to Community Development,* H. B. Long, R. C. Anderson, and J. A. Blubaugh, eds., pp. 9–24. Iowa City, Ia.: National University Education Association and The American College Testing Program.

Chin, R., and K. D. Benne. 1976. General strategies for effecting changes in human systems. In *The Planning of Change,* W. G. Bennis, K. D. Benne, R. Chin, and K. E. Coray, eds., pp. 22–45. New York: Holt, Rinehart and Winston.

Cohen, M. W. 1980. Professional roles as a community psychologist. In *Community Development in America,* J. A. Christenson and J. W. Robinson, Jr., eds., pp. 133–37. Ames: Iowa State University Press.

Extension Committee on Organization and Policy. 1966. Community resource development. Washington, D.C.: U.S. Department of Agriculture, Cooperative Extension Service.

Gallaher, A. Jr., and F. A. Santopolo. 1967. Perspectives on agent roles. *Journal of Cooperative Extension* 5(4):223–30.

Gibson, D. L. Professional certification for community development personnel. *Journal of the Community Development Society* 8(2):30–38.

Hamilton, V. E. 1980. Professional roles in Cooperative Extension Service. In *Community Development in America,* J. A. Christenson and J. W. Robinson, Jr., eds., pp. 120–28. Ames: Iowa State University Press.

Hawley, A. H. 1950. *Human Ecology.* New York: Ronald Press.

Huie, J. M., and R. T. Crouch. 1980. Professional roles in government. In *Community Development in America,* J. A. Christenson and J. W. Robinson, Jr., eds., pp. 115–20. Ames: Iowa State University Press.

Kelly, J. B., A. L. Balderrabano P., and E. Briseno L. 1986. The roles of community development workers in the U.S. and Mexico. *Community Development Journal* 21(1):11–22.

McCoy, P. E. 1980. Professional roles in the private sector. In *Community Development in America,* J. A. Christenson and J. W. Robinson, Jr., eds., pp. 103–8. Ames: Iowa State University Press.

Meyerson, M. 1956. Building the middle-range bridge for comprehensive planning. *Journal of American Institute Planner* 22:58–64.

Morris, R. 1970. The role of the agent in the community development process. In *Community Development as a Process,* L. J. Cary, ed. Columbia: University of Missouri Press.

Parsons, T. Professional certification for practitioners of community development. *Journal of the Community Development Society* 9(1):4–10.

Phifer, B., and F. List. 1971. *Community Development: A New Dimension of Extension.* Columbia: University of Missouri, Extension Division.

Ratchford, C. B. 1970. The community development profession in today's society. *Journal of the Community Development Society* 1(1):5–13.

Robertson, W. E. 1987. Nominees for officers, board chosen. *Vanguard* 64:1–10.

Ross, M. G. 1967. *Community Organization: Theory, Principles, and Practice,* 2d ed. New York: Harper and Row.

Stogdill, R. 1974. *Handbook of Leadership: A Survey of Theory and Research.* New York: Free Press.

7

The Practice of Community Development

MARIE ARNOT FISCHER

T HE three general approaches to community development—self-help, technical assistance, and conflict—have been discussed in previous chapters. This chapter describes how those approaches are applied to the practice of community development in planning, needs assessment, community organizing, leadership, and fund-raising. These functions are representative, but not inclusive, of all that community developers do. Whatever approaches are used, the goal is to build community capacity. The role of the community development practitioner is to facilitate that process.

This chapter suggests some of the skills that a community development practitioner needs to cultivate and the manner in which those skills are applied (see Table 7.1). A thorough knowledge of techniques is stressed, as is the necessity for both astute observation and a commitment to consulting the user or constituency. The effective community developer combines technical and human relations skills with atti-

Table 7.1. Attributes of an Effective Community Developer

A good community developer
- has a thorough knowledge of group organizing techniques
- is an astute observer
- plans *with* people, not *for* them
- consults the users
- summarizes and integrates group efforts
- builds others' leadership skills and group capacities
- graciously withdraws as the group becomes self-directed

136

tudes directed toward building individual leadership and group capacity. Those attitudes result in behaviors that are nurturing and that provide positive reinforcement designed to build confidence in others. The community developer must also be able to summarize and integrate group effort. Finally, he or she must discourage dependency by withdrawing gradually, graciously, and unobtrusively as the group's capacity for self-direction increases.

Planning. Planning involves the visioning of a desired future state and the development of a systematic strategy for achieving that state. There are several approaches to the process of planning, all of which contain some common elements. Three approaches are presented here: model coherency, strategic planning, and a traditional planning process.

Model coherency involves establishing an ideal or model of a desired future state and then designing strategies that conform to or are coherent with the model. The technique integrates needs assessment, goal formulation, and development of an action plan and involves five steps: (1) identification of people or interests to be served, (2) identification of need, (3) identification of goals, (4) description of current activities, and (5) development of a goal-directed plan of action. Model coherency is a technique which strongly links planning and performance—it requires a clear statement of the desired future state, an analysis of the present state, and a specific plan of action for moving from the present to the future.

Strategic planning places heavy emphasis on a thorough analysis of the present state or condition. It involves seven steps: (1) a thorough and comprehensive examination of the effectiveness of the organization—its mission, structure, constituency, program, financing, etc.; (2) an analysis of external factors—social, economic, political, technological—that affect the organization; (3) a critical diagnosis of the various elements of the organization; (4) an analysis of the implications of the first three steps; (5) the articulation of objectives and subobjectives; (6) the development of a strategy for implementation; and (7) monitoring and feedback. Perhaps the greatest strength of the strategic planning process is its emphasis on analyzing the milieu, or context, within which planning is to take place. The first three steps are sometimes referred to as the "WOTS": weaknesses, opportunities, threats, and strengths (So 1984).

The following example illustrates how a community group used the strategic planning process in developing a five-year plan. The group began by forming these committees: mission, history and accomplishments, constituency, organizational structure, program, and finance. The history and accomplishments committee finished its work; the mission committee recommended that some of the modifications of the mission statement be acted on at a later stage in the planning process; and the constituency, organizational structure, program, and finance committees described the current situation. Next the constituency, organizational structure, program, and finance committees analyzed the external factors that affected the organization and then listed the weaknesses, opportunities, threats, and strengths (WOTS) that were suggested by the analysis. This process led to a critical examination of existing objectives, the articulation of some new objectives, and, eventually, a modification of the mission statement.

Planning is never done in a vacuum; and unless it is undertaken by an organization or group which is just being formed, the group, by virtue of the fact that it exists, has been involved in planning to some degree. Thus it is important to analyze both the group's internal factors, including the planning that has been done, and the external factors that affect the organization.

Traditional planning involves (1) assessing needs, (2) establishing goals, (3) determining objectives, (4) considering alternatives and deciding on a course of action (method), (5) implementing action, and (6) documenting and evaluating processes and accomplishments (Arnot, Cary, and Houde 1985). In assessing needs, the question arises as to whose needs are to be served and whose perceptions of need are to be considered. Professional planners are bound by a code of ethics which states that, "a planner's primary obligation is to serve the public interest. . . . A planner must strive to give citizens the opportunity to have a meaningful impact on the development of plans and programs, . . . [and] must strive to expand choice and opportunity for all persons, recognizing a special responsibility to plan for the needs of disadvantaged groups and persons, and must urge the alteration of policies, institutions, and decisions which oppose such needs" (AICP 1981). Thus planners must be astute in analyzing the stakes of various players in any planning effort and assiduously avoid being co-opted by any special interest group.

Confusion abounds in distinguishing between goals, objectives, and methods (see Table 7.2). Semantics—whether one refers to "goals and objectives" or "objectives and subobjectives"—are of minimal im-

Table 7.2. The Differences between Goals, Objectives, and Methods

Goals	Objectives	Methods
Why is this being done?	*What* is to be done?	*How* will it be done?
What *values, belief systems,* or *guiding principles* prevail?	What are the *impacts* or *results*? How much? How many? For whom? By when?	How *effective* will it be? Is it manageable? Is it appropriate? What are the risks? Who are the legitimizers and will they approve?
General description of future state	*Specific* description of achievements at certain points in time	Instructions, policies, and guidelines for accomplishing objectives

portance. What is important is that certain questions are addressed. Basic to any planning effort, but often not articulated, is what are called "goals," which deal with the question of the philosophical basis for a planning effort: *Why* is this being done and what values, belief systems, or guiding principles prevail? For example, public housing projects are based on the premise or belief that all people are entitled to safe, sanitary, and decent housing. These become the goals.

A second important question is, *what* is to be done? What is the objective? Objectives should focus on the impact or the results, stated in measurable and time-referenced terms. The need is the *before;* the objective is the *after.* How will the world be different as a result of the planning effort? For example, suppose that the state association of planning commissions believes planning commissioners need additional training and that it has approached a university planning department to ask their help in developing an appropriate training program. The objective might be to provide training for planning commissioners in thirty communities by the end of December. At the end of the session, planning commissioners will understand (1) state statutory and case laws related to planning and zoning; (2) the authority and responsibility of planning commissioners; (3) the kinds of issues planning commissioners deal with, the alternative courses of action that might be taken, and the implications of each course of action; and (4) how planning commissions make decisions. (See Table 7.3.)

The method addresses the question *how.* In the example above, how should the training be delivered? The central question is, of course, *will* the method chosen achieve the desired result? In addition, when considering alternative methods at least four other things should be examined: Is it manageable? Is it appropriate? What are the risks? Who are the legitimizers and will they approve? To illustrate, training for planning commissions might be delivered through regional or statewide conferences, a correspondence course, or on-site training. Each alternative should be carefully examined before the method of training is chosen. Inasmuch as documentation and evaluation is ongoing, it seems useful to diagram the traditional planning process as illustrated in Figure 7.1.

A PLANNING EXAMPLE. Recently a human service agency in a midwestern city engaged a community development worker to assist in developing a long-range plan. The worker began by introducing several planning models. The planning committee used a traditional planning process and divided into work groups, each of which was

Table 7.3. Goals, Objectives, and Methods: A Plan of Action

Goal: (Why?)
   To equip planning commissioners with the knowledge and skills necessary to serve the public interest.

Objectives: (What?)
   To provide training for planning commissioners in thirty communities by December of this year. Commissioners will learn (1) the state statutory and case laws related to planning and zoning; (2) the authority and responsibility of planning commissioners; (3) the variety of issues planning commissioners deal with, the alternative courses of action that might be taken, and the implications of each course of action; and (4) how planning commissions make decisions.

Method: (How?)
   Ten regional workshops, each of which will involve planning commissioners from three communities.

Tasks	Deadline	Resources Needed	Persons Responsible
1. Identify communities	Jan. 15	List of existing planning commissions, addresses, phone numbers	Project director with executive director, League of Municipalities
2. Prepare letter to planning commissions asking their input	Jan. 30	List of existing planning commissions, addresses, phone numbers	Project director
3. Analyze responses to letter	Feb. 28	Time and a plan for analyzing responses	Project director and assistant
4. Develop training plan and materials	April 30	Training materials used in similar projects, state statutes, results of responses, etc.	Project director, assistant, secretary, and graphics specialist

Figure 7.1. Traditional Planning Reviews

responsible for compiling one element of the plan. Over a period of several months the agency director, planning committee chair, and community development worker met prior to each committee meeting to assess progress and plan the next steps. At the committee work sessions, subgroups spent approximately one and one-half hours working and writing and one-half hour in reporting progress, sharing information, and making decisions. Between work sessions committee members, assisted by agency staff, gathered additional information. Finally an editing committee put together the final draft. Each copy was placed in a notebook with dividers to facilitate making changes. The plan included a calendar that specified when and how each element was to be updated. As the planning process developed, the group became increasingly confident and less dependent on the community development worker.

What happened in the above scenario was highly participatory in nature and difficult to achieve. It required a good sense of timing, allowing enough time to complete assignments between meetings but moving rapidly enough to maintain momentum. It meant accurately assessing individual and group abilities, providing enough support to ensure success but not so much as to create dependency. It involved inspiring and encouraging the participants. It entailed clearly articulating expectations and holding people accountable. Most important, it necessitated nurturing a sense of group ownership and competency so that the product and the process belonged to the group.

The principle is, of course, that community development workers plan *with* people, rather than *for* them. If planning is to be a dynamic process, and if plans are to be implemented, the process and the product must be owned by the constituents. However, all too frequently planners approach their tasks with an "I know what's good for you" attitude. Berger and Neuhaus (1977, p. 37) comment on this type of professional-client relationship: "The purpose of the professions is to serve society—not the other way around. Too often professionals regard those they serve as clients in the rather unfortunate sense the Latin word originally implied. The clients of a Roman patrician were one step above his slaves in the social hierarchy, not entirely unlike some of today's servile dependents upon professionals. Such a notion has no place in democratic society." The situation is further complicated by the fact that frequently a group or organization wants and/or expects a planner to do the planning for them.

Ideally, professional planners contribute concepts, theories, analyses, processed knowledge, new perspectives, and systematic research procedures while constituents contribute intimate knowledge of the context, realistic alternatives, norms, priorities, feasibility judgments, and operational details. The relationship between the two groups is characterized by mutuality: planners and constituents learn from each other (Friedmann 1973). The results are planning processes that are in place and understood by the constituents, plans that are implemented, and groups that are empowered.

Needs Assessment.   Before embarking on any course of action, it is important to define the problems or assess the needs. More than one technique should be used since perception of problems and needs differ depending on the technique used and on the individual performing the needs assessment.

TECHNIQUES. Butler and Howell (1980) divide needs assessment techniques into two categories: techniques for using existing information, such as the census and content analysis; and techniques for using new information, such as participant observation, the case study, social network analysis, the survey, key informant involvement, life histories, nominal group process, the delphi technique, advisory groups and task forces, community forums, and community impressions. Several of these techniques, presented in a less sophisticated form, might be suggested to a community betterment group: (1) search out information already available on the community; (2) list what you like best about other communities; (3) list what you think needs to be improved in the community; (4) make observations; (5) ask community leaders about the community; (6) interview community residents; (7) interview potential users of a particular service; (8) have community residents fill out a questionnaire; and (9) bring people together to discuss community needs (Arnot, Cary, and Houde 1985).

Often several techniques can be used simultaneously. For example, in a small town a rural community worker invited all community organization leaders to a town meeting to discuss how the community might best participate in the state community betterment program. She began by asking the group to brainstorm in response to the question, "What do you like best about our town?" Written responses were displayed at the front of the room. Then she asked, "What would you like to see improved?" Someone said, "Fix the potholes in the streets"; another said, "Develop a meals-on-wheels program"; a third said, "Expand library hours"; and a fourth said, "Start a downtown improvement program." As these suggestions were made, the community development worker grouped them into four categories: public improvements, culture and the arts, human services, and economic development. Subsequently she asked those interested in public improvements to meet in one corner of the room, those interested in culture and the arts to meet in another, and so on. The tasks of each group were to suggest specific improvements that could be made and to develop a plan for implementing action to accomplish those improvements. The process involved using existing information, identifying what needed to be improved, asking community leaders about the community, and bringing people together to discuss community needs—all valid needs assessment techniques.

In addition to selecting more than one technique for assessing needs, the techniques chosen must be appropriate and manageable. A popular technique for needs assessment is the survey. Surveys can be very effective; however, they are often time consuming, costly, and may require a good deal of expertise. In determining whether a survey is an appropriate technique for needs assessment, the following questions should be asked: (1) Is the information already available? (2) Has a careful analysis been done as to why a survey is necessary? (3) What kind of survey (e.g., personal interview, telephone, or written) is most appropriate? (4) Exactly what information is sought? What questions should be asked? (5) Who should be surveyed—that is, what demographic characteristics (e.g., age, sex, residence, education, and marital status) are relevant? (6) Who will design the survey? Is expertise available to design it? (7) Is it feasible to do a pretest? (8) How will the information be tabulated and analyzed? Who will do that? (9) How and to whom will the information be reported? (10) How will the information be used? (11) How much will the survey cost? and (12) How much time is needed?

CONSULTING THE USERS. In the process of problem analysis or needs assessment, the community development worker must make every effort to consult the potential user or beneficiary whose needs and problems are being considered. That is not to say that the perceptions of community leaders, a cross section of residents, providers, advisory groups, or others, are invalid. It is merely to reaffirm that constituents should be consulted.

Community Organizing. The purposes of community organizing and the distinctions between citizen participation and community development are offered by Koneya (1978). The primary concern of the community developer is to build community capacity. In the process of building community capacity, the community developer may assist a group in creating a viable and continuing organization, in identifying community problems and needs, in mobilizing internal and external resources to meet those needs, and in developing strategies for effective action. The ultimate goal, however, is that a mature and dynamic community organization will evolve, one in which community groups can exercise power within the political arena without being dependent on outside leadership.

Saul Alinsky defined power as the ability to act. Effective action depends on good organizational skills and using a consensus or collaborative strategy. Sometimes groups operate in an arena in which they encounter little opposition. Such is often the case with community betterment programs which exist in many states in both small towns and urban neighborhoods. As shown in Figure 7.2, community betterment groups tend to be structured according to one of three models.

COMMUNITY BETTERMENT. In Belvidere, a village of 270, the General Federation of Women's Clubs decided to initiate community involvement in the state community betterment program. As a first step they chose improvement of the village park. Plans were made to hold a

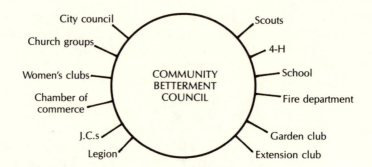

A community council consists of representatives from organizations within the community.

An existing organization spearheads the effort, inviting other organizations to send representatives to the council.

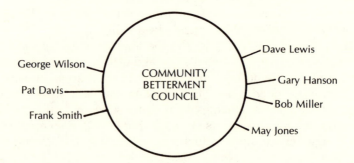

The council is formed of interested individuals.

Figure 7.2. *The Composition of Community Development Councils.* Courtesy of Otto Hoiberg. 1975. *Nebraska Community Improvement Program Manual.* Lincoln, Nebr.: Department of Economic Development.

workday in the park. The event was widely publicized and was held on a Saturday so that almost everyone, including children, could help. Representatives from the steering committee went to the school to talk about the workday. All rural families in the area were called and invited to participate. The steering committee outlined many projects and asked people to sign up to help with the ones in which they were interested. Ground was tilled; trees were planted; homemade playground equipment was built, painted, and put in place; flower beds were started; picnic tables were constructed; and work began on a footbridge. Everyone helped—men, women, children, persons with mental retardation, senior citizens, townspeople, and farm families. With the work well underway, a potluck luncheon was eaten in the park. During the luncheon the chairperson asked people to share their ideas about Belvidere and about community betterment. That day was a great beginning for what proved to be a very successful program.

Although this was a very simple project, it illustrates several sound community organizing techniques: involving the total community, beginning with a project that is manageable and highly visible, capitalizing on people's interests and abilities, building on continuity, laying the groundwork for establishing an ongoing organization, and having fun and fellowship.

HUMAN SERVICES. The St. Anthony Park Block Nurse Program in St. Paul, Minnesota, is somewhat more complex than the Belvidere program in that it distinguishes between the roles of professionals, volunteers, and natural helpers and involves all three in accomplishing the program's objectives. Professionals usually have special education and credentials, are salaried or charge fees for professional services, and work within a scheduled time period. Volunteers customarily organize on their own initiative or are recruited by an agency or institution to help that agency or institution carry out its mission. Although they are not paid, they often attend special training or orientation sessions to help them carry out their assignments. Natural helpers are people to whom community residents turn for help in coping with problems of living. An individual's natural helpers are persons in close relationship such as a spouse, neighbors, friends, relatives, and coworkers (Collins and Pancoast 1976).

There are not now, nor will there ever be, enough *professionals* to meet all human service needs; that would not even be desirable. In community organizing efforts, the community development worker needs to recognize and value the contribution of professionals, volunteers, and natural helpers and to foster a cooperative relationship among them. The Block Nurse Program draws upon all three to provide nursing, chore, and companionship services to older neighbors who otherwise might have to enter nursing homes. It is designed to help a family meet the needs of its members by supporting the family's resources and by supplementing those resources with services from the neighborhood (e.g., nursing, counseling, transportation, errands, chores, physical therapy). These services are coordinated by the public health nurse who sees the community as her client. Registered nurses living within the neighborhood and neighborhood residents trained in home health care provide professional services; other neighborhood residents trained as peer counselors serve as volunteers, and neighbors and friends offer help and support as natural helpers (The St. Anthony Park Block Nurse Program n.d.).

PUBLIC SERVICE. The Communities Organized for Public Service (COPS) in San Antonio has been especially successful in negotiating with city hall for public improvements. Some of the COPS leaders received training at the Industrial Areas Foundation in Chicago, started by Saul Alinsky, which focuses on wresting power from establishment groups. However Ernesto Cortes, one of the COPS leaders, contends that it is just as important to help people to attain dignity as it is to help them to acquire power. And he believes that "the best community organizing empowers people according to their best values which he has found to be those traced to Judeo-Christian and American democratic traditions: cooperation, participation, integrity of the whole person, free expression, concern for others, reciprocity, respect for the past, love, concern for the weak, and justice" (Boyte 1984, p. 159).

The above illustration would suggest that we take a new look at the conflict approach. Alinsky's advice to cut the issue, to freeze the target, and to go to war was based on a somewhat cynical approach to wresting power from those who had it, with the emphasis on the means. The COPS example advocates that community development workers would be well advised to recognize that "the dignity and example of ordinary people who take values that are widely and facilely espoused with utmost seriousness [gives] them discipline, depth, and clout" (Boyte 1984, p. 159).

ECONOMIC DEVELOPMENT. The community development examples in Chapter 1 (particularly MACED) suggest that some community organizing efforts are very sophisticated and require a great deal of specialization and expertise. The community developer may be a specialist who offers technical assistance in such areas as housing or finance, or may be an expert in packaging community development efforts. Or, he or she may develop and facilitate the processes that help the organization bring together community residents and staff specialists to achieve the organization's objectives.

Many examples can be found that deal with empowering people and building community capacity. Berger and Neuhaus (1977) suggest that one important means of empowering people is to strengthen community institutions, namely, the family, neighborhood, church or synagogue, and voluntary association. They describe these community institutions as mediating structures which stand between the individual in his or her private life and the megastructures which characterize much of public life.

In discussing building community capacity, McKnight (1985) presents yet another view—three visions of society: (1) the *therapeutic vision* which implies that professionals are available and competent to meet every need; (2) the *advocacy vision* in which people are protected by advocates and advocacy groups; and (3) the *community vision* in which each person is enabled to contribute his or her gifts, contributions, and capacities—the sum of individual capacities representing the power of the group. In summary, the community developer is engaged in community organizing primarily for the purpose of building community capacity.

Leadership.
Shared leadership is a concept which seems consistent with community development theory relative to capacity building. Leadership is a function shared by members of a group rather than the property of an individual (Arnot, Cary, and Houde 1985). In writing about the relationship of the leader to the group, Gardner states:

> Perhaps the most promising trend in our thinking about leadership is the growing conviction that the purposes of the group are best served when the leader helps followers to develop their own initiative, strengthens them in the use of their own judgment, and enables them to grow and to become better contributors. (1986a, p. 23)

Shared leadership or team leadership enhances the possibility that different styles of leadership can be brought to bear simultaneously. If the leader is a visionary with little talent for practical steps, a team member who is a naturally gifted agenda-setter can provide priceless support. No one knows enough to perform all the functions in our most demanding leadership posts today.

Corporate boards understand this better than most. The CEO does not have to be good at everything. Some are financial wizards. Some are superb managers. Some have gifts in public relations or selling. The important thing is not that the leader covers all bases but that the team collectively does so. (1986*b*, p. 16)

Shared leadership requires that a relationship of trust exists between the leader and the group. The leader instills trust by conveying, through behavior and attitude, that he or she believes that each member of the group has something to contribute; by treating all members with respect; by creating channels of open communication; and by being fair. In the examples below, Larry demonstrates his belief that leadership is a shared function, George shows a fear of sharing leadership, and Susan sees leadership in terms of the property of an individual.

Larry, who directed a community development agency in state government, had an extraordinarily energetic, enthusiastic, and capable staff. He had a low-key leadership style. He consulted with staff members individually and as a group about agency decisions. Moreover, in selecting staff he deliberately chose people who had abilities he did not possess, thereby creating a strong, competent team with varied talents and interests.

George, Larry's successor, was much more tense and autocratic. In choosing staff members he sought applicants whose ideas and abilities were very much like his own. He appeared to be threatened by people with different opinions and by people who had expertise in areas in which he lacked strength. His staff could be likened to peas in a pod. A certain air of caution and inflexibility prevailed throughout the organization.

Susan, who worked for a community agency, initiated a much-needed program for teenagers. She was very active and successful in gaining community support. She also organized an advisory committee which acted as a liaison between the community and the agency's board of directors. Soon the program came to be identified not as an agency effort but as Susan's program. She spoke of the constituents as "her" young people. Over a period of time the advisory committee became a cadre of her loyal supporters and the relationship between that group and the board was strained. Ultimately Susan and the executive director had a confrontation and Susan resigned in a huff, saying that she would take "her" staff with her.

These examples illustrate the basic principles of the practice of community development: (1) the best leaders are committed to building leadership in others; (2) shared leadership functions build stronger, more effective organizations; and (3) there is no place for autocratic selfishness in community development. No one person owns a constituency, staff, program, or agency. Community organization belongs to the public.

FUNCTIONS. The tasks or functions of leadership are described in many different ways. The functions may be grouped into two broad categories: task functions, which entail getting the job done; and maintenance functions, which involve nurturing the group as an effective unit. Cary adds a third function: meeting the needs of the members (Arnot, Cary, and Houde 1985). Boyatzis describes the functions of leadership as follows: (1) to make other people feel strong and help them to feel that they have the ability to influence their future and their environment; (2) to build others' trust in the leader; (3) to structure cooperative relationships rather than competitive relationships; (4) to resolve conflicts by mutual confrontation of issues rather than by avoiding or forcing a particular solution; and (5) to stimulate and promote goal-oriented thinking and behavior (Boyatzis n.d.). Gardner (1986c) suggests nine functions of leadership, although he does not present them as a definitive list: envisioning goals, affirming values, motivating, managing, achieving a workable level of unity, explaining, serving as a symbol, representing the group externally, and renewing.

In working with groups, the role of the community developer is to nurture leadership in others as a necessary component of group capacity building. Thus the purpose of shared leadership is not only to build leadership in others but also to foster group productivity through group solidarity – in short, to build a team. An effective leader enables groups to see themselves as they are *and* as they can become (Robinson and Clifford 1980). When leadership is shared, the leader's performance depends on group performance. If the leader assumes too much responsibility, he or she is perceived as autocratic and the group is likely to feel not needed and to lose interest. If the leader assumes too little responsibility, the organization may flounder because members lack a sense of direction. A positive relationship between the leader and the group coupled with the shared leadership function is empowering (Arnot, Cary, and Houde 1985).

CONTINUITY.   Sometimes groups are so caught up in the present that they forget to link the past with the future. A community development worker can provide valuable insight and technical assistance in this area. Establishing simple, systematic documentation is an important but often neglected aspect of building continuity. Providing each board member with a three-ring notebook that contains essential information such as current bylaws; names, addresses, and phone numbers of members; lists of committees; the budget; agendas; and minutes of meetings contributes to a group's effectiveness, provides an incentive for keeping documents current, and ensures that necessary records are available to pass on to successors. A system of mentoring, which may involve having a cochair who succeeds the chair, is another way of ensuring continuity.

Providing a means for leaders to continue to serve the group after their official term has ended is also useful in ensuring continuity as is illustrated by the following example:

> Amelia chaired the community council for many years before stepping down. Throughout her term she had kept excellent records which she shared with her successor. She offered to help in any way that she could in order to make the new leader's transition smooth and pleasant and to ensure the organization's continuity. As a result, the new chair viewed Amelia as an elder statesperson who did not interfere or try to exert control, but who was there to call upon when needed.

INCLUSIVENESS.   A great deal has been written and said about community power structures. The popularly held notion seems to be that the most significant power or influence within a community is vested in a small monolithic group of movers and shakers. Leadership surveys often ask people to identify the most influential people in the community. When the question is asked in that way, most of the people identified as leaders in this country are white males. This traditional approach to identifying the participants in the community power structure often overlooks the active and effective leadership provided by women and other groups such as ethnic and religious minorities, older people, young people, and low-income individuals (Bokemeier and Tait 1980; Cook, Howell, and Weir 1985; Perry 1980). For example, a study of the community of Zenda indicated that for the most part, community analysts have defined and analyzed communities with a focus on men. Although women are active and influential in community life, they tend to be backstage and rarely receive rewards commensurate with their contributions (Stoneall 1983).

The implications for community development practice are clear: (1) the concept of community power structures needs to be reexamined with an eye to inclusiveness; (2) leadership surveys should be refocused so that instead of asking, "Who are the most influential leaders?" the question might be, "To whom would you go if you had a particular concern or wanted to initiate action to get something done?" and (3) additional research on the role of women and others who are traditionally excluded from community decision making is long overdue.

Fund-raising.   Fund-raising offers a wealth of opportunities for practicing good community development principles and techniques (see Table 7.4). All fund-raising efforts require planning, conceptualizing programs, writing and speaking, active listening, visioning, delegating tasks, doing research, negotiating, creativity, and assertiveness.

DEVELOPING THE CASE FOR SUPPORT.   When asking others for money to support a program, cause, or organization, the person or group asking must, above all, have commitment. That is, the fund-seeker must be convinced of the need for the project and the merit of the proposal to address that need; any other motivation merely results in chasing money. The problem or need must be focused on the user, that is, on the constituency who will benefit. In addition, those seeking funds must supply the potential donor with enough data to enable him or her to make an informed decision. Further, a budget must be prepared which includes an explanation of all sources of funds, not just the amount being requested.

What does a potential donor need to know about the agency or organization seeking funds? That is, what are the components of the case for support? Any proposal for funding should address the following issues (see also Table 7.4): (1) Who is asking for support? What are the applicant's goals? What evidence is offered relative to credibility and capability? (2) What is the problem or need that is being addressed? (3) What are the objectives? That is, what is to be done to address the problem or meet the need? How much is to be done? Within what period of time? With what impact? (4) How will the objectives be achieved? (5) How much money is needed? (6) How will the project be funded in the future? (7) How will the project or program for which funds are sought be evaluated? (Kiritz 1980).

Table 7.4. *Advantages and Disadvantages of Types of Fund-raising*

				Source of Funds			
	Annual Fund Drive	Foundations	Corporations	Service Clubs	Special Events	Churches	Other
Advantages	Stable and predictable	Eliminates uncertainty; precise amount of grant is known	Builds a base of local support; gives visibility to organization	Local support; may develop into stable source of funding	Involves a lot of people; gives visibility to organization	Local support; may develop into stable source of funding	Direct mail provides broad base of support
Disadvantages	A lot of work— takes time and energy from other activities	Funds are for only one year; requires time and expense to prepare applications	Requires a lot of research	Requires constant nurturing	Requires a lot of work; may not result in much profit	Requires constant nurturing	Takes several years to generate a profit

FINDING THE FUNDING SOURCE. A first rule for those seeking funds is, "Know thy donor." In other words, know the donor's priorities, interests, patterns of giving, range of giving, and any other information that will be helpful in matching the need of the applicant with the agenda of the donor.

The Catalog of Federal Domestic Assistance is the most comprehensive listing of federal grants and is available in most public libraries and in many government offices. A first-time user should study the introductory pages to become familiar with the contents and learn how to use the catalog before plunging into specific kinds of programs. It should also be kept in mind that not all federal grants programs are listed in this catalog. As is true with all grants-seeking efforts, it is important to try to establish a personal contact with a potential funding source before submitting an application. Often a staff person in a federal regional office can assist an applicant with questions of eligibility, requests for proposals (RFP) that may be forthcoming, and funding programs that may not be listed in this catalog.

In cooperation with The Foundation Center (888 Seventh Avenue, New York 10106 [212-975-1120]), at least one library in every state houses a collection of references on foundations. The librarian in charge of the collection can offer valuable assistance on how to use it. This collection is helpful in locating appropriate potential donors.

Among other sources of funds are corporations, businesses, service clubs, the United Way, churches, and individuals. Successful fund-raising involves research directed toward matching a need with donors' interests. Asking for funds for a worthy cause is not begging or selling; it is exchanging something of value for something of value. That is, the applicant has a valuable service or project to offer and the donor wants to use money to improve the world in some way. Thus, applicant and donor become partners.

PRESENTING THE CASE. If the case for support is written, one or more competent persons should be asked to proofread it. In addition, it should be subjected to the "grandmother test" – someone who loves the author enough to be very frank in criticizing the content should read it (Kiritz 1980).

If the case is to be presented orally to several potential donors (i.e., businesses, individuals), the group seeking funds should be involved in developing a list of prospects. Solicitors should be assigned on a peer-to-peer basis. It is useful for solicitors, especially those with limited experience, to role-play asking for the gift. This can be valuable practice and can be fun as well.

HAVING FUN. Fund-raising should be fun. A neighborhood association, for example, decided to plan a special event to raise funds. The members began by brainstorming the type of event they wanted to hold. Suggestions included a barbeque, bake sale, car wash, block party, dance, carnival, and talent show. When a carnival was decided on, a story-board was helpful in listing all the tasks and activities involved. Individuals wrote tasks in very brief form on three-by-five-inch cards and read them aloud while handing them to the facilitator who posted them before the group. Some ideas included games, parking, ticket sales, child care, animals, balloons, a permit to block the street, booths, dance music, cleanup, food, prizes, and publicity. After the tasks had been identified, the cards were grouped into functional categories (e.g., publicity, equipment, entertainment), and group members volunteered to serve on committees related to the functions. A great deal of enthusiasm and goodwill was generated in the process and the group was off to a good start.

PACKAGING. One of the areas in which the community development professional can offer particularly useful technical assistance is packaging. There are at least two elements in packaging: to help a group determine possible sources of funds and to decide the most appropriate sources. A third element in packaging is negotiating with potential funding sources. For example, some local foundations will participate or contribute the amount requested only if other local foundations agree to participate. Sometimes a donor issues a challenge grant. In all of these instances the worker might negotiate with the donor and the group in finding and pulling together a funding package that is acceptable to all.

Here are some definite dos and don'ts for an effective fund-raiser: (1) Write proposals that are readable, understandable, specific, straightforward, and free of jargon. (2) Avoid circuitous reasoning (e.g., "the problem in this state is that planning commissioners have no training; the need in this state is to train planning commissioners"). (3) Do not use unjustified assumptions (e.g., "everyone knows what the problem is"). (4) Be positive in your presentation and manner without being a Pollyanna; don't plead poverty, don't use sermonettes or guilt, or don't preach doomsday. (5) Know yourself well enough so that if there is something wrong, you will know what to do about it or at least how to approach it. (6) Tell the prospective donor who you are, what you want to do, how you are going to do it, what it will cost, what is wanted from him or her. (7) Document the "need" thoroughly. (8) Obtain endorsements of applicant's credibility. (9) Think objectives through methodically and state them clearly in detail. (10) Make sure that the budget accurately reflects what is needed. (11) Make an evaluation plan and describe it in the proposal. Remember—the greater the detail, the more prepared you are to "hit the ground running" when your proposal is funded.

Developing a funding proposal provides an individual, organization, or agency with a wonderful opportunity for planning, for envisioning a program, and for carrying it through from beginning to end. It also affords a means for people to work together in preparing a case for and in soliciting support. And finally, it enables those who are alert to problems and unmet needs to form partnerships with those who have resources that they want to use wisely in solving problems and meeting needs.

Summary.   The principles for community development practice are (1) professionals plan *with* people, not *for* them, (2) community developers are concerned with empowering people and building community capacity consistent with democratic traditions, (3) people should be asked about their needs and helped to speak on behalf of themselves, (4) a group must be committed to its cause before asking for external support, and (5) shared leadership results in effective organization. In summary, the purpose of community development is to help people help themselves.

References

American Institute of Certified Planners (AICP). 1986. *AICP Code of Ethics and Professional Conduct.* Washington, D.C.: American Institute of Certified Planners.

Arnot, M., L. J. Cary, and M. J. Houde. 1985. *The Volunteer Organization Handbook.* Blacksburg, Va.: Center for Volunteer Development.

Berger, P. L., and J. Neuhaus. 1977. *To Empower People.* Washington, D.C.: American Enterprise Institute for Public Policy Research.

Bokemeier, J. L., and J. L. Tait. 1980. Women as power actors: A comparative study of rural communities. *Rural Sociology* 45(2):238–55.

Boyatzis, R. E. n.d. *Leadership: The Effective Use of Power.* Cambridge: Harvard University, Department of Social Relations.

Boyte, H. C. 1984. *Community Is Possible.* New York: Harper and Row.

Butler, L. M., and R. E. Howell. 1980. *Coping with Growth.* Corvallis: Oregon State University, Western Rural Development Center.

Collins, A. H., and D. L. Pancoast. 1976. *Natural Helping Networks.* Washington, D.C.: National Association of Social Workers.

Cook, A. K., R. E. Howell, and I. L. Weir. 1985. Rural leadership programs and changing participation of men and women in public affairs. *Journal of the Community Development Society* 16(1):41–56.

Friedmann, J. 1973. In *Retracking America: A Theory of Transactive Planning.* New York: Doubleday and Company.

Gardner, J. W. 1986a. *The Heart of the Matter.* Washington, D.C.: Leadership Studies Program, Independent Sector.

_____.1986b. *The Nature of Leadership.* Washington, D.C.: Leadership Studies Program, Independent Sector.

_____.1986c. *The Tasks of Leadership.* Washington, D.C.: Leadership Studies Program, Independent Sector.

Kiritz, N. J. 1980. Program planning and proposal writing. Los Angeles: The Grantmanship Center.

Koneya, M. 1978. Citizen participation is not community development. *Journal of the Community Development Society* 9(2):23–29.

McKnight, J. L. 1985. Regenerating Community. In *From Consumer to Citizen.* Toronto: Canadian Mental Health Association.

Perry, H. L. 1980. The socioeconomic impact of black political empowerment in a rural southern locality. *Rural Sociology* 45(2):207–22.

Robinson, J. W., Jr., and R. A. Clifford. 1980. Leadership roles in community groups. North–Central Regional Extension Publication No. 36–3. Urbana: University of Illinois, Cooperative Extension Service.

The St. Anthony Park Block Nurse Program. n.d. Working paper. St. Paul, Minn.

So, F. 1984. Strategic planning: Reinventing the wheel? *Planning* 50(2):16–21.

Stoneall, L. 1983. Bringing women into community studies: A rural midwestern case study. *Journal of the Community Development Society* 14(1):17–29.

8

Teaching
Community Development

LEE J. CARY

T HE potential community development practitioner engages in a community development education program to prepare for the professional practice of working with community groups. The dilemma the practitioner faces is simple: real community development has yet to evolve into a freestanding profession with an operational theory of its own. The potential practitioner and the community development educator cannot wait for the theory to evolve. (See Chapter 14.) Therefore, the teaching of community development must move ahead based on the most relevant social science knowledge, the best of current practice experience, and an understanding of major societal changes underway in the world. The interaction of student and educator and the joint venture on which they are embarked may themselves be the most effective process for the growth and refinement of an operational theory for community development.

Four major concepts are central to understanding community development. *Human groupings,* from families and neighborhood clusters to national and international organizations, and how individuals relate to and work with such groupings is a central interest of community development practice. Why do people join groups? How long and under what conditions do they remain active? How essential is interdependency to the vitality and accomplishments of a group? Understanding human groupings and being able to work effectively with people in group situations is at the very core of community development practice and a major theme in community development education.

An understanding of and the ability to focus on *communication, power,* and *leadership* in group situations is a second important concept. The necessity of communicating both within groups and among groups, as well as the ability to understand the proper uses of power, draws heavily on social science theory, as discussed by Blakely in Chapter 14. Leadership is an essential ingredient in a group's formation, in developing the individuals who make up the group, and in strengthening the group itself.

A third major concept deals with *social change.* Of all the changes going on in the world at any given moment, which ones can be effectively sped up or slowed down by conscious, effective group effort? More difficult to determine, in which of these social changes do we want to intervene? What are our values? Our knowledge of social change is limited, and yet community development practice aims to help bring about or reduce the effects of social change.

Finally, trying to understand and deal with *human relations* is central to any field of professional practice. How people behave and why is so important yet so broad a subject of inquiry that community development practitioners find it necessary to deal constantly in human relations although they have only a limited understanding of what is taking place and of the consequences of intervention. Now let us look at each of the four major concepts in detail.

Major Concepts.   *Human groupings* is an umbrella term
that covers a number of other concepts important to teaching community development. There are two major classifications: primary groups, which are intimate face-to-face associations, and secondary groups, which are larger and composed of more formal clusters of people. Community development takes place in both types of groups, but the positions and roles of individuals and the relationships between individuals in primary and secondary groups are quite different. Important too are the intensity, duration, and frequency of interaction in human groups as well as the relationships among various groups.

Interaction between groups may follow several patterns including cooperation, competition, and conflict. Warren (1978) has referred to these as situations of issue consensus, issue difference, and issue dissensus, calling for, respectively, a collaborative, a campaign, and a contest strategy. Interaction between groups also has an impact on interaction within a group. Over time, repeated contact between groups can lead to adjustments, accommodations, and even assimilation of the groups into one.

The concept of human groups raises questions concerning what brings individuals into groups and what holds groups together. A comprehensive response to these two inquiries is beyond the limits of this discussion, but several important factors can be cited. Geography is a factor to the extent that physical proximity increases the opportunities for interaction, while distance decreases such possibilities, although new telecommunication mediums overcome some of these problems. Sutton (1970) maintains that the important point is not what is "local to" but what is "collective for" a particular population, placing the emphasis more on common needs and interests than on common terrain. Other factors bringing individuals together and holding them together are identification with the group purpose or goal and, after joining, the experience and satisfaction found in working together. Finally, boundary maintenance is important in keeping a group together. Through a variety of techniques, including celebrations and the use of symbols, the unity of the group is maintained; because of these efforts to achieve boundary maintenance, individuals are less apt to leave to join other groups.

The second broad concept—*communication, power,* and *leadership*—focuses on a system of social relationships and the instruments that help to coordinate and harmonize these relationships. These three concepts are closely related and are difficult to consider alone. However, for our purposes we will consider each separately. Communication is essential to any group activity and basic to any human interaction. The structure of communication is a central concern as is an understanding of the potential blocks to effective communication. One of the most common blocks is misunderstanding because of differing definitions and lack of precision in the use of language. Feedback, communication as a two-way process, can help to reduce the danger of misunderstanding. Power, the ability to exercise control, is an important instrument of coordination. The larger the group, the more essential is the coordinating function and the more complex the power relationships. Power is frequently granted or allocated by a group to those who can help to fulfill the group's needs and expectations. Individuals accorded sufficient power and prestige are identified as leaders and may be called on to perform a variety of leadership roles. As the roles become established, they may rotate among members of a group as the members assume specific roles. Leadership training helps individuals learn how to perform roles essential to a group's task accomplishment and maintenance.

The third concept is *social change,* which is a very complex and continuous process occurring everywhere and constantly altering social relationships. One part of social change is concerned with changes that are planned, and some portion of these planned changes are carried out through a process identified as community development. In teaching community development, it is important to identify the major practice variables that apply specifically to this process and to determine how they differ from those associated with other processes of planned change. The concept of social change poses a number of difficult questions. What constitutes progress or desirable change? Who decides what planned changes to undertake and how they should be carried out? Change carried out through an open and democratic process involves certain value assumptions about the way in which change is brought about. Most basic is the orientation that people should participate fully in the decisions that affect their lives, and all those who are affected should have open access to the process. Whether we have yet developed adequate mechanisms for putting this principle into practice is open to question.

The fourth concept is *human relations.* The theory and practice of human relations is primarily concerned with the most effective ways of helping people organize to accomplish specific objectives. The behavior and attitudes of individuals change, in part because of changes in the relationships among individuals. Cooperation develops from joint activity and from an individual's attitudes toward others in an organization and toward the organization itself. The individual's behavior is conditioned by the social systems within which the individual functions. Each social system and each organization is made up of two interrelated systems, one formal and the other informal. The formal system focuses on the rational relationships among the parts and appears on the organization's chart. The informal system results from informal ties within the organization and is created by members. In understanding and working with these relationships within an organizational structure, it is important to recognize the vital role played by effective two-way communication. Involvement, common experiences, and shared symbols that signify belonging are equally important in developing an individual's positive feelings and cooperative attitudes in an organization.

While these four concepts are quite broad and their presentation here is somewhat simplistic and generalized, understanding them is basic to an understanding of how individuals in groups carry out a community development process in the context of their immediate community and the larger society. A task force of the National Association of State Universities and Land-Grant Colleges published a report in 1975 that listed over thirty concepts considered central to community development (ECOP 1975). What we have presented here embraces a number of the more basic concepts in the task force report and focuses attention on the importance of social science theory as a basis for community development teaching and practice.

Values and Ethics.

The place of values and ethics in professional education and practice is an umbrella issue that supercedes these four concepts. We attempt to be explicit about the concepts and skills needed to become a competent community development professional. However, we are much less explicit about values, about a code of ethics which communicates these values and governs conduct, and about how we go about helping beginning professional practitioners to internalize these values.

What distinguishes community developers from other professional practitioners is based as much on how we go about our work as it is on what we do. It is a collective ideology that sets community developers apart as a profession, distinct from all others. It is most important that more attention be given to a code of professional ethics and principles of good practice. These need to be clearly articulated and widely accepted principles by which individual performance can be judged.

In teaching community development we teach values. We talk about community groups making their own decisions, which is a value. We talk about open democratic participation in the community development process, which is another value. The question is not whether we transmit values or not. The question is, What values do we transmit, and how do we transmit them? The answer, at present, is not at all clear. We do not have an agreed-upon code of ethics, although we do have a code of good practice (see Chapter 6). Until some agreement is reached on these values, a discussion of how to transmit them is premature.

What should these values be? What should a code of ethics contain? Frank Fear, a former chairperson of the Community Development Society's Professional Improvement Committee, has given considerable time and thought to these questions. In an issue of the Society's *Vanguard,* Fear (1984) proposed a code of ethics and also suggested a procedure for reviewing the proposed code. Background information on what ethics are and why professions have codes of ethics was included.

Using information gathered from a literature review and a random sample survey of Community Development Society members, the Professional Improvement Committee identified five phases of the community development process that are anchored in good practice principles. These phases are (1) establishing the relationship, (2) diagnosing the problem, (3) selecting the appropriate solution, (4) implementing the solution, and (5) terminating the relationship (Fear 1984). The fact that a code of ethics for community developers is not yet a reality in no way minimizes the essentiality of such a code to the profession.

Although there is neither an established code of ethics nor agreed-upon minimum standards for professional education in community development, many programs seem to share a common philosophy, a number of similar courses, and similar degree requirements. Also, most who teach in these programs share a concern for maintaining a relationship and balance between theory and practice and between teaching in the classroom and teaching in the community. The primary objective is to prepare students for beginning professional practice in community development. The success of these teaching efforts can be measured, in part, by the ability of graduates of these programs to perform effectively in community settings as community development professional practitioners.

Toward an Operational Theory. Teaching
community development must be based, in part, on the most relevant social science theory and research. The challenge, however, is not only to grasp the vast range of social science knowledge that has some contribution to make to community development, but to make use of that knowledge in the day-to-day practice of the community developer.

An ideal operational theory for community development would bring together social science theory and knowledge, as well as the best of current practice experience. An example of one effort that focuses on a specific aspect of community development process is Linneman's (1983) attempt to document the disengagement strategies of community development practitioners based on relevant social science knowledge and current practice. Two major areas of her inquiry deal with when to disengage and how to disengage. From the information provided by respondents, Linneman developed a list of twelve observable indicators used in determining readiness of a group to disengage. Listed in order of decreasing frequency, they are as follows: increasing group confidence, decreasing need for practitioner input, increasing group skills in linkage or information gathering, increasing degree of idea generation within the group, emerging effective group leadership, maturing group process, increasing accuracy in role perceptions, increasingly assuming the community development role, increasing perception of internal resources, increasing degree of goal attainment, broadening of group perspectives, and increasing proportion of group requests being of a technical nature.

Linneman also identifies ten strategies for achieving disengagement and notes that some are appropriate in many situations while others have limited application. Among these strategies are *intentional absence,* to encourage group members to assume greater responsibility; *referral* to other resource persons or invitation to meetings as such resources are appropriate; and *cutoff date,* a strategy in which the practitioner agrees to work with a group for a specified length of time or until a particular objective is reached.

While new practitioners should find this information helpful, Linneman recognizes that these indicators and strategies do not represent an exhaustive list or the only list. And even if this list is complete, it leaves a number of issues undecided. Where a group is with respect to any of the indicators is a matter of judgment, and when and how specific strategies are used will need to be based on considerable experience. Linneman's work moves us a step closer to developing a small part of an operational theory, but it also clearly points out how much more work needs to be done.

A recent effort to present a conceptual model addressing both task and process goals is the work of Daley and Kettner, which also stresses the importance of operational models. These authors propose that "community development can fulfill its commitment to process and capacity building while achieving specific social and economic development objectives (including working for social justice) if operational models are developed that address both task and process goals" (Daley and Kettner 1986, p. 55). Their "episode of purposive change" recognizes that common elements of change efforts at both the organizational and community levels can contribute to balanced practice results.

The episode of purposive change has five phases and is described by Daley and Kettner as a planned intervention model which helps to direct the professional practitioner. The phases are (1) assessing antecedent conditions, (2) preparing for change, (3) planning change,

(4) implementing change, and (5) assessing change residue and its implications. What is a particularly helpful addition to a growing operational theory of community development is that this model identifies task and process goals as well as task and process considerations for each of the five phases.

Community development, as a field of professional practice, must draw on experience to enrich the social science knowledge presently available and to suggest ways this knowledge can be used in practice, in working with people. Physicians, dentists, attorneys, and other professionals prepare themselves for practice through attending formal courses but also through hands-on experience. Teaching community development calls for this same mix of formal instruction and learning through doing.

The potential community development practitioner may have a wealth of social science knowledge, but what to do and say (or not do and say) at a particular point in a community meeting rests heavily on that person's interpersonal skills and abilities and on whatever he or she has gained from past experiences. Teaching community development calls for a very high quality of field instruction and supervision. While all the burden should not be placed on the student, much of the synthesis of theory and practice occurs within the student in the field experience or internship, or in the first professional practice position.

Societal Changes
and Development.
There are major societal changes underway in the world that impact directly on community development. The changing world economy is, perhaps, the most important of these. Two changes to be considered here, however, are particularly relevant for community development education. The first is the changing perception that individuals have of themselves and their roles in society. These individual changes include the individual's growing sense of empowerment, increasing potential for self-actualization, and greater opportunities for meaningful involvement.

The second is the changing power and status of small informal local groups in terms of their ability to develop effective local controls, create group solidarity, and demonstrate that most social change is initiated and carried out by relatively small groups and not by individuals, organizations, or institutions. Ravitz points out that community development may be the instrument through which people at the local community level create the means to invigorate our society. "Given the crisis of our economy, our politics, our social relations, and given too the confused condition of our guiding values, it may be that community development which is the democratic process at the level of our domestic lives has its best opportunity to be applied" (Ravitz 1982, p. 10).

The possible gains for both individuals and the community groups they are a part of make community development potentially a very strong strategy for change. Much of what is going on in the world today can be viewed as the enhancement and empowerment of people, both individually and collectively. How community development reacts to these two major social changes will profoundly affect the future of community development. Will community development be seen as a way for local people to get together to carry out modest community improvements, or will it be seen as a process for societal change throughout the world based on changes in individuals and their groups?

Khinduka (1969) identifies community development as a slow, incremental process to help bring about adaptations in the social system. He sees it as a rather "soft" strategy for social change because of what he identifies as inadequacies built into the basic ideology of community development. These inadequacies emphasize—perhaps overemphasize—citizen involvement, consensus, localism, and gradualism. These make community development a useful but limited approach to adjustments and improvements at the local level. Warren (1978) also questions some of the assumptions on which community development practice is based. He notes that there is a decline in the notion of the single public interest as well as a decline of trust in collaborative strategies. He recognizes the usefulness of collaborative strategies in consensus situations but points out that in many community situations there is not a single public interest or community good shared by all. Various groups frequently have different legitimate interests and concerns.

If community development teaching emphasizes the more traditional approach as outlined by Khinduka and Warren, then beginning professional practitioners will be able to work effectively in small communities and homogeneous neighborhoods where a common interest can be identified, consensus can be achieved, and participation can be inclusive. The limits placed on such practice have to do with size and issues. Only a relatively small number of people can be involved directly in the process and only issues on which there is little or no controversy can be addressed.

If, however, community development teaching emphasizes a review and, where appropriate, a revision of the earlier "principles" of practice, and if other approaches to helping people organize are recognized and studied, then the beginning professional practitioner will be challenged to work in different ways with any number of different community groups. The limits placed on such practice will be the newness of this approach and, therefore, the lack of adequate back-up support from those currently engaged in the teaching and practice of community development. At this point no decision has been made about what change in direction, if any, should be taken for the teaching of community development. When this decision is made, the teaching of community development will be the key to bringing about a new vitality and purpose to community development or to helping it continue in a more traditional way.

Components in Community Development Curricula.

In 1974 Naylor (n.d.) attempted to identify the major components in community development curricula. The six most frequently found were (1) introductions to the field, (2) theoretical perspectives, including social science theory as it applies to the change process, (3) community development process and program development, (4) group dynamics and group processes; (5) research and analysis of data, and (6) field experience or internship.

Introductory courses attempt to provide a general understanding of community development through a study of its historical and philosophical perspectives. Concepts, values, and principles are examined as an introduction to theory and practice. Courses on the theoretical perspectives focus on efforts to influence human, social, economic, and political development. Major interpretations of change, as found in the various disciplines, are reviewed to create a conceptual understanding of the mechanics of planned change at the community level. Courses in process and program development are offered to engage the student in a study of how to apply community development theory in specific situations through the establishment and operation of the process in programs and projects. Courses in group dynamics and group processes combine theory and laboratory experience with an emphasis on understanding interpersonal competence and small group behavior, working in small group situations, and using group techniques. Research and the analysis of data provide an introduction to social science research methods and techniques, including the basic tools and procedures for conducting research relevant to community development situations. It is believed that these courses also help to meet the needs of students planning individual research projects. Finally, field training or internship provides practice in a professional setting where the student can test and develop skills under a qualified field instructor. Together these courses help to prepare the student for professional practice by combining theory and practice and by contributing to the student's knowledge, skills, and experience in community development.

A 1976 survey report of community development education programs included data about courses and related activities for the twenty-two programs offering advanced degrees with an emphasis in community development (Cary 1976*a*, 1976*b*). Although respondents were not specifically asked about the six categories established by Naylor (n.d.), they did furnish information on course offerings that tended to lend support to the six components identified earlier. All but one of the twenty-two programs offered and frequently required community development core courses, usually covering such topics as introduction to the field, theory and practice, and program development. Sixteen required field experience or internships, and fifteen required research and/or a research project. Respondents for nearly two-thirds of these programs (fourteen of twenty-two) indicated that their programs also allowed for electives or optional courses. Course information was not provided on one of Naylor's six categories, group dynamics and group processes, even though this information was considered important and was provided through various course offerings and workshops.

Another item in this survey dealt with program emphasis. Respondents were asked to identify whether a development, planning, or action emphasis most nearly described the community development approach of their staff. To aid respondents, definitions for these three approaches were offered in the questionnaire. The definitions were similar to those used by Rothman (1970) in his conceptualization of three practice models of community organization. Respondents for eight of the twenty-two programs indicated a development emphasis, while three indicated a planning emphasis. Four other respondents felt they emphasized all three approaches, two emphasized development and planning, one indicated a development and action emphasis, and four gave no indication of program emphasis.

A study of master's degree programs in community development in the United States and Canada was completed by the writer with the aid of two graduate assistants (Cary, Azer, and Turley 1977). At the time of the study, five universities in the United States and one in Canada awarded master's degrees in community development: University of Missouri–Columbia, Southern Illinois University–Carbondale, University of Louisville, University of Maine–Orono, University of California–Davis, and University of Alberta. Again, using the Naylor framework, all six institutions include courses in process and program development and research and analysis of data. Five of the six have a field experience or internship requirement and offer course work in the theoretical perspectives of community development. Three of the six have introductory courses in community development and courses in group dynamics and group processes.

The *Directory: Community Development Education and Training Programs,* prepared by Robertson (1987), lists thirty-nine institutions of higher education that offer a total of fifty-two programs. Some of these programs lead to degrees in community development while others lead to degrees in related fields with an emphasis in community development. Robertson identifies seven programs in the United States that offer master's degrees in community development. In addition to the five listed in the 1977 study (Cary, Azer, and Turley), the directory includes Georgia State University and New Hampshire College. The master's program at the University of Alberta, included in the earlier report, has been discontinued. Robertson also provides information on seventeen institutions of higher education in the United States and one in Canada that offer advanced degrees with an emphasis in community development.

Of the seven institutions in the United States that offer master's degrees in community development, certain program similarities can be identified. First, all of the programs have faculties who have varied backgrounds and represent a range of disciplines including, but not limited to, community development, anthropology, sociology, rural sociology, psychology, economics, geography, social work, and adult education. This is similar to the composition of the faculties reported in 1977. Second, there is movement toward specialization which was much less developed by these programs ten years earlier. In addition to core (required) courses in community development, areas of specialization are offered and encouraged by at least five of these seven programs. Of the twelve different specializations offered, the one mentioned most frequently is planning. Four other specializations are mentioned three times each: economic development, urban affairs, rural development, and administration. Also mentioned are social development, program development and evaluation, community organization, education, research, youth work, aging, and international development.

The areas of specialization raise a number of questions that not only should be asked here but also need to be addressed by community development educators. Are these specializations simply responses to the job market, or are they seen as basic components of a community development curriculum? If they are perceived as basic to the community development curriculum, does this indicate that community development process is too basic or too general to equip the practitioner for professional practice? Is the objective to prepare the community development practitioner to use the community development process in his or her specialization, which would make community development a method as defined by Sanders (1966), or to use the specialization to augment the process?

There is some evidence to support the concern among many community developers that more and more professional practitioners, representing a wide range of disciplines, are "discovering" community development as a way or a method to carry out their work in the community. Although community development educators may be pleased that they have been "discovered," the down side is that community development increasingly is becoming a way to carry out a program or to accomplish an objective that has not involved, in any meaningful way, those who will be impacted by the program that emerges or by the objective that is achieved. This issue needs the careful attention of community development educators and practitioners.

References

Cary, L. J. 1976*a*. Community development education: An overview of programs throughout the world. *Journal of the Community Development Society* 7(2):115–21.

———., ed. 1976*b*. *Directory: Community Development Education and Training Programs throughout the World.* Columbia, Mo.: Community Development Society.

Cary, L. J., S. Azer, and R. Turley. 1977. Master's degree programs in community development in the United States and Canada: A status report. Columbia: University of Missouri, Department of Community Development. Mimeo.

Daley, J. M., and P. M. Kettner, 1986. The episode of purposive change. *Journal of the Community Development Society* 17(2):54–72. Extension Committee on Organization and Policy. 1975. *Community Development: Concepts, Curriculum, Training Needs.* Task Force Report. Columbia: University of Missouri, USDA, Cooperative Extension Service.

Fear, F. A. 1984. A Code of Ethics for Community Development. *Vanguard* 53(Spring):1, 6–7.

Khinduka, S. K. 1969. Community development: Potentials and limitations. In *Social Work Practice,* E. Berlatsky, ed., pp. 15–28. New York: Columbia University Press.

Linneman, J. A. 1983. Disengagement strategies of community development practitioners. *Journal of the Community Development Society* 14(1):63–72.

Naylor, H. L. n.d. Working paper on core curricula in community development. Columbia: University of Missouri, Department of Community Development. Mimeo.

Ravitz, M. 1982. Community development: Challenge of the eighties. *Journal of the Community Development Society* 13(10):1–10.

Robertson, W. E. 1987. *Directory: Community Development Education and Training Programs.* Columbia, Mo.: Community Development Society.

Rothman, J. 1970. Three models of community organization practice. In *Strategies of Community Organization: A Book of Readings,* F. M. Cox, J. L. Erlick, J. Rothman, J. E. Tropman, eds., pp. 20–36. Itasca, Ill.: Peacock.

Sanders, I. T. 1966. *The Community: Introduction to a Social System,* 2d ed. New York: Ronald Press.

Sutton, W. A., Jr. 1970. The sociological implications of the community development process. In *Community Development as a Process,* L. J. Cary, ed., pp. 57–83. Columbia: University of Missouri Press.

Warren, R. L. 1978. *The Community in America,* 3d ed., Chapter 12. Chicago: Rand McNally.

9

Community Economic Development

RON SHAFFER
GENE F. SUMMERS

THERE is a basic tension in the field of community development between those whose primary goal is development *of* the community and those who seek primarily to achieve development *in* the community. Adherants of the development-*of*-the-community perspective view community as a quality of the relationships among residents of a locality which serves as a causal factor in determining the residents' well-being. Thus, the creation and maintenance of activities, organizations, and institutions that strengthen interactional ties among residents are deemed essential. Community development, therefore, requires attention to these cohesive and integrative structures (Kaufman 1959; Wilkinson 1972, 1979, 1985, 1986; Reitzes and Reitzes 1980, 1987).

By contrast, development-*in*-the-community proponents see the community as a locality in which social, political, and economic activities occur regularly and through various organizational forms. Community is essentially a territorial setting for social processes which may enhance the lives of people who reside there and may improve the locality's standing relative to that of other localities. Community development is therefore an effort to improve one or more of the processes in the locality as a means to achieve a goal (or goals) of residents. However, it is altogether possible that achieving development in the community may produce development *of* the community.

Community economic development is a clear example of the development-*in*-the-community orientation. The goal is to create appropriate jobs and raise the real incomes of residents. The locality is treated very much as if it were a business firm. Consequently, attention is given to the efficient use and maintenance of productive resources as well as to adaptability to changes in the external environment – the markets and the supply of materials needed for production (Isard 1956, 1975; Thompson 1965; Pulver 1979; Harmston 1983; Shaffer 1988; Summers et al. 1988).

Community Economic Vitality.   In the discussion that follows, we are assuming the existence of a market economy. While we are accustomed to thinking about private sector firms operating in a market characterized by competition, we are frequently oblivious to the fact that communities also compete. And it is the local state which represents the community interest in such competition.[1] There are conflicting interest groups in every community based on class, ethnic, race, age, religion, education, occupation, or other social categories. Superimposed on them is the local state whose authority and power coincide with the territorial perimeter of the local system and whose primary instrument is the apparatus of local government. The future well-being of the community depends primarily on actions of the local state, although not exclusively so. At times local state policies and actions may coincide with those of other corporate interest groups, but that occurrence is coincidental because the ultimate interest of the local state must be the continued existence of the social system which occupies its territory. The competition with other local states contains at least three significant dimensions of comparison: economic, social, and political. While they are not empirically independent, they are analytically separable; our discussion dwells on the economic competition among communities which is made dynamic largely by actors representing the local state. Firms compete in the private economy, and their managers only incidentally consider the interests of the community and the competition among local states. In particular, the private sector is only marginally interested in the territorial or spatial dimensions of the competition. The distinction between these arenas of competition is crucial because it allows one to recognize the basis for the sometimes alarming lack of common interests between local officials and local business owners and managers.

The latent policy goal for a community's economic development is the desire to remain vital through time as change occurs. Vitality is the ability to survive, to persist in generating desired outcomes. It is a very broad normative and functional concept. One can only know what factors influence survival, system reproduction, and continued creation of desired products of systems by observing successes and failures from which inferences may be made.

In addition to the subjective and *ex ante* nature of vitality, there also is a competitive aspect to it which is observable only through comparison. Usually, perhaps always, there is a competition among systems—whether they are individuals, groups, communities, or other social formations—to at least maintain, if not improve, their relative standing. Thus, one must not be lured into false inferences by rising indicators of output. Other units in the competition may be climbing even more rapidly. Consequently, a system that is doing a better job of producing its outputs today than it did yesterday may nevertheless have lost its ability to survive.

Community economic vitality is the capacity of a local social system to continue generating income and employment in order to maintain, if not improve, its relative economic position. Past observations of growing, stable, and declining communities lead one to conclude that the institutional apparatus is critical. Vital communities possess social constructions, with underlying assumptions, which encourage and permit the orderly and efficient use of economic resources, ensure their maintenance, and allow adaptation to changes in the environment.

It is our contention that community economic vitality is a long-run concept that requires more than just the efficient use of resources in the short run to generate profits, jobs, and income for current community residents. Any discussion of vitality must recognize the longer-run concepts of community maintenance through time and the adapatability of the community to changing conditions both within and outside itself. A theme that also must be part of the concept is that outcomes of the economic system must approach some form of equity among residents of a community, among communities, and over time. This elusive concept must be high on the list of important elements of community vitality. On the following pages we share the construct that community economic vitality requires recognition of efficient use of economic resources, maintenance of resources, and flexibility to changing conditions.

Orderly and Efficient
Use of Resources.   When the community is perceived as
an economic decision-making unit attempting to maximize profits, utility, or reward from the use of its resources, the parallelism between
theory of the firm, resource owners, and consumer behavior and that
of community economic vitality becomes apparent. A community's output (employment or income) is a function of what it can supply and
what is being demanded. What it can supply is derived from the types
of resources the community has. How many resources does it have?
How are these resources used? Demand incorporates the products that
are created and their relative values in the marketplace. How much
can be sold? What are the prices that they can be sold for? Where are
markets located? How are markets changing? Acceptable economic
actions and the manner in which economic decisions are made are
crucial elements that set the institutional framework for demand and
supply decisions. Furthermore, these actions occur among spatially
separated economic units. This section examines demand and supply
and their application to the condition of community vitality. Then the
discussion expands to institutions and community vitality.

SUPPLY AND VITALITY.   The supply aspect of vitality emphasizes the
importance of capital, labor, and other factors of production in creating
output and income (Borts and Stein 1964; Leven 1985; Richardson
1969; Thompson 1965). The supply approach suggests that growth in
the output, employment, or income for communities is precipitated by
one or more economic actions regarding resource use. A community
can increase its output by increasing its stock of capital through invest-
ing local savings or importing capital from other areas, or by shifting
capital from less to more productive uses within the community. A
community can increase output by increasing its labor force through
new entrants to the labor force, through in-migration, by hiring previously unemployed workers, or by shifting labor from less to more
productive uses. Finally, a community can adopt new technology which
permits increased output or uses unemployed resources.

     There are two basic assumptions important to the present discus-
sion. The first assumption is that labor and capital resources are mobile among places and uses. The second assumption is that technology
is distributed instantaneously over space and uniformly over time. After briefly reviewing the first assumption, the focus of this discussion

shifts to technology because of its inherent ability to be disruptive or to create new opportunities for existing resources.

Markets bring together demanders and suppliers of products and resources and permit them to negotiate a transaction agreeable to both. However, if they cannot reach an agreement, the market needs to send signals so they will change their behavior. Furthermore, that signal needs to indicate the type of change needed. Not only must the signal be sent, but the actors within the market must be able to receive and respond to that signal in an appropriate fashion. Any economic development/vitality strategy attempts to reduce either barriers to economic development or imperfections in the market (e.g., market failures).

Imperfections in the resource market hamper community economic vitality. A major source of market failure is resource immobility. Immobility of resources among uses and places can prevent the appropriate adjustment of factor and product prices.

There are two forms of resource immobility. The first is when resources fail to perceive and respond to long-run economic opportunities or signals from the community. This could be the failure of capital and labor to move into or out of a community toward higher returns. The second form of immobility is when resources are not used in the community in their most productive manner. This occurs when labor or capital in a community is used to produce something that has a lower than expected maximum–possible-use value to society.

In a dynamic setting some barriers to the efficient utilization of resources include lack of entrepreneurship; the high cost of adjustment, such as the cost of creating additional highly skilled labor or of sophisticated machinery; uncertainty about governmental fiscal policy and monetary policy or labor skills required; institutional rigidity such as tradition; a lack of decision-making capacity of both institutions and human resources; a lack of key resources or key organizations to support the development process; and a lack of integration or coordination among key parts of the economy or political systems (e.g., an adversarial relationship among the public and private sector).

The spatial diffusion of technology or innovation significantly affects differences in vitality among communities (Borts and Stein 1964; Molle 1982; Richardson 1969). Technological change does not occur at a constant pace, nor is it uniformly adopted over space. The spread of technology is largely a result of social communication and interaction. The adoption of technology is a result of learning, accepting, and making a decision. The noninstantaneous spread of technology reveals a market imperfection preventing every community equal access to the same production processes. The end result is that some communities grow more rapidly than others because they use more advanced technology.

There are a variety of forces retarding the transmission of technology over space. The first and probably the most important reason is differences in the rate at which management accepts and adopts technology. The adoption of new technology usually does not occur immediately on receipt of information about the technology. Rather the manager may require repeated messages about the technology coupled with new information about how the technology (i.e., a management strategy to reduce risk) has performed for similar firms. Second, the transmission costs of technology are not zero. There are costs involved in becoming aware of the new technology, figuring out how the new technology can be applied, disrupting production, and training workers in the use of new technology in a particular plant. Third, it takes time to incorporate new technology into the capital stock. The amount of time depends on whether the new technology requires completely new production processes or requires only minor changes. Fourth, communities have different industrial sectors present, and the rate of technological transformation among industrial sectors varies. Therefore, communities with sectors experiencing rapid technological change will themselves experience more rapid technological change. Fifth, the instantaneous transmission of technology among communities may be hampered by patent agreements and secrecy in the use of the technology and by the failure of the technology owners to offer it to all locales.

In summary, the economic vitality of a community can be linked to forces generally labeled *supply forces.* Imperfections in the market signals sent and received along with the nonuniform or noninstantaneous transmission of technology creates differences in theoretical and actual outcomes. These failures of the market cannot be ignored, but neither should their importance be inflated in a dynamic setting.

DEMAND AND VITALITY. The demand aspect of community economic vitality contends the vigor of a community depends on the development of its export industries (North 1956; Pfister 1976; Richardson 1969; Thompson 1965; Tiebout 1956*a,* 1956*b*). The critical force in the community's economic vitality is the demand external to the community, not the community's ability to supply capital, labor, or use technology. The timing and pace of the community's economic vitality is determined by the success of its export sector, the characteristics of the export sector, and the disposition of income received from export sales.

The export sector is the carrier of external economic forces into the community. The characteristics of the export sector and the disposition of its income are the internal dynamics of the community's economy that translate those external forces into community economic vitality. The impact of changes in the export sector on the rest of the community depends on the number and strength of the linkages between the export and nonexport sectors (e.g., characteristics of export sector). Furthermore, the distribution of income from the export sector and the ownership of resources used in the export sector are important elements in translating changes in the export sector into community economic vitality. For example, if the ownership of export base resources is external to the community, then changes in the export sector may have a minimal impact on the community because the income is not reinvested in the community. Likewise, the availability of skills that permits the local labor force to work in the export sector also contributes to the success of translating external demand into local economic change.

The nonexport sector is equally important to community economic vitality because it is the mechanism that converts the external economic stimuli into local economic activity. Without the nonexport sector, the local effects of the external economic stimulus will be minimal.

The volume of exports from a community can either increase or decrease over time. The increase (decrease) may occur because there has been a rightward (leftward) shift in external demand; or the good or service exported has a high (low) income elasticity; or there has been an increase (decrease) in income levels in nearby areas; or there has been an improved (reduced) comparative advantage in the community (e.g., altered costs of labor, capital, or changes in technology); or because of the factor endowment of the community (e.g., a depletion of the natural resource base or technological changes has altered input combinations in which this community previously had an advantage). If a community does not adjust to the forces that might alter its volume of exports, the community will find itself stranded outside the economic mainstream with a relatively or even absolutely worsening economic position.

In summary, the economic vitality of a community is dependent on external demand for the community's output. This is a necessary condition, but not sufficient for community economic vitality. The translation of external demand into local economic activity is crucial. This leads to a need to examine the institutional dimensions of the community.

INSTITUTIONS AND VITALITY.   Institutions are basic to any form of social interaction, although they are usually not recognized except when changes are proposed or when they are not performing satisfactorily. The interest here is much more restrictive: only those institutions facilitating or impeding community economic vitality will be examined.

Institutions are the rights and obligations or the social, political, and legal rules that govern what has to be taken into account in the use of a community's resources (production), exchange, and the distribution of rewards (Davis and North 1971). Institutions are the traditions, the customs, the attitudes, and the governmental arrangements that set the framework in which economic units (households, businesses) make consumption and production decisions. Institutions are concerned with decisions and with decision making. Two crucial decisions that vital communities make are the maintenance of economic resources and the adaption to change.

Maintenance of Economic Resources.[2]   An institutional matrix which

assures orderly and efficient use of economic resources does not, in and of itself, secure the vitality of a community. The long-run stability and growth of income and employment require a set of mechanisms to maintain the quantity and quality of local economic resources. Provision of the necessary institutional arrangements usually involves both the local private and state economies.

In the short run (ten years or so), vitality may depend largely on the existing export base and on the mechanisms in place that enable the locality to capture the money generated by it. But markets for products and services come and go. Consumer demand today is vastly different than it was fifty or one hundred years ago. Therefore, the longevity of any community ultimately depends on its ability to renew its export base; that is, the longevity depends on the community's capacity to invent, to innovate, or to acquire new exports.

Thompson (1965, p. 53) made this point forcefully when he said,

"The local social overhead – the infrastructure – that has been amassed is, more than export diversification, the source of local vitality and endurance." A rich infrastructure facilitates the adjustment to supply and demand changes by providing social and economic institutions and physical facilities needed to initiate new enterprises, to transfer capital from old to new uses, and to retain a skilled, healthy, and motivated labor force.

This view is in sharp contrast to the simple export base interpretation that leads many community leaders to "give away the store" in order to attract new export firms. Such a simple export thesis emphasizes the multiplier concept, which is in reality a cash flow model of local economies, and ignores the causal mechanisms involved in long-term development, for example, long-run use of community resources. It encourages profit taking rather than development behavior. Community economic vitality requires public and private sector support of a local network of services and facilities which ensure the continued availability of factors of production, especially land, labor, and capital.

LAND. Land is the economic resource most controlled by the community. All production occurs somewhere; it must have a spatial location. Communities also occupy space, and because of prerogatives of the modern state they have a great deal of control over their territories. Since land is an essential economic resource, the control of land gives the community – the local state – a substantial ability to direct its own economic vitality.

Land varies in its economic potential and therefore in its value. Because it does so, its potential dictates the economic vitality of the community to a large extent. Historically, great cities have emerged where land had great economic potential. Breaks in modes of transportation made land in the immediate vicinity valuable since it was needed for freight transfer activities and for housing workers and provisioning their needs. Breaks in transportation gave us harbor cities, railroad junction cities, and river cities. Today, air transportation and motorways have diminished the transportation break as the basis of land value in these cities. Where other uses have been found for the land and the value has remained high, the city economy has retained its vitality. In some instances, once thriving transportation break cities have declined and shrunk to near extinction. Communities whose birth was sired by immobile natural resources face a similar threat once the resource is depleted. But every community must take steps to ensure the continued economic value of its land.

The cases of transportation and natural resource extraction imply that changes beyond community control determine local land values. To some extent that is true, since no community is totally autonomous. But communities can exercise considerable control over future land-uses and therefore land values. The local state can determine land uses to a great extent through planning future land-use patterns; exercising the power of eminent domain; regulating the size, type, and use of construction; and establishing discretionary provision of public services. The location of roads, streets, highways, sewers, gas lines, bridges, tunnels, parks, and schools all impinge on future land uses and land values.

The public investments that shape future land uses and land values are immobile. They cannot migrate to another community as other factors of production can. Rather, they create a magnet for attracting and retaining labor and capital needed for production. Many students of community politics note that land is the focal point of local politics. It cannot be otherwise because land is the economic resource over which the local state exercises greatest control.

LABOR. Skilled workers are relatively scarce in the labor force, a situation which allows them to demand higher wages. They also are concentrated in firms and industries where innovation is occurring through research and development. This gives a firm the monopoly power that results from an early lead in a new industry and the higher profit margins are passed on, in part, to labor. Labor that is better educated, and generally more intellectually agile, constitutes a resource to the community in noneconomic arenas.

There are options that communities can use to enhance their ability to retain and attract a skilled labor force. Through zoning laws they can ensure adequate land for middle-class residences. They can build and maintain parks, recreation facilities, high-quality schools, and adult educational programs. Provision of public services seldom used by middle-class residents can be kept to a minimum or eliminated, thereby reducing the tax burden on skilled labor. Lowered taxes translate into a higher benefit/tax ratio for skilled workers (i.e., increases their real wages) and thereby increase the competitive position of the community in attracting and retaining skilled workers. This strategy is rational from the perspective of the local state's interest in community economic vitality (i.e., maintaining or improving its economic position). It also coincides with the economic interests of middle-class workers.

However, this market-based option largely ignores the interests of unskilled and semiskilled workers.

To maintain equity among classes under the conditions of a market-oriented public economy, it is necessary for the national state to assume responsibility for the redistributive function. For the local state operating in a market economy, it is irrational to adopt policies that increase the benefit-to-tax ratio of taxpayers who already are above the average ratio; that is, the poor, the handicapped, and the dropouts (Peterson 1981). Thus, equity becomes a responsibility of both the national and local states, but the national state is the dominant partner. The national state sets the rules for competition among local states. Local states have considerable flexibility in responding to those rules or pushing them further. The constraint for the community is that it cannot exceed the national norms of equity without making itself less competitive relative to other communities. Only within the limits of the national state's rules do local attempts to redress inequitable outcomes of the market not enter the realm of intercommunity competition.

CAPITAL. Unlike nation states, local states have very limited tools with which to control the flow of capital into and out of their territories. Tariffs, price and wage controls, monetary policies, and deficit spending are mechanisms reserved for the national state. Therefore, communities are left largely to the use of devices that minimize the local cost of capital investment in enterprises within their territories or that create investment opportunities and thereby generate a competitive advantage.

Cost reduction is the strategy most often pursued by local states. They can reduce the tax burden for firms by minimizing public services, especially to taxpayers with above average benefit/tax ratios and to nontaxpayers. They can offer public land at a discount price, or perhaps free of charge. They can provide tax holidays where law allows such practice. They can exempt or discount the assessment of real property—that is, land, buildings, machinery, and equipment. They can reduce or ignore regulations such as safety and pollution codes. Such public subsidies can attract capital to the community, but the extent to which the local state can reduce costs to capital without jeopardizing its economic vitality is a matter of considerable debate.

There is a form of capital which has been largely unnoticed perhaps because of its newness. Cash transfer payments and investment income paid to retirees constitute a significant proportion of personal income in most industrially advanced nations. In the United States it accounts for nearly one-third of the aggregate personal income. As retirees, the recipients of these payments are spatially quite mobile, and when attracted to a locality they bring their benefit payments and dividends with them. These dollars function in the local economy in the same manner as any other export money flow, provided the locality can capture them. Thus, another strategy involves making the community more attractive to retirees with substantial cash transfer and investment incomes, and creating ways of capturing the capital they bring with them.

Adapting to Change.   The underlying theme in the discussion to this point has been that dynamic conditions in the economy create a need to be flexible and adaptable as well as to make decisions to adjust to the change. A variable affecting community economic vitality is the capacity to perceive and accommodate change. This is the ability of the local community to distinguish problems and symptoms and to create an appropriate response. This dimension of the community's institutional structure is typically embodied in its ability to assemble both private and public capital, labor, and technology (Ruttan 1978; Schmid 1972; Schultz 1968). The public dimension is the ability of local government and community organizations to anticipate and influence change, to make intelligent decisions about policy, to develop programs, to implement policy, to attract and absorb resources, to manage resources, and to evaluate current activities to guide future actions (Honadle 1981). In essence the institutional capacity question of community vitality becomes, Can communities appropriately define problems and use the internal and external resources available to guide their own economic development? The discussion of institutions and community economic vitality leads to a series of questions about institutions influencing resource use, the incentives and aspirations of individuals, orderly change through time, entrepreneurship, capital accumulation, technological change, labor supply, and geographic and occupational mobility of labor. These dimensions of community vitality were addressed in the preceding discussions of supply and demand forces. The focus now shifts from describing their importance to recognizing them and how they affect community economic vitality.

Entrepreneurship is a key institutional ingredient in community economic vitality. Entrepreneurs bring together the resources, take the necessary risks, have the ideas, provide the ingenuity and the energy to create new products and services, and search out markets (Shapero 1981). By definition they are responding to change and trying to capture the opportunities embodied in change.

While entrepreneurs are created, not born, there are certain personal characteristics associated with the entrepreneur versus the average person. Entrepreneurs generally possess the following characteristics: (1) A disposition to accept new ideas and try new methods.[3] This means that the individual is comfortable, both with uncertainty and risk, and is inclined to undertake innovative behavior. (2) A need to achieve. In other words, there is some internal drive to succeed that permits the individual to accommodate risk and seek new innovative ideas to reach that achievement. (3) A tendency to set moderately difficult goals. Entrepreneurs are very result-oriented but do not set goals for themselves that are either unachievable or present no challenge. (4) An ability to accept and act according to feedback. In other words, they are sensitive to feedback; they adjust to it, accept it when valid, and use feedback to make adjustments to accommodate variations from where they expect to be and where they actually are (Pryde 1981, p. 525).

Some particular entrepreneurship skills that appear to be relevant to this discussion include the following: (1) an ability to perceive market opportunities accurately and to devise effective strategies for exploiting them; (2) the capacity to identify and meet resource needs (e.g., determine what resources are in short supply and find either substitutes or alternative sources); (3) skills in the management of political relationships (e.g., capability of working with people in the community, especially local government, to implement an idea); and (4) an ability to manage interpersonal relationships, because the individual cannot do it alone. Successful entrepreneurs are able to build a team of people to work with them in creating an effective business organization (Pryde 1981, p. 525).

There are several features of communities that seem to encourage entrepreneurial innovation. First, it is important for a community to create an atmosphere of immunity or indifference that permits individuals to experiment with ways of doing things that are different from those specified by the existing norms. Without this, tradition becomes the standard and change is virtually nonexistent. Second, community social institutions are characterized by considerable differentiation, not uniform traditional patterns. Thus, diversity is common rather than unique. Third, power within the community is relatively diffused rather than concentrated (i.e., vested interests have less control). Fourth, the source of economic power is diversified rather than coming from only one or two sources. A narrow common source is likely to resist emerging market forces and become isolated. Finally, the means for social mobility are widely available rather than narrowly restricted. Thus, individuals perceive opportunities for themselves to become upwardly mobile.

Institutions can be both facilitators and barriers to economic vitality. Traditionalism is a barrier to economic vitality, while the willingness to accept change and technological innovation is a positive element supporting economic vitality. Economic institutions provide decision rules for adjusting and accommodating conflicting demands among different interest groups within society. Economic theory typically assumes that the necessary institutions either exist or will develop. However, the creation of an institutional framework supportive of community economic vitality is not automatic, and it may be the critical element in a community's economic development efforts.

Comprehensive Strategies for Community Economic Development.[4]

Community economic vitality and economic development imply a condition of change and dynamics. If communities are to foster conditions of vitality, they need to engage in policies and strategies that capture the opportunities available to the community to provide the jobs and incomes desired through time. These efforts cannot be limited to single-purpose or single-dimensional efforts. Communities that limit their activities to just one or a few of these methods do exactly that—limit themselves in achieving the desired outcome.

There are several ways a community can actively alter its income and employment base. The options are attracting new basic employers, capturing existing markets, improving the efficiency of existing firms, encouraging the formation of new firms, and reacquiring dollars taxed away by higher levels of government. There is nothing mystical about these five, nor are they mutually exclusive.

Attracting new basic employers—the traditional attempt to bring a manufacturing plant to the community—remains an important option, but the idea of attracting a basic employer needs to be broadened to include all activities that bring dollars into the community. Health care, retirees, regional shopping centers, regional headquarter functions, and tourism all meet these qualifications. This is an obvious application of the concepts embodied in the demand orientation to community vitality. The principle used is bringing external income into the community.

Capturing existing markets acknowledges that bringing dollars into the community is only part of the task. There must be some place for people and firms to spend the funds locally or the funds will leak to other locales. Furthermore, this also applies to income currently in the community but not used there. This option means the community tries to understand who its customers are, what they want, what is available locally or nearby, and what might be feasibly offered in the local economy. This is another application of demand-oriented principles of community vitality. The key focus is increasing and strengthening the linkages between the export and nonexport sectors.

Improving the efficiency of existing firms means the community explicitly considers the profitable operation of local businesses that have provided jobs and income in the past. The supply-oriented dimensions of this strategy appear in efforts to use appropriate management practices, marketing strategies, and production technologies, and in efforts to maintain a well-trained work force. The institutional dimensions of this strategy involve recognition that the working relationship between the local private and public sectors is crucial. It is a relationship where each party recognizes the role of the other and how they must cooperate for success.

Encouraging the formulation of new businesses is an option attaining increasing significance. There is a mounting body of evidence that the difference between growing and declining areas is less a difference in the rate of firms' deaths and contractions than it is a difference in the rate of firms' births and expansions. Obviously, all three theoretical dimensions of community economic vitality appear in this strategy.

There are dramatic differences among communities in the perception of the reasonableness of starting a new firm. A community can promote firm start-ups through identifying entrepreneurs, assisting people with business ideas in determining whether the ideas have merit, and creating a core of mentors to guide start-ups around or through the early mistakes. If business start-ups are viewed as experiments — Do people want this product at this location and price or not? — the threat of potential failure becomes less ominous. This does not suggest the death of a business is to be encouraged but recognizes that frequently the market is misread or uncertain until the experiment is attempted.

Reacquiring dollars taxed away by higher levels of government builds on the idea that those tax dollars represent potential local spending that escapes. Furthermore, there often are public investments that create the preconditions for other economic development activities. These tax dollars can return in the form of support for the local schools, highway aids, special purpose grants, and even Social Security benefits. Regardless of how they return, they represent an injection of income into the local community's economy and often represent the agglomeration of resources exceeding what the community could do by itself. Furthermore, the use of programs of senior governmental units to address local economic needs often displays imaginative community decision making and creative interpretation of administrative rules.

When communities engage in comprehensive economic development efforts, they need to recognize the variety of activities possible. No single activity is sufficient, nor is success assured by a multitude of activities. The application of community economic development theories within the context of the shifts in the larger economy and society leads to the components of a comprehensive community economic development strategy just reviewed.

Socioeconomic Impacts of Industrial Development.

While communities need to pursue a wide variety of economic development activities, one particular activity that provides some insight into the types of community changes arising from an economic development event is industrial development. What follows is a brief review of expectations and empirical evidence of socioeconomic changes in communities. Unfortunately, a quarter of a century of studying socioeconomic changes from industrial development indicates expectations and reality often do not coincide.

EMPLOYMENT. It has been a common expectation that new industry (manufacturing) would create jobs for the unemployed, the underemployed, and low-income people in rural communities. Studies now show that local labor markets operate in ways that often work against the needs of the people for whom rural industrialization was promoted. There are at least three reasons why this is so. First, many of the new jobs are filled by commuters from outside the community. In many rural areas the commuter shed has a radius of seventy-five miles or more. Thus, workers at a new plant often live in communities scattered throughout a multicounty area and the jobs leak out of the local community in which the plant is located. Second, a sizable portion of the new jobs are filled by in-migrants who either transfer to the community from another plant operated by the firm or who migrate to the area to take advantage of the new jobs. Finally, new jobs often are filled by persons who previously have not been in the labor force. Consequently, only a small fraction of the jobs created by a new industry provide employment for those people in the community it was intended to help.

Even so, there is evidence that the rate of unemployment declines in communities receiving new industry. But the benefits are small relative to the magnitude of the problem. One should also note that the largest declines in unemployment have been observed in cases involving multiple plant locations. There appear to be several reasons for the modest improvements in the unemployment rate. Leakage of jobs to commuters and in-migrants certainly is a major reason. Also, new entrants often are less stable in the labor force than are experienced workers. Consequently, residents who had not been counted as unemployed because they had not worked previously are counted as unemployed after they have entered the labor force and then left their jobs. Similarly, in localities experiencing economic growth it is common for workers to move from job to job with the consequence that at any given moment some will be unemployed. Thus, increasing job opportunities in a community or locality almost never eliminates unemployment. However, the fact that the strongest declines in unemployment occur in situations where there are multiple plant locations suggests the presence of underemployment in local economies which must be substantially reduced before unemployed workers are called into the work force. In rural areas unemployment is likely to be quite high, and this slack in the local labor market must be taken up before the local unemployed persons find jobs.

INCOME. New industry has a positive effect on income, in the aggregate or on the average. Industrial jobs typically pay a higher wage than the locally prevailing rate. But if one examines the distribution of income gains among local residents, the positive effect is less clear. New industry may raise the average income in a community while depressing the relative income status of some segments of the population — particularly the elderly, the unemployed, and others whose incomes are not increased by the new industry, directly or indirectly. In general, people who do not possess resources or assets for which there is an increased demand generated by the new industry will experience a relative decrease in income. This is a particularly significant issue because in many rural communities 40 to 50 percent of the population is over sixty-five years of age and not in the labor force. These people live on fixed incomes which are devalued by localized inflation associated with new industry.

INCOME-EMPLOYMENT MULTIPLIERS.   The logic of rural industrialization leads to an expectation of income and employment multiplier effects in the local economy. Jobs and income added to the community by the new industry should stimulate further income and jobs in businesses in the secondary sector as plant workers spend their payroll and the plant makes purchases of goods and services locally.

Experience shows that there are multipliers, but their magnitudes are far smaller than expected. They range from virtually none to as high as 3.0, but the average is more in the order of 1.3. That is, it takes about three manufacturing jobs to generate one additional job in the local economy.

There are at least three reasons why the multiplier effect is so low. First, payroll and jobs leak out of the local community. This occurs through commuting of workers, area-wide trading patterns, recreation travel outside the area, payment of taxes to nonlocal units of government, and other transactions which take residents' dollars outside the community. Second, most rural communities have many facilities — commercial, residential, industrial, and public service — which are underutilized. Until utilization reaches near full capacity, additional construction seldom occurs. The dampening effect here is similar to the underemployment effect on the unemployment rate. The slack must be removed from the system before the anticipated effect of multipliers will be realized.

Finally, many industries locating in rural communities purchase their supplies, production materials, financial services, legal services, and marketing and advertising services outside the local community. Similarly, the product of the plant is shipped immediately to nonlocal sites for additional processing, warehousing, or sale. Thus, very few backward or forward linkages of the manufacturing plant are located in the community. The payroll of the plant work force is the principal contribution to the local economy and, as already noted, much of that leaks out. Consequently, the income and employment multiplier effects of new industry generally are rather modest.

POPULATION STABILITY. To the extent that stabilizing the population of rural communities is a goal of industrialization, it is very successful. Unequivocally, new industry halts population decline. It appears this is mainly from increased in-migration and unchanged or slightly decreased out-migration. New industry, however, does not mean that large numbers of young people will cease to leave their rural hometowns in search of work and education. It does mean that as they leave, other young families move in to take their place. Consequently, rural communities with new industry have migration flows that resemble those of larger cities and metropolitan areas. One should note also that the changed demographic structure means future changes in the types of services and products demanded by community residents of local businesses and government.

All the above-mentioned changes associated with rural industrialization have a stimulating effect on local trade and commerce, even though the impact is less than hoped for. Real estate and retail sales are particularly worth noting because they represent the major components of the revenue base of local governments: property tax and sales tax.

REAL ESTATE. The inventory of parcels of real estate on tax books generally increases with new industry, especially residential parcels. This is consistent with the evidence of population growth, of course. Most communities experience little growth in commercial and industrial parcels, which is probably due to the underutilization of existing facilities and the backward and forward linkages of the new industry. On the other hand, assessed valuation of real property virtually always increases in all categories: residential, commercial, and industrial. Clearly, the property tax base is enhanced by rural industrialization.

RETAIL SALES. Similarly, retail sales increase with new industry. This reflects both the aggregate growth in income and the population increase. The magnitude of growth is often relatively modest and less than expected, but this experience is consistent with the leakage of payroll and jobs already mentioned. Clearly, there is private sector growth resulting from new industry, and it is not surprising, therefore, to find local merchants, bankers, and real estate developers active in promoting new industry.

LOCAL GOVERNMENT FINANCE. One of the primary goals of the rural industrialization policy was to improve the fiscal base of local governments. As just noted, the tax base generally is increased in communities with industrial growth. But that is only one side of the public ledger. To local governments, people cost money and more people cost more money. Where new industry brings population growth, it often strains the public service delivery systems and increases the costs to local government. Experience shows that the increased expenditures occur in the provision of schools, police protection, highways, streets and roads, and health services and facilities. All of these are quite reasonable consequences of a growing population with school-age children.

Of course, the ultimate question with respect to local fiscal impacts of new industry is its net effect on government revenues and expenditures. This is not well studied and most analyses are rather short run, performed less than five years after the location of a new industry. However, the evidence clearly suggests that in the short run increased costs outweigh gains in the fiscal base. Positive net gains have been observed where no local subsidy was offered to industry and where there was little or no population increase.

Summary.   Community economic vitality is concerned with the efficient use of the community's resources, the maintenance of those resources through time, and the adaptability of the community to changing conditions. This has several implications for efforts to examine or define community economic vitality. Vitality is a long-run, dynamic concept that cannot be replaced by short-run "resource exploitation" for the current residents of the community. Community economic vitality is a function of local and nonlocal economic, social, and political forces. Any discussion of community economic vitality must start with the external forces affecting a community. National demand and national economic conditions are critical, because they provide an expanding (contracting) market for locally produced goods and services. For a community to respond to external demand requires the appropriate economic sectors. There must be businesses existing in the community either selling to or capable of selling to the external market. These businesses should be a significant force in the local economy (i.e., have strong linkages back into the rest of the community). Additionally, the availability of resources must be considered. A community needs to possess the natural and manmade resources, plus the public and human capital used to produce the goods or services demanded either locally or nonlocally. Anyone examining the resource base of the community needs to be cognizant of the mobility of those resources into and out of the community as well as the potential uses of those resources in the community.

Typically a community's resource base is given, as is demand for a community's goods and services. Thus, the variable is how the community interprets that demand and allocates its resources to produce the appropriate output. This is the capacity of the community to identify problems and perceive solutions, and to enable the community to overcome many demand-and-supply–related obstacles. Likewise, it may permit the community to utilize existing resources in unique fashions to generate new potential for the community.

There are both internal and external forces impacting on the community. Furthermore, these forces create constant change that both generates new opportunities and closes previous alternatives. An important difference between communities characterized with vitality and those characterized as lacking vitality is how they respond to changes in themselves and their external environment. Dramatic changes in the external environment mean that historic approaches to community economic development are no longer sufficient. Successful community economic development recognizes the opportunities change creates, moves to capture those opportunities, and is not limited to just a few types of efforts.

Such a comprehensive strategy should at least attract new basic employers, including nonmanufacturing firms that export goods and services, provide assistance to existing employers, encourage and assist new business start-ups, enhance the ability of communities to capture dollars already existing in the local economy, and facilitate the ability of local units of government to secure funds available from nonlocal units of government.

Notes

1. *Local state* is used to refer to all subnational governmental entities.
2. This section follows closely the arguments advanced by Thompson (1965) and Peterson (1981).
3. Individuals likely to engage in entrepreneurial innovation have a minimal commitment to existing norms and institutional arrangements. Because they have this minimal commitment, they can perceive alternative behavioral patterns and ways of doing things.
4. This section is derived from Pulver (1979).

References

Borts, G. H., and J. L. Stein. 1964. *Economic Growth in a Free Market.* New York: Columbia University Press.

Davis, L., and D. C. North. 1971. *Institutional Change and American Economic Growth.* London: Cambridge University Press.

Harmston, F. K. 1983. *The Community as an Economic System.* Ames: Iowa State University Press.

Honadle, B. W. 1981. A capacity building framework: Search for concept and purpose. *Public Administration Review* 41(Sept.-Oct.):575–80.

Isard, W. 1956. *Location and Space Economy.* New York: Wiley.

———. 1975. *Introduction to Regional Science.* Englewood Cliffs, N.J.: Prentice-Hall.

Kaufman, H. F. 1959. Toward an interactional conception of community. *Social Forces* 38(Oct.):8–17.

Leven, C. 1985. Regional development analysis and policy. *Journal of Regional Science* 25(Nov.):569–92.

Molle, W. 1982. Technological change and regional development in Europe. *Papers of the Regional Science Association* 52:23–38.

North, D. C. 1956. A reply. *Journal of Political Economy* 64(Apr.):170–72.

Peterson, P. E. 1981. *City Limits.* Chicago: University of Chicago Press.

Pfister, R. 1976. Improving export base studies. *Regional Science Perspectives* 6:104–16.

Pryde, P. L. 1981. Human capacity and local development enterprise. In *Expanding the Opportunities to Produce: Revitalizing the American Economy through New Enterprise Development,* R. Friedman and W. Schweke, eds., pp. 521–33. Washington, D.C.: The Corporation for Enterprise Development.

Pulver, G. C. 1979. A theoretical framework for the analysis of community economic development policy options. In *Nonmetropolitan Industrial Growth and Community Change*, G. F. Summers and A. Selvik, eds. Lexington, Mass.: Lexington Books.

Reitzes, D. C., and D. C. Reitzes. 1980. Saul D. Alinsky's contribution to community development. *Journal of the Community Development Society* 11(2):39–52.

_____. 1987. Alinsky in the 1980's: Two contemporary Chicago community organizations. *The Sociological Quarterly* 28(June):265–84.

Richardson, H. W. 1969. *Regional Economics: Location Theory, Urban Structure, Regional Change*. New York: Praeger.

Ruttan, V. W. 1978. Social science knowledge and institutional change. *American Journal of Agricultural Economics* 66(Dec.):549–59.

Schmid, A. A. 1972. Analytical institutional economics: Challenging problems in the economics of resources for a new environment. *American Journal of Agricultural Economics* 54(Aug.):893–901.

Schultz, T. W. 1968. Institutions and the rising economic value of man. *American Journal of Agricultural Economics* 50(Dec.):1113–27.

Shaffer, R. 1988. Community economic development theories. Chapter 2 in *Community Economics Analysis: Study of the Economic Structure and Change of Smaller Communities*. Ames: Iowa State University Press.

Shapero, A. 1981. The role of entrepreneurship in economic development at the less than national level. In *Expanding the Opportunity to Produce: Revitalizing the American Economy Through New Enterprise Development*, R. Friedman and W. Schweke, eds., pp. 25–35. Washington, D.C.: The Corporation for Enterprise Development.

Summers, G. F., L. E. Bloomquist, T. A. Hirschl, and R. E. Shaffer, eds. 1988. *Community Economic Vitality*. Ames: Iowa State University, North Central Regional Center for Rural Development.

Thompson, W. R. 1965. *A Preface to Urban Economics*. Baltimore: The Johns Hopkins Press.

Tiebout, C. M. 1956*a*. Exports and regional economic growth. *Journal of Political Economy* 64(Apr.):160–69.

_____.1956*b*. The urban economic base reconsidered. *Land Economics* 31(Feb.):95–100.

Wilkinson, K. P. 1972. A field theory perspective for community development research. *Rural Sociology* 37(1):43–52.

_____. 1979. Social well-being and community. *Journal of the Community Development Society* 10(1):5–16.

_____. 1985. Rural community development: A deceptively controversial theme in rural sociology. *The Rural Sociologist* 5(2):119–24.

_____. 1986. In search of the community in a changing countryside. *Rural Sociology* 51(4):1–17.

10

Local Organizations and Leadership in Community Development

LORRAINE E. GARKOVICH

C ONSIDER a tale of two communities. Both had the opportunity to obtain a sizable amount of money for local economic development *if* they could generate matching funds. The responses of these two communities serve as a paradigm for the main focus of this chapter. "In the first community, local residents, businesses, and organizations immediately responded to what they viewed as a challenge to the entire community. In a matter of weeks, pledges and donations had exceeded the amount required by more than 30 percent. Meanwhile, the second community was thrown into turmoil trying to decide who should be responsible for matching the grant money. In the end, they fell far short of the amount required and, subsequently, failed to receive the grant" (Ryan 1987, p. 1).

The moral of this tale is that access to resources is a necessary but not a sufficient condition for community development. If people cannot mobilize and organize to use available resources, community economic development fails. This chapter focuses on the role of local organizations and leadership in the community development process.

The delineation between development *of* the community and development *in* the community has been employed throughout this book to illustrate two supposedly divergent approaches to community development. The first refers to a focus on fostering interactional ties among residents so as to promote a cohesive and integrated community. The second refers to a focus on primarily economic and, to a lesser extent, political and social structures and processes that contribute to the enhancement of community well-being. This distinction is a matter of convenience rather than reality, for development *in* the community must be grounded in development *of* the community through the building of local capacity.

In its typical use, *capacity building* has been applied to efforts to enhance the functioning of local governments (Honadle 1981*a*, 1981*b*). However, in this chapter it will be argued that local capacity is also a defining characteristic of the general community. Local capacity in this context symbolizes the ability of residents to articulate needs and to identify actions to solve these needs. Local capacity also represents the ability of residents to mobilize and organize local or extra-local resources in the pursuit of communally defined goals (Ryan 1987). Simply put, local capacity engages organizations, leadership, and citizens in the community development process. This chapter will describe the theoretical importance of capacity building, then briefly review conceptual literature in this area, and conclude with examples of strategies for capacity building within the general community. But first it is necessary to establish why capacity building of the general community is so critical for the future of people, particularly rural people.

Capacity Building and the Future of Community Development.

Since the early 1980s, communities, especially rural communities, have confronted a social, economic, political, and demographic environment substantively different from that of the first part of this century. These changes can be subsumed under three topics: restructuring, devolution, and revitalization (Wellar 1984). *Restructuring* is "characterized by greater spatial integration, greater population mobility, expanded and more complex industrial and commercial linkages, and greater dependency (or vulnerability) of local economies and local governments upon broad market forces beyond their direct control or even influence" (Wellar 1984, p. 32). World, national, regional, and state events now impinge on community life through changes in employment or demand for local products, through the arrival of migrants who bring their own cultural baggage, or through regional shopping malls just down the new intrastate highway. *Devolution* is characterized by the changing relationships among different levels of government, specifically, the delegation of fiscal and functional responsibilities to local governments. Services that once had been funded and organized by larger governmental units now are the responsibility of local governments, as are the costs of developing and maintaining infrastructure (water and sewage treatment, roads, etc.). *Revitalization* is characterized by the diversification of the socioeconomic base of rural communities with the arrival of new people and new industries. Rural communities are less homogeneous today in terms of class, ethnicity, economic base, power, and interests than they were yesterday, and they will be even less so tomorrow.

These changes present a tremendous challenge to communities and local government officials. For example, the amount of legal authority that local government officials may actually exercise varies considerably. As a result, although the new federalism may have transferred primary responsibility for programs and services to local governments, many officials do not have the legal authority necessary to deal effectively with these new responsibilities. Associated with this is the ability of local governmental units to generate financial resources. "Financial resources are the sine qua non of governmental action" (Reid 1984, p. 20). Yet, local governments have differential access to the various means of generating such resources (such as bonding authority, occupational taxes, etc.). Third, a critical barrier to dealing effectively with these changes is the lack of adequate information that identifies and confirms trends, monitors changes, predicts outcomes, and defines alternatives for action. As Wellar (1984, p. 32) notes, "Very few rural governments possess, or know how to acquire on their own, the professional, technical, and financial capability to cope with the information problem." Moreover, "small rural jurisdictions can seldom afford to hire professional staff, and they must rely principally on part-time, noncareer, citizen officials for much of their leadership talent" (Reid 1984, p. 26). This points to the final problem confronting rural governments in this new era – their "management capacity." As components of management capacity, Reid (1984, p. 20) includes "the quality of government leadership and the strength of its supporting institutions." While these comments refer specifically to the supporting governmental institutions, such as planning divisions, personnel departments, or budget offices, it will be argued in this chapter that local officials must rely increasingly upon the support of nongovernmental local organizations and leadership if they are to successfully meet the challenges of this new era.

A Framework for Understanding Capacity Building.

While there are many different theoretical approaches to the phenomenon of the community, the one of relevance to capacity building is the community action approach or social field paradigm (Sanders 1975; Warren 1978). A brief description of this framework provides a context for understanding local capacity building in community development.

A community can be viewed as a dynamic and emergent configuration of groups and activities addressing a constantly changing variety of "interest fields" (Kaufman 1985; Sanders 1975). Basic concepts, then, include: "associations, actors, actions and interest configurations" (Kaufman 1985, p. 55). Associations are organizations or groups based within the community that focus on providing services or resources or coordinating local efforts. Actors are the leaders and members of associations and the other residents of the community who await mobilization. Actions are projects, policies, or other activities that actors perform in order to achieve identifiable community-based goals. Interest configurations are the bundle of community concerns as represented by associations, actors, and actions. In this sense, associations are organized embodiments of single or multiple interests within the community, actors are motivated to become involved in particular interests, and actions are oriented toward satisfying or accomplishing particular interests. Kaufman (1985, p. 59) argues that "community development is expressed through both structure and task accomplishment. Development involves associations and networks of actors, on the one hand, and actions and the community image of their realization, on the other hand."

Associations represent the "interorganizational field" of communal life (Sanders 1975, p. 373) and can be viewed as "an aggregate of organizations (associations), which appear, disappear, change, merge, and form networks of relations with one another" (Turk 1970, p. 1). The importance of associations in understanding social action can be viewed in this way: "Individual behaviors depend upon the presence of organizations that encourage or accept them and . . . organizations must be assumed to be both the formulators and the means of the individual action" (Turk 1970, p. 2). Associations, then, provide the locus in which individual interests are articulated and translated into action goals, and human and other resources are mobilized for goal accomplishment.

Social action is the pivotal element in the social field paradigm. It is in social action that various associations and actors come to orient their activities around overlapping interests. There have been several frameworks or models proposed for analyzing this action system. For example, Green and Mayo (1953) identify four stages: the initiation of action, articulation of goals and means, implementation of the action plan, and action outcomes. Both Kaufman and Wilkinson (1967) and Holland, Tiedke, and Miller (1957) identify five stages. But perhaps the most encompassing approach to the community action system is the five-stage model proposed by Warren (1978, pp. 316–21).

First, the "initial systemic environment" contains both the sources of possible dysfunction contributing to the emergence of felt needs or interests and the organizational basis for responding to these needs. Second, the "inception of the action system" involves the identification of action objectives and the appropriate components of the systemic environment to respond to these needs. Third, "expansion of the action system" entails mobilizing associations or individuals outside the original associations and/or actors. Of particular concern here are the reasons underlying the expansion of the action system, such as financial resources, popular support, or technical assistance. Fourth, the "operation of the expanded action system" involves the specific task-oriented activities designed to achieve the identified objectives. Finally, the "transformation of the action system" reflects the various outcomes stemming from the action effort, including achievement of the action objective followed by dissolution of the coalition of actors or the reorientation of the action system toward a new set of needs. In effect, this final phase focuses on the systemic residue of the community action. What is left from the action, systematically, after the action episode is terminated? (Warren 1978, p. 320).

The utility of this model is that it both identifies key factors in and highlights the complexity of community action. Community action entails the coincidence of many components of the community system in a concerted effort toward a consensually defined goal. In this context, development depends on the local capacities, or the abilities of residents to organize and mobilize their resources for the accomplishment of consensually defined goals. Hence, as noted in the beginning of this chapter, the availability of resources for a development project simply is not sufficient to guarantee a particular development outcome. While necessary, these resources must be organized and allocated through the efforts of local organizations and leaders in order to accomplish particular development outcomes.

Local Organizations. Local organizations represent the associations component of the social action model of community development and are a key aspect of capacity building. Community systemic environments vary in the number and viability of local organizations, and indeed, the fostering of such organizations has been a goal of many community development efforts. The reason is that "local organizations can equip local publics with the voice and capacity to make credible demands on government and on others who control resources" (Esman and Uphoff 1984, p. 27). Studies in the United States and many other countries suggest that local organizations are a necessary condition for development and that development is limited or impeded by the absence or the rudimentary nature of such associations (Esman and Uphoff 1984).

The presence and viability of local organizations are especially critical in economic development efforts. Based on their cross-cultural study of sixteen nations, Esman and Uphoff (1984, p. 50) argue: "Technology, resources and organization are like the economic factors of land, labor and capital—complementary elements of larger processes. Any of them can constitute a bottleneck, but unless the other two are appropriately increased in amount and quality, increasing one by itself will produce diminishing returns." Ryan (1987, p. 2) argues for a similar conclusion, stating, "Community development is instrumental to the success of economic development." For Ryan, community development entails the concerted efforts of local people to improve their situation, and local organizations provide a vehicle for citizen participation in development efforts.

However, all too often development efforts and resources are not directed toward the fostering of local organizations or network building among local organizations. The reasons for this are varied, but Esman and Uphoff (1984, p. 50) suggest that "establishing local organizations is a more organic than mechanical process. . . . It is not predictable, takes time, and does not obviously 'move money' in large amounts" and so is less attractive as a development strategy than other alternatives such as construction projects. Yet, development efforts that have long-term benefits for a people or a community rarely proceed in leaps and bounds; rather, they move with small steps, carefully constructing a solid foundation of citizen participation that leaves behind a self-starting community when the development project ends. Furthermore, moving large amounts of money into local communities is not necessarily community development if it results in a citizenry dependent on someone else. Real development efforts empower people by teaching them the skills that allow them to do for themselves.

Why are local organizations a key component of local capacity and so important in development efforts? Esman and Uphoff (1984) identify four critical tasks such organizations perform. First, *interorganizational tasks* entail the myriad of ways in which local organizations serve as intermediaries between local citizens and the state. These include activities such as providing information about community needs, interests, and concerns; brokering the competing priorities of local citizens or groups and establishing hierarchies of needs to present to extra-local agencies; or assisting in the implementation of programs so that they take into account community lifeways. Second, *resource tasks* involve the mobilization of local resources (labor, capital, materials, information) and the management of these resources in the accomplishment of development goals. Third, *service tasks* may involve the actual delivery of services that reflect development goals or coordinating their delivery in the local community. Fourth, *extra-organizational tasks* entail presenting local demands to bureaucracies or organizations outside the community and buffering local residents from intrusions by external agencies. Thus, local organizations function at the inception, expansion, and operation stages of the social action system, and are a factor in the transformation of the action system.

There are many types of local organizations and these may be distinguished on the basis of variation along three continua—size, structure, and function. Size ranges from small (under ten members) to large (over one hundred members). Structure has several components including stability (duration of existence), accessibility (degree of openness to new members), degree of formalization (frequency and formality of meetings), and nature and extent of extra-local affiliations (number and types of linkages to associations outside the community). Function also has several components reflecting aspects of goal orientation, including single versus multiple goals, locality-oriented versus cosmopolitan goals, or short- versus long-term goals.

Local organizations, then, include economic development associations, agricultural cooperatives, health-services boards, tenants' associations, water-users' groups, business and professional associations, parent-teacher associations, church groups, neighborhood organizations, youth groups, extension adivsory boards, voluntary associations, and any other group of local persons who come together to accomplish consensually defined goals that will produce benefits for both their members and the larger community. But the mere existence of a variety of active local organizations does not guarantee adequate local capacity for development. The other essential building block is leadership.

Leadership.

There is a considerable body of literature on leadership (Burns 1978; Hunt and Larson 1979; Kellerman 1984; Santora 1983; Yukl 1981). The purpose here is not to review this extensive literature but to briefly address why leadership is a significant aspect of local capacity and a critical component in the development process. In the social action framework, the underlying process is one in which associations are linked through common interests to act in concert toward mutually defined goals. This process hinges on effective leadership, leadership that can anticipate change, contribute to informed decisions, identify action programs, stimulate support, attract resources, and manage group behavior. Leadership involves, then, both the ability to organize and sustain task performance and the ability to arouse or stimulate others to join in the task. Although directed toward the management of public programs, the following comment is most appropriate to the broader issue of leadership. "To manage a program is to make things happen through people. Therefore, management involves human as well as technical systems" (Garcia-Zama 1985, p. 5).

How does leadership emerge and function within the community? There are several theoretical approaches to the understanding of leadership, but the situational-contingency approach best fits the social action model of community development. The situational-contingency theory proposes that leadership emerges from the interaction of individual leader traits or behaviors with the characteristics of other persons and within a particular situation. In other words, the effectiveness of leadership is a function of its fit with the situation in which it occurs. The situation includes other actors (both leaders of other local organizations and followers) and the action toward which leadership is directed. This approach emphasizes the flexible and adaptable nature of community leadership. It suggests that leadership is activated in response to particular interests, is variable in its enactment, and is sensitive to the needs of its followers. Furthermore, it suggests that leaders may specialize in interest fields, emerging to offer their skills and knowledge when appropriate situations develop. Communities, then, contain many potential leaders, and efforts must be made to both activate and nurture this leadership.

Within the context of community development, leaders perform many functions that either contribute directly to the accomplishment of a particular development objective or contribute indirectly through the empowerment of citizens. Leaders anticipate change; that is, they not only act to correct deficiencies in the local environment, but they also can note "a community situation in which an opportunity for positive action and advantage is envisaged" (Warren 1978, p. 317). While local government leaders are often overwhelmed with the day-to-day problems of managing official community affairs and so react to situations, the leadership of local organizations is often proactive. Leaders can stimulate citizens to articulate their interests and concerns and help citizens to create a vision of the community in which they want to live. In this sense, it is important to acknowledge that although we often think of local leaders as acting out of self-interest, altruism is also a motivating force. Community efforts directed toward historical preservation, beautification, the construction of recreational or cultural facilities, or more effective planning represent activities that will enhance the quality of social life without necessarily producing economic benefits for one person or group.

Leaders contribute to informed decisions by providing the input or defining the context for such decisions. Knowledge and information are the currency of social change. Communities can never have too much information available for use in decision making, but equally critical is information that is appropriate to the decision under question. This function of leadership and, by extension, of local organizations is even more important for development efforts given the critical need of rural government officials for access to useable information. The identification of relevant information, its acquisition, and the organization of this information within a decision-making context are all aspects of how leadership contributes to informed decisions. Ryan (1987, p. 8) argues that "information brokers" may be necessary to provide a linkage between "knowledge providers and local decisionmakers," and this is a role that local organization leaders may be able to perform. For example, local leaders can identify members of their groups who have special technical skills or can sponsor seminars by providers of technical assistance from outside the community.

Leaders identify potential action programs. This is a direct outcome of the first two functions, for action programs are the logical extension of envisioning a desired future and gathering the information necessary to defining its character. The transformation of this information into specific proposals for action is an aspect of the inception of an action system. Ideally, leaders will present several strategies for action, each with an accompanying scenario of possible consequences.

Leaders stimulate support for action among citizens and local organizations. Mobilizing support entails making things happen through people and, in its finest form, empowers the citizens of a community because they become participating partners in the development process that will affect their lives. Leaders also work to attract the resources necessary to sustain action efforts, soliciting funds from community members and sometimes external sources, or organizing contributions of materials or labor for local development projects.

Both of these functions depend on the strength and complexity of the networks that link local organizations together (horizontal linkages) and those that tie the local community to external organizations and leadership (vertical linkages). One study of Wisconsin communities found a relationship between the number of contacts local leaders maintained with elites in metropolitan centers or at the state and federal levels and their local community's share of economic growth. This study suggests "a major part of growth promotion activity takes place outside of the public domain through the privately coordinated actions of developers, bankers, utility owners and others with strong proprietary interests in growth" (McGranahan 1984, p. 538). This analysis is based on Molotch's (1976) concept of the city as a "growth machine," wherein the primary concern of local elites or influentials is the promotion of economic growth. Molotch argues that the distribution of growth among communities reflects as much the relative effectiveness of local leaders in influencing extra-local events and decisions as it does the relative ecological advantages (access to highways or railroads, availability of water, etc.) of particular communities.

Finally, leaders manage group dynamics. A key component in the effectiveness of any group is the quality of its leadership. Effective leaders recognize individual variations among members in their ability and willingness to do a job and assign work roles accordingly. Effective leaders are sensitive to the natural cycle of commitment to long-term projects and provide the psychological support necessary to sustain commitment over prolonged periods. Moreover, many community development efforts entail the cooperative efforts of several local organizations and often government officials at several levels. In these situations it is critical that a leader emerges to coordinate the efforts of the various participating groups.

Thus, from the perspective of the social action theory of development, it is clear that all communities share unfulfilled needs (a lack of facilities or services deemed important to the welfare of the community) as well as unfulfilled desires (the presence of facilities or services deemed to enhance the quality of life in the community). The variable success rate of communities in satisfying these needs and desires reflects inherent differences in the local capacities of communities. In other words, "with strong capacities, communities can build on what exists by devising new structure, processes and innovations to create new strengths. In effect, communities become self-driven, requiring little if any outside assistance" (Ryan 1987, pp. 7–8). Given the theoretical framework of this chapter, local capacity is the basis for the inception, expansion, and operation of the local action system. The two key components of local capacity are the number and viability of local organizations and the pool of leadership in the community.

In summary, local organizations are the structural foundation for social action and community development. Local organizations bring together people with common interests, giving direction and form to their activities and linking them with others who share similar interests. Local leadership is the human foundation for social action and community development. Leaders initiate development efforts and make them work by mobilizing and harnessing the natural desire of people to live in a "good" community. The importance of both leadership and organization is perhaps best summarized in the following comments about the management capacity of governments: "Just as inspired leadership can sometimes attain difficult objectives by stretching limited resources, poor leaders have always been able to consume large quantities of personnel and materials to little advantage. Leadership alone is usually insufficient to meet the challenges. . . . Organizational support is also needed" (Reid 1984, p. 20). Not only governments but also citizens need effective local organizations and leadership if they are to become partners in the development process. The question for community development specialists is: What strategies will foster and nurture local organizations and leadership?

Strategies for Local Capacity Building.

The rationale for local capacity building bears repeating here: local governments alone simply do not have the human resources to cope effectively with the changing social, political, and economic environments which they now confront. If the base of human resources that local governments can draw upon is not expanded, then communities and people will never achieve the quality of life they want and deserve.

Three general types of strategies for local capacity building will be discussed. These are expanding the base of citizen involvement, enhancing the leadership pool, and enlarging the information base of local communities (Ryan 1987). While each is important, it is together that they establish a solid foundation for citizen participation in community development. These strategies have multiple purposes and outcomes. They contribute to capacity building by nurturing and strengthening local organizations, by generating citizen interest to participate in community decision making and actions, and by increasing the vehicles for citizen involvement.

EXPANDING THE BASE OF CITIZEN INVOLVEMENT. Action research and neighborhood associations are two strategies to expand the base of citizen involvement in community development. Action research has a long history in the practice of community development, and several reviews of this approach are available (Garkovich and Stam 1980; Johnson et al. 1987). Table 10.1 illustrates the issues and approaches in action research. In general, action research is designed to engage citizens, local organizations, and local officials in identifying needs, assessing services, or conceptualizing alternative futures. In some cases, action research entails asking the people of a community what it is they want or hope for; in other cases, it involves the gathering of secondary data about the community.

The research can be self-studies, wherein the members of the community plan, conduct, and analyze the results with technical assistance from extra-local advisors (Ryan 1987). This approach maximizes the level of citizen involvement because local people are identifying issues in the context of their knowledge of the history and traditions of the community. Or, specialists from outside the community can perform the action research in consultation with local organizations and leaders (Garkovich 1979). Depending on the nature and level of cooperation among the participants, this approach may be uplifting or excruciating. In its ideal form, this approach operates as "a community-research partnership in which the parties jointly determine mutually acceptable decisions concerning what is to be accomplished during the project and how it is to be accomplished" (Truman et al. 1985, p. 107). With respect to specific outcomes, action research can be utilized to describe a community, to set goals for the future, or to develop specific action recommendations.

Table 10.1. Issues and Approaches to Needs Assessment

What Needs Will Be Assessed?	Who Will Do the Assessment?	How Will the Assessment Occur?	How Will Assessments Be Utilized?
Action Preferences	Policymakers	*Primary Analysis*	*Focus of Data Analysis*
Type of action		Type of sampling	Descriptive
general	Community organizations	random	general
specific		purposive	specific
Type of goal	Citizens		Goal setting
general		Method of data	general
specific	Extra-local agencies	collection	specific
		mailed questionnaire	Action recommendations
		personal interviews	general
Concerns and Issues			specific
Quality of life concerns		*Secondary Analysis*	
actual community		Census data	*Recipients of Data Analysis*
ideal community		State and local government	Policymakers
Quality of services and		Private organizations	Community organizations
program issues			Citizens
actual community			
ideal community			
Availability and Utilization of Services and Programs			

The other strategy for expanding the base of citizen involvement focuses on encouraging the emergence of neighborhood associations. The neighborhood as a unit for social action once figured prominently in the research of rural sociologists (Loomis, Ensminger, and Wooley 1941; Ryan 1944) and remains an important concept for urban practitioners. The neighborhood remains a viable social entity in many rural communities, organized around local institutions such as schools, churches, or county roads. In some cases, these neighborhoods are incipient, waiting to be activated by a common concern. In other cases, they are already actors in the community life. The important point is that neighborhood associations are an integral component of local capacity, one that activates individuals who might not otherwise become involved in community affairs since they are not part of business, professional, or political associations. But neighborhood associations, because they invoke issues immediate to the individuals' home and family, can bring new actors into the community arena, actors who have a vested interest in the intergenerational continuity of a preferred way of life.

ENHANCING THE LEADERSHIP POOL. Strategies for enhancing the leadership pool focus on increasing the pool of potential leaders, augmenting the personal resources of leaders, and encouraging entrepreneurs. If we assume that leaders are made, not born, and that most people have within them the basic skills and abilities to assume leadership positions, then one strategy for local capacity building is to promote the emergence of such individuals. The larger the pool of leaders in a community, the greater the opportunities for things to happen in that community. Moreover, research demonstrates the existence of leadership specialization; that is, different leaders are involved in different kinds of action projects and draw on distinct networks of participants. This underscores the need to expand the pool of potential leaders in order to ensure a sufficiently broad base of leadership skills available to the local community.

Several national programs exemplify approaches to fostering the emergence of leaders and enhancing their skills. Since the mid-1960s, the Kellogg Foundation has funded Rural Leadership Development programs through private organizations and universities. These programs identify young adults with the potential for leadership and, through "structured group-centered educational experiences," facilitate the "acquisition of signficiant leadership skills by these individuals"

(Voland 1986, p. 565). The Kellogg programs have been very successful in expanding the pool of rural leaders (Howell, Weir, and Cook
1979), and in Pennyslvania, where one of the first operated, "alumni
have developed a sponsoring organization and are contributing funds
to foster its continuation" (Voland 1986, p. 565). Here local capacity
building efforts become self-driven. Similar projects have been established by other organizations. For example, both Reynold Industries and Phillip Morris, Inc., have sponsored programs to foster the
emergence of agricultural leaders, and several states (Missouri, North
Dakota, South Carolina) have established leadership development programs.

An integral component of these efforts to expand the pool of local
leadership is the focus on augmenting leadership skills (Rossing and
Heasley 1987). Activities designed to help potential or current leaders
understand the leadership process—different styles of leadership, patterns of leader-member interaction, or methods of mobilizing support—and to enhance their information base are representative of this
strategy. For example, all of the leadership projects just described
allocate time to each of these issues, and several bring program participants together with state and federal institutional elites in an effort to
expand the linkages between local and extra-local leaders. This latter
point appears to be especially critical since some research suggests
that knowledge of and the ability to tap extra-local sources of support
are key factors in successful development efforts (McGranahan 1984;
Preston 1983). One respondent in a study of community action illustrates the importance of this effort: "I can remember sitting on the
floor in somebody's living room, pouring over the Federal Register
looking at program after program, shopping for something we could
use and were eligible for" (Richards 1984, p. 77).

A third strategy for enhancing the leadership of a community is
the fostering of entrepreneurs. Entrepreneurs are specialized leaders
who translate local comparative advantages in local resources, skills,
or talents into new approaches to existing business activity patterns.
Entrepreneurial ventures exploit local strengths, are models that stimulate other entrepreneurial efforts, and are an important aspect of local
capacity building. The importance of entrepreneurs in stimulating
community economic development cannot be overstated. Of the estimated 14.5 million new jobs added to the economy since 1981, nearly
all have come from small business starts and expansions. In the rural
South, the rate of new business formation was greater than in the rural
areas of the rest of the nation. Employment growth in industries dominated by small businesses was nearly six times greater than that in

industries dominated by large firms between 1984 and 1985. Moreover, small businesses are more likely to hire the formerly unemployed and to provide jobs to new workers. Finally, entrepreneurial ventures by women represent a substantial proportion of these new business starts. This broadens the pool of economic actors in a community, providing new avenues of participation for a segment of the community that has not traditionally been heavily involved in economic development.

Entrepreneurs are made, not born, and there is a need for "entrepreneurial excavating," that is, identifying potential entrepreneurs and assisting them in developing potential new ventures. The Rural Women's Proprietorship Project in rural southeastern Kentucky is an example of a community development project designed to expand the pool of entrepreneurs in a rural area. The project provides technical assistance and educational support to women considering new business ventures. The educational program includes issues such as defining markets, selecting a business location, product pricing, terms of sale, advertising, inventory control, personnel management, financial planning, cash flow analyses, and legal and insurance issues. At the completion of the training program, participants have developed a complete business prospectus that will be the basis for soliciting financial support from local institutions. In the first six months of the project, 130 women participated in the educational programs. Even if all of these participants do not start their own businesses, the program has expanded the pool of potential economic leaders in the community and has heightened citizen awareness of the complexities and challenges of economic development.

In Missouri, Alternatives for the '80s is a multidisciplinary effort of the University of Missouri to assist communities in identifying alternative approaches to economic development. One program focuses on identifying craftspeople who work from their homes and providing technical assistance in defining market demands and marketing products. Another program thrust is the Rural Entrepreneurship Clearinghouse that provides technical assistance to persons seeking to develop their own businesses. Still another program thrust brings together a variety of organizations and leaders in small communities to discuss community strengths and resources as the first step in identifying alternative paths to economic growth.

EXPANDING THE INFORMATION BASE. The final strategy for local capacity building focuses on enlarging the information base of local communities. Clearly, efforts to expand the base of citizen involvement and to enhance the leadership pool entail enlarging the local informa-tion base. Action research produces information about the community and its people that, in all likelihood, would not otherwise be available. Leadership development helps leaders acquire new skills or hone their existing talents; encourages new specialists to become part of the leadership pool; and, by fostering linkages with leaders and organiza-tions outside the community, broadens the base of information avail-able to local leaders. But the information needs of communities in this rapidly changing environment exceed the capacity of the available technical and human resources. In Table 10.2 Wellar (1984) highlights several of the information consequences of the changing rural environ-ment and provides a starting point for considering strategies to enlarge the information base of local communities.

Expanding the local information base must address two interrela-ted needs: the need for information and the need for knowledge (Cleve-land 1982). "Information is specific facts and ideas, bits and pieces of data that serve as building blocks for knowledge. Knowledge is the organization of facts and ideas within a logical structure that links these isolated facts within a broader context. Knowledge, then, is in-formation made useful in content and form to the needs or interests of a client" (Garkovich 1985, p. 262). This dichotomy is useful, for it forces community development practitioners to recognize that in some cases, communities do not have access to all the information they need for good decision making. But in other cases, they suffer from an information overload; that is, they have either too much information or information in a form that does not contribute to good decision making. Strategies must be developed, then, that address both the need for information and the need for knowledge.

Technical assistance has been the primary vehicle for expanding the information base of local communities. Typically, technical assist-ance has involved experts or specialists from agencies outside the com-munity (Cooperative Extension Service, universities, state-supported regional agencies, or private firms) providing information resources for specific projects. While such an approach often yields the specific in-formation that is immediately required by local communities, this strategy does not necessarily build a local capacity for coping with information needs in the future.

More beneficial to communities in terms of the development of an enduring capacity to deal with information needs are strategies that build on existing talents and skills within the community. Programs designed to encourage local businesses to contribute human and tech-

Table 10.2. *Impacts of Social Structurings, Devolution, and Revitalization on Information Decision Making in Rural Governments*

New Development	New Information Implications	New Information Capabilities Required of Rural Governments
Restructuring Movement by societies to new population, economic, spatial, and public-private sector dynamics, patterns, and linkages	Need for intelligence and soft data or early warning information on incipient changes of dynamics, patterns, and linkages Need for hard data to identify and confirm trends, to monitor change, and to predict alternative socioeconomic futures and market tendencies	Networks of contacts operating at international, national, and regional scales of socioeconomic intelligence gathering, analysis, and synthesis. Professional and technical staff, and information systems and services support, to acquire and process socioeconomic data and conduct studies at regional and extra-regional scales using methods and techniques that are state of the art in other levels of government and the private sector.
Devolution Transfer or shift of fiscal and functional responsibilities from central/federal to local (rural) governments	Loss or disruption of rural-area data collection in censuses and surveys, and rural area statistical series Loss or disruption of rural-area socioeconomic and environmental studies, and professional/technical expertise and consultation Need for data to evaluate existing programs (for continuation), and as basis for creating new or replacement programs	Professional and technical staff, and information systems and services to define, produce, and maintain rural-area data for statistical series, and to produce data on an as-needed basis. Professional and technical staff to conduct socioeconomic and environmental studies, evaluate existing programs for continuation, initiate and evaluate new programs originating with rural government, and evaluate project proposals made by the private sector or other levels of government.
Revitalization Rapid expansion or diversification of economic base, population profile, housing market, social services support systems, physical infrastructure, land use activities, etc.	New data needed on available and required land, infrastructure, social services, and (local) finances to accommodate or promote revitalization New data or intelligence needed on private sector intentions, development spin-offs, and citizen preferences on rate, scale, and direction of revitalization	Professional and technical staff to identify needed data on land use, labor force, infrastructure, housing, educational, medical, and social services, etc. Information systems to acquire and process small area data (down to individual lot and enterprise level) that are timely, reliable, and accurate for monitoring rate, scale, and direction of revitalization (diversification and expansion). Professional and technical staff, to (1) analyze and synthesize data and prepare land use and financial plans according to management and fiscal capacity of rural governments; and (2) to conduct impact assessments of revitalization initiatives, including evaluation of associated or follow-up development activities.

Source: Barry S. Wellar. 1984. Information for decision making by rural public authorities. In *Local Leadership and Rural Development: Implications for Research and Extension*, Organization for Economic Cooperation and Development with the U.S. Department of Agriculture and the Virginia Cooperative Extension Service, p. 37. Washington, D.C.: U.S. Department of Agriculture.

nical resources to the information base of the community exemplify this approach to greater citizen participation in community development. In this case, the provision of technical assistance is designed to help local organizations, leaders, and officials identify the many ways that they can become partners in development. This may involve matching the information needs of the community with the information resources that already exist within local organizations. For example, some firms provide release time for employees to participate in community activities such as teaching classes in local schools. This concept can be extended to assisting local governments in preparing financial plans or grant proprosals, or in conducting business climate evaluations as part of a larger economic development strategy. In this way, local organizations become partners with local government by making "in-kind" contributions to information and knowledge-building activities.

Similarly, voluntary associations bring together local citizens with a variety of skills and interests. Such organizations can be encouraged to inventory the talents of their members and to determine if and how their members would be willing to work with other organizations or local government when there is a need for their particular skills. A guide to voluntary action resources could then provide information on the community's human resources and serve as the basis for network building among the community's local organizations.

Finally, communities need to know what works. Knowledge of action programs that have been developed to meet specific problems is valuable to the decision-making process. A strategy that focuses on illustrating the who, what, and how of actual development projects contributes to the knowledge base of a local community with what is, in effect, an action workbook of demonstration projects. Preston (1983, p. 92) developed such a program, Rural Community Action: Three Case Studies, that provides a case study report, a leader's guide, and a slide/tape set for local officials who are planning a community development project. The various materials outline how different types of community projects moved from initiation to implementation and highlight problems and issues that affected the outcomes. This strategy not only adds to the information base of the community but also builds the confidence of local decision makers since they have available reality-tested guides to action. But, as Preston notes, it requires comparative studies of underlying patterns in community development projects as well as realistic assessments of project outcomes. Unfortunately, there is not yet an adequate research base for this strategy.

Citizen Participation in
the Future.

A critical reading of the community development literature of the recent past would produce the question: What ever happened to citizen participation? While much lip service is given to the importance of citizen participation in community development activities, it has not always been emphasized in reality. Too often, community development has been done *to* a community of citizens rather than *with* them. The tragedy of this approach is explained by the proverb: Give a man a fish and he eats for one day, teach him to fish and he eats for a lifetime.

A critical evaluation of community development efforts over the last two decades, then, would have to conclude that many of these efforts have produced passivity and dependence on external agencies and have failed to empower the citizens of local communities. In a centralized political and economic environment wherein national governments have defined the parameters of development efforts, these outcomes may have been only ethically questionable. But today, with the devolution of so many functions to local governments and the explosion of responsibilities confronting these communities, the customary approaches to community development are pragmatically questionable.

If community development as a discipline and a practice is to be relevant to the needs of the communities of tomorrow, the challenge is to shift the focus of training and activities to the more difficult and time-consuming, yet eminently more effective, strategy of local capacity building. Blakely and Bradshaw (1982, p. 118) argue that "the basic problems in rural communities today are not related to resource deficiencies but to resource organization and allocation." These authors and others (Honadle 1982; Reid 1984) then suggest that governmental capacity building will be a critical community development activity in the future. But local capacity building that stops at the doors of county courthouses or local government offices will not succeed in the long run. There are many reasons, but primary among these are that local officials serve for relatively short periods of time, local governments do not have the resources to maintain large staffs of specialists, and most importantly, the field of local social action encompasses far more actors and organizations than do local officials and administrative units.

Thus, if community development efforts are to be enduring and to produce maximal results, they must engage all the people and organizations of a community in coordinated activities to improve their quality of life (Voth and Bonner 1978). It is in this broader meaning of local capacity building—expanding the base of citizen involvement, enhancing the leadership pool, and enlarging the information base of the community—that a successful future for community development will be found.

References

Blakely, E. J., and T. K. Bradshaw. 1982. New roles for community developers in rural growth communities. *Journal of the Community Development Society* 13(2):101–20.

Burns, J. M. 1978. *Leadership.* New York: Harper and Row.

Cleveland, H. 1982. Information as a resource. *The Futurist* 16(Dec.):34–39.

Esman, M. J., and N. T. Uphoff. 1984. *Local Organization: Intermediaries in Rural Development.* Ithaca, N.Y.: Cornell University Press.

Garcia-Zama, J. C. 1985. *Public Participation in Development Planning and Management.* Boulder, Colo.: Westview Press.

Garkovich, L., 1979. What comes after the survey? A practical application of the synchronized survey model in community development. *Journal of the Community Development Society* 10(1):29–38.

_____. 1985. Serving small community information needs through academic programs. In *Research in Rural Sociology and Development: Focus on Community,* Vol. 2, F. A. Fear and H. K. Schwarzweller, eds., pp. 257–73. Greenwich, Conn.: JAI Press.

Garkovich, L. and J. M. Stam. 1980. Research on selected issues in community development. In *Community Development in America,* J. A. Christenson and J. W. Robinson, Jr., eds,, pp. 155–86. Ames: Iowa State University Press.

Green, J. W., and S. C. Mayo. 1953. A framework for research in the actions of community groups. *Social Forces* 31(2):320–27.

Holland, J. B., K. E. Tiedke, and P. A. Miller. 1957. A theoretical model for health action. *Rural Sociology* 22(2):149–55.

Honadle, B. W. 1981*a. Capacity Building (Management Improvement) for Local Governments: An Annotated Bibliography.* Economic Statistics Service (Mar.). RDRR-28. Washington, D.C.: U.S. Government Printing Office, U.S. Department of Agriculture.

_____. 1981*b* A capacity building framework: A search for concept and purpose. *Public Administration Review* 41(Sept./Oct.):575–80.

_____. 1982. Managing capacity building: Problems and approaches. *Journal of the Community Development Society* 13(2):65–74.

Howell, R. E., I. L. Weir, and A. K. Cook. 1979. Public affairs leadership development. Pullman: Washington State University, Department of Rural Sociology.

Hunt, J. G., and L. L. Larson, eds. 1979. *Crosscurrents in Leadership.* Carbondale: Southern Illinois Press.

Johnson, D. E., L. R. Meiller, L. C. Miller, and G. F. Summers, eds. 1987. *Needs Assessment: Theory and Methods.* Ames: Iowa State University Press.

Kaufman, H. F. 1985. An action approach to community development. In *Research in Rural Sociology and Development: Focus on Community.* Vol. 2, F. A. Fear and H. K. Schwarzweller, eds., pp. 53–65. Greenwich, Conn.: JAI Press.

Kaufman, H. and K. P. Wilkinson. 1967. Community structure and leadership: An interactional perspective in the study of community. Social Science Research Bulletin 13. Mississippi State, Miss.: Mississippi State University.

Kellerman, B., ed. 1984. *Leadership: Multidisciplinary Perspectives.* Englewoods Cliffs, N.J.: Prentice-Hall.

Loomis, C. P., D. Ensminger, and J. Wooley. 1941. Neighborhoods and communities in county planning. *Rural Sociology* 6(4):339–41.

McGranahan, D. A. 1984. Local growth and the outside contacts of influentials: An alternative test of the "growth machine" hypothesis. *Rural Sociology* 49(4):530–40.

Molotch, H. 1976. The city as a growth machine: Toward a political economy of place. *American Journal of Sociology* 82(Sept.):309–32.

Preston, J. C. 1983. Patterns in nongovernmental community action in small communities. *Journal of the Community Development Society* 14(2):83–94.

Reid, J. N. 1984. Rural government capacity: Institutional authority and local leadership. In *Local Leadership and Rural Development: Implications for Research and Extension.* Organization for Economic Cooperation and Development. Proceedings from the Conference on Local Leadership and Rural Development. Colonial Williamsburg, Va., April 19–30.

Richards, R. O. 1984. When even bad news is not so bad: Local control over outside forces in community development. *Journal of the Community Development Society* 15(1):75–86.

Rossing, B. E., and D. K. Heasley. 1987. Enhancing public affairs participation through leadership development education: Key questions for community development research and practice. *Journal of the Community Development Society* 18(2):98–116.

Ryan, B. 1944. The neighborhood as a unit of action in rural programs. *Rural Sociology* 9(1):27–35.

Ryan, V. D. 1987. The significance of community development to rural economic development initiatives. Chapter 16 in *Rural Economic De-*

velopment in the 1980's: Preparing for the Future. Agriculture and
Rural Economy Division, ERS Staff Report No. AGE870724. Wash-
ington, D.C.: U.S. Government Printing Office, U.S. Department of
Agriculture.

Sanders, I. T. 1975. *The Community,* 3d edition. New York: Ronald
Press.

Santora, J. C. 1983. *Leadership: A Selected Guide to Periodicals, 1972–
1982.* Public Administration Series: Bibliography P-1190. Monti-
cello, Ill.: Vance Bibliographies.

Truman, B., C. H. Grether, L. Vandenberg, and F. A. Fear, with J. J.
Madden, L. Joesting, and W. J. Kimball. 1985. When the tire hits the
pavement: A case study of the dilemmas associated with conducting
action research. *Journal of the Community Development Society*
16(1):105–16.

Turk, H. 1970. Interorganizational networks in urban society: Initial
perspectives and comparative research. *American Sociological Review* 35(1):1–19.

Voland, M. E. 1986. Leadership and rural America. In *New Dimensions
in Rural Policy: Building upon Our Heritage* Joint Economic Committee Report, pp. 561–66. Washington, D.C.: U.S. Government Printing Office, June.

Voth, D. E., and W. S. Bonner. 1978. Citizen participation in rural development: Concepts, principles, and resource materials. SRDC Synthesis Series #6. Mississippi State, Miss.: Southern Rural Development Center.

Warren, R. L. 1978. *The Community in America,* 3d edition. Chicago:
Rand McNally.

Wellar, B. S. 1984. Information for decision making by rural public
authorities. In *Local Leadership and Rural Development: Implications
for Research and Extension.* Organization for Economic Cooperation
and Development. Proceedings from the Conference on Local
Leadership and Rural Development. Colonial Williamsburg, Va.,
April 19–30.

Yukl, G. A. 1981. *Leadership in Organizations.* Englewood Cliffs, N.J.:
Prentice-Hall.

11

Evaluation for Community Development

DONALD E. VOTH

Community Development. We must have a common conception of what community development is before we can evaluate it. Community development may be defined in many different ways. As a science, it is a description and analysis of the process of change in human communities. As a social movement, it is a set of values and aspirations, supported by a loose network of "believers." As social engineering, it is a set of applied strategies for bringing about change in communities. As a program, it is specific agencies which implement concrete interventions in communities to achieve specific objectives. (See Chapter 1, Table 1.1.) And, as a product, it is something that is available for the public to adopt and use, that is more or less attractive and more or less effective in achieving what the public wants from it.

Ordinarily, when evaluation of community development is considered, the universe of discourse is narrowed to community development as social engineering and/or as program. To us, then, it is (1) situations in which a group, usually locality-based (such as a neighborhood or local community), attempts to improve its social and economic situations through its own efforts with professional assistance and perhaps also through financial assistance from the outside, and with maximum involvement of all sectors of the community or group; or (2) situations in which a group or agency external to target communities sets about to try to achieve the same objectives as above. Usually community development involves the organization or mobilization of a local group with responsibility for guiding the community development process, the identification and mobilization of local leadership, the mobilization of citizen participation, the execution of needs assessments, and the implementation of selected projects.[1]

There seems to be relatively widespread agreement about certain core objectives of community development. These involve concrete improvements in communities, such as amenities and level of living, and, more abstractly and profoundly, improvements in the ability of collectives to make rational decisions about things that affect them and to bring these decisions to fruition through various forms of collective action. In some instances, more emphasis is placed on substantive achievements (e.g., improvements in economic well-being), and the community development process is there to achieve these.[2] In other instances, more emphasis is placed on the process aspects of community development. Nevertheless, the objectives listed above would probably be accepted by most community developers.

Analytically, however, this brief definition of community development leaves much to be desired. There remains a huge "black box"[3] of the processes whereby community improvements actually occur, and much disagreement about which strategies are most effective. Economists and geographers fill the black box with theories of regional science, central place theory, or economic processes derived from input/output theory. Political scientists focus on the formal and/or informal power and decision-making structures, and how they function. Sociologists fill the box with several alternative theories, from social movements, to power and the realignment of power relationships, to the logic of social networks or fields. In reality, of course, these are not mutually exclusive. Community development is simultaneously economic, political, and social; each represents a particular aspect of the community and of community change.

Whatever community development is analytically, in practice it is purposive interventions that are designed to achieve some or all of the goals identified above. A wide variety of interventions may be used; they vary in style and approach among agencies, among phases in the community development process, and among community development practitioners. The interventions are intended to influence generic community processes (the black box), with resulting improvements in economic well-being, decision-making ability, quality of life, and so on (see Table 11.1).

In the context of a particular set of interventions, a particular view of the community processes, and a particular set of outcomes, community development evaluation may try to answer the following ques-

Table 11.1. The Community Development Process

Inputs ⟶	Throughputs ⟶	Outputs
Community development interventions	Generic community development processes (the black box)	Community development impact

tions: (1) Were the interventions actually carried out, and to what extent? (2) Is the community development effort worthy – is community development a good "product"? (3) How can community development interventions be improved? (4) Did the interventions influence the community processes in the way expected or did they not influence them at all? (5) Did the interventions and the ensuing community processes lead to the expected outcomes or to any outcomes of significance? and (6) What unexpected results or side effects do the community development interventions have?

Evaluation Research. One of the important recent developments is that evaluation research is merging back into general social science research. Evaluators are less likely now than they were ten years ago to consider evaluation something unique and separate from the broader field of social research.

WHAT IS EVALUATION? Evaluation is not distinguished from social research by a particular methodology, but by (1) the imposition of specific forms of discipline on the collection and interpretation of information, (2) the variables examined, and (3) certain normative criteria – evaluation should be addressed to identifiable audiences that have a purpose for evaluation, and it should be designed and performed in such a way that they can use it (Patton 1978).

DISCIPLINED INQUIRY. Cronbach and Suppes (1969, p. 12) discuss the discipline of evaluative research as follows: "Disciplined inquiry has a quality that distinguishes it from other sources of opinion and belief. The disciplined inquiry is conducted and reported in such a way that the argument can be painstakingly examined. The report does not depend for its appeal on the eloquence of the writer or on any surface plausibility. The argument is not justified by anecdotes or casually assembled fragments of evidence."

Each subject matter has its own peculiar form of discipline. However, all involve the assumption that the argument must be susceptible to "painstaking examination" by others so that, using the same data and the same logic, others could be expected to reach the same conclusions. In the broadest sense, then, the scientific element in evaluation research is present to deal with the question of validity—validity of measurement and validity of the logic whereby conclusions are reached. And, it is important to note that the criterion of scientific validity applies to all methods, including qualitative methods. At the least, even with qualitative methods, it is desirable to know that another researcher could have reached the same conclusions by being explicit about how they were reached.

POLICY-RELEVANT VARIABLES. Evaluation is concerned with answering questions that someone can do something about. That is, it focuses on policy-relevant variables, at least some of which are manipulable, rather than on the generic concepts that underlie those variables.[4] These policy variables include, of course, the community development interventions themselves. But they also include environmental conditions leading to their success or failure.

STANDARDS FOR EVALUATION. The literature on evaluation has always had a strong normative tone, and, of course, evaluation is inherently a normative activity. Originally, this involved primarily arguments about which models of evaluation should be used and, in particular, exhortations to improve the technical adequacy of evaluation practice (Rossi 1969; Patton 1982, pp. 15–16). More recently, with the development of evaluation as an autonomous field of professional practice, professional standards for evaluation practice have been developed. They concern themselves with more than mere technical adequacy. The Evaluation Research Society has developed a set of standards (Patton 1982, pp. 16–18, 297–99; Evaluation Research Society 1980, 1982, 1984; Cronbach 1984). The same has been done for educational evaluation by the Joint Committee on Standards for Educational Evaluation, headed by Daniel L. Stufflebeam (Joint Committee on Standards for Educational Evaluation 1981). Standards also are available from the General Accounting Office and from the Office of the Auditor General of Canada (Evaluation Research Society 1984, p. 681).

Stufflebeam (1980) summarized the Joint Committee's work as follows:

> The standards that will be published essentially call for evaluations that have four features. These are *utility, feasibility, propriety,* and *accuracy.* And I think it is interesting that the Joint Committee decided on that particular order. Their rationale is that an evaluation should not be done at all if there is no prospect for its being useful to some audience. Second, it should not be done if it is not feasible to conduct it in political terms, or practicality terms, or cost effectiveness terms. Third, they do not think it should be done if we cannot demonstrate that it will be conducted fairly and ethically. Finally, if we can demonstrate that an evaluation will have utility, will be feasible and will be proper in its conduct, then they say we could turn to the difficult matters of the technical adequacy of the evaluation. (P. 90).

The Evaluation Research Society standards are arranged into six sections: (1) formulation and negotiation, (2) structure and design, (3) data collection and preparation, (4) data analysis and interpretation, (5) communication and disclosure, and (6) utilization. "These are listed roughly in order of typical occurrence, and all six of these phases are normally included in front-end analysis, evaluability assessment, formative evaluation, impact evaluation, and program monitoring. Secondary evaluations, however, may not include any new data collection or analysis. . . . The standards themselves take the form of simple admonitory statements" (Evaluation Research Society 1984, p. 684).

The norm that evaluation should have utility to someone—a dominant element in all of these standards—derives from the long and sad experience of evaluators who have learned that, unless there is an audience for evaluation, and unless the goals of this audience[5] are taken into consideration, the evaluation will not be used.

HISTORY OF EVALUATION. Evaluation has developed and matured since the original widely used volume by Suchman (1967); the influential work of Campbell and Stanley (1966); the development of professional and quasi-professional organizations of evaluators (American Evaluation Association, Evaluation Network, the Evaluation Research Society) and of evaluation newsletters and journals (*Evaluation Review, Evaluation Practice,* etc.); and the publication of annual reviews of evaluation since 1976—all of these works attest to a vigorous literature on evaluation.[6]

Much of the impetus for the development of evaluation research was the plethora of social programs of the 1960s, especially the War on Poverty but also the programs before 1960 to improve rural life in the United States and rural community development in the less developed countries. Community developers, of course, played key roles in the design of those programs, and many of the philosophical and operational tenets of community development were embodied in them. The literature on these programs contains important accounts of evaluation methods being devised and refined in turbulent social settings (Annals 1969; Clark and Hopkins 1970; Vanecko et al. 1970). Still, during its maturation process the evaluation research literature seems to have virtually abandoned community development. Indeed, it is very difficult to find any mention of community development, or social programs similar to community development, in any of the literature on evaluation, and community development literature seldom deals with evaluation.

TYPES OF EVALUATION. There are, of course, many different types of evaluation and indeed, many different ways of classifying the types (Forester 1975; Hudson 1975; Burton and Rogers 1976; Perkins 1977; Cosby and Wetherill 1978; Worthen and Sanders 1973; House 1980; Evaluation Research Society 1980; Patton 1981, 1982). The major methods of classifying evaluation research – when the classifications are analytical rather than ad hoc – involve the dimensions of purpose or intent of the evaluation; methodology, including types of data and analytic techniques used; the particular phase of the policy or program in which the evaluation is carried out; the nature of the relationship between evaluator and what is being evaluated; and, finally, the level of abstraction or epistemological perspective of the evaluation.[7]

However, the most frequently encountered classifications of types of evaluation are simply ad hoc, and, like evaluation methodologies themselves, tell as much about the classifier as about evaluation. House (1980), for example, classified evaluations into eight major types – systems analysis, behavioral objectives, decision-making, goal-free, art criticism, professional review, quasi-legal, and case study – admitting, all the while, that there are others he could have added. Patton (1982, pp. 45–47) identified thirty-three different types in a similar ad hoc fashion. Previously, having allowed his imagination free rein, Patton (1981, pp. 186–93) had listed 132 types, some of which are facetious but instructive.

The Evaluation Research Society Standards Committee classified evaluation into six types based on purpose or intent of evaluation and the evaluative activities carried out: front-end analysis, including such things as feasibility analysis; evaluability assessment, which focuses on determining whether—and how—a more formal evaluation can be carried out; formative evaluation, which provides developmental information for program improvement; impact evaluation, which aims to determine program or project results and outcomes; program monitoring, which includes a variety of in-course program tracking activities carried out by management; and evaluation of evaluation (Evaluation Research Society 1980, pp. 3–4, as quoted in Patton 1982, p. 44).

The criterion of classification that has stimulated the most debate is that of method. Evaluation literature shows a distinct bifurcation into two broad schools, which were referred to by Patton in 1978 as the "natural science paradigm of hypothetico-deductive methodology" (p. 203), on the one hand,[8] and a "holistic-inductive," or "qualitative" paradigm, derived most directly from anthropological field methods, on the other (p. 207).[9] The former, in its purest form, is characterized by the evaluation literature produced by quantitatively oriented sociologists, as found in the popular handbook by Rossi, Freeman, and Wright (1979). It hardly recognizes that other alternatives exist. The extensive evaluation literature of Campbell and Stanley (1966) and Cronbach (1979) also follows this paradigm, though not so dogmatically. The holistic-inductive paradigm is represented by the extreme, "goal-free" position taken by Scriven (1972), and, in highly usable form, by the works of House (1980), Stake (1975, 1978), and Patton (1978, 1982).[10]

Recently evaluation has become more and more eclectic, advocating use of multiple methods and de-emphasizing the contrasts between the extremes of methodology (Mark and Shotland 1987).

Evaluation of Community Development.

Although the history of community development does not make one optimistic that more or better evaluative information, if available, would have a significant influence on the popularity of community development to policymakers, we cannot abandon the responsibility of making such information available.[11]

What types of evaluation apply? What has been done in the literature? What unique problems arise? and What implications do all of these have for the future of evaluation in community development?

For community development, we classify evaluation along three of

the dimensions mentioned above: (1) the *function* of evaluation research, (2) the *phase* of the community development process within
which evaluation occurs, and (3) the research *method* or logic that is
used.

FUNCTIONS OF EVALUATION. The functions of evaluation can be arrayed along a continuum that represents the relationship of evaluation
to the community or communities (or the community development
process) being evaluated.[12] At one extreme, evaluation is part and par-
cel of that process. This is evaluation *in* community development and
is the first function of evaluation for community development. At the
other extreme, evaluation stands outside the process, examining the
entire community development enterprise. This is evaluation *of* community development, or, in the broadest sense, external evaluation.

Thus we identify three major functions of evaluation for community development. There is an internal function—contributing to the
process—and two external functions—assessing specific programs
and/or projects, and assessing the community development enterprise
as a whole.

Function 1: Contributing to the process. Evaluation plays an extremely important role within the community development process itself. It may be a central element in the community development intervention—it may even stimulate the action. Evaluation in community
development may include engaging community people themselves in
research, perhaps in a process of self-study (Truman et al. 1985),
through use of survey techniques, simulations, etc. (Woods and
Doeksen 1984). Evaluation is also a particular stage in the community
development process when community development follows these
phases: (1) determining goals, (2) setting priorities, (3) assessing resources, (4) engaging in action, and (5) evaluation.

Horst et al. (1972, pp. 302–4) point out that many current social
programs have specific goals and objectives that are characterized by
uncertainty and discretion. This is particularly true of community development. In fact, to many community development *is* assisting the
community to exercise its own discretion. Thus, this form of evaluation, where the target systems set their own goals, is important in
community development, especially in the formative stages of projects. Formative evaluation thus may frequently be used to serve the
function of evaluation *in* community development (Rutman 1977, pp.
57–71; Morris and Fitzgibbon 1978, pp. 24–68; Patton 1978). This

function of evaluation is similar to—perhaps the same thing as—social action research (see Voth 1979; Truman et al. 1985). Needs assessment also plays an important role in evaluation *in* community development.

Function 2: Assessing programs and projects. This is, perhaps, the most important role of evaluation for community development. Administrators and planners/evaluators, as well as community development practitioners, are the users of program and project assessments. Such research may be internal, in which case it usually focuses on comparisons of different approaches or on the processes whereby a program is being carried out. When conducted or demanded by an external source, it may be concerned with evaluating program implementation or impact with a view toward making decisions about the program or project (i.e., continuation, termination, expansion). External evaluation is concerned primarily with inputs and outputs and only secondarily with community processes, whereas internal evaluation, while not trying to generalize about these processes, focuses on explicating and improving them (see Table 11.1).

Function 3: Assessing the enterprise. This important function involves at least three somewhat distinct sets of questions. First, can community development achieve its stated objectives? Has it ever done so? The only evidence that is needed to answer these questions is one positive case. If it has been successful once, then we know that it can be successful again. And, of course, the evidence in this case is overwhelmingly positive. (See also Chapter 13.)

The second set of questions is more difficult. It concerns whether community development has, in general, achieved its objectives, or how the methods community development has used compare with alternative methods for achieving the same objectives. Even though community development can achieve certain objectives when programs or projects are properly implemented, attempts to achieve objectives certainly can also result in failure due to various factors (e.g., shoddy implementation, overextended efforts). And, of course, other approaches may be equally effective or more effective. Historical assessments, such as those done by Holdcroft (1978, 1984) and Blair (1981) have tried to answer these questions.

Third, both generic community research and community development evaluation contribute to generalizations about the community development process. It is to such research and evaluation that we look for general information about community development processes, and about how community development works and can be made to work.

PHASES OF COMMUNITY DEVELOPMENT PROJECT OR PROGRAM.
One of the most widely recognized distinctions among types of evaluation is that which is based on the stage of the project or program
during which the evaluation is performed. The distinction between
formative and summative evaluation is perhaps one of the most widely
accepted, and it is based on this criteria. Formative evaluation is performed early to help determine what a project or program can and
should achieve; summative evaluation is performed later to assess impact.[13] Another key concept is evaluation of implementation. It is
clear—as has been pointed out above—that potentially effective strategies of community development may fail if they are not implemented
correctly. Indeed, this is one of the most serious problems in carrying
out social interventions such as community development and may well
be one of the major reasons for the alleged failure of community development in the 1950s and 1960s.[14] Community development did not
really fail in the large-scale schemes that tried to implement it then; it
was never really tried because of ineffective implementation.

Thus, we have in typical sequence: (1) evaluation of implementation, (2) formative evaluation, and (3) summative evaluation. The latter
two could, perhaps, be referred to as "evaluation of process" and "evaluation of impact." Obviously the functions performed by evaluation
differ from one phase to another. To a significant extent the methods
vary as well.

METHODS OR MODES OF EVALUATION.   The most frequently used
typologies of evaluation, and much of the early debate about evaluation, are based on the methods used and focus heavily on questions of
the technical adequacy of these methods (Patton 1982, pp. 15–16). We
classify evaluation methods into four general categories (see Appendix
11.1).

The first three methods discussed below are usually concerned
with determining—in some way—input/output relationships from existing interventions. Their results are *ex post.* It is their nature that they
cannot be performed before the project or program is implemented,
since the input/output relationships are determined from the program
or project that is evaluated. The fourth set of evaluation methods is a
group of *derived* designs, which extrapolate the consequences of
known or assumed input/output relationships, either *ex post* or *ex ante.*

The classical experimental design, which frequently serves as the
ideal model for evaluation methodology, is commonly contrasted with
various less rigid, more qualitative methods.[15] We find evaluation de-

signs to be arrayed along a continuum from classical or quantitative designs to intuitive, descriptive, or case-study designs. The continuum has at least two important thresholds—the first as one moves from comparative to noncomparative designs, and the second as one moves from goal-based to nongoal-based designs.

Comparative, Goal-based Designs. Designs in which effect parameters (input/output relationships) are estimated by making explicit comparisons between experimental and control groups or across the range of independent variables, and in which community development objectives are predetermined, explicit, and measurable, are comparative, goal-based designs.[16] Originally, the ideal model was that of the classical experiment, and the work of Campbell and his associates on various evaluation designs referred to as "quasi-experimental" has always had this as its point of reference (Cook and Campbell 1979; Campbell and Stanley 1966). These designs focus on validity issues and thus provide the strongest possible basis for making causal inferences. But there have always been problems with their application in evaluation of social programs, and especially of community development. Researchers usually cannot exercise the control they require or imply; the designs usually allow estimation of only one parameter or a very limited number of parameters, and because of that they cannot avoid being very different from the processes that actually occur in community development; the results are usually not available in time— or, in any case, until the end of the project; and they cannot provide information about questions not posed in the original research design or facilitate midcourse corrections in program interventions.

Experimental and quasi-experimental designs are illustrated in Figure 11.1. This is Campbell and Stanley's (1966) basic design and determines or estimates one parameter (the treatment effect, T) at one

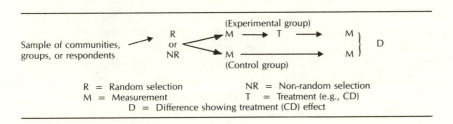

Figure 11.1. Experimental and Quasi-Experimental Comparative Goal-based Designs

time. Random assignment (R) makes the two groups completely equivalent, so the possibility that other differences might actually have caused the observed effects is eliminated, giving the design high internal validity. However, random assignment usually is impossible, so quasi-experimental designs must be used. This design frequently uses various measurements of the differences between the treatment and control groups, which introduces the following group of comparative goal-based designs.

More recently, multivariate designs and structural equation models of econometrics have gained in popularity, at least in the literature about evaluation if not in community development evaluation practice (Hawkes 1974; Miller, Voth, and Chapman 1984). In principle they can overcome the narrow focus of experimental and quasi-experimental designs through their ability to model a much larger proportion of the relevant social system in question. Measurement is one of the persistent problems in social program evaluation. Most key variables cannot be measured directly, leading to the frequent use of multiple indicators of underlying constructs. Significant recent progress has been made in causal systems modeling, which allows simultaneous estimation of measurement error and errors in equations so that the separate impact of these errors can be assessed (Miller, Voth, and Chapman 1984).

Still, there has been very little use of these sophisticated statistical models in evaluation in general, and especially in evaluation of community development. And, it seems unlikely that they will be widely used in the future. The reasons are evident from some of the problems peculiar to evaluating community development mentioned elsewhere. The demands that these models place on both theory and data are unrealistic for the current state−or, perhaps, the inherent nature−of community development.[17]

Noncomparative, Goal-based Designs. Disillusionment with comparative designs has been widespread for a variety of reasons. And, in some situations (e.g., evaluation of implementation) comparison is neither possible nor very meaningful. Thus, some evaluation concerns itself essentially with the question of whether predetermined norms or goals have been achieved, without making explicit comparisons of any kind.[18] A variety of evaluation models fall into this category. One that was popular in the late 1960s and 1970s was the discrepancy evaluation model developed by Provus and his associates (1968, 1969*a*, 1969*b*) and elaborated in a manual by Yavorsky (1977). Bennett and Nelson's (1975) widely quoted evaluation model for community development could easily be put into this category.

And, it is here that we find the style of evaluation that is, evidently, the most frequently used: assembling a team or task force of specialists—perhaps accompanied by an evaluation professional—to evaluate a program or project. Comparative data are used if they are available, but the essential evaluative judgments are a team or group process, judging performance against predetermined objectives and existing possibilities. Frequently, extensive evaluation reports are issued, complete with summaries of program goals, objectives, outputs, and inputs, and recommendations for future directions. The U.S. Agency for International Development (USAID) uses its "logical framework," which is very similar to the discrepancy evaluation model, to provide the essential causal frame of reference for project design, management, and evaluation.

Although these goal-based or norm-referenced, noncomparative evaluation methods appear simple, they can become very complex. Their essence is the establishment of measurable goals or standards of achievement—measurable objectives, in the terminology of education—and evaluation of performance against these goals or standards, within the context of key causal and environmental assumptions. These methods should specify the cause-effect logic whereby goals and objectives are to be achieved, detail specification of the system in which they occur, and explicate assumptions necessary for them to be realized. One of the most detailed contemporary examples is the project design and evaluation scheme used by the USAID, and presented in their project design and evaluation manual (USAID 1980). It emphasizes clear specification of the cause-effect relationships in the project, starting at the most abstract level with project goals, moving down to project purposes, then to project outputs, and, finally, to project inputs. In between project inputs and outputs are, of course, the whole gamut of project activities and processes, which are further explicated in other portions of a project proposal. As one proceeds from the more to the less abstract levels, the preceding (lower) levels are regarded as necessary but not sufficient conditions for achieving the following (higher) levels. This logic is, in turn, summarized in tabular form in the "logical framework" in Appendix 11.2. Another way to work out the details of a program's or project's cause-effect process is some form of activity networking, like activity precedence diagramming (see Appendix 11.3).

Thus, the essence of noncomparative, goal-based designs for evaluation is the prior explication of objectives, in measurable form, and the step-by-step causal process whereby the project is supposed to work. This has the effect of emphasizing the need for a close relationship between project design and project evaluation.

Noncomparative, Nongoal-based Designs.   As in the case of comparative designs, there has been dissatisfaction with noncomparative designs that still focus on predetermined goals or objectives, and with the determination of whether or not, or to what extent, these goals have been achieved. Thus there is a second major threshold in distinguishing evaluation research methodologies, including "goal-free" evaluation and other qualitative, more intuitive methods of evaluation. Goal-based designs are criticized for overlooking side effects, for bias resulting from attention to stated goals, and for inflexibility (Scriven 1972). Perhaps even more serious are distortions introduced into program or project implementation itself that arise from the expectation of being evaluated with goal-based or norm-referenced designs. Program staffs become strongly motivated to work toward the measures rather than toward genuine program or project objectives.

Weiss and Rein (1972), Cohen (1976), and Deutscher (1976) have advocated intuitive evaluation methodologies somewhat similar to the qualitative methodologies of social anthropology and functional sociology. Intuitive evaluation was also suggested by Patton (1978, pp. 220–28). Scriven (1972), the originator of goal-free evaluation, has consistently taken the most extreme position by proposing the disregard of program or project goals entirely, on the assumption that attention given primarily and often only to stated goals leads to bias and invalidity in evaluation design. He argues that a truer picture can be obtained through a process whereby the evaluator performs his or her own needs assessment,[19] rather than depending on stated goals and objectives, and then applies observation, design of checklists, interviews, and other research tools to draw out all pertinent information on program effects and outcomes. This includes both negative and positive effects that may have been unanticipated, judgments about ethical issues, and the intrinsic worth of program or project objectives.

Scriven has recently expanded his position by advocating the adoption of methods and approaches used in product evaluation, which is not the least concerned with manufacturer goals or objectives but rather focuses on market desires and needs and how well the product meets them. This follows what he refers to as a "consumerist" ideology (1981; 1984, pp. 68–69). Stake (1975) has taken a similar–though not so extreme–position, advocating a case study approach. Recently the term *naturalistic evaluation* has been added to the lexicon of reaction to hypothetico-deductive methods (Guba 1987).

Derived Designs.   Several other methods of evaluation are concerned not with estimating initial program effects, but with using known or assumed effect parameters to reach conclusions about over-all consequences. Whereas goal-based comparative designs are used to estimate input/output relationships *(ex post)*, these derived designs apply known input/output parameters *(ex ante)* in an attempt to anticipate the impacts of community changes before they occur and thus to evaluate them. Several different names can be found (they are not mutually exclusive): (1) policy simulation, (2) cost-benefit and cost-effectiveness analysis, (3) community impact modeling, and (4) *ex ante* financial and economic analysis of projects.

In community development, community impact modeling is probably the most widely used, especially for assisting community leaders to systematically project the economic, financial, and demographic effects of anticipated changes in the community's economic base (Woods and Doeksen 1984). In agricultural and rural development, the bible of *ex ante* financial and economic analysis of projects is Gittinger's *Economic Analysis of Agricultural Projects* (1982). This classification of types of evaluation for community development is summarized in Appendix 11.1; an indication of key sources and applicability to different situations is given for each type.

What Has Been Done in Community Development Evaluation?

As was pointed out above, the quantity of evaluation literature on community development is small and does not seem to be growing. The *Journal of the Community Development Society* has published only fourteen articles even vaguely dealing with evaluation since its beginning in 1970, six of which were published in the 1970s and eight in the 1980s.[20] One looks in vain for any treatments of community development in any of the general evaluation literature since the early 1970s. But, then, except for the late 1950s and early 1960s, when community development seemed to hold promise as a reform and development strategy for U.S. urban ghettos and rural areas and for less developed countries (LDCs), the professional literature has never published much of what was going on in community development. During the 1960s and early 1970s community development evaluation work was closely associated with various federal programs, and there was a substantial investment in evaluation of these programs.[21] More recently, since the demise of public interest and investment in community development programs, there has been little incentive for the kinds of evaluation of the community development enterprise or of community development programs that find their way into publications. And, evaluation *in* community development is virtually never written up, not to mention submitted to social science journals for publication.[22]

In fact, an evaluation literature, per se, could hardly be expected to arise from evaluation *in* community development, since the community people performing it have little reason to publish. The same holds true, to a lesser extent, for evaluation *of* community development programs and projects. Such evaluation is only stimulated when community development is part of the programs of major bureaucracies. Because support has declined, the reasons for a literature of community development evaluation—except for the concern of some academicians about understanding community development processes—have receded.[23]

Still, some research is available which dates back to the 1960s. In 1979 Congress mandated a national evaluation of the Cooperative Extension Service's programs. This resulted in an evaluation of community resource development nationwide (Extension Service 1980; Mulford et al. 1980; Davie and associates 1979; Science and Education Administration-Extension 1980). Voth and Miller expanded on previous evaluations of community development in southern Illinois (Voth 1975*a*, 1975*b*; Miller and Voth 1982) and performed a careful, comparative analysis of the impacts of community resource development in Arkansas during the years when these programs were popular (Voth, Miller, and Chapman 1983; Miller, Voth, and Chapman 1984). Lackey, Peterson, and Pine (1981) reported on a case of evaluation *in* community development in Missouri. At a more general level, Holdcroft published his obituary on community development in less developed countries (1978, 1984), and Blair (1981), in direct contrast, showed significant but quite unexpected consequences of the community development movement of the 1950s and 1960s.

Unfortunately, the predominant results of the evaluation of the community development enterprise as a whole have not been encouraging. The congressionally mandated evaluation viewed community resource development as a product to be evaluated by opinions of key actors who knew of the program. It concluded that community resource development had been positive, but, because of its peculiar perspective, it could say little about the ultimate impacts of it. The comparative studies performed by Voth and Miller (Voth 1975*a*, 1975*b*; Miller and Voth 1982; Voth, Miller, and Chapman 1983; Miller, Voth, and Chapman 1984) have been able to show only minor impacts, and some of these are perverse. Holdcroft's assessment was primarily a historical reconstruction and explanation of the "failure" of community development (see Chapter 13), and Batten's assessment of international community development agreed with that of Holdcroft's (1978). Earlier studies of community development in the War on Poverty (Vanecko, Orden, and Hollander 1970; Clark and Hopkins 1970) were no more encouraging in demonstrating general success of the community development enterprise or in estimating its precise impacts.

However, Blair (1981), who focused on the long-term empowerment of the poor, was impressed with the positive consequences of the community development movement both in LDCs and in the War on Poverty in the United States, even though the consequences were not exactly those that had been anticipated. And, although we have not been able to demonstrate with hypothetico-deductive methods that the rural community development efforts of the 1960s worked, it is now a matter of history that the decade did show a major rural renaissance. There is also substantial and continuing anecdotal evidence that community development can work, both in LDCs and in the United States.[24]

Characteristic Features of Community Development Evaluation.

There is, then, an anomaly. On the one hand, generalized, comparative evaluations of community development have seldom been able to demonstrate much in the way of impact. On the other hand, there is clear evidence that community development has frequently been successful. Most of the latter evidence is case study or anecdotal in nature. Finally, the current crisis in rural America and in poor communities makes community development attractive, even though evidence of its efficacy is not easy to find. What does this mean for evaluation? Most of all, it requires attention to the peculiar features of community development which complicate evaluation. These are discussed elsewhere (Voth 1979). The major peculiarities identified are (1) ambiguity of goals in community development, (2) absence of a model of the community development process; (3) inability of the researcher to control assignment to treatments; (4) weak effects, crude measurement, and small samples; and (5) political problems in the relationship between evaluation and program administrations. This assessment reflected the extraordinary concern with the technical adequacy of evaluation methods. At the present time two additional aspects of community development seem to be especially important for more effective evaluation: (1) the black box of community development, and (2) the scale at which community development occurs.

THE BLACK BOX OF COMMUNITY DEVELOPMENT PROCESS. It is clear that the processes whereby communities develop are complex and poorly understood. The black box is exactly that. This leaves the evaluator without knowledge about what he or she should focus on, what he or she should measure, or—more profoundly—what model of evaluation to use. This shortcoming becomes more evident as evaluators place greater emphasis on the use of program theory in evaluation (Bickman 1987). Community development, like many social programs, implies changes in values, attitudes, and behaviors of individuals, and even more, implies institutional and social structural changes. This is especially true of those programs that emphasize the process objectives of community development. Seldom have practitioners or community scholars been able to state with precision the operational measures of these changes or the processes whereby they occur.[25] Nor have they been able to specify in operational terms how one would distinguish a more developed community from a less developed one. This raises the initial question of whether community development can be evaluated at all (evaluability assessment) and justifies insistence on the need for basic analytic work on these community processes.

There do seem to be two somewhat distinct models of how community development works. The first is the administrative model and the second, the social movements model. The *administrative* model implies the need for careful attention to each and every detail, to each and every actor, in order for community development to succeed in the community. The responsibility of the community development practitioner, and of local leadership, is heavy. There are no significant social multipliers in the sense that, once begun, community development proceeds on its own. This was how community development was viewed by Mayer (1958) in the early, successful community development work in Upper Pradhesh in India. It can also be found in the attention to detail of the practical guides to community development prepared by early practitioners, both in the United States and in international community development.[26] This attention to detail is almost inevitably lost when community development goes nationwide as a large-scale bureaucratic program as well as when community development is implemented in a partial fashion by agencies such as the Cooperative Extension Service, whose commitment is only to certain phases or portions of the total community development process.

The *social movements* model, far more common in the literature of community development, implies that once community development practitioners and local leaders stimulate local community processes, local movements begin to operate on their own, resulting in significant social multipliers and a self-sustaining process. Thus, for example, community development has been characterized as the stimulation of local social movements (Richmond 1974). This view made community development very attractive to national planners in less developed countries. It implied a fortuitous efficiency—a short-cut—for development that was almost magic (Batten 1973, p. 36).

The evidence does not support the social movements model. Perhaps this is why so many failures have been observed. Expectations for community development were unrealistic; outcomes were both smaller and different from what was expected. We have found little evidence in comparative evaluations that community development has ever led to either broad-based changes in attitudes and behavior or autonomous community-wide improvement campaigns. During the War on Poverty, community development seldom led to major changes in community power structures. It has, however, been able to achieve certain specific, limited objectives; and it has frequently had unexpected impacts (Miller, Voth, and Chapman 1984).

Even more fundamentally, the administrative and social movements perspectives both imply an engineering or an intervention model of community development. Some agent provides an input, and the community changes in some predicted direction as the consequence. There are alternative views of what community development is, and the models of evaluation needed vary significantly (Shapiro 1984). For example, if community development is viewed as a product in a marketplace of ideas and strategies, as Scriven's view of evaluation might suggest, then the interventionist input-output analogy is no longer interesting. The rates of acceptance, the manner of use, and the relative satisfaction become dominant considerations.

THE SCALE OF CAUSE-EFFECT IN COMMUNITY DEVELOPMENT. The second fundamental problem community development poses for evaluation concerns the question of the scale at which it works when it is successful. Generalized, comparative evaluations ordinarily assume that community development is a highly localized process in which each local community responds to local community development inputs.[27] It makes sense, then, to compare experimental communities with control communities. It has always been recognized – in principle, at least – that this was inconsistent with such important views as the "mass society" perspective introduced by Vidich and Bensman (1958) in the 1950s and the closely related "great change" view introduced into the community and community development literature by Warren first in 1963. These views, the disappointing results of comparative evaluations of community development, as well as the intriguing argument of Blair, suggest that the consequences of community development are not to be found so much at the community level as in society-wide impacts on the position of the poor, in local government behavior, etc. To the extent this is true, cross-sectional comparative evaluation designs will not detect real effects, even when – as was done by Voth (1975*b*) and Miller, Voth, and Chapman (1984) – they use difference measures with a variety of lags. Indeed, sorting out the question of scale and appropriate comparative evaluation designs seems to be one of the most important current tasks for researchers interested in evaluating community development. If we could do this effectively, we might be able to determine what, if any, impact the various community and rural development programs had in bringing about the rural renaissance of the 1970s and the ghetto depopulation in urban areas during the same time period (Lemann 1986*a,* 1986*b*). It seems reasonable to suppose that Blair was right, that their impact was far greater than has been recognized, even though the consequences have left much to be desired.[28]

So, What Advice Can We Give?

What is most important in evaluation is the ability to (1) use a wide variety of methods; and, in doing so, to (2) match methods with the model of community development being evaluated, the stage in the community development program or process, and, most importantly, the major stakeholders' needs for the program and its evaluation. Evaluation functions very differently when community development itself is conceptualized differently. Of particular interest on this point is Shapiro's (1984) treatment of different models of organizational decision making, and the implications of such differences for evaluation, as well as Scriven's (1984) very intriguing suggestion that bureaucratic *outputs* might best be viewed as *products* in a free market and be evaluated as such. Shapiro (1984, pp. 635–39) identifies four models: (1) rational choice, (2) bureaucratic politics, (3) organizational process, and

(4) cognitive processing. The rational choice model is that assumed by most early evaluation literature which, at the same time, frequently mourned the fact that evaluation was seldom actually used. Shapiro also quotes Weiss' (1972, p. 2, as quoted in Shapiro 1984, p. 640) influential article: "Evaluation research is viewed by its partisans as a way to increase the rationality of decision making. With objective information on the outcomes of programs, wise decisions can be made on budget allocations and program planning. Programs that yield good results will be expanded; those that make poor showings will be abandoned or drastically modified." And, clearly, if community development is viewed as a product in a marketplace of ideas and strategies, the functions and methods of evaluation are drastically affected. The methods of the Consumers' Union and their *Consumer Reports* come to mind.

Even for the four views of community development identified earlier – science, social movement, social engineering, and program – evaluation tends to perform different functions and uses different methods. In view of this dependence of evaluation logic on program logic, evaluators have begun to place greater emphasis on explicit use of program theory in evaluation, bringing evaluation much closer to the broader field of social research than was previously the case (Bickman 1987). Thus, evaluation needs to be more closely tied to community development program theory, design, and implementation.

Depending on the nature of the community development interventions, the position of the stakeholders who want evaluative information may vary tremendously. In many cases, community people themselves are the major and, perhaps, only significant stakeholders in the process. The varying perspectives, again, imply the need for evaluation practice to respond eclectically.

Thus, evaluators must have a wide variety of skills and be able to use a wide variety of methods in *each* evaluation. Large-scale comparative evaluations based on complicated systems modeling and/or structural equation models require data that are not likely to be available and are of interest primarily to academics since policymakers frequently do not use them anyway. And, in any case, we already know that (1) community development can work, and (2) many – especially the rural and the poor – have no alternatives. What community developers need is evaluation to improve their practice, and, thereby, to defend their position, not evaluation to estimate whether all of their efforts put together add $1 million or $2 million – or nothing – to the GNP.

Patton has for some time emphasized the need for evaluators to be "grounded in the fundamentals." Part of what he means is that community developers must master a wide range of skills—all the skills needed for quantitative, comparative designs on the one hand; as well as the process skills needed to work effectively with groups in tense and difficult settings on the other; and, perhaps most important, the wisdom to know which is required when. The same point has been emphasized more recently by Chelimsky (1987), the director of the Program Evaluation and Methodology Division of the General Accounting Office. Some of the skills needed for evaluation are, fortunately, community development skills. So, community developers should not have too far to go to become good evaluators.

Still, we should simultaneously be paying attention to larger-scale evaluation, putting together comparative data sets with historical depth. Surely this is now possible, at least within states and perhaps nationally. It seems remarkable that government, colleges and universities, and major foundations have stimulated and supported community development in various ways for such a long period of time, but evidently not one has shown any sustained interest in compiling a comprehensive data base on what has been tried and what the consequences have been. When and if this is done, it will require that careful consideration be given to the relationship between the "middle range" theory of how community development happens and research design, including cross-sectional designs, time series designs, and the scale of effects.

Finally, community developers would do well to give attention to the systematic development and writing up of the many specific evaluation models, measurements, and so on that fall within each of the major approaches being used. This could result in a comprehensive resource, as have similar treatments in other fields where evaluation has been applied for some time (e.g., Cooley and Lohnes 1976).

Appendix 11.1. Classification of Types of Evaluation, Functions of Evaluation for Community Development, and Applicability

Model or Method of CD Evaluation Research	Functions of CD[a] Evaluation		
	Function 1: Facilitate CD Process	Function 2: Assess CD Project/Program	Function 3: Assess CD Enterprise
Comparative, Goal-based Designs: Experimental Quasi-experimental Causal systems modeling Recommended references: Campbell and Stanley (1963); Rossi, Freeman, and Wright (1979).	Seldom or never used	Occasionally used in large-scale comparative studies	Occasionally used in large-scale comparative studies
Noncomparative, Goal-based Designs: Discrepancy evaluation model Logical framework "Measurable objectives" Team of experts Recommended references: Yavorsky (1977) and USAID (1980).	Occasionally used, can be very useful to help CD group "work through" project	Very frequently used. This is the most common form of evaluation	Not applicable, except as such studies cumulate to provide evidence about the CD enterprise
Noncomparative, Nongoal-based Designs: Goal-free evaluation Responsive evaluation Consumer marketing model Recommended references: Scriven (1967, 1983); Patton (1980).	Frequently used. Seems to have potential for CD	Frequently used. Seems to have potential for CD	Not applicable
Derived Designs: Policy simulation Cost-effectiveness and cost-benefit analysis Impact modeling and assessment Project economic and financial analysis Recommended references: Gittinger (1982).	Impact modeling frequently used. Others useful for *ex ante* and "what if" analysis	Impact modeling frequently used. Others useful for *ex ante* and "what if" analysis	Probably not applicable, except in very special situations.

References recommended covering variety of designs: Patton (1978, 1980, 1981, 1982); House (1980); Miller (n.d.).

[a]Community development.

Appendix 11.2. The Structure of the "Logical Framework" or Logframe

Goal Levels			
Major Goal or Goals	Verifiable indicators	Means of verification	Critical assumptions

Purpose (Objective) Levels			
Purpose 1	Verifiable indicators (or end of project status)	Means of verification	Critical assumptions
Purpose 2	Verifiable indicators (or end of project status)	Means of verification	Critical assumptions

Output Levels			
Output 1	Verifiable indicators	Means of verification	Critical assumptions
Output 2	Verifiable indicators	Means of verification	Critical assumptions

[It is here, between project inputs and outputs, where the processes (the "black box") of the project are detailed. Typically this would be described in a detailed "technical analysis." (See Activity Precedence Diagramming in the learning exercises at the end of the book.)]

Input Levels	
Input 1	Quantitative and qualitative parameters
Input 2	Quantitative and qualitative parameters

The lower levels are necessary but not sufficient conditions for those immediately above. In the left column the item itself is described, in the next column indicators of achievement are identified, in the third column methods for verification are identified. Finally, in the fourth column critical assumptions necessary for the cause-effect relationship to be effective are made explicit. When a project is designed in this way, and the community development logframe is kept updated, evaluation becomes straightforward.

Appendix 11.3. Activity Networking

Another tool frequently used in project design, when, as with noncomparative goal-based evaluation designs, evaluation is either built into project design, or project logic must be reconstructed for evaluation to be carried out, is a set of methods of activity networking. The most well-known is Program Evaluation and Review Technique (PERT) which was developed in the 1950s. PERT can become very complicated.

A simpler version, which is very useful for evaluation, is called Activity Precedence Diagramming (APD). It is closely related to the input-throughput-output scheme of Table 11.1, and involves, simply, diagramming all key activities in terms of their order of precedence. An example for early phases of a typical community development project is given below:

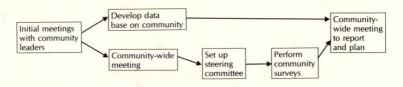

This allows the evaluator not only to identify key aspects of a community-development-project implementation process where measurements can be made, but also allows him or her to assist the project by identifying where problems may have occurred.

Notes

1. This is inherently a sociological definition of community development in that it focuses on what people do purposively and in groups and sees this as the cause of other changes. And, for poor communities and communities of limited resources, the sociological aspect is paramount, since social organization is the only resource at their disposal.
2. This is especially true of poor communities, in the United States or in less developed countries. Having few resources and less power, poor people find they have no alternative but to use local community development techniques to try to improve their lot.
3. No doubt many practitioners would dispute this. To them the process of organizing and mobilizing a community is neither mysterious nor complicated. And, perhaps social scientists err in inferring deep and complicated processes that can be understood only by profound thought, extensive reviews of "the literature," and expensive empirical research. Still, basic questions—whether community development can be expected to catalyze or ignite a local social movement which proceeds under its own momentum; or whether its effects are felt community-by-community in a highly localized fashion, responding directly to local level inputs; or whether community development efforts influence society in general; and similar questions—each imply completely different evaluation approaches, each beg for answers.
4. Of course, this distinction can easily be overemphasized. Without some understanding of underlying, generic community processes, appropriate policy variables usually cannot even be identified, or measured.
5. Strictly speaking, evaluations do not have an audience. They have audiences, referred to by evaluation specialists from political science as "stakeholders." A most important group of stakeholders for most evaluations, including community development evaluations, is the community and those within or outside the community who are attempting to bring about community development.
6. Rossi, Freeman, and Wright (1979, pp. 18–29), House (1980, pp. 21–43), and Patton (1978, pp. 14–19) provide brief overviews of the background and history of evaluation research.
7. See especially Scriven's (1984) discussion of evaluation ideology for a comparison of different ways of looking at evaluation.
8. This captures much of what House (1980, pp. 22–26) evidently means by his "systems analysis" type of evaluation, which includes both quantitative science methods for estimating effect parameters (*ex post*) and for extrapolating or applying those parameters (*ex ante*).

9. House (1980, pp. 39–40) refers to this as the "case study (transactional) approach" and points out that the "responsive evaluation" of Stake (1975, 1978) appears to be of this type as well.

10. It is misleading, however, to suggest that the qualitative approach rejects the use of quantitative techniques. Most of its advocates actually use a variety of methods, including qualitative methods, both because of the insights to be gained and because quantitative methods simply are not always applicable. It is also important to note that educational evaluators such as Campbell and Cronbach, who were originally identified with the hypothetico-deductive approach, have more recently advocated multimethod approaches (Patton 1982, p. 203). (See also Stuffelbeam 1972, 1974.)

11. This pessimistic assessment about the importance of evaluation is not unique to community development. In the early literature on evaluation, both Weiss and Rein (1972) and Patton (1978) concluded that significant use of evaluation in bureaucratic decision making was rare. Indeed, this important observation seem to have been decisive in Patton's own evaluation career as well as in that of many other evaluators. For Patton it resulted in a series of creative explorations and experiences designed to make evaluation used and useful (1978, 1980, 1981, 1982). Leviton and Boruch (1984) suggest, in a more recent article, that evaluators may have learned their lesson and may now be far more influential than they were originally.

    Chelimsky (1987) agrees, and traces a pattern of very significant growth and maturation in evaluation since the early 1970s. Patton's writing implies—at least to the extent this growth and maturation is real—that it may be because early evaluators focused upon the hypothetico-deductive method and emphasized primarily technical adequacy, but more recently evaluators have been able to adopt a much wider variety of methods and approaches. This is a change to which Patton himself contributed.

    Still, one could trace the history of strategy fads that have come and gone in U.S. rural and urban development and in U.S. international development efforts and find that not only community development, but virtually all of these development projects, have been adopted with little advance evidence of their efficacy, and most have been abandoned with little subsequent evidence that they succeeded or failed. Ideological considerations, turf battles by disciplines and bureaucracies, and the need for new administrators and new practitioners to implement their "new" ideologies and methods seem to be far more important than evaluative evidence.

12. This discussion, of course, takes an idealistic view. That is, we assume that the major function of evaluation is—in some sense—to evaluate. It is not cynicism but simple realism to acknowledge that a

very large proportion of evaluation is actually done to perform other functions such as to inject various more or less hidden agendas, to avoid or evade decisions about doing or not doing something, to create an environment favorable for implementing decisions already made, etc. There is little to be gained from cursing this reality. Hopefully, an eclectic approach can help to make the best of even some of the most thoroughly booby-trapped evaluations.

13. Patton (1982, p. 48) discusses the formative/summative distinction as follows:

> The summative versus formative distinction was originally made by Scriven (1967) to call attention to different evaluation purposes. Summative evaluations are done for the purpose of making judgments about the basic worth of a program. Formative evaluations are aimed at program improvement. Summative evaluations tend to focus on outcomes (though not necessarily to the exclusion of evaluating implementation), and formative evaluations tend to focus on program processes (though not necessarily to the exclusion of measuring outcomes). Over time these tendencies have led to an unfortunate deterioration in the precision of usage such that summative evaluation is sometimes taken to mean outcomes evaluation, and only outcomes evaluation, while formative evaluation is treated as equivalent to a process focus.

14. On this failure, see Holdcroft (1978, 1984), Blair (1981), and Chapter 13.

15. It is out of this "ideal" that the rich evaluation literature associated with Campbell and his various associates in education and others such as Rossi in sociology emerged. This literature has focused heavily on solving problems of design validity and — more recently — measurement validity in a comparative context using quantitative data.

16. Or, we could say comparative, *norm-referenced* designs.

17. Still, in principle, it should be possible to aggregate large community data bases for large-scale, aggregate analysis of community development in the United States, as was attempted, for example, by Voth, Miller, and Chapman (1983) and Miller, Voth, and Chapman (1984). Unfortunately, the data are not available, and data sources have deteriorated seriously during the last few years.

18. The term *norm referenced* means, essentially, the same thing as my *goal-based.* The key feature of these evaluation designs is the extent to which they focus on assessment of the achievement of predetermined goals and objectives.

19. And, thereby, independently determines client needs.

20. This judgment is, of course, somewhat arbitrary. I have been as inclusive as possible, but have no doubt missed some articles that dealt with evaluation tangentially. Following are the ones we identi-

fied: Cohen (1976); Daley and Winter (1978); Davie (1983); Gibson and Worden (1984); Hobgood and Christenson (1973); Lackey, Peterson, and Pine (1981); Mackeracher, Davie, and Patterson (1976); Phifer (1983); Truman et al. (1985); Vaughn (1972); Voth, Miller, and Flaherty (1982); Williams (1981); Woods and Doeksen (1984); and Yoak (1979). Of course, other social science journals do carry some evaluative literature on community development. Still, the small amount that appears in the discipline's major journal is an indication of the importance given to it.

21. See Voth and Jackson (1980) for a review of the evaluative literature on citizen participation in rural and urban community development. Most of the evaluative literature on community development, including early evaluations of the Community Development Block Grant (CDBG) program, is reviewed there.

22. But, see the interesting article by Lackey, Peterson, and Pine (1981).

23. Even this role has not been easy to sustain. Nothing can make an academician less popular than to volunteer independently to evaluate someone's favorite program. Part of the reason for the lack of interest in community development evaluation may be that sociologists – and rural sociologists – closely associated with it have learned this lesson too well.

24. The most remarkable case, which is reviewed more thoroughly elsewhere in this volume (see Chapter 13), is the early community development work supported by the Ford Foundation in the 1950s. It had very significant early successes, even in increasing agricultural production before the miracles of the green revolution had been heard of.

25. We must go back as far as 1976, to the important essay by Cottrell, to find a serious attempt to conceptualize the goals of process-oriented community development; or to the earlier and more abstract conceptualizations of Kauffman (1959) or Wilkinson (1972). However, these both involve aspects of community relationships that are so fundamental that one wonders whether it ever made sense to suppose that practitioners could manipulate or engineer them one community at a time.

26. See, for example, Poston (1953*a*, 1953*b*, 1976), and Warren (1963).

27. Thus, Voth (1975*b*) compared fifty-one southern Illinois communities, some of which had community development projects and some of which did not, over a period of twenty years. The logic was, of course, that the individual communities that had community development should have "done better" than those that did not.

28. It is encouraging to note that evaluation practice is now tending to merge back into the social sciences from which it emerged as, it was frequently argued, a "different" kind of research. This trend is being

expressed in terms of the need to use program theory in evaluation (Bickman 1987). For too long it has been assumed that evaluation could be carried out without the aid of social theory.

References

Annals of the American Academy of Political and Social Science. 1969. Special issue on the War on Poverty, Vol. 385 (Sept.).

Batten, T. R. 1973. The major issues and future direction of community development. *Journal of the Community Development Society* 4(2):34–44.

Bennett, C. F., and D. L. Nelson. 1975. Analyzing impacts of community development. State College: Mississippi State University, Southern Rural Development Center.

Bickman, L., ed. 1987. *Using Program Theory in Evaluation.* San Francisco: Jossey-Bass Publishers.

Blair, H. W. 1981. The political economy of participation in local development programs: Short-term impasse and long-term change in South Asia and the United States from the 1950's to the 1970's. Ithaca, N.Y.: Cornell University, Rural Development Committee.

Burton, J. E., Jr., and D. L. Rogers. 1976. A model for evaluating development programs. Ames: Iowa State University, North Central Regional Center for Rural Development.

Campbell, D. T., and J. C. Stanley. 1966. *Experimental and Quasi-Experimental Designs for Research.* Boston: Houghton Mifflin Co.

Chelimsky, E. 1987. What have we learned about the politics of program evaluation? *Evaluation Practice* 8(1):1–21.

Clark, K., and J. Hopkins. 1970. *A Relevant War against Poverty: A Study of Community Action Programs and Observable Change.* New York: Harper and Row.

Cohen, M. W. 1976. A look at process: The often ignored component of program evaluation. *Journal of the Community Development Society* 7(1):17–23.

Cook, T. D., and D. T. Campbell. 1979. *Quasi-Experimentation: Design and Analysis Issues for Field Settings.* Boston: Houghton Mifflin Co.

Cooley, W. W., and P. R. Lohnes. 1976. *Evaluation Research in Education.* New York: Wiley.

Cosby, A. G., and G. R. Wetherill, eds. 1978. A synthesis: Resources in evaluation for rural development. State College: Mississippi State University, Southern Rural Development Center, SRDC Synthesis Series, No. 2.

Cottrell, L. S., Jr. 1976. The competent community. In *Further Explorations in Social Psychiatry,* B. H. Kaplan, ed. New York: Basic Books.

Cronbach, L. J. 1979. *Design of Evaluations.* Stanford: Stanford Evaluation Consortium.

———. 1984. In praise of uncertainty. In *Evaluation Studies: Annual Review,* R. F. Conner, D. G. Altman, and C. Jackson, eds., Vol. 9, pp. 693–702.

Cronbach, L. J., and P. Suppes. 1969. *Research for Tomorrow's Schools: Disciplined Inquiry for Education.* New York: Macmillan.

Daley, J. M., and T. Winter. 1978. An evaluation: Intercultural use of community development. *Journal of the Community Development Society* 9(2):62–75.

Davie, L. 1983. Community development in the Cooperative Extension Service. *Journal of the Community Development Society* 14(2):95–106.

Davie, L. and associates. 1979. *Community Resource Development: A Description Based on the Analysis of 52 Case Studies Using the Shared Process Evaluation System.* Toronto: Lynn Davie and associates.

Deutscher, I. 1976. Toward avoiding the goal-trap in evaluation research. In *The Evaluation of Social Programs,* C. Abt, ed. Beverly Hills, Calif: Sage.

Evaluation Research Society. 1980. Standards for evaluation (draft). Washington, D.C.: Evaluation Research Society.

Evaluation Research Society, Standards Committee. 1982. Evaluation Research Society standards for program evaluation. In *Standards for Evaluation Practice (New Direction for Program Evaluation, No. 15),* pp. 7–19. New York: Jossey-Bass Publishers.

———. 1984. Evaluation Research Society standards for program evaluation. In *Evaluation Studies Annual Review,* R. F. Conner, D. G. Altman, and C. Jackson, eds. Vol. 9, pp. 680–92.

Extension Service, USDA. 1980. Community and rural development: National Extension evaluation project. Washington, D.C.: Agricultural Extension Service, U.S. Department of Agriculture.

Forester, J. 1975. The practice of evaluation and policy analysis. Washington, D.C.: Institute of Urban and Regional Development, Working Paper No. 257.

Gibson, L. J., and M. A. Worden. 1984. A citizen's handbook for evaluating community impacts: An experiment in community education. *Journal of the Community Development Society* 15(1):27–44.

Gittinger, J. P. 1982. *Economic Analysis of Agricultural Projects.* Baltimore: The Johns Hopkins Press.

Guba, E. G. 1987. What have we learned about naturalistic evaluation? *Evaluation Practice* 8(1):23–43.

Hawkes, R. 1974. Structural equations in evaluation research. Paper presented at the Institute on Methodological Concerns in Evaluational Research, Loyola University.

Hobgood, T. N., and J. A. Christenson. 1973. A systematic perspective of applied research in community development. *Journal of the Community Development Society* 4(1):100–108.

Holdcroft, L. E. 1978. The rise and fall of community development in developing countries, 1950–65: A critical analysis and an annotated bibliography. East Lansing: Michigan State University, Department of Agricultural Economics, MSU Rural Development Paper, No. 2.

_____. 1984. The rise and fall of community development, 1950–65: A critical assessment. In *Agricultural Development in the Third World,* C. K. Eicher and J. M. Staatz, eds., pp. 46–58. Baltimore: The Johns Hopkins Press.

Horst, P., J. N. Nay, J. W. Scanlon, and J. S. Wholey. 1972. Program management and the federal evaluator. *Public Administration Review* 34(4):300–308.

House, E. R. 1980. *Evaluating with Validity.* Beverly Hills, Calif.: Sage.

Hudson, B. 1975. Domains of evaluation. *Social Policy* 6(2):79–89.

Joint Committee on Standards for Educational Evaluation. 1981. *Standards for Evaluations of Educational Programs, Projects, and Materials.* New York: McGraw-Hill.

Kaufman, H. F. 1959. Toward an interactional conception of community. *Social Forces* 38(1):9–17.

Lackey, A. S., M. Peterson, and J. Pine. 1981. Participatory evaluation: A tool for community development practitioners. *Journal of the Community Development Society* 12(1):83–102.

Lemann, N. 1986a. The origins of the underclass. *The Atlantic Monthly* 257(6):31–55.

_____. 1986b. The origins of the underclass. *The Atlantic Monthly* 258(1):54–68.

Leviton, L. C., and R. F. Boruch. 1984. Contributions of evaluation to education programs and policy. In *Evaluation Studies: Annual Review,* R. F. Conner, D. G. Altman, and C. Jackson, eds., Vol. 9, pp. 597–632.

Mackeracher, D., L. Davie, and T. Patterson. 1976. Evaluation and development: Shapes approach. *Journal of the Community Development Society* 7(2):4–17.

Mark, M. M., and R. L. Shotland, eds. 1987. Multiple methods in program evaluation. In *Volumes on New Directions for Program Evaluation.* San Francisco: Jossey-Bass Publishers.

Mayer, A. 1958. *Pilot Project, India.* Berkeley: University of California Press.

Miller, M. K., and D. E. Voth. 1982. Evaluation of rural health service programs using pooled cross-section and time series data. *Evaluation Review* 6(1):7–59.

Miller, M. K., D. E. Voth, and D. D. Chapman. 1984. Estimating the effects of community resource development efforts on county quality of life. *Rural Sociology* 49(1):37–66.

Morris, L. L., and C. T. Fitzgibbon. 1978. *Evaluator's Handbook.* Beverly Hills, Calif.: Sage.

Mulford, C., G. E. Klonglan, R. D. Warren, R. C. Powers, M. L. Maas, and L. M. Tillotson. 1980. Impact of Extension's community resource development projects: A study involving state program leaders, Extension workers, and knowledgeable citizens. Ames: Iowa State University, Department of Sociology and Anthropology, Sociology Report, No. 146 (January).

Patton, M. Q. 1978. *Utilization-Focused Evaluation.* Beverly Hills, Calif.: Sage.

_____. 1980. *Qualitative Evaluation Methods.* Beverly Hills, Calif.: Sage.

_____. 1981. *Creative Evaluation.* Beverly Hills, Calif.: Sage.

_____. 1982. *Practical Evaluation.* Beverly Hills, Calif.: Sage.

Perkins, D. N. T. 1977. Evaluating social interventions: A conceptual scheme. *Evaluation Quarterly* 1(4):639–56.

Phifer, B. 1983. Review of community and rural development: National Extension evaluation project. (Washington, D.C.: Agricultural Extension Service, U.S. Department of Agriculture, 1980). *Journal of the Community Development Society* 14(1):96–98.

Poston, R. W. 1953*a. Democracy Is You: A Guide to Citizen Action.* New York: Harper and Row.

_____. 1953*b. Democracy Speaks Many Tongues.* New York: Harper and Row.

_____. 1976. *Action Now! A Citizen's Guide to Better Communities.* Carbondale: Southern Illinois University Press.

Provus, M. 1968. *Discrepancy Evaluation.* Berkeley: McCutchan.

_____. 1969*a. Discrepancy Evaluation Model, 1969.* Pittsburgh: Pittsburgh Public Schools.

_____. 1969*b.* Evaluation of ongoing programs in the public school system. In *Educational Evaluation: New Roles, New Means,* R. W. Tyler ed., pp. 242–83. Chicago: National Society for the Study of Education.

Richmond, L. 1974. Active community thought: Myth and reality of a community development program. Master's thesis, Southern Illinois University, Department of Community Development.

Rossi, P. H. 1969. Practice, method, and theory in evaluating social-action programs. In *On Fighting Poverty,* James L. Sundquist, ed., pp. 217–34. New York: Basic Books.

Rossi, P. H., H. E. Freeman, and S. R. Wright, eds. 1979. *Evaluation: A Systematic Approach.* Beverly Hills, Calif.: Sage.

Rutman, L. 1977. *Evaluation Research Methods.* Beverly Hills, Calif.: Sage.

Science and Education Administration-Extension. 1980. Evaluation of economic and social consequences of Cooperative Extension programs. Washington, D.C.: SEA-Extension, U.S. Department of Agriculture (January).

Scriven, M. 1967. The methodology of evaluation. In *Perspectives on Curriculum Evaluation,* R. Tyler, R. Gagne, and M. Scriven, eds. AERA Monograph Series on Curriculum Evaluation, No. 1. Chicago: Rand McNally.

———. 1972. Pros and cons about goal-free evaluation: Evaluation comment. *Journal of Educational Evaluation* 3(4):1–4.

———. 1981. Product evaluation. In *New Models of Program Evaluation,* N. Smith, ed. Beverly Hills, Calif.: Sage.

———. 1984. Evaluation ideologies. In *Evaluation Studies: Annual Review,* R. F. Conner, D. G. Altman, and C. Jackson, eds. Vol. 9, pp. 49–80.

Shapiro, J. Z. 1984. Conceptualizing evaluation use: Implications of alternative models of organizational decision making. In *Evaluation Studies: Annual Review,* R. F. Conner, D. G. Altman, and C. Jackson, eds., Vol. 9, pp. 633–45.

Stake, R. E. 1975. Program evaluation, particularly responsive evaluation. Kalamazoo: Western Michigan University, Evaluation Center, College of Education, Occasional Paper No. 5. Also in *Rethinking Educational Research,* W. B. Dockrell and D. Hamilton, eds. 1980. London: Hodder and Stoughton.

———. 1978. The case study method in social inquiry. *Educational Research* 7(2):5–8.

Stuffelbeam, D. L. 1972. Should or can evaluation be goal-free? Evaluation comment. *Journal of Educational Evaluation* 3(4):4–5.

———. 1974. Meta-evaluation. Kalamazoo: Western Michigan University, Evaluation Center, College of Education, Occasional Papers, No. 3.

———. 1980. An interview with Daniel L. Stuffelbeam. *Educational Evaluation and Policy Analysis* 2(4):85–90.

Suchman, E. A. 1967. *Evaluative Research: Principles and Practice in Public Service and Social Action Programs.* New York: Russell Sage Foundation.

Truman, B., C. H. Grether, L. Vandenberg, and F. A. Fear with J. J. Madden, L. Joesting, and W. J. Kimball. 1985. When the tire hits the pavement: A case study of the dilemmas associated with conducting action research. *Journal of the Community Development Society* 16(1):105–16.

U.S. Agency for International Development (USAID). 1980. *Design and Evaluation of Aid-Assisted Projects.* Washington, D.C.: The U.S. Agency for International Development.

Vanecko, J. J., S. R. Orden, and S. Hollander. 1970. Community organization efforts, political and institutional change, and the diffusion of change produced by community action programs. Rep. 122. Chicago: National Opinion Research Center.

Vaughn, G. F. 1972. Evaluating a community development institute. *Journal of the Community Development Society* 3(1):30–39.

Vidich, A. J., and J. Bensman. 1958. *Small Town in Mass Society.* Princeton, N.J.: Princeton University Press.

Voth, D. E. 1975*a*. Problems in evaluating community development. *Journal of the Community Development Society* 6(1):147–62. Also in *Community Development Research: Concepts, Issues, and Strategies,* E. J. Blakely, ed., 153–74. New York: Human Sciences Press, 1979.

_____. 1975*b*. Evaluation of community development programs in Illinois. *Social Forces* 53(4):635–46.

_____. 1979. Social action research in community development. In *Community Development Research: Concepts, Issues, and Strategies,* E. J. Blakely, ed. New York: Human Sciences Press, pp. 67–81.

Voth, D. E., and V. N. Jackson. 1980. Evaluating citizen participation: Rural and urban community development. Washington, D.C.: Center for Responsive Governance, Working Paper Series, No. 80-01.

Voth, D. E., M. K. Miller, and D. M. Chapman. 1983. Estimating the effects of community resource development efforts on county quality of life: A final report. Mississippi State, Miss.: Southern Rural Development Center, Final report submitted in completion of a cooperative agreement for research on the impacts of Community Resource Development.

Voth, D. E., M. K. Miller, and J. Flaherty. 1982. The impact of differential communication structures on rural community development efforts. *Journal of the Community Development Society* 13(1):43–58.

Warren, R. L. 1963. *The Community in America.* Chicago: Rand McNally.

Weiss, R. S., and M. Rein. 1972. The evaluation of broad-aim programs: Difficulties in experimental design and an alternative. In *Evaluating Action Programs: Readings in Social Action and Education,* C. H. Weiss, ed., pp. 236–49. Boston: Allyn and Bacon.

Wilkinson, K. P. 1972. A field-theory perspective for community development research. *Rural Sociology* 37(1):43–52.

Williams, A. S. 1981. Training rural citizens: An evaluation of a leadership training program. *Journal of the Community Development Society* 12(1):63–82.

Woods, M. D., and G. A. Doeksen. 1984. A simulation model for community development planning. *Journal of the Community Development Society* 15(2):47–58.

Worthen, B. R., and J. R. Sanders. 1973. *Educational Evaluation: Theory and Practice.* Worthington, Ohio: Charles A. Jones.

Yavorsky, D. K. 1977. Discrepancy evaluation: A practitioner's guide. Charlottesville: University of Virginia, Evaluation Research Center.

Yoak, M. O'Neill. 1979. Research and community development: A practitioner's viewpoint. *Journal of the Community Development Society* 10(1):39–48.

12

An Overview of Community Development in America

BRYAN M. PHIFER
with
E. FREDERICK LIST
and BOYD FAULKNER

C OMMUNITY DEVELOPMENT in America has had its roots in rural life, basically since the late nineteenth century. Some would argue that its roots go back further–even to Jamestown. Using the criteria of self-reliance and initiative, they would certainly have some ground for this argument. On the other hand, the earliest communities in America were often directed in an authoritarian manner and survival was the prime objective. By the time of Alexis de Tocqueville's tour of the country in the 1830s, both democracy and a concern for self-improvement were evident. His book *Democracy in America* provides rare insight into what made the country tick, both philosophically and socially. Indeed, he observed that

> Americans of all ages, all stations in life, and all types of dispositions are forever forming associations. There are not only commercial and industrial associations in which all take part, but others of a thousand different types–religious, moral, serious, futile, very general and very limited, immensely large and very minute.
>
> Americans combine to give fetes, found seminaries, build churches, distribute books, and send missionaries to the antipodes. Hospitals,

prisons, and schools take shape in that way. . . . In every case, at the head of any new undertaking, where in France you would find the government or in England some territorial magnate, in the United States you are sure to find an association. (Tocqueville 1966, p. 485)

The proponents of community development are a varied lot and have established a confusing number of models. Examples include the following:

1. Utopian movements or planned types of religious communities such as the Shakers, Dunkards, Mennonites, Amish, Hutterites, and Mormons, who formed isolated groups of communities, most of which supported tradition rather than change and were highly authoritarian

2. Special movements or settlements such as Brook Farm

3. Cooperatives, credit unions, farm organizations, community organizations, neighborhood councils, and the like, all of which tend to support change

4. Civic and service clubs

5. Business and industrial groups such as the Sears Foundation and utility companies which support community improvement efforts

6. Community organizations and health and welfare councils with a strong social work emphasis

It is ambiguous to include all activities based on a self-help concept under the rubric of community development, since community development is holistic and not focused on special interests or piecemeal projects. It goes beyond sporadic joint efforts, such as barn raisings or clean-up, paint-up campaigns; neither is it social welfare for others. Self-help has long been a part of the American heritage. Community development as we know it today—the purposeful attempt to improve communities under democratic conditions of participation— did not begin to emerge until the late nineteenth and early twentieth centuries. It did not burst on the scene suddenly. Instead, a convergence of a number of influences ultimately grew into the field of community development.

Roots of Community Development.   Major recognition of the need to improve rural life came as a result of the Country Life Movement and President Theodore Roosevelt's Country

Life Commission. The radical agrarian mood and proposals of the Populist party "had grown increasingly ugly in response to the farm crisis that had escalated during the last quarter of the nineteenth century. . . . The Country Life Movement emerged as an urban sponsored alternative to the radical economic proposals of the Populists" (Summers 1986, p. 348). Many of the concerns voiced by the movement and articulated more sharply by the commission centered on the inadequacies of rural communities. Commission recommendations gave impetus to the growing demand for the U.S. Department of Agriculture (USDA) and the land-grant colleges to take a more active role in the life of rural Americans. Out of this movement arose the Cooperative Extension Service as provided by the Smith-Lever Act of 1914. The report of the House Committee on Agriculture in submitting the bill included these guidelines:

> The theory of the bill is to extend this system to the entire country by providing for at least one trained demonstrator or itinerant teacher for each agricultural county, who in the very nature of things must give leadership and direction along all lines of rural activity – social, economic, and financial. . . . He is to assume leadership in every movement, whatever it may be, the aim of which is better farming, better living, more happiness, more education, and better citizenship. (U.S. Congress 1915, p. 5)

This philosophy of extension was in keeping with that proposed by the Committee on Extension Work of the Association of American Agricultural Colleges and Experiment Stations. The association had been working for a number of years to obtain federal support for extension work to help meet the growing demand for such education. In the *History of Agricultural Extension Work,* Alfred Charles True (1928) states:

> During the first decade of the twentieth century, the work connected with farmers' institutes and other forms of agricultural extension work in which the land-grant colleges participated increased so rapidly in extent and variety that these institutions had great difficulty in meeting the demands on them in this direction without impairing their resident teaching and research. A demand therefore arose for federal appropriations for extension work, partly to stimulate increased state appropriations for this purpose. (P. 100)

At the meeting of the association in Portland, Oregon, in August 1909, the Committee on Extension work repeated its recommendation for federal appropriations for extension work and developed a proposed plan that "defines extension work broadly yet closely. Defines agriculture and rural life so as to include instruction and aid in any phase of this field—in subjects technical and scientific, concerning business management, home making, sanitation; and economic, social, and moral subjects. Indicates that extension work is for adults and youth and children, and for people *in towns and cities as well as in the open country*" (True 1928, p. 102).

The influence of the Cooperative Extension Service on community development, especially in rural areas, has been widely recognized. In his annual report of extension work for 1923, C. B. Smith, then director of the States Relation Service of the USDA, stated, "The maxim that all programs of extension work should be based on an analysis of local or community needs has been given increasing support, as shown by the greater number of community programs developed throughout the United States. More than 21,000 communities . . . have local committees or clubs which join with Extension agents in developing and working out local programs of work" (True 1928, p. 175).

Thus it was apparent from early extension workers' experiences that the involvement of local people in identifying needs and developing programs was essential to successful extension work. True points out, "Extension forces were also realizing that they could not reach large numbers of people effectively without the active cooperation of many local leaders. They therefore increased their efforts to get beyond the county organization supporting their work and to build their programs on a community basis" (True 1928, p. 175).

Whether this philosophy was basically self-serving or whether it truly sought to meet community needs is impossible to determine. Suffice it to say that the successful extension worker had to develop programs with people rather than for people.

The earliest community clubs under the sponsorship of the Cooperative Extension Service started in the South in the 1920s. This movement for organized communities was directed at improving the welfare of the people not only in communities but also in the surrounding countryside. The community club or organized community movement probably originated in Mississippi (Kaufman 1978), and one such club in Mississippi, Oktoc, has been active for nearly sixty years. Gradually, the organized community movement spread to other southern states. Although extension work in the South was segregated at that time, community clubs also were widely used in black communities. J. A. Evans of the USDA observed in 1923, "Some form of community organization . . . is utilized in each county that has a Negro agent.

Community clubs elect local leaders, help make programs of work, raise funds for club equipment, and for premiums at local fairs and exhibits, provide social entertainment, and assist generally in promoting various phases of the extension program for their community and county" (True 1928, p. 191).

Although the early Cooperative Extension Service centered much attention on community development, not until the mid-1950s did it take formal action to institutionalize community development as a major program effort nationwide.

Rural Community Organization.   President

Roosevelt's Country Life Commission determined that a major problem of rural people was lack of organization. As a result, several states (including Georgia, Kentucky, Mississippi, Missouri, New York, North Carolina, West Virginia, and Virginia) undertook community organization work. Many states used a community scorecard for measuring and scoring community efforts. Much of this early effort was under the direction of rural sociologists from colleges of agriculture, and many of these persons were ordained ministers who were sensitive to the need for social improvement in rural areas.

Rural sociologists concentrated on rural community organization in the years following World War I, with much work being stimulated by research grants offered by the USDA. Carl Taylor, a leader in both the area of rural community organization and research related to rural communities, observed in a review of early rural sociology research, "Indeed it is more than possible that the opportunities for these early studies would not have opened if the building of research methodology or social theory, instead of interest in situations, had been insisted upon" (Taylor 1958, p. 188).

Some claim that for several years immediately following World War II sociologists "virtually abandoned the rural community as an object of study on the assumption that it had been eclipsed by the great changes of mass society" (Summers 1986, p. 349). This view was very shortsighted and, in fact, rural America increasingly became the object of large-scale public and private development efforts from the mid-1950s through the 1970s.

One of the first books on community development was Frank Farrington's *Community Development: Making the Small Town a Better Place to Live in and a Better Place in Which to Do Business,* published in

1915. It is a handbook and guide in community organization that focuses on the economic aspects of community improvement, business and commercial organization, and the role and importance of service clubs. Farrington intended his book to be used by towns of less than 10,000 population, but his ideas also proved useful to larger towns. Although the emphasis of this work is on local initiative, its concept of community development is narrow by today's standards.

External Influences. In reviewing the history of community development in the United States, one cannot overlook early work overseas and its influence on such efforts at home. In 1908 the Indian poet Tagore urged young people to work together for village welfare. In 1914, with the assistance of Leonard Elmhurst, an Englishman, Tagore founded a rural institute that was associated with his government and had contact with government agencies.

In the early twenties the Indian colonial government introduced its first rural development operation under another Englishman, F. L. Brayne. He published his books, *Village Uplift in India,* in 1927, and *Rural Reconstruction,* in 1934. These individual attempts led to national community development programs in India and other British colonial areas. The Indian colonial government started the Village Rehabilitation Scheme in 1944 and its full-scale community development program in 1952. At that time it was stated that "community development is the method and Rural Extension the agency through which the Five-Year Plan seeks to initiate a process of transformation of the social and economic life of the villages" (Taylor et al. 1965, p. 169).

Community development was introduced in Thailand by Prime Minister Pebunsongkram in 1942. About four hundred workers drawn from minor officials and elementary school teachers were selected through examination for intensive training. They were then assigned to community development work in different Tambols—geographic areas similar to U.S. counties (Ministry of the Interior 1979).

Pakistan's national Village Aid program started in 1953. Like India's program, it focused on community development as the method and extension as the vehicle for development. Bangladesh's well-known Camilla Project started in 1959.

The emergence of community development in many parts of Africa had a British colonial influence that lasted longer than in India. The British and French both initiated community development in African villages by promoting literacy and self-help in their territories. The next chapter will explore these issues in more detail.

Role of Educational Associations.   In the United States, various associations and organizations have been involved in community development for several decades. One of the most influential of these is the National University Extension Association (NUEA). At its first conference in 1915, President Charles Van Hise took a firm position on the importance of "informal community service," and in 1919 recognition was given to the "human community," a step away from the limited physical or geographic area. In 1924 the term *community development* appeared in the NUEA proceedings, while in 1935 a plea was made for university-sponsored community development workers. Through the World War II years the movement in universities was given impetus by NUEA leaders Howard McClusky of the University of Michigan, Jess Ogden of the University of Virginia, and Baker Brownell of the University of Montana.

A community organization committee was established in the NUEA in 1948, followed in 1955 by a Division of Community Development. In 1960 Katharine Lackey wrote an extensive report of the status of community development in member institutions of the NUEA. This report covered the Universities of Michigan, Wisconsin, Indiana, Nebraska, Washington, Utah, Minnesota, Michigan State, Pennsylvania State, Purdue, Kansas State, Northern Michigan, and Southern Illinois.

Another organization that has given support to community development over the years is the Adult Education Association, which has a section for community development in its structure. Membership in this group overlaps considerably with membership in the NUEA Division of Community Development. The 1960 *Handbook of Adult Education* (Knowles 1960) contains a chapter on community development authored by Howard McClusky.

Early University Efforts.   One of the pioneers in university-sponsored efforts in North America is St. Francis Xavier University in Antigonish, Nova Scotia, which has provided a distin-

guished community development training program for more than fifty years. Through its Coady International Institute, the university attracts many foreign nationals seeking training for work in their home countries. The institute emphasizes true grassroots methods of training, through which students become involved with community residents in dealing with community issues.

An interesting event in the history of community development that had far-reaching effects was the Montana study conducted by Baker Brownell in the late 1940s while he was on the staff of the University of Montana. This study was directed at determining the potential for revitalizing dying lumber towns in the Northwest. Richard W. Poston was commissioned to record the activities conducted during this study; the result was a book entitled *Small Town Renaissance* (Poston 1950), which gained him a reputation as a student and practitioner of community development. The remarkable phenomenon observed was that although the discussion groups in the various lumber towns were not organized for action, several took significant action that saved their towns from the otherwise inevitable cycle of boom and bust.

After writing about Brownell's Montana study, Poston was invited to the University of Washington to direct the activities of its Bureau of Community Development. There he developed a vigorous field program with a staff of eight consultants working in small communities throughout the state. The Washington approach was oriented toward citizen participation with study committees, town meetings, and action projects dominating community life through the initial period of the effort. Always present was the realization that most communities needed some economic stimulus. Consequently, many projects had economic development overtones. These efforts, combined with more traditional community development approaches, proved to be sound methods of achieving both community and economic development.

Meanwhile, Baker Brownell went to Southern Illinois University at Carbondale in the early fifties to help organize an area services unit, including a community development division, for this fast-growing institution. In 1953 Richard Poston joined the staff to begin a new operation similar to that at the University of Washington. Many of the community problems were similar, but the economic and employment needs in southern Illinois were so great that Poston soon added a factory location specialist to this staff. The activities of this specialist were partially supported by the two major power companies in the region. The Community Development Institute was founded in 1959 and the Department of Community Development in 1966.

William Biddle's program at Earlham College in Richmond, Indiana, began in 1947. Known as "community dynamics," this effort combined graduate study with community experience in the student's pursuit of the master's degree. The goal was to provide a training program at the graduate level with a democratic philosophy toward community development. The program continued for thirteen years until a change in college administration in 1960 established other priorities. Biddle continued his work in community development, however, and became one of the field's most prolific writers.

Since the early 1960s, Springfield College in Massachusetts has offered the degree of Master of Education in Community Leadership and Development. This program emphasizes group work, community organization, and community development.

For many years West Georgia College in Carrollton has used a variety of cultural studies and experiences to broaden the perspective of adult students. The goal is to promote interest and develop the ability to deal with all aspects of community life.

The University of Missouri's community development program began in the mid-1950s with a dual thrust from the General Extension Service and the Cooperative Extension Service. The first three area rural development agents were placed in the field in 1956 through special funds provided by the USDA. These two extension programs were combined in 1960 and the field staff has expanded over the years to twenty area community development specialists at present. The Center for Community Development was established on the Columbia campus in 1960 to meet the need for formal training and backup support of field staff. The center became the academic Department of Community Development in 1962 and began offering courses leading to a master's degree.

Over the years about a third of the master's degree students in the Department of Community Development have been foreign nationals. In 1966 the department began a diploma program in community development designed for those who either do not qualify for entrance into the master's program or who cannot spend the time required for the master's degree. In 1965 the department began its annual International and Community Development Institute designed to provide short-term, intensive training for foreign nationals. By 1986 more than 750 persons from sixty-five countries had completed the program.

By 1976, some sixty-three other institutions of higher education offered majors in community development (Cary 1976). The 1987 directory of institutions providing community development training, diploma, or degree programs lists thirty-four U.S. and Canadian institutions plus several in other countries (Robertson 1987).

Community-based Efforts

CITY DEPARTMENTS OF COMMUNITY DEVELOPMENT.   Kansas City, Missouri, was the first city in the United States to have a division of community development. It was established in 1943, primarily to combat wartime juvenile delinquency, but it later grew into a pioneering effort in citizen participation through community and neighborhood organizations. It remained a very active part of Kansas City's life, with an emphasis on community development rather than funding, until the early 1980s when its role was diminished. Today many cities have departments of community development, although most are funding agencies for government programs, such as community development block grants, and are not philosophically or practically oriented toward community development as it is defined by professionals.

"Citizen participation" is a requirement for cities receiving federal funding under the Community Development Act. However, there is a wide variation of interpretations as to what it means. They range all the way from simple legal notices in newspapers and public hearings to fulfill legal requirements, to true effort to involve citizens in the developmental process. Almost every city receiving community development funds has either a director of community development or a department of community development or both.

COMMUNITY EDUCATION. Community education, stimulated through grants from the Kellogg and Mott foundations and carried out primarily through school systems, has had a great influence on community development in the United States. The community education movement has encouraged communities to utilize their schools for a broad range of after-school activities, ranging from the more traditional adult education and recreation activities to citizen involvement in the resolution of community issues.

Seay and Crawford (1954) have observed:

> The Community School Service Program was first developed in five small, widely separated Michigan communities where the people at-

tempted to use the educative process in solving their problems. They brought together through educational activities their resources—the natural, human, technological, and institutional resources—and applied them to their local problems in health, recreation, agriculture, and other aspects of community life. Thus, education was seen as a power in the solution to the problems of people. (P. 17)

In June 1945 Eugene B. Elliott, State Superintendent of Public Instruction in Michigan, proposed to the W. K. Kellogg foundation that it underwrite an experimental community education program. He wrote, "Set down in simple terms, our proposal is this: We want to take all we know about a community, put it together in a working program of community self-improvement, and observe the results. We who are in the Michigan State Education Authority feel that the community school idea, now spreading rapidly in Michigan and in other states as well, should be put to a rigorous experimental test" (Seay and Crawford 1954, p. 15).

In July 1945 the Kellogg Foundation agreed to subsidize the project. This research project continued in formal operation until 1953 with Kellogg Foundation support. The Mott Foundation later underwrote similar highly successful work in Flint, Michigan. In the same spirit, the National Community Education Development Act was passed in 1974, providing seed money to state departments of education and local school systems to further community education.

COMMUNITY ORGANIZATION. *Community development* and *community organization* have been closely associated over the years; indeed the terms have been used almost interchangeably by many, as reflected by the literature. For example, Murray Ross wrote *Community Organization: Theory and Principles* in 1955; and an article, "Community Organization and Community Development: Similarities and Differences" by Tom Sherrard, appeared in 1962 in the *Community Development Review* published by the Agency for International Development.

While community development and community organization might share some similar objectives, there are basic differences between them. "The difference," according to Roland Warren (1963, p. 327), "is in the kinds of settings and tasks and personnel with which they have been associated." Community organization gives greater attention to the established social service organizations, which deal with a specific clientele. Community development, on the other hand, might involve the establishment of an entirely new organizational structure, using people from all segments of the community, to reach an agreed-upon goal. Community organization is more apt to involve the use of social services for others. In the community development context, those involved in the major effort might themselves be the beneficiaries of that effort—the result is self-help on an organized, community-wide scale.

Distinctive Community Development Literature.   A body of literature distinct to community development began to emerge in the 1940s. Ogden and Ogden published *These Things We Tried: A Five-Year Experiment in Community Development* in 1947. In 1953, Ruopp edited *Approaches to Community Development* and Poston wrote *Democracy Is You: A Guide to Citizen Action.* In 1955, the United Nations published *Social Progress through Community Development,* which was widely regarded as a cornerstone of community development literature at that time. The first issue of the *Community Development Bulletin* published by the International Cooperation Administration appeared in 1956.

Other literature began to follow, including Batten (1957, 1967), Sanders (1958), Mezirow (1962), Warren (1963), Ogden and Ogden (1964), Clinard (1966), Biddle (1965), Cary (1970), Littrell (1971), Phifer (1975), Roberts (1979), Christenson and Robinson (1980), and this book.

The first issue of the *Journal of the Community Development Society* was published in the spring of 1970 under the editorship of Bryan Phifer. Establishment of the society and its journal greatly stimulated the publishing of articles on community development.

Alternative Approaches

SOCIAL WORK APPROACHES.   Purists argue that some of the early social movements or projects are not accurately classified as community development. Others maintain that a significant relationship exists and that these movements deserve mention in a historical context.

One such project in 1917 was known as the Cincinnati Social Service Unit Project (Steiner 1925). It was a citywide effort to support a demonstration project concentrated in the Mohawk-Brighton district of Cincinnati. The purpose was to develop an ongoing child health program. Organizational units at the neighborhood and block levels worked together to launch and carry out the services as needed. Care was taken to involve the local residents in the decisions and actions required so that the total effort was well distributed throughout the population and was not considered a top-down operation. Not only was the health program very beneficial to the children, but the whole project was a demonstration of democratic community organization.

SETTLEMENT HOUSES. The settlement house movement was more related to community organization and social work than to community development in that its primary focus was to do things for people. Settlement houses played a unique role in large American cities around the turn of the century. The first settlement house, founded in a crowded section of London in 1884, was named Toynbee Hall since it grew out of the work of Arnold Toynbee. In 1887 Stanton Coit founded a settlement house in New York City, and in 1889 Jane Addams and Ellen Gates Starr founded the famous Hull House in Chicago.

Early settlement houses in this country were directed primarily at helping newcomers to large cities adjust to their new environment. One of the highest priorities was the Americanization of immigrants, who generally settled in crowded inner cities, could not speak English, and worked at menial jobs. Courses in the English language were emphasized and other adult education classes were provided. Settlement houses also provided day care centers, baths, community centers, and libraries; organized savings banks and community clubs; and provided recreational facilities.

Crusaders such as Jane Addams made a tremendous contribution to the social and economic welfare of newcomers to large cities through the settlement house movement. As the great wave of foreign immigrants began to wane after the turn of the century, and other social service agencies arose, settlement houses gradually lost the unique role they once played; although as late as the early 1960s some two hundred affiliated groups belonged to the Federation of Settlements and Neighborhood Centers.

CONFLICT APPROACH. The Back of the Yards movement, organized by Saul Alinsky (1969) in Chicago in the 1930s, began a social experiment in neighborhood stabilization. The Polish workers, as Alinsky said, were not so much trying to keep others out as they were trying to keep their own people in. Gains were slow, but significant progress was made over the years toward a better neighborhood environment for these blue-collar workers. In 1940, Alinsky organized the Industrial Areas Foundation in Chicago, which (after initial organizational work there) later embarked on major projects in several other cities. Alinsky's purpose was to help the segments of population that had traditionally been without power to develop influence through organized effort. This approach to social change came to be known as a conflict, or confrontation, approach. Much of the support for his activities came through local church-related organizations. All-out effort was made to acquire power for disenfranchised groups of people and to encourage the people to participate in decisions immediately affecting them and their neighborhoods. Over the years Alinsky launched major projects in Chicago, Rochester, and Kansas City, and in southern California with the farm workers. His work demonstrated that power and participation could be acquired through intensive organizational effort. The challenge remains, however, how to channel such power most effectively—whether to get representation within the establishment or to remain highly organized in order to exert pressure from outside the establishment. Summers (1986, p. 355) comments that "although he used a radical vocabulary, his organizational strategy emphasized democratic citizen participation and community cohesion."

Urban Development Programs.   Many diverse programs for curing urban ills have been proposed and carried out over the years. Some of these, such as urban renewal, centered on housing and left monuments to ignorance. As Biddle points out, most of these programs did things to or for people rather than with people (Biddle 1965, p. 184). The result often was huge housing projects resembling upended dominos in a barren wasteland, filled to overflowing with people who did not want to be there. The notorious Pruitt-Igoe project, built from 1953 to 1955 in St. Louis, earned the infamous distinction of being labeled the worst public housing in the United States by the secretary of Housing and Urban Development (HUD) before it was razed in the mid-1970s.

Biddle (1965, p. 184) identified the core of the problem when he described the missing elements in many urban development programs, whether in job training, slum clearance, or industrial development: "All these aims are good, but they lack the essential personal development experience. Community development processes are addressed to this essential need. These processes provide, not the answers, but the means by which citizens shall seek the answers."

Moreover, many urban programs have been directed at single issues, disregarding the larger community's interests, need, and involvement. "Continuous community improvement," as Hurley H. Doddy observed, "requires the resources and involvement of all types of groups working on many facets of community problems" (Biddle 1965, p. 185). Biddle continues:

> The sociologist Morris Janowitz has criticized his fellow sociologists for finding urban society impersonal, self-centered, and barren, because they believed the importance of local community had declined into disorganization and a mass society. According to Janowitz, these sociologists have failed to take into consideration that "impressive degrees and patterns of local community life exist within . . . metropolitan limits" (Janowitz 1952, p. 241). Such patterns of community life are often visible only to those who are especially discerning and compassionate. And when patterns of community have been discovered, the problem is to find ways for utilizing them to expedite development. (P. 185)

Brokensha and Hodge (1969, p. 141) point out that "often the failure of urban community development is due to the inability of city dwellers to associate with the agency workers; the latter seldom realize that the poor have a visible way of life." In this connection, Gans (1962, p. 10) eloquently describes the communication gap in a Boston project: "Their way of life constituted a distinct and independent working-class sub-culture that bore little resemblance to the middle class and the communication between the agency workers and the people is even less perfect, when lower-class, as opposed to working-class, people are involved."

Thus, urban development programs may concern themselves with community development projects and yet fail to meet the democratic participation requirements of true community development.

Urban Institutes. Urban institutes have emerged as a means of studying and proposing solutions to urban ills and as a way to recruit members of minority groups for civic and political leadership roles. For example, the Urban Institute in Washington, D.C., was organized in 1968 to meet the need for an independent, broadly based research organization to study and propose solutions to a number of urban problems. It works closely with governmental policymakers and administrators seeking insights about pressing urban problems and alternatives to existing policies, with special emphasis on social and economic aspects of urban problems. The Urban Institute has close links with urban researchers in government, universities, and social and economic research organizations; maintains a large library; issues a bimonthly publication entitled *Policy and Research Report;* and publishes books, papers, and reprints of relevant articles.

The Urban Affairs Institute (UAI), formerly the Urban Affairs Foundation, was founded in 1967. It was supported by the Ford Foundation. Its objectives were to seek ways to recruit potential political and governmental leaders from minority groups and to increase awareness of urban students on issues affecting education, public affairs, and government. Early programs of the UAI included fellowships and internship training; public services training; New Opportunities Development, which was a means of encouraging and developing interest in public affairs among secondary school students; Higher Horizons, a multifaceted cultural enrichment program for elementary students; a joint program with Occidental College in Los Angeles to award a Master of Urban Studies degree; and urban scholarship assistance. UAI published the *Urban Fellow* newsletter and the *Black Politician* journal.

The Urban Affairs Association founded in 1969 supports university teaching, research, and service programs in urban affairs. Headquartered at the University of Delaware, it publishes a journal, papers, and a directory of university urban programs.

The Private Sector.   A unique effort in the private sector is the community improvement program sponsored by the General Federation of Women's Clubs and Chevron USA. This program was started in 1955 and was cosponsored by Sears, Roebuck and Co. for the first twenty-seven years. It makes use of training and consultation by university community development specialists with program leaders and in participating communities.

Several public utility companies have sponsored community development activities for more than thirty years. One of these, Planned Progress (sponsored by Union Electric, Missouri Edison, and Missouri Power and Light companies), involved high school students in community study and action projects. This program was organized in the mid-fifties. Some utility-sponsored programs encourage cooperative efforts among citizens, businesses, and the utilities. Northern Natural Gas Company and United Telecommunications were active in this regard in the 1970s. Utilities often help with the financing of state-sponsored community development award and recognition programs.

As mentioned earlier, many Cooperative Extension Service workers have viewed their roles as encompassing much more than agricultural production. In addition to their work with communities, many of these workers also started "organized community" programs directed at helping communities organize for a variety of self-improvement efforts, including improved agricultural production. Sponsors such as utility companies and chambers of commerce made annual awards much like today's community betterment programs sponsored by some state governments.

Rural Development. The mechanization of agriculture and the result—vast out-migration of farm labor after World War II—was a turning point in rural America. As small towns and counties lost population, they found it difficult to maintain basic services, and without services they could not attract business and industry. This cycle only compounded the out-migration as people left to seek employment elsewhere. The USDA and the Cooperative Extension Service took official recognition of this dilemma in 1956 with the revision of the Smith-Lever Act. Section 8 of the revised act authorizes rural development, or community development work, as an official extension function.

The first nationwide rural development program was started by the USDA land-grant college extension system in 1956 with the employment of rural development agents in pilot counties throughout the country. Special funds were authorized by Congress for this purpose.

Rural development was the brainchild of Under Secretary of Agriculture True D. Morse. Before joining the Eisenhower administration, Morse was associated with the Doane Agricultural Service in St. Louis, which had earlier made a study for the Asheville, North Carolina, area. Out of this study grew an effort toward community and area revitalization. Successes from the Asheville experiment gave Morse the incentive to try it on a nationwide scale.

When President John F. Kennedy took office in 1961, his adminis-

tration looked for a new major thrust for rural America; rural development was that thrust. The name of the program was changed to Rural
Areas Development and at the same time the Area Redevelopment
Administration came into being. Together, they made a productive
marriage of educational resources and money for carrying out community and area-wide projects. The Area Redevelopment Administration
required that "overall economic development plans" be made by local
committees of concerned citizens and governmental officials as a prerequisite for grants. Citizen Rural Areas Development committees
were organized and assisted by extension workers throughout the
country to facilitate this work. By the mid-sixties there were active
Rural Areas Development committees in more than half the counties in
the country.

Community Resource Development. With
the expanded rural development effort came reallocation of staff resources among many extension services. Staff members were assigned
at both the campus and field levels to provide leadership for rural
development. By 1963 the Extension Service, USDA, had established
the division of Community Resource Development and the term *CRD*
began to be applied to staff having responsibility for rural and community development. Eventually, many states shortened this designation
to *community development,* and the literature of the Cooperative Extension system began to reflect the broader concepts of community development in contrast to the earlier emphasis on economic development.

The Extension Service, USDA, changed its usage of CRD from
Community and Resource Development to *Community and Rural Development* in the late 1970s. By 1980, it reported that nearly one thousand
Extension specialists and agents whose major assignment is CRD ac-
counted for more than half of the total staff time devoted to this work.
The remaining staff inputs were from workers in agricultural, home
economics, and youth programs. Community and Rural Development
work represented 8.3 percent of Extension's total program effort and
budget in 1980 (U.S. Department of Agriculture 1980*a*) or 1,386 staff
years.

The Extension Service undertook three major evaluations of CRD
in the 1970s. One was the national evaluation of CRD mandated by the
Food and Agricultural Act of 1977 and was conducted in 1979 using
the Shared Process Evaluation System (SHAPES) developed by the

Ontario Institute for Studies in Education. The report of this evaluation, entitled *Community and Rural Development: National Extension Evaluation Project,* was published in 1980. It identified four major outcomes of CRD work:

> The *first outcome* (consequence/impact, result) of Extension work usually recognized by local clients is a sense of direction. Clients often say they knew they had a problem but that they just didn't know what to do about it. Extension assistance often allowed them to determine the direction they should move to get what they wanted.
>
> The *second outcome* most often identified by clients is the existence of a community facility or service, a new industry, more jobs, or whatever it was they determined was needed.
>
> The *third outcome* most often identified by clients is a sense of accomplishment and recognition that they have been able to deal with controversial community issues and to influence the formulation of public policies that affect them.
>
> The *fourth outcome* is a sense and a belief that those involved in a successful development effort are now better able to solve their own problem without federal, state, or other outside assistance. (U.S. Department of Agriculture 1980*b*, p. 887)

In 1977 a national task force conducted an "Evaluation of Community Organization and Leadership Development" in Cooperative Extension's Community Development Program. The Mississippi Cooperative Extension Service assumed leadership for the study with assistance from task force members from other institutions. A third study was entitled "Impact of Extension's Community Resource Development Projects" and was conducted in 1979 by Iowa State University in cooperation with the USDA Extension Service. Findings of this study were published in 1980 (U.S. Department of Agriculture 1980*a*, 1980*b*).

Despite the positive findings of all three studies regarding participation in and outcomes of CRD work, the USDA chose to reduce funding for CRD work in the 1980s and place emphasis on more traditional extension work. This occurred despite the finding of the national SHAPES study that "clients felt strongly that Extension CRD programs serve the needs of local people and that they were determined by local people" (U.S. Department of Agriculture 1980*b*, p. 90).

With reduced USDA funding for and emphasis upon CRD work, staff years devoted to community development work also have declined in the 1980s. From a high of nearly 1500 staff years in 1979, CRD work represented only 949 staff years in 1985 (Nelson 1986)—a 37 percent decline.

Several states which chose to nearly eliminate CRD work soon found themselves in dire straights as they saw traditional extension work severely cut in the early to mid-eighties as farm families increasingly left agriculture. The impact upon rural communities was similar to that resulting from the out-migration from agriculture and rural areas in the 1950s.

By 1986, the USDA again recognized the plight of rural America and the need for rural revitalization. A report entitled *Revitalizing Rural America* states:

> The survival of rural America, both the farms and smaller communities, is dependent upon the expansion of income and employment opportunities in rural areas. Recognizing the growing challenge for local leaders and the contribution that educational assistance can make, the Cooperative Extension Service has identified Revitalizing Rural America as a priority program effort for FY 88-91. . . . Revitalizing rural America is not only in the best interest of the 63 million people who live there, but also is in the best interest of the entire nation.
>
> Of the 39,000 general purpose local governments in the United States, 73 percent have populations of less than 2,500 and most of them are run by volunteer leaders. These rural communities must begin to work now on stopping the loss of human capital. One way to do this is by developing new and innovative leaders who can empower rural people to effect rural revitalization. By eliminating maintenance management in favor of leadership with vision, viewing change as inevitable and as a situation filled with unlimited possibilities for positive responses, and fostering an internal organizational environment that encourages creativity and honest communication, rural leaders can take the lead in empowering individuals to bring about community change. (U.S. Department of Agriculture 1986, p. 19)

Time will tell whether the Agricultural Extension Service and U.S. Department of Agriculture recognize that more than traditional extension work is needed to revitalize rural America. *Rural community revitalization will demand nothing less than a renewed commitment to community development and staff resources to do the job.*

Federal Government Thrusts. With the Johnson administration came a flood tide of federal programs offering assistance to communities, beginning with the War on Poverty in 1964, President Johnson's first major domestic program. Community action

agencies were organized nationwide and within two years the Office of Economic Opportunity had a multibillion dollar budget. President Johnson stated in his 1969 budget message that $27 billion would be spent on antipoverty programs in fiscal year 1969 by ten government agencies. This was a big leap – from practically nothing earmarked for antipoverty efforts prior to his inauguration to a vast outpouring of social and community service programs. In his 1969 budget message, President Johnson stated:

> In the application of this priority system, my budget provides selective increases for a number of urgent domestic programs, particularly manpower training, model cities, programs to control the rising crime rate, family planning, and health care for mothers and infants, air and water pollution control, and research in better methods of education. . . . These and other selected programs for which I am recommending increases respond to the most urgent needs of our nation today – the basic problems of poverty, crime, and the quality of our environment. (U.S. Congress 1969)

As scripture says, "Where the carcass is, the vultures will gather" (Matt. 24:28). With such high stakes, not only did interagency fighting over control of programs occur but also many quasi-governmental organizations emerged to take advantage of readily available money. Within two years, most of the Office of Economic Opportunity (OEO) budget was earmarked for specific programs such as Head Start. Moreover, local control was lost by community action agencies and OEO not only lost its grassroots support but also its federal dominance. Major funding programs were transferred to the Department of Health, Education, and Welfare (HEW); the Department of Housing and Urban Development (HUD); and the Labor Department. Thus, OEO, which started with a meteoric rise, began its not so spectacular demise. Today, local community action agencies have to generate their own funding and have a much narrower range of program efforts than originally envisaged by OEO.

One can best appreciate the change in national priorities during the 1960s by looking at federal government outlays during the period 1959–1969. Total expenditures increased from $92 billion to $186 billion. Defense spending did not even double during the period despite the Vietnam War, increasing from $46 to $79 billion. Space exploration and technology peaked during this period with an expenditure of nearly $6 billion in 1966 as compared to $145 million in 1959. Expenditures for housing and community development jumped from $30 million in 1959 to $1.5 billion in 1969 – a five-hundredfold increase. This was the era of "big government" spending, which saw the birth of HUD and the emergence of secondary and higher education as major forces in the Department of Health, Education, and Welfare. HUD's forerunner, the Federal Housing Administration, and the U.S. Office of Education were transformed almost overnight from little known agencies with little influence to multibillion dollar operations.

Title I of the Higher Education Act also came into being during the Johnson administration. This act provided grants for community development to institutions of higher education. However, Title I never was institutionalized within university structures to the extent of Cooperative Extension work, since grants were made only in response to approved proposals. Funding of this program ceased when its enabling legislation expired in the 1970s.

When the first catalog of Federal Domestic Assistance Programs was published in the mid-sixties, more than eleven hundred federal programs were identified. Many of these programs provided funding for community projects. The proliferation of federal grant-in-aid programs of the 1960s almost overwhelmed the capacity of local governments to utilize them effectively. Moreover, restrictive categorical grant programs not only made a science out of grantsmanship but also created situations in which local funds that should have been spent on priority needs often were used for match money to get grants for whatever projects were currently being funded. The government's carrot-and-stick philosophy was so pronounced that local governments and citizen groups began demanding change in funding procedures.

The Revenue Sharing Act of 1972 resulted from increasing demand for local control over federal funds for community improvements. This act lasted until the budget cuts of 1986. Special revenue sharing and community development block grants enabled units of government to concentrate on their own priorities to a greater extent than was possible under the more restrictive categorical grant programs. The community development block grants also combined numerous former categorical grant programs into six broad categories and eliminated much duplication, red tape, and paper work. However, revenue sharing had its drawbacks. It created a monetary dependency upon the federal government that was even more detrimental to local initiative and to local units of government than the negative aspects of the categorical grant programs.

Today, we find a hodgepodge of programs under the label of community development. Many cities have departments of community development for administering block grant programs, while almost all states have regional planning commissions or councils of government.

The range of local, state, and federal efforts runs the gamut from true citizen initiative and effort to those almost wholly directed by governmental units.

State Government Efforts.   Many states have

community betterment programs which offer recognition and cash awards for community improvement efforts. The Missouri program, called the "Missouri Community Betterment" has been in existence for nearly a quarter century and includes six classes of cities plus neighborhoods. Judges rate cities and neighborhoods using criteria developed to measure local initiative, participation, and accomplishments. An annual award program and banquet is the highlight of the program for participating communities. The governor makes presentations to winning entrants amidst much vocal support and fanfare from contestants.

Most states have departments of community and economic development which provide technical assistance and administer grant programs. States offer special economic incentives for development in depressed areas and most have tax incentives to promote economic development. Missouri's Neighborhood Assistance Program goes even further by providing tax write-offs to business and industry for investments in neighborhood and community development projects.

International Assistance Programs.   The

U.S. government's involvement in community development is not limited to the domestic scene. The Marshall Plan directed at rehabilitating war-torn countries following World War II led into foreign assistance programs for underdeveloped countries. Most direct U.S. foreign assistance is now provided through the Agency for International Development (AID) and much indirect assistance is provided through U.S. contributions to the United Nations and the World Bank. Each of these agencies has a long, although varied, history of community development efforts. The Peace Corps, which celebrated its twenty-fifth anniversary in 1986, has emphasized community development self-help principles in its training of the thousands of volunteers who have served overseas.

The U.S. private sector, notably the Ford Foundation and the Rockefeller Foundation, also has been actively involved in community development work internationally since World War II. Other private organizations such as the Summer Institute of Linguistics and World Vision, church-related agencies, and other groups too numerous to list have had a major community development emphasis in their assistance programs.

Community Development Society. The Community Development Society was founded in 1969 at Columbia, Missouri, in response to the need of practitioners and others interested in community development to form an organization devoted to continuous study of the field, improvement of practice, and sharing of knowledge and experience. Lee J. Cary was the society's first president. Within ten years the society had approximately 850 members. Since then its membership has fluctuated considerably. The purpose of the society is to provide:

1. A forum for the exchange of ideas and experiences and the development of common interests
2. For publication and dissemination of community development information to the public
3. Advocacy of excellence in community programs, scholarship, and research
4. Promotion of citizen participation as essential to effective community development

The society publishes the *Journal of the Community Development Society,* and *Vanguard,* a quarterly magazine, for its members and holds an annual conference. Several state chapters conduct periodic meetings throughout the year and publish state newsletters.

The Challenge Ahead. Community development has emerged as a vital twentieth-century force in democratic participation for community self-help. It moved from a primary emphasis on economic development in its embryonic years to a holistic approach

toward community capacity building. Whether it retains this emphasis depends largely on the courage, vision, and initiative of citizens and professional practitioners; it is much easier to look to government for solutions than to take the hard road of self-reliance.

In the future, more issues—such as the environment, quality of life, and economic stability—will take center stage in the public policy arena. How we decide these issues could determine whether we remain a democracy. Community development can help us realize that these issues have community as well as national and international aspects, and it can be a means for addressing such issues on both the micro and macro levels.

References

Alinsky, S. D. 1969. *Reveille for Radicals.* New York: Random House.

Batten, T. R. 1957. *Communities and Their Development.* London: Oxford University Press.

_____. 1967. *The Non-Directive Approach in Group and Community Work.* London: Oxford University Press.

Biddle, W. W. 1965. *The Community Development Process: The Rediscovery of Local Initiative.* New York: Holt, Rinehart and Winston.

Brokensha, D., and P. Hodge. 1969. *Community Development: An Interpretation.* San Francisco: Chandler.

Cary, L. J., ed. 1970. *Community Development as a Process.* Columbia: University of Missouri Press.

_____. 1976. *Directory: Community Development Education and Training Programs Throughout the World.* Columbia, Mo.: Community Development Society.

Christenson, J. A., and J. W. Robinson, Jr. 1980. *Community Development in America.* Ames: Iowa State University Press.

Clinard, M. B. 1966. *Slums and Community Development.* Glencoe, Ill.: Free Press.

Farrington, F. 1915. *Community Development: Making the Small Town a Better Place to Live in and a Better Place in Which to Do Business.* New York: Ronald Press.

Gans, H. J. 1962. *The Urban Villagers: Group and Class in the Life of Italian Americans.* New York: Free Press.

Janowitz, M. 1952. *The Community Press in an Urban Setting.* New York: Free Press.

Kaufman, H. 1978. Personal conversation with Bryan Phifer. Knowles, M., ed. 1960. *Handbook of Adult Education.* Washington, D.C.: Adult Education Association.

Lackey, K. 1960. Community development through university extension. Community Development Publication, No. 3. Carbondale: Southern Illinois University.

Littrell, D. W. 1971. *The Theory and Practice of Community Development: A Guide for Practitioners*. Columbia: University of Missouri Press.

Mezirow, J. D. 1962. *The Dynamics of Community Development*. New York: Scarecrow Press.

Ministry of the Interior. 1979. *Community Development in Thailand*. Bangkok: Ministry of the Interior.

Nelson, D. L. 1986. Update of CRD programs. Unpublished report. Washington, D.C.: Agricultural Extension Service, U.S. Department of Agriculture.

Ogden, J., and J. Ogden. 1947. *These Things We Tried: A Five-Year Experiment in Community Development*. Charlottesville: University of Virginia.

_____. 1964. *Small Communities in Action*. New York: Harper and Row.

Phifer, B. M., ed. 1975. *Community Development Concepts, Curriculum and Training Needs*. Published for the Agricultural Extension Service, U.S. Department of Agriculture. Columbia: University of Missouri.

Poston, R. 1950. *Small Town Renaissance*. New York: Harper and Row.

_____. 1953. *Democracy Is You: A Guide to Citizen Action*. New York: Harper and Row.

Roberts, H. 1979. *Community Development: Learning and Action*. Toronto: University of Toronto Press.

Robertson, W. E. 1987. Community development education and training programs. Columbia, Mo.: Community Development Society.

Ross, M. 1955. *Community Organization: Theory and Principles*. New York: Harper and Row.

Ruopp, P., ed. 1953. *Approaches to Community Development*. The Hague: W. Van Hoeve.

Sanders, I. T. 1958. *The Community: An Introduction to a Social System*. New York: Ronald Press.

Seay, M. F., and F. N. Crawford. 1954. *The Community School and Community Self-Improvement*. Lansing, Mich.: Clair L. Taylor, Superintendent, Public Instruction.

Sherrard, T. 1962. Community organization and community development: Similarities and differences. *Community Development Review* 7(1):11.

Steiner, J. F. 1925. *Community Organization: A Study of Its Theory and Current Practice*. New York: Century.

Summers, G. F. 1986. Rural community development. *Annual Review of Sociology*. 12:347–71.

Taylor, C. C. 1958. *Adult Education* 8(3):188. Review of *The Growth of a Science—A Half Century of Rural Sociological Research in the United States* by Edmund Brunner. New York: Harper and Brothers, 1957.

Taylor, C. C., D. Ensminger, H. Johnson, and J. Joyce. 1965. *India's Roots of Democracy.* Bombay: Orient Longmans.

Tocqueville, A. de. 1966. *Democracy in America, 1835. A New Translation* by George Lawrence. J. P. Moyes and M. Lerner, eds. New York: Harper and Row.

True, A. C. 1928. History of agricultural extension work in the United States: 1785–1923. USDA, Miscellaneous Publication 15. Washington, D.C.: USGPO.

UN Bureau of Social Affairs. 1955. *Social Progress through Community Development.* New York: United Nations Bureau of Social Affairs, Sales #551U.

U.S. Congress. 1969. Budget Message to the Congress. Washington, D.C.: USGPO.

U.S. Congress, House. 1915. Committee on Agriculture. Cooperative Agricultural Extension Work: Report to Accompany H.R. 7951. 63rd Congress, 2d session, House of Representatives 110.

U.S. Department of Agriculture. 1980a. Community and rural development. Washington, D.C.: Science and Education Administration, USDA.

U.S. Department of Agriculture. 1980b. Community and rural development: National extension evaluation project. Washington, D.C.: Agricultural Extension Service, USDA.

U.S. Department of Agriculture. 1986. Revitalizing rural America. Washington, D.C.: Agricultural Extension Service.

Warren, R. L. 1963. *The Community in America.* Chicago: Rand McNally.

13

An Overview of International Community Development

DONALD E. VOTH
MARCIE BREWSTER

THIS chapter provides a brief historical overview and an assessment of the current status of international community development. We define what is meant by international community development, describe its origins and its typical application in a historical context, and, finally, make a brief assessment of its rapid demise as a major public sector strategy for development.

The term *international community development* is itself ambiguous. Generically it could, of course, refer to all methods, models, and styles of community development practiced in the world, including community development applied in other developed countries. However, we limit our discussion to a much smaller range of community development applications. We focus on community development as it has been and is being applied in developing countries, either as a local self-help strategy in the private sector, as a limited function community-focused activity within specialized bureaucracies, or, perhaps most importantly, as a major national strategy for development. In the last form it has frequently had major outside donor support from foundations, governments, and United Nations agencies.

Community development was, for a period of time in the late 1950s and early 1960s, the major strategy whereby external agencies of the free world supported the development of less developed countries (LDCs). The backbone of the programs were village level workers (VLWs). They worked in the local communities, acting as a catalyst for the local development effort, and were provided with varying degrees of technical assistance and expertise. Support and training for these workers came from a high-level, national community development bureaucracy that was aided and assisted by the foreign donor country or agency, usually the USICA (U.S. International Cooperation Administration), the UN, or, in the case of *Animation Rurale,* the French equivalent of community development, France.

The international community development movement's prominence was relatively short lived. It began in the early 1950s and reached a peak in 1959, after which support from the assisting agencies was rapidly phased out. The supposed failure of international community development was that it did not provide the expected outputs. Community development can be a slow and cumbersome way to increase agricultural production; the anticipated spontaneous development movement and thus local support and direction never materialized. Without external support, and lacking the expected momentum of a grassroots movement, community development as a national development policy was in effect abandoned by the middle 1960s. Instead, leaders turned to more direct ways to address their immediate and growing need to increase food production.

After a period of infatuation with the possibilities of the high technology of the green revolution, the human side of development again began to emerge in the 1970s in both farming systems research and in various participatory development schemes. And, community development itself still exists within various specialized agencies such as ministries of social welfare. Even more importantly, community development remains a viable strategy within reformist and church-based private development organizations, which is where it originated.

If there is anything to be learned from the international community development experience, it is that community development can be effective, but it must remain close to and under the control of the people in the communities being "developed." This is the same lesson that was learned from the U.S. experiment with community development during the War on Poverty. Large-scale bureaucratic schemes of community development suffer from both internal and external contradictions that prevent them from being effective and can easily make community development into a sham.

Some key phases in the history of international community development are as follows:

Late 1940s: Ford Foundation Etawah Community Development Project started in Uttar Pradesh, India.

Early 1950s: India's community development program established with
U.S. assistance.

Mid-1950s to mid-1960s: Period of intense interest in international
community development; and major aid programs, journals, centers, and training programs established.

Early 1960s: Community development began to decline as a major
development strategy, and the national planning movement
emerged.

Mid-1960s: Scare of the "population bomb," result of 1960 Census data,
and promise of the green revolution demanded immediate technical solutions and accelerated the reduction of the role of community development for social scientists.

Mid-1970s to late-1970s: Emergence of green revolution failures, successes of participatory development schemes and farming systems
research, and passage of the New Directions mandate of the U.S.
Congress in 1973 brought some community development methods
back.

Early 1980s: Emphasis on private sector role in development provided
new opportunities for community development.

What Is International Community Development?

Definitions of com-
munity development applied to developing countries abound in the
literature, but fortunately they have much in common and are, for the
most part, similar to that given in Chapter 1. Thus, we examine community development as it was implemented by the U.S. International
Cooperation Administration (USICA) and the United Nations (UN),
which closely parallels British practice. We also examine the French
strategy of *Animation Rurale.*

**COMMUNITY DEVELOPMENT IN USICA AND UN–ASSISTED PRO-
GRAMS.** The form of community development adopted in the immediate postwar period by the USICA and UN agencies emphasized certain key features. Miniclier, former chief of the community
development division of the International Cooperation Administration
(now the Agency for International Development or USAID) states:

Community development is the term which describes a complex of processes now used by many governments to reach and involve the bulk of their people in self-help endeavors to raise standards of living, increase productivity and achieve certain political objectives. . . . The United Nations describes community development as the processes by which "the efforts of the people themselves are united with those of governmental authorities to improve the economic, social and cultural conditions of communities, to integrate these communities into the life of the nation, and to enable them to contribute fully to national progress." It is defined by ICA as "a process of social action in which the people of a community organize themselves for planning and action; define their common and individual needs and problems; make group and individual plans to meet their needs and solve their problems; execute these plans with a maximum reliance upon community resources; and supplement these resources when necessary with services and materials from governmental and non-governmental agencies outside the community." (Miniclier 1956, p. 1)

Miniclier (1956, p. 1) then elaborates, "Manpower is the greatest resource of most developing countries. By capitalizing on the imagination, initiative and energy of people community development is producing better health, agriculture and education." Carl Taylor (1956, pp. 35–36), a key advocate of community development at that time, also emphasized the importance, in community development, of developing a dynamic and positive relationship between local people and governments as well as the capability of local people to organize and plan for themselves. Thus, community development in this early period placed especially heavy emphasis on (1) the fact that it was particularly appropriate because of the resource constraints of LDCs, (2) the active involvement of local people in both implementing projects and decision making and planning, and (3) the need to develop a positive relationship between the people in local communities and government—and the unique contributions that community development could make to achieving this.

ORIGINS OF COMMUNITY DEVELOPMENT. The origins of international community development are complex. They involve the end of colonialism, the emergence of development, and the implementation efforts of specific political ideologies. As a field of practice, though, community development has its origins in specific development and assistance projects. It began with mostly small-scale projects carried out in the private sector, frequently administered and supported by church groups and other reformist groups and agencies; or with relatively small-scale programs or projects carried out in close cooperation with citizen groups by colleges, universities, or regional development organizations.[1]

The original popularity and support community development obtained from the U.S. foreign aid agency was largely due to the postwar success with the Marshall Plan in Europe, the cold war attitude, and the promise and optimism of community development's strategy for the developing world. Community development's promise was to use the developing world's most abundant resource, human capital, to aid and direct its own development using a process that was expected to be self-fueling. At the same time, the community development strategy was seen as a means of promoting development along democratic lines, thus stemming any rising communist movements. Community development was also expected to provide tangible benefits, especially in the form of increased agricultural production.

The community development movement gained momentum during the late 1950s partly because American leaders began to see a combined military and economic assistance to the developing nations as the best foreign policy instrument available to combat the threat of international communism. Rostow's (1960) highly influential book, *The Stages of Economic Growth,* and the existing paradigm of community development which anticipated the stimulation of a more or less automatic process of growth toward local participatory democracy and development — a view strongly enforced by such advocates of community development as Poston (1962) — were consistent in suggesting that communist takeovers could be prevented by largely temporary interventions designed to get the process started. Communism posed two threats: (1) from external military aggression, and (2) from internal revolution by the large, disenfranchised, agrarian population in developing nations. Community development could combat the latter as the democratic alternative to totalitarianism. With its focus on citizen participation and government supervision, it had the potential of building grassroots democratic institutions and improving the material welfare of rural people within the general framework of the existing political and economic order, and particularly within the general framework of the free world.

The community development movement expanded rapidly in the 1950s, in great part due to the support it received from both the United States and the United Nations. By 1960, over sixty programs of either regional or national scope had been started in African, Asian, and

South American countries. India's well-publicized project, begun in 1952, served as the prototype until 1956. The Indian program provided consultants and training materials for other countries in Asia wishing to launch community development programs.

Supporters of community development in the United States included sociologists and anthropologists along with some educators, economists, agriculturalists, political scientists, and social welfare specialists (Holdcroft 1978, p. 16). A community development division was set up in 1954 as part of the Washington headquarters of the foreign aid agency, and community development offices were established in some foreign aid missions as well. The community development division was an outspoken proponent of community development around the world.

In 1955 three foreign aid teams composed of prominent community development advocates from the United States visited the newly begun community development programs in Bolivia, Egypt, Iran, Jamaica, Peru, Puerto Rico, Gold Coast, India, Pakistan, and the Philippines. Glowing reports of success in terms of numbers of village workers trained, numbers of village projects constructed, and the acceptance of community development by both governments and villagers helped spur community development programs in other countries.

The community development program in India was begun in 1952 with massive support from the Ford Foundation and the U.S. foreign aid agency. Over the next few years, the United States assisted the launching of major programs in Iran and Pakistan in 1953, the Philippines in 1955, Jordan in 1956, Indonesia in 1957, and Korea in 1958; smaller programs were begun in Iraq in 1952, Afghanistan and Egypt in 1953, Lebanon in 1954, and Ceylon and Nepal in 1956. Assistance for community development programs reached a peak in 1959. At that time, twenty-five nations were aided in implementing programs, and the foreign aid agency employed over one hundred people as community development advisors, either directly or through contract. The United States channeled most of its funds directly into programs as bilateral foreign economic assistance, and a smaller amount through the UN agencies that were also funding community development programs, spending some $50 million supporting community development during the ten-year period ending in 1962 (Holdcroft 1978, p. 18).

THE FRENCH VERSION: *Animation Rurale.* *Animation Rurale* was a strategy of village-based development which came from France and was, in many respects, similar to the community development of the U.S. International Cooperation Administration and the United Nations. As a methodology, *Animation Rurale* relied on governmental support and the existence of a governmental bureaucracy to initiate and foster a participatory strategy carried out at the village level. Its objectives were similar to those of community development: improvement in the quality of village life through improved services, increased agricultural production, and increased education, in addition to attitudinal change of the residents and the integration of small communities into national development plans.

Ideologically, *Animation Rurale* was different from community development.[2] Community development came to prominence on the international scene in the post–World War II years and was promoted as a democratic alternative to communism in the developing nations. It was seen as a way of shaping the political development of the populace in a democratic direction and the economic development along basically capitalist lines. In contrast, *Animation Rurale* was born out of the utopian socialist vision of society held by the French Catholic Left and directly from the work of Father L. J. Lebret which, though deeply infused with ideology and political philosophy, had its origins in work with poor peasants in fishing villages of France. IRAM (Research and Application of Development Methods Institute), founded in 1956 in France, used Lebret's principles of development combined with the communitarian socialism of Emmanuel Mounier to fashion the strategy for rural change which was *Animation Rurale* (Gellar, Charlick, and Jones 1980, p. 41). Mounier rejected both communism and capitalism as models for development, relying instead on political education and radical transformation of economic structures to achieve his communitarian socialism (Gellar, Charlick, and Jones 1980, p. 36). While community development worked within the existing local hierarchy, *Animation Rurale* had as an objective the transformation of society from the village base up. This ideological difference also affected operational methods. *Animation Rurale* was more sensitive to local and national class and caste distinctions, more likely to use a conflict-oriented strategy (Rothman 1970), and more likely to focus heavily on consciousness raising among low-income village residents and peasant farmers.

Implementing Community Development.

Both USICA and UN–supported community development and *Animation Rurale* were designed to be major, national-level development strategies.

USICA AND UN–IMPLEMENTING STRATEGIES. In countries showing an interest in implementing community development, the first step was usually the formulation of a preliminary program proposal by a team of "experts" working in cooperation with local government officials. Then a host government community development agency and a community development division in the U.S. Country Mission (U.S. Overseas Mission, USOM) would be established. Government leaders usually attended one of the international conferences on community development which were held in Iran (1955 and 1956); the United States (1957); Libya (1958); Ceylon, now Sri Lanka, (1959); and Korea (1961); and visited countries where community development programs were already underway. The conferences were sponsored by the United States and provided a forum for an exchange of ideas and experiences between representatives of participant countries as well as an opportunity for prospective participants to be encouraged to start their own program. Once a program in community development was decided on, training of community development officers either in the host country or in another participant country would begin. The U.S. government or the UN, as the case might be, provided most of the needed support for getting the training underway, including advisors, supplies, and equipment in addition to most of the financial support needed for program implementation.

Usually a national community development bureaucracy was created, with a top administrator above the secretarial or ministerial level—frequently within the executive office of the president.[3] This bureaucracy had, as its key component, specially trained civil servants called village level workers, or multipurpose village level workers. These were the persons responsible for activating the community development program through stimulating local organization, participation, planning, and implementation. These village level workers were generalists, having received a minimal amount of training in some subject matter areas such as health, agriculture, and working with local groups. These community development organizations usually were affiliated with an agency that was responsibile for training village level workers, other local leaders, and, even local people.

The operational strategy was to work with village residents in identifying their felt needs and in assisting them to organize to meet these needs with a combination of self-help and governmental assistance. Ordinarily funds, technical assistance, and in-kind assistance were available in limited amounts for villages to request. As with the Office of Economic Opportunity (OEO) in the United States, there were often certain packaged programs that were made available for promotion by village level workers. This village-level operational strategy included some version of the community development process, in which the village level worker would lead community people through needs and resource assessment, priority setting and project selection, project implementation, and evaluation. Frequently local councils or other types of local organizations within which this activity could be carried out were created (Holdcroft 1978, p. 13).[4]

UN procedures for aiding establishment of community development programs were generally similar to those of the United States, although on a smaller scale. They included capital assistance for pilot programs, international conferences, and the publication of numerous materials on community development.

***Animation Rurale* IMPLEMENTATION STRATEGY.** *Animation Rurale,* as it was envisioned by its designers, was also to be instituted on a comprehensive national level in a country. Its immediate goal would be to find and recruit local *animateurs* who would be trained by the government's Animation Service in problem identification and organizational and problem-solving techniques (Charlick 1980, p. 1). In addition, *animateurs* were to be given training in simple techniques that could be used to improve agricultural productivity and basic rural conditions. They could then demonstrate these techniques to their village residents. For such a program to succeed, much depended on the dynamism of the *animateur* to activate the consciousness of the peasants, to help them organize for the completion of small local projects, and to put in motion the processes that were thought to lead to changes in attitude among both the rural people and government workers. As the village became more "animated," the *animateurs* would assist in the organization of village development committees, cooperatives, and other groups working to solve specific problems at the village level. "Specialized groups would select 'representatives' to be trained by *Animation Rurale* and technical service agents in such areas as primary health care, functional literacy, agricultural extension, village hygiene and cooperative activities" (Charlick 1980, p. 1).

Characteristics of International Community Development.

Several characteristics are common to international community development in the era discussed this far. First, community development became a national program in quite a number of countries, and, as such, it involved a national community development bureaucracy. Because of its urgency, and its goal of integrating specialized services, this bureaucracy was usually headed by an agency above the ministerial level in the executive office of the president.

Second, community development was advocated for reasons that were, in part, peculiar to developing countries. The main reasons were (1) a shortage of financial resources but an abundance of human resources, with community development being given the task of mobilizing these human resources in the national development effort; (2) the belief that development, once initiated by the community development strategy, would proceed automatically without significant additional external investments;[5] (3) a history of "top-down" administrations, especially during the colonial era—with government officials being seen as inspectors, tax collectors, or regulatory officials—and a desire to use community development to create new, more positive relationships between the population and government (Sussman 1980, p. 104); (4) an emphasis on integrated rather than specialized or sectoral development which was based on the assumption that, in developing countries, specialized or sectoral approaches would be retarded and inhibited by sociocultural factors resisting change;[6] and, finally, (5) an optimism or idealism about ordinary village people, which not only assumed that they could and would participate in the national development task at the local level, but which was willing to attempt—in the first instance at least—to help them meet their felt needs at the community level, and to give them decision-making authority about what activities the government should engage in throughout their villages.

Finally, community development had emerged as a proposed strategy because of successes it had obtained in small, private sector initiatives. These had focused on organization of poor communities to pool their resources and help themselves with basic subsistence, and to gain power and influence in the larger community.

National-level, Community Development Schemes.

It is useful now to examine some specific examples of community development as it was adopted. Each case is different, of course, but the overall pattern within each case is similar. Because of its importance, community development work in India can be used as an example of the USICA and UN community development strategy (Sussman 1980; Mayer 1958; Holdcroft 1978; Blair 1981). Community development work in Senegal can be used as an example of *Animation Rurale.*

INDIA: USICA AND UN. Blair (1981) (see also Sussman 1980; Mayer 1958) describes early community development work in India as follows:

> The Community Development Program in India began officially in 1952, but its actual origins go back a number of years before to the Etawah Project in Uttar Pradesh, which began and flourished under the leadership of Albert Mayer, a well-known town and regional planner from the United States. During several years of trial and error mixed with theory, Mayer and his team developed a model for rural development that was in essence an elaborate extension system. At the local level, a trained Village Level Worker (VLW) would determine the "felt needs" in the several villages under his aegis and serve as a multipurpose extension agent in meeting those needs. There would be backup support from the next higher administrative level, where a team of specialists in education, public health, agronomy, irrigation and other fields stood ready to help him. (P. 15)

There were also a variety of rural development efforts in the private voluntary sector to stimulate and manage rural development in India, including fifteen projects funded by the Ford Foundation. The massive, nationwide effort that began in 1952 had been preceeded by an expansion of the Etawah Project to fifty-five pilot projects (Sussman 1980, p. 120). These projects all emphasized use of local resources, experimentation with village level workers, and an integrated approach: "As stated by the chairman of the Grow More Food Enquiry Committee, 'All aspects of rural life are interrelated and no lasting results can be achieved if individual aspects are dealt with in isolation'" (Sussman 1980, p. 106).

Organization of the projects during this stage was not left to chance. The multipurpose VLW, a concept that was systematized for the first time by Etawah, was hired with some experience in rural life or agriculture and given more training. The VLW, who concentrated on ascertaining local problems and organizing on the village level, was well supported with specialized expertise from project headquarters. More organizational and logistical support was centered at the district office.

During this early stage, concentrated pilot projects achieved very substantial successes, paralleling the early stages of rural community development in the United States and in other countries (Poston 1950). Sussman (1980) summarizes:

> Measured both in terms of service inputs and production outputs, the gains at Etawah were impressive. The projects completed included the construction of drains, storage tanks, roads, and canals; the delivery of improved health measures, sanitation, and adult and primary education; the introduction of better implements, technology, and improved seed in agriculture; the use of better feed and breeding in animal husbandry; and even the publication of a village newspaper. Although the project had social and cultural benefits, its underpinning was economic development. One of its accomplishments was in the field of small industry—the development of brick kilns. This local industry was encouraged because the brick making process was simple and easy to learn, materials were readily available, the kilns were not difficult to construct, the cost was low, and the industry was labor intensive. In addition, the brick molding season didn't conflict with agricultural operations and the market was potentially great. The Etawah Project had shown that by considering local conditions and resources, needed and economically profitable efforts could be designed to benefit the local people.
>
> The major emphasis of Etawah as a production experiment was in agriculture. It was the introduction of a new variety of potato, the Patna Phulwa, which provided the early breakthrough for the project. Project workers facilitated the sale of seed at cost to the farmers and provided technical information. Because the price of the new seed was less than the local variety, the size of the potato larger, and the yield greater, it was quickly adopted by local farmers. The average potato crop yields more than doubled. The history of the introduction of wheat as the major crop in the area was similar. (P. 113)

The demonstrated successes at Etawah helped spur the Indian community development movement. With government and outside assistance, VLWs attempted to transfer the design from what were small closely monitored and efficiently organized private programs to a large government bureaucracy. The VLW concept was duplicated elsewhere in India, but where adequate technical support, organizational efficiency, or commitment to village development along villager-based lines was missing, the transfer was not altogether successful.

SENEGAL: *Animation Rurale.* *Animation Rurale* was attempted in Senegal, Niger, Cameroon, Upper Volta, and Madagascar during the 1960s. Only in Senegal was it adopted on a broad, comprehensive scale as it had been intended, and it continued there for only a brief time. *Animation* techniques in piecemeal form resemble classic community development so we will look more closely at Senegal, where, from 1959 until 1962, *Animation Rurale* enjoyed strong support from the national government. Serious efforts were made to organize the peasants directly, bypassing the traditional political and economic institutions and "thereby reducing the power of conservative local authorities and foreign traders" (Charlick 1980, p. 3).

The government's objectives during the initial years of *Animation Rurale* stressed national political and economic integration; diversification of the national economy, which was heavily dependent on the peanut trade; modernization of the rural economy; and socialization of people in the countryside. The *Animation's* role was to (1) raise the consciousness of the rural masses, (2) stimulate adoption of new ideas and techniques, and (3) organize communities to participate in self-help development projects and government-initiated development programs (Gellar, Charlick, and Jones 1980, p. 104). *Animation Rurale* was part of a triad of development programs that were to work together in Senegal; this triad also included the Rural Expansion Centers (CER) and multifunctional cooperatives (Gellar, Charlick, and Jones 1980, p. 53). The CERs were to be fully staffed centers that would provide assistance and expertise in a broad range of areas. The cooperatives, which expanded rapidly due to strong support by the government, were to be fully independent after a two-year apprenticeship. *Animation Rurale* was the third part of the government's strategy. *Animation Rurale's* role was to promote discussion between the local people and the state-level governments, to preach African socialism, to encourage participation in cooperatives, and to foster change by encouraging people to make more demands on the technical service agencies. Second, *Animation* was seen as a way to challenge the traditional conservative political and economic forces and to help in the establishment of alternative structures. Its third function was to train animateurs, reorient the local bureaucrats to the socialist perspective, and work with the people directly to improve health care and agricultural productivity.

Animation Rurale had certain successes in its early years in Senegal. It worked best in those areas where certain national political leaders had more powerful influence and in the Casamance region where isolation from the rest of Senegal and the lack of a developed cash economy made the *Animation Rurale* services more attractive and less resisted. The *Animation Feminine* also seemed to work well. Programs were organized around traditional women's roles. Women organized groups to take advantage of the government's social and health care services. They organized small agricultural projects, using the proceeds to purchase simple tools needed for their villages, even though women were excluded from direct membership in the co-ops (Gellar, Charlick, and Jones 1980, pp. 117–18). Women's projects appealed to the men because the women were doing work that would contribute to improvements from which they too could benefit. Moreover, since women were generally outside the traditional hierarchy, their efforts did not come into conflict with the local power structures.

Especially among women, but among other groups as well, *Animation Rurale* had the effect of raising expectations and demands of the rural people. For women, "it had an important and lasting impact . . . in providing them with experience in dealing with government officials and organizing their own small-scale projects. In the late 1970's, Senagalese rural women were becoming more vociferous in their demands for a greater role in Senegal's political and economic life and, in the process were becoming a potentially potent force for pressuring the government to do more to help satisfy the basic needs of Senegal's rural population" (Gellar, Charlick, and Jones 1980, p. 119).

According to a survey in the late 1960s, the rural population "had a favorable opinion of the animation program, and of the work of village 'animateurs.' . . . Many farmers cited the fact that they had received good advice on agricultural techniques from the 'animateurs' and that this had contributed to improving their quality of life . . . Nearly two-thirds of those with a good opinion of the Animation Service attributed this to the impact of the program on rural women" (Gellar, Charlick, and Jones 1980, p. 114).

The Decline of Community Development.
The community development movement reached its peak in 1959. By 1960 many community development programs were already faltering, and by 1965 most

national programs had been either terminated or drastically cut back. The rapid decline of the international community development movement can be attributed to two main factors: (1) disillusionment of developing nation leaders with the performance of community development in meeting its goals, and (2) dramatic reduction in support from the major donors. These two causes were interdependent and mutually reinforcing. Leaders became disillusioned because community development failed to demonstrate success in building grassroots democratic institutions, improving the economic and social well-being of rural people, or making any clear contribution to national economic goals.

INTERNATIONAL COMMUNITY DEVELOPMENT'S DECLINE IN USAID. In spite of the fact that the Foreign Assistance Act of 1962 reiterated the continued and greater support of the U.S. Congress for community development efforts, actual support for community development continued to decline. Assistance was withdrawn from six nation's community development programs and the number of U.S. community development advisors dropped from 105 to 68 between 1959 and 1960. By 1963 the community development division of the U.S. foreign aid agency had been abolished along with most of the community development offices in the developing nations. Since the United States had provided the major support for these programs, community development in these nations was either terminated or greatly reduced.

There were two general factors that combined within the United States to undermine support for the community development effort on the international scene. There was concern over the lack of support that community development received from the host countries, but there was also an internal conflict between the community development personnel and the technical services personnel; that is, the generalist against the specialist. Ultimately, it was the technical services, which were bureaucratically better established, that took the lead influence in development policy away from the more abstract social scientist. Holdcroft (1978) states:

> Under the Kennedy Administration, the leadership of the United States foreign aid agency in the early 1960's was concerned not only with the lack of host country support of community development programs, but was also disillusioned with the widespread internal conflict and animosity between United States community development and technical serv-

ices personnel, particularly agriculturalists. This conflict permeated the foreign aid agency both in Washington and field missions, and it spread to host country ministries and agencies. It was an ideological battle which pitted the generalist against the technologist, the pluralist against the monist. Usually these conflicts were resolved in favor of technical services personnel who were bureaucratically more established and less abstract in their perception of development process. (P. 22)

In the developing nations, where support for a community development program was generally tied to one political leader or party, changes in political leadership meant that community development programs were relegated to divisions of other ministries, such as agriculture, where their influence was subordinated to other ends.

A general pattern of evolution in community development project emphasis can be recognized in the developing nations. India again provides a representative example. During the initial phases, the project emphasized social welfare goals, public works projects, and changes in villagers' attitudes. Increasing food production was the second major emphasis, changing in the early 1960s to a focus on local self-government and the establishment of cooperatives as technical agricultural development came to replace the broad community development approach.

Animation Rurale. After 1962 and the fall of Mamadou Dia (*Animation Rurale*'s major supporter in the Senagalese government) from power, the program was undermined and relegated to successively less prominent positions in the government's development plans. The situation at the national level reflected controversy that the Animation Service was engendering elsewhere in the country. Where *Animation* succeeded in organizing the peasants and increasing their expectations and demands, it threatened the local powers who stood to lose their dominance of the cash economy. It also put pressure on the government to supply services and personnel where local projects had built schools, clinics, and pharmacies; thus, its very successes in these areas hastened its decline. *Animation Rurale* was cited as a failure in its efforts to improve agriculture production, but *Animation* was intended to work with the technical services. Technical instruction for the animateurs was often insufficient, and the relationship between *Animation* and the technical services failed to materialize. Charlick (1980, p. 6) says, "As long as they [members of the technical services] remain unconvinced that they need the willing cooperation of local-level people to improve their performance in ways significant to their career, they are unlikely to facilitate 'animation techniques' and they may well sabotage them. 'Animating' the technical service agent may be one of the most intransigent bottlenecks in participatory rural development programs."

Current Status of Community Development.

Thus, in the form of the major national programs that existed in the late 1950s and early 1960s, community development no longer exists. Community development activities and techniques do exist, however, on very limited scales, within specialized technical services such as social welfare, planning, and agriculture. As such, in spite of their attempts to perform as generalists and to use the techniques of community development, community developers have frequently been relegated to facilitating the delivery of specialized services. This is true of the several forms of community development discussed here. Animateurs are found in many specialized agencies—for example, agricultural extension—in francophone, less developed countries, but few countries retain major national community development bureaucracies.

At the same time, as the result of disillusionment with the green revolution, the New Directions mandate of the U.S. Congress in 1973, and similar significant changes in direction within the World Bank and related agencies, participatory approaches to development have again become popular. This revival included the short popularity of Integrated Rural Development, and now includes the training and visit system popularized by the World Bank and the farming systems research approach now widely accepted by USAID, World Bank, and a number of the International Agricultural Research Centers.[7]

Large-scale, publicly supported, community development approaches, however, have not experienced a resurgence. These new participatory approaches, although very similar to community development in their stated philosophical orientation, tend to be firmly established within one or more technical services—usually agriculture—and generally have no ties to the programs of other services within the countries or the project areas where they operate. Indeed, there is even conflict within the field of agriculture as to whether farming systems research should be located in research or extension. Thus, we have experienced essentially a rediscovery of significant elements of the community development movement by biological scientists, agricultural economists, and others who have been, until now, largely oblivious to community development, community development expertise, and community development literature.

In the private sector, especially among churches and other reformist organizations and agencies from which it emerged in the first place, community development continues to be a widely used and viable strategy in many LDCs.[8] Key elements in these programs are (1) their structure for implementing community development, (2) their staffing, (3) their community development process, and, finally, (4) the local community structures they support.[9] As such, community development is clearly the preferred – perhaps the only available – strategy of the weak and the powerless and of those who are willing to take the risks to identify strongly with the weak and powerless.

STRUCTURE FOR IMPLEMENTATION. Contemporary Haiti provides us with an example of a situation in which, though a national *Animation Rurale* program existed in the past and still exists in the organizational charts, the real effectiveness of community development is in the private sector.

The community development programs which exist in Haiti are carried out by regional organizations with limited geographical responsibility. There is a central office within the region, which is responsible for policy, program guidance, employment and training of central staff, etc. All organizations obtain at least some outside support, generic support as well as support that is tied to specific programs, but each depends primarily on support from its constituency, the poor farmers and villagers of Haiti. Perhaps even more important than their specific agricultural development agendas, the real raison détre of these central offices is to stimulate and support any organization and development activities in communities within their region.

The private programs in Haiti have both generalist community organization staff (animateurs) and subject matter specialists in the areas of agriculture, health, and education. Some staff members serve both as specialists and as community organizers. Although they may have professional training, staff selection is based more on performance than on formal credentials, and a large portion of staff training is in-service.

There are usually three levels of staff: two within the community itself and the other outside the community. The staff that works outside the community is more likely to be made up of full-time agency employees, to be professionally trained, and to be more experienced than the staff that works inside the community. Local community staff include community organizers or animateurs who are selected as extensions of the community development agency, on the one hand, and elected officials of the local community organization on the other. The community organizers are usually local community members who have shown capability and initiative and, consequently, have been selected to take responsibility for community development activities for their own local organization. These community organizers are usually paid small salaries and work part-time. Generally, some of the money to pay community organizers comes from the community itself. Community officials are, of course, local people who serve within the local organizational structure; they almost always serve without pay.

All of the staff persons in the Haitian community development agencies are carefully trained by the agency itself. Community organization training is vital. Both community organizers and technical specialists also may attend training sessions offered by specialized agencies and vocational schools.

A typical pattern of community organization training is that offered by Integrated Rural Development, a regional community development agency of the Haitian Baptist churches. Candidates are recruited and are given several weeks of training. Then, after a preliminary evaluation of a candidate's capabilities, a decision is made whether or not to employ him or her on a probationary basis. This is followed by another period of two to three weeks of training, which is followed by four to six weeks of the candidate working in a community and with the community development program staff under close supervision. If successful, the candidate is employed as a community organizer; additional training of approximately two days per month is provided for an extended period of time. The training mainly emphasizes methods for working with people in groups and in community organizations.

THE COMMUNITY DEVELOPMENT PROCESS. A standard community development process is used. The main objective is to form a local community organization. Ordinarily the initiative for the community development activity comes from the community.[10] The agency staff then responds by taking the originating group, then the larger community of which it is a part, and subsequently a select group of community leaders through a series of meetings involving needs assessment and problem identification, planning, organization for action, and implementation.

LOCAL COMMUNITY STRUCTURE. A formally organized, local community organization forms the core of each of these community development programs. These formally organized, local community programs may differ in their internal structures, yet they are bound together by a central organization. Each local committee program is represented on the board of the central organization. This, perhaps more than anything else, limits the extent to which such organizations can expand. As they become larger their ability to respond to the needs of all of their community organizations diminishes.

Community development activities like these are ubiquitous in LDCs, and cases can be found where they have been successful in a wide variety of environments—urban and rural—and with a wide variety of issues including health, education, and agriculture.

Effectiveness of International Community Development.

The conventional wisdom is that international community development failed, which stems from the fact that the programs and efforts to evaluate them were so rapidly abandoned. Blair (1981) has recently questioned this conventional wisdom, suggesting that, like the War on Poverty in the United States and other participatory development programs, although community development may have failed in the short run, it actually was successful in the long run even though the successes were not exactly what the proponents had expected. The successes were, essentially, the beginning of political and economic claims by rural people and the lower classes, and the development of constituencies—some of them organized—which in one way or another consistently supported these claims, with the result that the welfare of the lower classes has become a permanent part of the political and economic agenda (Blair 1981, pp. 1–3). More specifically, with respect to India, Blair (1981) states:

> Community development and Panchayati Raj can be pointed to as major factors in bringing about the transformation of agrarian structures that has taken place in large parts of the country over the last two decades.

> Through these institutions a middle-level farmer class, poor by interna-
> tional standards, was able to get a political foothold in various state
> machineries to implement policies that started a flow of goods and serv-
> ices toward itself, thereby promoting its own advancement as a class.
> Following in its wake is the increasingly conscious and militant class of
> the truly poor – the landless laborers and marginally employed, mostly
> from the lowest and even untouchable castes – who are learning from the
> successes of the rising middle class how to use the weapons of political
> and economic action themselves to claim a place in the system. (P. 3)

In addition to this, one must add that, if the unanimous assessments of the effects of the pilot programs in India – as well as those in
other countries (Poston 1962) – are correct, they demonstrated that
community development could achieve its more immediate objectives,
including making significant contributions to agricultural development
even before the "miracles" of the green revolution were available.

Blair (1981, pp. 64–126), in part agreeing with Holdcroft (1984)
and others who claim that community development failed in the short
run, attributes this short-term failure of community development to
five things: takeover by local elites, structural contradictions in the
programs, over-rapid expansion, the "compulsion for measurement,"
and the dilemma of "supervision versus autonomy." Other reasons
given are the failure to contribute to economic or agricultural development and the expansion of social services without concomitant increases in productive activities to support those services (Holdcroft
1978). And, perhaps most importantly, the hoped-for autonomous process of development that community development was to stimulate
never occurred. This is quite clear from the successes of the Etawah
Project, which succeeded because of continuous, meticulous planning
and supervision, with those in charge leaving nothing to chance. It was
never a question of the project stimulating something that would be
continued on its own. The same appears to be true of successful projects in radically different environments that used similar strategies –
for example, the USDA Rural Development programs which occurred
during the same era (Miller and Voth 1984).

The bureaucratic and administrative context within which community development operated is one dilemma that is partially captured
in Blair's over-rapid expansion argument, but which includes broader
considerations. It is, we feel, as relevant to community development's
alleged failure in the United States' War on Poverty as it is in developing countries' programs. Sussman (1980, p. 122) states, "The lesson of
Etawah and community development in India is that the calculus involved in the development of a national program is complex and de-

pends even more on political and bureaucratic perspectives than it does on what is learned in the field trial, the pilot project, or the demonstration project."

Blair implies, in his argument of the rapid expansion from the pilot project to the national level, that had the process progressed more slowly, community development may have succeeded at the national level. Be that as it may, there are other considerations which suggest that what was possible in the pilot projects might never be possible on a national scale. Sussman (1980, pp. 115–20) suggests this, implying that the environment for leadership and management was changed so much that community development could not operate effectively. We want to identify two elements of this bureaucratic environment which affect the implementation of similar projects on a large national scale.

First, as has been discussed above, the bureaucratic environment involved conflict between the generalists and the generalist bureaucracy on the one hand, and the specialists and their specialized bureaucracies on the other. This, more than anything, weakened community development, especially when the threat of rapid population growth (the population bomb) and the promise of the green revolution—both, incidentally, popularized primarily by biological scientists—captured the imagination of scholars and policymakers. Then the complex integrated strategies of community development, which depended heavily on citizen involvement and input and were uncertain and slow, were rapidly abandoned because of the urgency of the need to "feed the world." Eminent agricultural scientists, as well as prominent foundations, stood in the wings with dramatic solutions (Stakman, Bradfield, and Mangelsdorf 1967; Dahlberg 1979). The social scientists who had supported community development, already dissuaded by the political volatility and complexity of community development, had little courage to fight back. Even when community development worked, as the Senegal case suggests, community development strategies were opposed, precisely because their success was seen as a threat.

Second, there is some question about whether participatory strategies such as community development and *Animation Rurale* could ever have been expected to have "worked" at a broad national level except in special cases where peculiar political environments allowed governmental bureaucrats to engage in what is, in essence, political work. This was possible for a time in Senegal. It has been, in general, possible in single-party states, as long as no major ideological shifts occur.

In countries like the Philippines and India, because they had at least the formality of multiparty systems, it was never possible for village level workers to engage in ideologically grounded mobilization.

The result of this was that (1) village level workers were limited in the extent to which they could – even if they wanted to and were trained to – try to deal with local political issues, including citizen mobilization about development objectives, and (2) change in governments almost inevitably resulted in changes in the community development program, because its essence was greatly tied to the current political ideology. In this respect the private or quasi-private sector of the pilot project was qualitatively different from the governmental sector.

This same assessment can be made of the War on Poverty in the United States. The program was adopted almost entirely from the Ford Foundation's Grey Areas projects and embraced as a government program (Rubin 1969). It is one thing for Ford Foundation executives to support citizen organizations that attack city hall; it is quite another for one level of government to fund and stimulate such attacks on another level of government.

Thus, although the record clearly shows that community development can be an effective instrument in developing countries, it also shows that nationwide publicly funded programs of community development confront formidable obstacles that are both bureaucratic and political, and for which no easy solutions are apparent. Still, it is clear (1) that the method of community development remains one of a few tools available to poor communities, (2) that it can be effective if implemented in close cooperation with people in poor communities, and (3) that key elements of community development methodology – such as client participation and sensitivity to felt needs – are viable elements of any development strategy, whether pursued by the public or by private sectors.

Notes

1. In the United States, the discovery of methods for linking public agencies with local citizen groups, referred to by David E. Lilienthal as "democratic administration," was very influential in persuading policymakers that local community initiative and responsibility could be effectively linked with the planning and implementation of major public inititatives (see Selznick 1966).
2. It is interesting to note that, with some very minor exceptions, France did not try to use community development as a way to resist the anticolonial revolutions in her colonies. Indeed, *Animation*

Rurale was never an "official" governmental strategy, as was community development in the United States.

3. This organizational pattern is similar to that adopted in 1964 for the Office of Economic Opportunity, which was located in the Executive Office of the President of the United States for exactly the same reasons that the national community development bureaucracy was located within a high office in a developing country. This was to give the agency enough visibility and authority so that it could coordinate the respective specialized services at all levels, and especially at the local village level.

4. This was almost always emphasized by advocates of community development in rural communities of the United States at the same time (Poston 1976), thus essentially bypassing local governments. As in Tocqueville's model, the local voluntary sector, rather than government, was to be the major locus of self-help and self-improvement in the United States.

   In developing countries the ambiguity of this private sector strategy was, perhaps, more apparent and less frequently pursued on a consistent basis. Consequently, in India, for example, the local organizational stimulus of the community development program contributed to the reform of local government and the creation of the "Panchayat Raj" structure, locally elected government councils with some genuine decision-making authority that exist to the present and are a very important part of Indian polity (Blair 1981, p. 16).

5. Thus, community development never consumed very large investments, but this was intended. As Blair (1981, p. 37) has pointed out, it was seen as a "pump-priming operation; . . . the major part of the resources would eventually be furnished by the beneficiaries. The modestly financed national component would become self-liquidating as each local project gained its feet and moved off under its own power. . . . In the words of one careful student of the Indian development process, A. H. Hanson (1966, p. 420; see Blair 1981, p. 37), '[CD's] ultimate objective is a self-liquidating one, to be achieved when the process of development becomes self-generating and self-sustaining.' "

6. This is somewhat in contrast with the reasons for emphasizing integrated development in developed countries. There, frequently opposite reasons were given (i.e., that economic and/or technological development was already occurring so rapidly that an integrated strategy was needed to "protect" society from possible negative effects on community social organization).

   In any case, advocates of community development in both contexts emphasized being truly interdisciplinary and coordinative, using both specialized disciplinary expertise and specialized service agencies with a generalist trained to help integrate these inputs at the village level.

7. Of special importance is work done at Cornell University on "participatory development." The most well-known is that done by Whyte (1981). However, the Rural Development Committee of the Cornell University Center for International Studies published a newsletter on development participation, and a series of bibliographies, monographs, and special studies, all dealing with participatory development from the middle 1970s through the early 1980s. Of particular interest are Cohen and Uphoff (1977); Uphoff, Cohen, and Goldsmith (1977); and Cohen et al. (1978).

8. The same is true, perhaps to a lesser extent, in the United States. The continued viability of organizations like ACORN (Association of Community Organizations for Reform Now), which represent the poor and disenfranchised, is evidence of its continued utility.

9. The following comments are based on descriptions of three private voluntary organizations in the Les Cayes region of southern Haiti, Integrated Rural Development (IRD), a program of the Baptist churches of Haiti; Developpement Communautaire Chretien d'Haiti (DCCH), supported by Caritas and international Catholic agency; and Union des Cooperatives de la Region du Sud (UNICORS), supported by the Oblate Fathers of Canada.

10. This is a rather subtle point in any community development activity. Public relations efforts for the agency can greatly influence the extent to which local communities will show their own initiative. And, when dealing with specialized issues or programs such as irrigation or soil conservation issues, in which more initiative may be taken by the agency, it is important that all producers participate.

References

Blair, H. W. 1981. The political economy of participation in local development programs: Short-term impasse and long-term change in South Asia and the United States from the 1950's to the 1970's. Ithaca, N.Y.: Cornell University, Rural Development Committee.

Charlick, R. 1980. *Animation Rurale:* Experience with "participatory" development in four West African nations. In *Rural Development Participation Review.* Ithaca, N.Y.: Cornell University, Rural Development Committee.

Cohen, J., and N. Uphoff. 1977. Rural development participation: Concepts and measures for project design, implementation, and evaluation. Ithaca, N.Y.: Cornell University Center for International Studies, Rural Development Committee, Monograph No. 2.

Cohen, J., G. Culagovski, N. Uphoff, and D. Wolf. 1978. Participation at the local level: A working bibliography. Ithaca, N.Y.: Cornell University Center for International Studies, Rural Development Committee, Bibliography No. 1.

Dahlberg, K. A. 1979. *Beyond the Green Revolution.* New York: Plenum Press.

Gellar, S., R. B. Charlick, and Y. Jones. 1980. Animation Rurale and Rural Development: The Experience of Senegal. Ithaca, N.Y.: Cornell University, Rural Development Committee.

Hanson, A. H. 1966. *The Process of Planning: A Study of India's Five-Year Plans, 1950-1964.* London: Oxford University Press.

Holdcroft, L. E. 1978. The rise and fall of community development in developing countries, 1950-65: A critical analysis and annotated bibliography. East Lansing: Michigan State University, Department of Agricultural Economics, Rural Development Paper, No. 2.

_____. 1984. The rise and fall of community development, 1950-65: A critical assessment. In *Agricultural Development in the Third World,* C. K. Eicher and J. M. Staatz, eds., pp. 46-58. Baltimore: The Johns Hopkins Press.

Mayer, A. 1958. *Pilot Project, India.* Berkeley: University of California Press.

Miller, M. K., and D. E. Voth. 1984. Estimating the effects of community resource development efforts on county quality of life. *Rural Sociology* 49(1):37-66.

Miniclier, L. M. 1956. Community development defined. *Community Development Review* 1(Dec. 31):1-2.

Poston, R. W. 1950. *Small Town Renaissance.* New York: Harper and Brothers.

_____. 1962. *Democracy Speaks Many Tongues.* New York: Harper and Row.

_____. 1976. *Action Now! A Citizen's Guide to Better Communities.* Carbondale, Ill.: Southern Illinois University Press.

Rostow, W. W. 1960. *The Stages of Economic Growth.* London: Cambridge University Press.

Rothman, J. 1970. Three models of community organization practice. In *Strategies of Community Organization: A Book of Readings,* F. M. Cox, J. L. Erlich, J. Rothman, and J. E. Tropman, eds., pp. 20-36. Itasca, Ill.: Peacock.

Rubin, L. 1969. Maximum feasible participation: The origins, implications, and present status. *The Annals of the American Academy of Political and Social Science* 385(Sept.):14-29.

Selznick, P. 1966. *TVA and the Grass Roots.* New York: Harper and Row.

Stakman, E. C., R. Bradfield, and P. Mangelsdorf. 1967. *Campaigns against Hunger.* Cambridge, Mass.: Harvard University Press.

Sussman, G. E. 1980. The pilot project and the choice of an implementing strategy: Community development in India. In *Politics and Policy*

Implementation in the Third World, M. S. Grindle, ed., pp. 103–22. Princeton, N.J.: Princeton University Press.

Taylor, C. C. 1956. Community development programs and methods. *Community Development Review* 1(Dec. 31):34–42.

Uphoff, N., J. Cohen, and A. Goldsmith. 1977. Feasibility and application of rural development participation: A state-of-the-art paper. Ithaca, N.Y.: Cornell University Center for International Studies, Rural Development Committee, Monograph No. 3.

Whyte, W. F. 1981. Participatory approaches to agricultural research and development: A state-of-the-art paper. Ithaca, N.Y.: Cornell University Center for International Studies, Rural Development Committee, ARE No. 1.

14

Theoretical Approaches for a Global Community

EDWARD J. BLAKELY

Challenging the Assumptions of Community Development. The practice of

community development grew out of an era of rapid social and economic change. At the turn of this century, the nation was commencing a long and turbulent cycle of industrial transformation. Community development as a profession emerged from the difficult transition experience of millions of individuals and from the inadequacy of existing institutions to cope with the problems of the times. Community development practice was formulated to assist rural farm communities in adjusting to mechanized and scientific agricultural methods as well as to major alteration in societal values. At the same juncture in history, community development professionals were assisting newly arrived rural and foreign residents in dealing with changing work roles, altered neighborhood ethnic composition, and concentrated economic and political power in the growing American cities. Community development evolved from societal need for a social technology transfer profession rather than from any profound intellectual or theoretical propositions regarding social change or development. In many respects, community development has been shaped by conditions of the times rather than by an abstract view of societal order or theory. As a result, the only place we can search for the theoretical roots of community development practice is in contemporary conditions that are reshaping our entire society.

We are currently in the midst of a new and even more profound and rapid socioeconomic transformation than we were in the preceding era. The industrial era, which spawned community development practice, has now run its course. We are no longer in a transition period between an industrial era and an advanced or postindustrial era. We presently live at a time when the global society is undergoing total reformulation, creating an entirely new economic order linking communities to global economic conditions rather than to parochial and indigenous self-help and self-regulating economic systems that characterized earlier community development paradigms. As Peter Drucker states, we are in the midst of a socioeconomic system that has *"already changed* — in its foundations and its structure — and in all probability the change is irreversible" (Drucker, 1986, p. 768).

The world economy has changed in several fundamental ways, and this change has had a dramatic impact on individuals, communities, and nation-states. Moreover, the changed conditions have already altered the foundations of the community development profession, because as Drucker (1986) points out:

1. Primary products and goods production, which were heretofore the goal and measure of development, have been uncoupled from the industrial economy.

2. There has been an uncoupling of the traditional relationships among industries, employment, and community.

3. Capital movement is uncoupled from productive capacity resulting in an alteration between work and economic well-being.

4. Local economies, particularly large metropolitan systems, have uncoupled from the national economic system resulting in communities as global marketplaces.

5. There has been an uncoupling of general community economic growth and local community development.

This new context requires the formulation of a theory or set of principles to guide community development professional practice since "practitioners . . . cannot wait until there is a new theory. They have to act. And their actions will be more likely to succeed the more they are based on the new realities of a changed world economy" (Drucker 1986, p. 768).

Therefore, a new intellectual construct for community development is in the process of being formed to guide practice in a completely new environment. Theory for these changed circumstances provides a useful and recognizable framework or operational principle from which the profession articulates its way of interacting with the changing world. Theory in this context is usefully descriptive shorthand that the practitioner can apply in conventional settings. The problem that community development must address is that both the conventions and the setting have shifted, requiring the formulation of theories to match the new reality.

UNCOUPLED PRACTICE FROM THEORY. The existing community development paradigm is logically connected with the agriindustrial-industrial economy. Theories that support community development practice are derived from the socioeconomic concepts that have guided the long wave of industrial development. As such, existing paradigms rest on a geoeconomic and geopolitical view of the world. The basic conceptual notions that are formed within this paradigm generate a set of theories about people and places that emanate from a single notion regarding the relationships of people within shared physical and socioeconomic space. The real distance between the theories that support this concept of a global interconnected system creates a gulf between individual needs and operating realities (Jacobs 1984). As a result, community development professionals must seek a new base and rationale for their role in society.

The old premise of community development as shaped by an industrial social change paradigm suggests that (1) modernization is socially beneficial, (2) productive capacity can be locally generated and controlled, (3) the destiny of geographically identifiable communities is dependent on collective action, (4) power is a self-initiated (individual and collective) and developed process, and (5) professional or volunteer change agents can alter the socioeconomic potential of a community. In essence, the community development process is a positivist view of social intervention as the primary instrument for socioeconomic-economic change. The validity of these assumptions is undergoing significant challenge in the current environment, as depicted in Table 14.1.

Community developers are now encountering circumstances in which previous paradigms or historical reviews of the profession will not enhance the field's skill or language or their scholarship. They are no longer useful or relevant. As a result, community developers are acting "before there are any substantive activities that represent program; . . . in the absence of consciously applied procedures that would represent method, and even though the participants may have [an] emotional commitment similar to that found in [other] social movement[s], . . . its operations at the community levels do[es] not [now]

Table 14.1. Changes in the Community Development Profession: 1860 to Present

	Agricultural Society 1860–1910	Industrial Society 1910–1960	Advanced Industrial Society 1970–Present
Required Techniques and Skills	One-to-one client orientation	Variety of social and community-action techniques designed to build group solidarity	Sophisticated policy methods designed to broaden participation
Typical Positions and Institutional Settings	Advisor in College of Agriculture	Community organization/ development specialist in College of Agriculture and/or other social welfare agencies	Planner/developer in regional planning organizations and institutions
Professionalization	Adjunct to other professional roles	Specialists with emerging sense of professional potential	Quasi-professionals linked with planning, public administration, and related policy-oriented fields

Source: T. K. Bradshaw and E. J. Blakely. 1979. *Rural Communities in Advanced Industrial Society: Development and Developers*. New York: Praeger, p. 153. Copyright © 1979 by Praeger Publishers. Reprinted with permission.

have the scope usually associated with social movements" (Edwards and Jones 1976, p. 140).

Community development theory based on the agriindustrial-industrial construct is thin, because of its adaptation to conditions rather than to application of theoretical remedies. Nonetheless, there is a strong set of operational principles derived from field experiences and other allied sciences to provide direction for community development professional practice.

We have reached a new juncture in the nature and role of community as an institutional building block for society. It is at this critical juncture that new theoretical underpinnings must be identified. I will examine the radical changes in premises described by Drucker (1986) and other scholars who reflect on the new pressures on the existing theoretical framework. These new uncoupling forces or forces of change are reordering the nature of community and its relationship with the economic system. In addition, I will describe the impacts of large-scale forces on localities and the resultant impacts on conceptualizing community and designing a theory to support the action of professionals who operate at the local level. The concepts of place and social interaction still dominate community development theory. These concepts will have to be examined in an effort to find workable guidelines for future action as communities uncouple from the industrial base from which they were formed.

Uncoupled Production from Place. The traditional association between industrial production in the form of firm location and resultant corporate/owner community citizenship has collapsed. In the last decade, over 40 percent of American firms have reduced operations, changed ownership, or altered their production processes substantially. The very nature of industrial ownership and control has been fundamentally and permanently altered.

This transformation in the American and world economies is underscored by the fact that many world-leading manufacturing firms no longer produce only a single product, such as automobiles or steel, and the leading international producers are now footloose service organizations that produce such items as hamburgers, computer software, and financial services. In other words, the production process is no longer anchored in natural resources, skilled labor, or production capacity of certain places (Bluestone and Harrison 1982).

Community development is place oriented. As companies abandon their role in community, the very definition of community itself is transformed. What is the community economic unit without a traditional association with firms that utilize the locality's natural and/or human resources? The relationships between the work force, the company, and the community have all changed as firms become increasingly international in character. A company's productive output may be, and usually is, organized and assembled anywhere in the world. As a result, the logical and traditional link between people, place, and productive activity is no longer a base for conceiving development principles or theories.

Uncoupled Community Consciousness. The central concept of community has always inferred psychological, economic, and social relationships. Moreover, communities within the same geographic region have built integrated economic systems. The twin concepts of social and economic solidarity provided a foundation for theory building based on the notion of area economic growth, which sought to determine the factors and direction of development (growth pole), or integrative (functional or decentralized integration) theories that linked communities in the same areas to a common destiny. Community development within this framework aimed at ensuring that the social system of community was able to withstand the onslaught of the industrial system. Community social mobilization formed the bedrock of this theoretical construct.

At its base, community development is the science of commune. The concept of community as embodied in a set of institutions, people with shared aspirations and identity, is fundamental to community development. Community development literature is really the sociology of commune. Much of the rich literature of community development (Warren 1972; Alinsky 1972; Kim 1973) is designed to demonstrate the necessity of human settlement systems. The alteration of telecommunications as well as the development of transportation and individual amenities have created a more insular society rather than a more integrated one. While the notion of community retains some semblance of respectability, the underlying values and support systems are no longer in place. This is demonstrated by the sharp increases in anomie in both urban and rural areas. Surrogate communities linked by computers or other electronic methods are being formed faster than are traditional human interacting communities. These new communities do not share the basic elements of community such as shared space, common heritage, or intergroup relationships. Communities are now formed as networks seeking economic, political, and other relationships on a worldwide basis (Jacobs 1984). Community no longer serves as the strong, commonly understood base for conceiving of and implementing development strategies.

In many respects, the concept of development has lost its meaning for many people and many places. The norms of development and the rationale for development do not share a common identity with the current circumstances. A new theory of community development must now consider the absence of geographic or territorial consciousness rather than the presence of it.

Uncoupled Community Institutions.   Institutions are the social knitting mechanism of the community concept. In advanced industrial societies, institutions of all types are drifting away from a common integrated spatial and/or group base. Community, until recently, inferred a network of churches, schools, community associations, and sports and recreation groups as well as local political institutions. People are now being integrated into the social system through interests that cover large spatial areas sometimes international in character. Summers very correctly asserts that in today's world the parochial view of community as a geographic phenomena is overwhelmed by "the recognition that some issues transcend the proximate environment [leading] to collective actions on a broader scale" (Summers 1986, p. 353).

The traditional basis for forming neighborhood organizations as a building block for social and political integration has diminished as a result of greater social and economic mobility. Moreover, technology has created new information systems that stimulate interest groups outside the territorial system. The geographic community no longer serves as an institutional or values base for individuals or families. "We have looked at various ways Americans today separate out their ideas of self, family, religion, and work, and how they seek lifestyle enclaves to find the self expression missing in the rest of their lives . . . Breaking with the past is part of our past" (Bellah et al. 1985).

The recent break with the past is based on the creation of a whole new network of institutions that serve individuals in their roles or lifestyles rather than in their places. There are organizations for skiers, gays, dieters, runners, mothers, single parents, etc. These organizations are not institutions. That is, the organizations do not serve to build continuity and a base for community problem solving. Rather, they are temporary and fragmentary. We are confronted with institutional adhocracy. That is, institutions are no longer fixed but are ad hoc adaptations to the environment they serve. New institutions emerge or new patterns develop within the framework of existing long-term organizations. For example, a new form of church is designed to serve the gay community, a community of interest rather than a geopolitical-political area. There is no institutional base for community. It is this period of rapid change and uncertainty in the economic environment in which "community development has the potential for being effective, . . . [especially] when distrust of extra-local entities is high" (Summers 1986, p. 353). We have entered a critical juncture in the evolution of the American socioeconomic-economic system. At no time since the Great Depression has there been so much agreement on the need to rekindle the forces that build community at the fundamental level. As a result, there has been a major revision of community development theory to accommodate this transition in the fabric of American society.

Revising Theories of Community and Development.

The attendant phenomena that is endemic to the transformation of the underlying conceptual base of community development has created a gradual but noticeable bifurcation of *community theory* from *development theory*. This statement seems, on the surface, to represent a contradiction of terms. How is it that the concepts of community and development could become separated? How could there be any difference between them? Yet, we are faced today with profound and deep divisions in professional practice regarding the emphasis and even the rationale for the development professions because of this new and deepening separation in basic views of community as a place and development as a process. There are those who continue to view community as a social interaction form. The emerging dominant view is that of community as an economic system designed to meet the individual and collective needs of residents. Where these views tend to depart is on the emphasis of the qualitative versus the quantitative aspects of community. There is little doubt that the qualitative social mobilization concepts no longer satisfy contemporary reality. Moreover, as current community development theorists (Pulver 1979; Cary 1970; Blakely 1979; Castells 1983) indicate, the reality of an advanced industrial society alters the conceptual base of community so dramatically that the arena of development has shifted from development *of* the community to development *in* the community (Summers 1986).

This conflict in theoretical perspective is not entirely new. Kaufman (1959) drew a similar distinction in community development theory. His distinction emphasized the integration of social structures in a community over those processes that increased personal wealth and well-being as an outcome of collective actions. The concept *of* community within community development theory has always emphasized the sociopsychological concepts of belonging as well as the territorial notions, including political power associated with commonality of place. We are now witnessing a transformation of the meaning and conceptual territory of this concept to the realm of "collective association." Development *in* the community, on the other hand, recognizes the economic character and institutional framework associated with a common geographic entity. As external (regional, national, and international) forces have impinged on the local community, one response has been to revise local economic base theories to meet community-level requirements. Moreover, the conceptual position of a community as a competitive economic unit has gained ascendancy over community as a sociopsychological unit. That is, development of community is now an instrumental value bound in economic rationality. This conceptualization forms a new, increasingly separate established base for community theory. This reformulation of community as an economic unit can be observed on several levels. The gentrification of inner-city neighborhoods is a close, readily perceivable impact of external economic realities on small neighborhood geographic units. At the local jurisdiction level, plant closures and firm relocations have propelled local governments into unprecedented competition to create new employment, retain existing employers, and attract new firms. Local economic development is based on the concept of a locality as an economic unit which can alter firm behavior or alternatively assist in stimulating new entrepreneurs. Economics has overshadowed and subsumed all other theoretical orientations to community development.

Community development theory—based on these increasingly separate orientations to the nature of community and the functions of local institutions—can be conceived of in three sometimes interrelated conceptual areas. These are theories *in* economic/instrumental development; theories *of* social systems; and theories that merge these notions into "integrated or synthetic" community development theory. The first two theoretical perspectives are partial conceptualizations of an emerging intellectual framework that is integrated in the synthetic view. At this juncture in history, there is no concerted attempt to derive a strong theoretical perspective for the practice of community development. This could be, in part, because things are changing too fast or have changed too much for theorists to speak as definitively about the field today as others (e.g., Biddle and Biddle 1965; Sutton and Kolaja 1960; Cary 1970) were able to in earlier frameworks.

As Christenson, Fendley, and Robinson note in Chapters 1 and 2, community development theory does not guide community development practice. Rather, practice is derived from the problems that emerge from the activities that the development professionals face without reference to any particular paradigm. The normative structural approach to developing theory advanced initially by Oberle, Stowers, and Darby (1974) and refined by Blakely places theory "as a human creation and a human experience capable of being altered or changed in directions established by its own members" (Blakely 1980, p. 208). These theorists, who continue to dominate the intellectual center of the profession, stressed the need to base action on (1) organizing and forming groups, (2) planning as a process to promote change, and (3) developing common values and ethical rules to guide social actions. While all of these ideas remain part of the community development debate, they have not produced a framework for development theory. Rather, these ideas have been used to provide a common vocabulary for community developers regarding the objectives of the development process. On the other hand, they do not create a framework for actions within that process. The theories of development are challenged currently by a more mechanistic and deterministic perspective that is emerging in other literature, but is influencing community development professional practice.

Emerging Instrumental (Economic) Theories of Development.   Community development as development science is derived from the fundamental notion of whether or not the aim of the development process or intervention is to foster development *in* the community. That is, community development is instrumental and economic in character. Community economic theorists (e.g., Tiebout 1962) treat the community as a system of firms. Like any firm, the community must face the harsh realities of the marketplace and position itself to take advantage of its competitive assets and to capture its share of economic activity. The community economic paradigm views community as an interrelated system of mi-

crounits – individuals, households, and firms. Interaction among these units and their responses to the external environment will determine whether the community develops in ways that maximize its latent potential as well as actualize goals set by the residents with respect to the geopolitical-economic units' health. Moreover, there are theorists who argue that the national economic system is built from these geopolitical-economic units rather from the performance of firms (Blakely and Bowman 1986; Summers 1986; Shaffer 1985). These theorists argue that the total performance of the national economy will be determined by the ability of the smaller units to cooperatively marshall resources to compete with the world economy as a total geographic unit. Moreover, the employment problems of people in any locality can be resolved only by building employment opportunities that match the human resources rather than by altering the skill levels of the existing population to meet imported or incapable employment (Blakely 1985, Blakely and Bowman, 1986). Summers (1986, p. 356) points out that this conceptualization of community economy as the base for community development "constitute[s] a very potent force in academia and thus currently dominates the field of . . . community development. It is also the case that economic development concerns top the list of officials' perceived needs, and thus there is a 'strong market' for this approach to development."

This strong market has caused a revision in a number of partial geopolitical-economic theories to include an intellectual base for this activity. The sum of these theories, as articulated above, can be expressed as:

$$\text{Community Economics} = f \begin{cases} \text{Natural resources, labor, capital investment,} \\ \text{entrepreneurship, transport, communications,} \\ \text{industrial composition, technology, size,} \\ \text{export market, international economic situation,} \\ \text{government spending and policies} \end{cases}$$

The theoretical construct for community economics is derived from revisions of both neoclassical economics and alterations in regional development concepts of community microlevel analysis. These partial theories can be arrayed in a manner that depicts their relationships to the development of a new synthetic theory of local community economic development.

Neoclassical Community Theory and Development Theory.
Neoclassical development theory is used by many macroeconomists to explain regional growth and development. The background assumptions of neoclassical theory are not spatially oriented. Nonetheless, neoclassical theory models of large-scale economic systems can be applied to the notion of placing communities, like firms, into a world competitive position. If communities are the new base for wealth generation, then neoclassical theory forms an important base.

Neoclassical theory offers two major concepts to local and community development: equilibrium and mobility. These concepts suggest that all economic systems move toward some natural equilibrium. Economic activity that is unfettered (mobile) will produce better economic results than will limited economic activity. Moreover, the movement of capital provides communities with new opportunities to compete both internally and externally. Communities can compete with one another and this will benefit the entire economic system. Neoclassical theory provides the basis for the current wave of deregulation in the nation among private firms as well as public utilities.

Neoclassical development theorists would argue that a deregulated environment, including labor deregulation, serves the interests of communities as well as capital. Since capital and resources flow to the most advantageous place, then a community with a good business climate will be the ultimate beneficiary in a free market.

Neoclassical, local economic development advocates argue against restraints proposed for firm closures and worker dislocations as proposed by Blakely and Shapira (1984). Neoclassicists suggest that such concepts ultimately drive capital away from communities and nations, dry up entrepreneurship, and, worse, prop up outmoded firms or non-competitive communities. As the neoclassicists see it, firms that lose their markets and workers who might lose their jobs are the inevitable consequence of necessary economic reorganization.

There are many detractors to neoclassical theory as applied to localities. Neoclassical theory provides very little information on the reasons for capital movement and inadequate explanations as to how communities can compete for economic growth. On the other hand, neoclassical theory contains some very usable concepts for community development practice. First, all communities are fundamentally competitive economic units. Communities cannot hold firms captive nor produce profits merely by giving away civic assets. Second, a competitive resource base is more important than compensatory aid. That is, inner-city areas cannot and will not ever develop using transfer payments and other forms of welfare assistance. Therefore, it follows that building real wealth in disadvantaged communities rather than arguing only for greater public assistance must be the goal of development.

Building a capital base in disadvantaged urban or rural areas requires a model that is more capitalistic in nature than previous community development models. As a result of embracing a portion of neoclassicism as public policy, there is increasing attention being placed on efforts to ensure "black capitalism" and community and local equity participation in private ventures. This means that even the disadvantaged community is viewed as an undercompetitive entity rather than a zone of dependence.

Community Socioeconomic-Economic Base Theory.

As stated previously, communities are socioeconomic-economic systems. As whole systems, they operate in a free market environment; they trade and enter into negotiations with one another. Advocates of economic base theory (Tiebout 1962) suggest that communities are, in fact, trading zones with their growth determined by the demand for goods, services, and products from outside the boundaries of the community.

A substantial body of community economic development theory has emerged from the economic base theoretical model. The major components of this theory suggest that communities either generate wealth internally or attract firms that export products and/or services. The notion is to capture capital and build local economic wealth. The best current illustration of this model at work is the new focus on growing high-tech firms. Communities have invested in research parks, incubators, and other forms of direct and indirect assistance aimed at capturing these elusive technology-based firms in the belief that the products produced will generate substantial local wealth (Malizia 1985).

Community development practice that is derived from this approach tends to emphasize activities associated with so-called economic strategy planning. The basic idea is to organize local resources in a manner that will propagate new basic (export) firm starts in the community or area. This is currently an exceptionally popular activity and parallels the old community resource development model that was pioneered by Poston (1976) nearly four decades ago. The essential difference between the current approach and that of its predecessors is the increasing attention on community size (large vs. small), indigenous ownership or use of local resources, and new orientation toward achieving economic stability by maintaining an economic export base.

Casual Development Theory. The continuing

search for the cause(s) of companion social and economic decline of disadvantaged neighborhoods and rural areas has led more community development practitioners to couple their intervention techniques with rigorous theoretical constructs. Theories of cumulative causation suggest that the interplay of domestic and international capital forces in the disadvantaged community conspire to create a situation of increased economic divergence between disadvantaged areas and the socioeconomic system as a whole. Or more simply, the gap between rich people and neighborhoods or communities and poor people and poor neighborhoods is increasing rather than narrowing. Market forces, as Figure 14.1 indicates, pull capital, expertise, and resources away from disadvantaged communities. As a result, the most depressed areas become increasingly depressed because of the divergence in resources. Moreover, these communities become less and less able to compete with the external environment or to generate the capacity to revitalize themselves internally. Myrdal (1957) enunciated this theory as follows:

> Suppose . . . an accidental change occurs in a community, and it is not immediately canceled out in a stream of events, perhaps a factory employing a large part of the population burns down, and they cannot rebuild it, at least not at that locality. The immediate effect is that the firm owning it goes out of business and its workers become unemployed. This will decrease income and demand. A process of circular causation has been started with effects which cumulate in the fashion of a "vicious cycle." In turn, the decrease demand will lower incomes and cause unemployment in all sorts of other businesses in the community which sold to or served the firm and its employees . . . If there are no exogenous changes, the community will be less tempting for outside businesses and workers who had contemplated moving in. As the process gathers a downward spiral gains momentum, business established in the community and workers there will increasingly find reasons for moving out to seek better markets somewhere else. If they do, this will again decrease income and demand. (P. 23)

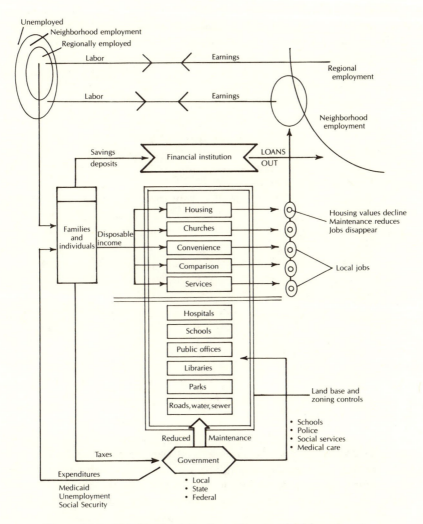

Figure 14.1. Neighborhood Decline – Structural Disinvestment

These causal factors as described by Myrdal also operate in a similar way with respect to employment options and opportunities. One development theorist, Galster (1986), suggests that the employment barriers of the disadvantaged are reinforced by their continuing plight which places them both physically and psychologically further from the employment market.

These backwash effects prevent low-income neighborhoods from developing the requisite internal capacity or capital for revitalization. At the opposite extreme, economically healthy areas feed on themselves and create more growth-inducing activities. As a result, capital and other factors of economic growth avoid less well-off inner-city and rural areas, and these disadvantaged places actually export both capital and labor to other areas. It is for this reason that community development practitioners advocate new community capitalism. This local capitalism places the emphasis on generating wealth within the disadvantaged community by increasing the number of jobs in the area, improving business and home ownership, and maintaining or capturing internal community income.

The community development corporation and rural development corporation are direct responses to the need for community-level capitalism in support of this theoretical construct (Mayer 1986). These development corporations are attempting to restore the market, to act as capital retainers or capital attractors, and to stabilize the market system in the disadvantaged area. Cumulative causation theory has much current appeal. Community development has embraced this notion as a new way to reconstruct both the institutional as well as the economic framework of communities.

Community Attraction Theory.   A new wave of community competitiveness has stimulated another theoretical perspective which is labeled *attraction theory*. Business promotion and attraction have been an unacknowledged part of community development for a long time. As community economic development becomes increasingly central, attracting new firms to a locality becomes a pragmatic response to employment decline. Initially, community development professionals formulated the various forms of boosterism associated with business attraction. However, more recently attraction concepts have gained a more legitimate status. In part, this is simply for political reasons related to the need for both local communities and professional community developers to demonstrate that they are doing something about the dwindling job base. Another reason why this movement should embrace attraction activities is the new evidence that the attractiveness of localities has a genuine impact on economic stability (Blakely and Bowman 1986).

A derivative of attraction theory emphasizes creating an attractive locale rather than promoting the business or industrial sector. The rationale for this approach, from a community development perspective, is that attractiveness goes well beyond advertising and providing incentives for branch plant locations. In the new context of attraction theory, the fundamental concept is to develop an appealing locality for business development, creation, or expansion. Tools for accomplishing this objective are associated with the old boosterism/promotion concept as well as the emergence of more sophisticated stratagems that rely on hard and soft infrastructures as inducers for the desired development. That is, the presence of a high-quality university with major research programs in certain rising fields may create an inducement for participating firms to locate in the area or for locals in the area to build on the momentum by opening their own enterprises in related fields. A university provides, in the attraction model, both hard and soft infrastructures which are required for certain types of firms.

The underlying principles of attraction theory are intuitively correct. Testing the theory is another matter. However, measures have been developed to determine the attractive capacity of localities and neighborhoods (Blakely and Bowman 1986).

Attraction theory has become an unheralded but important component of the development *in* the community thrust. In many respects, this aspect of community development is the core of the professional dimension of community development training. Students armed with basic, local, economic development training which emphasizes both business attraction and deal making are considered the best-prepared professionals for the emerging community and local economic development profession.

Further work must be done to perfect this theory. Some of this conceptual work is being developed by the private sector as geopolitical-economic science. There are some self-serving aspects to this development model since it may be viewed as a clever device of industrial development professionals to shake their old smokestack-chasing image. Nonetheless, there are essential image and projection concepts that need to be developed and codified.

Instrumental (Economic) View of Community.

It is important to discuss and describe the level and nature of practice intervention that flows from the instrumental (economic) view of community development. It is at this level that there is a major departure among community development practitioners.

Contemporary, economic development–oriented community development strategists generally favor macro- or large-scale interventions in the external economic environment in addition to locally based actions. An individual or basic community organization serving individual needs is far less important to the economic development specialist. The dominant intervention orientation among this group of community development professionals would be based on what Summers (1986) labels as *authoritative intervention.* That is, information is intervention. The specialist provides sufficient data to the client group which will subsequently provide alternative courses of action to community members. The specialist in this approach acts as an agent of the information rather than an agent of the client. As a result, expertise, data development, and manipulation form the core skill base for these community development professionals. This technocratic approach to development yields, as Lackey (n.d.) notes, is

> a veritable intellectual and cultural power structure. Its worldview of underdevelopment reality and its hierarchy of values determine the priorities, methodologies, and instrumentalities to be used in dealing with the conditions of underdevelopment. This monopoly that provides the . . . establishment with powerful normative and methodological controls over the "development" process. We could also refer to this particular monopoly as the power to perpetuate a dominant "paradigm" of development. (P. 1)

Nonetheless, there are important benefits in this approach. Information is power. Communities and groups that use information well will be in a better position to respond to the changing world economic circumstances. On the other hand, this highly technical and increasingly dense information system gives some members of the community greater control over others. There is little intuition in this approach as undereducated residents become increasingly marginalized from the decision-making process. Nonetheless, no community will remain competitive without the skills and information that are emphasized in this approach.

Community as Social Systems Theory.
Community development theory *of* the community is the historic base of the field. This social-institutional–network view of communities re-

lies heavily on the building block theory of communities. At the base of the community structure lies the individual and family supported by schools, churches, and civic institutions. The interaction of the various components of this system forms the template for community development activities. These activities might range from rebuilding this network to mobilizing people for constructive action in the community. The community in this intellectual construct is viewed as a single entity. As a result, changes in any component of the human-institutional framework can be viewed as a threat or, alternatively, an improvement in the social fabric.

This view of community continues to have considerable theoretical respectability within community development, albeit for different reasons and for serving very different needs. In the current context, the basic set of building blocks have been altered considerably. Neighborhoods are no longer the primary social organization serving as the base for community. This recent configuration of basic human/community institutions includes a new web of family-centered institutions that are surrogates for extended family functions. These include the development of everything from various support groups to child care centers and care centers for the elderly. Functions previously performed in the family or by the church or school are now performed by extraterritorial institutions. These institutions are viewed as family-like. The services of these institutions are similar to those previously performed within the neighborhood or the community (Pilisuk and Hillier 1987). As a result, this transformation or uncoupling of the central community framework has changed development theory. The active community is viewed as an antidote to the cold industrial world. Preserving community is now an art and an important component of community development practice. However, it must be pointed out that this area of community theory is in disarray among practitioners and theorists alike.

Localism as Community Theory. Place or
venue has been rediscovered in a highly competitive and increasingly socially distant socioeconomic setting. However, the underlying rationale for place theory or theory of belonging is no longer hinged entirely on mutual protection. The new goal of local orientation is to deal constructively with the frayed links between individuals and the massive forces beyond local control. This idea is increasingly manifest in what Castells (1986, p. 13) depicts as a shift from "a space of locali-

ties to a space of flows," or in other words, *think globally act locally*. In many respects, the forces that drive people apart also pull them together. The big picture is, in fact, too big for most of us. We seek shelter in more proximate social-institutional arrangements. In very eloquent yet simple language, Bellah et al. (1985, p. 158) portray modern American community theory through the eyes of one of their interviewees: "Many people feel empty and don't know why they feel empty. The reason is we are all social animals and we must live and interact and work together in a community to become fulfilled. . . . Loneliness is a national feeling. . . . I live in a spectrum that includes the whole world. I'm part of all of it."

Berger (1974) elaborates on the underlying counterresponse to the instrumental view of community as taking away the sense of a person being "at home." He suggests that this countermovement toward the microfamiliar is based on "the reality of loss. . . . Its cumulative effects have been cataclysmic" (Berger, p. 23). Thus, we now have a new theoretical construct of *community as lost* as an antimodern form in comparison to the earlier conceptualization of community as the device for achieving collective modernism. In this sense, community becomes a quest for the self as manifest in others. This view focuses on community as an alive concept, which is far removed from the static nature of community as perceived by spatial-institutionalists.

Community development practitioners, working within the old paradigm, find themselves increasingly out of step with the new social meaning of community. Devising a community program based on this active conceptualization of community is much more difficult since it responds to the nascent, collective aspirations of groups. It is precisely this aspect of collective consciousness that is on the decline in most communities since few individuals continue to share a territorially based social attachment. Yet, it is within this milieu that the community aspect of community development theory must be fashioned to meet contemporary needs.

Attempts to develop community with modern social and residential mobility as a development goal have frustrated the intervention approaches of practitioners. Creating social cohesion as a community development objective of forming "neighborhoods" is especially difficult.

Community as Network Theory.

There are few words as powerful in contemporary lexicon as *networks*. Networks are best defined in community development as "intersection points of interests." That is, so-called networks are artificial configurations that serve some end. These ends are increasingly diverse. In some instances, networks refer to access to power and/or resources. In other instances, networks refer to mutual carrying (e.g., child safety or environmentalism). Finally, a network may reflect a new means of responding to old problems, such as providing personal assistance to or counseling for family members. Networks represent a new set of shadow institutions that either help people meet their goals or act as replacements or surrogates for historic basic institutions. As Kanter (1972, p. 3) suggests, "the network metaphor and the concepts it produces offer a tool kit which emphasizes the process of organizing." The network addresses the fundamental issue: whether the individual is independent or dependent. Increasingly, the evidence in support of this theoretical position is that the individual is now able to determine or choose his or her dependencies. The network perspective was empirically examined by Wellman (1979) in a careful study of relationships in Toronto. In this work, he shows that a network analytical perspective explains the new inter- and intracommunity relationships that

> avoid[s] the individual-as-unit . . . their inherent social psychological explanatory bases, [and avoids] seeing internalized attitudes as determined social relations. . . . Thus, complex networks of chains and clusters are ultimately connected via a common network node. Social solidarity analyzed from this perspective, may be an outgrowth of the coordination of activities through *the network process rather than of the sharing of sentiments through common socialization.* (P. 1226, italics added)

These networks can be ego-ego–centered or socioeconomic-ego–centered. Ego-ego–centered networks are those that are organized to provide an individual need thorough collective means—for example, the provision of personal adjustment services through support groups, or surrogate family activities. The socioeconomic-ego–centered view of community provides an institution-building context. Individuals and organizations within this context have a boundary that is recognized by all participants and offers all members an overview of activities. This, in turn, provides each member with unique contextual knowledge. This knowledge base gives all participants access to resources that are not available to outsiders. Proximity promotes increased network density. This point has become the centerpiece in technology innovation theory. Social science researchers have found the knowledge network to be the key to high-technology growth in certain areas of the world.

The local community is an organizing structure or boundary system for the community network system. Figure 14.2 shows the components that form the base for community networks. Community begins with self-identification of the individual with the community/network, and with the acceptance of this person or member by the community/ network. This enables the member to gain access to the network resource bank. The potential resources are specialized and organized for access by those who value the system's goods, services, infrastructure, and values. The model in Figure 14.2 further illustrates that the individual member of the network, both directly and indirectly, builds a global network through local/contextual associations. This elaboration of the internal resources of the local and global networks transforms the capacity of the individual or organization. The network in this perspective is an empowering tool.

Community development theorists are only now beginning to assess the implications of network theory on community development practice. It is apparent, however, that the link from individual to global community is through these new systems of human interaction. The means to enhance community theory with network concepts is not altogether clear. However, it is apparent that this new form of community without spatial walls but building from a proximate/local base is a permanent change in community as an institution.

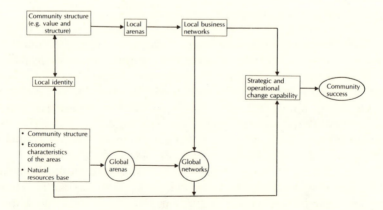

Figure 14.2. Community Development: A Network Approach

Practice Implications of Community Social Systems.

The preceding discussion leads to a reconceptualization of community as aspatial/ solidarity units. In this perspective, urbanites are seen as limited members of several social networks that extend beyond their neighborhoods. It is the range and strength of these ties that provides a basis for forming solidarity activities and sentiments. The goal of the community development specialist — mobilizing the network — becomes one of appealing to a sense of common geographic destiny.

Community development intervention is network creation and institutional capacity building to fulfill both individual and collective needs. That is, community development practice means forming a "network of networks" (Wellman 1979). Mobilization and the formation of coalitions (e.g., helping networks or natural support systems) are the new intervention terminology. Methods to achieve this form of development outcome, as well as theoretical guides to fashion it, are still being designed by field practitioners. Aspatial community development techniques require a reconceptualization of the goals and processes of intervention from strategies designed to build individual connections to strategies designed to build institutional networks that support individual actions.

A Synthetic and Contemporary Theory of Community Development.

Conditions as opposed to abstractions form the conceptual and thereby the theoretical basis for a theory in community development. In the current context, the form of community as well as the interaction processes within social systems creates a new milieu for the formulation of theory. As localities become part of the *space of flows,* contemporary theory must deal simultaneously with behavior and groups. In addition, a working theory of community development has to focus on the relationships among groups within the socioeconomic system (see Figure 14.3).

Finally, theory must accommodate the notion of the coordinated movement of networks and systems rather than that of the participation of individuals (Spaulding 1987). A new working theory of community development emerges from the current social alteration in human

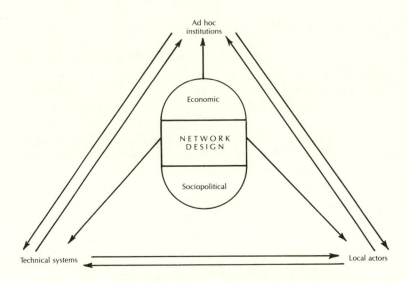

Figure 14.3. A Synthetic Theory of Community Development

interactions and from personal as well as institutional networks. Community development practice should not attempt to control the forces of postindustrial change to preserve some atavistic notions of agriindustrial–industrial geographic solidarity, but should build within the conditions a theoretical framework. It is within the process of change rather than the identification of past values that the community development practitioner must find theory.

This contemporary community development theory does not emerge as a complete, well-articulated body of knowledge. Rather, it is in the process of being built from a series of well-known conceptual positions that are based on the conditions and situations of contemporary reality. Community or local development is a human creation from this theoretical framework, and it provides an image of development, an institutional form for social change, an operational and systematic form, and an intersection of actors and/or interest which create a momentum for change. The theories that flow from this are discussed below.

A THEORY OF ADVOCACY. Transformation of the social system requires the development of new responsive institutions. These institutions are the products of the situation and are maintained in response to the situation. Each social situation develops new requirements that have a life coterminous with the human condition rather than with a spatial form. Community development requires dealing with drugs, teenage pregnancy, local crime, and other societal problems. In a similar manner, local community economic situations require new organizational forms for public/private partnerships and related continuously changing circumstances which require some organizational form.

The community development theoretical proposition that emerges from the formation of adhocracies is that all human conditions require some legitimizing institutional context to deal effectively with individual or collective needs. That is, community is formed from the situation and for the circumstances. The operational, theoretical proposition would hold that the community developer builds temporary institutions rather than merely mobilizing (organizing) the community to express its needs to the existing social/political institutional forums. In essence, the community developer acts as a catalyst and expert in designing institutions to meet group needs across any space required to articulate those needs.

A THEORY OF DEVELOPMENT TECHNOCRACY. Information technology is forming a new branch of learning which is influencing the basic framework for community development theory. Information technology is the basic mode of community economic development where both data and process flows determine outcomes. The methods that emerge from information technology form a new technocracy embodied in certain analytical practices or methods that are more opaque to the citizen participant than were previous community-oriented modes of professional practice. One of the best illustrations of this transformation is the difference between the tools of the community organizer and those of the community economic specialist. While both professionals are involved in community development, the organizer transfers the essential organizational skills to the participants, which reduces their dependency. On the other hand, an understanding of community economic analysis is not easily transferred and thus creates a greater need for expertise and separation or differentiation between the skills of the professional and those of the layperson.

Operationally, this theoretical construct leads to a notion of a more democratic and educative form of technical information and decision-making process. Thus, the community development specialist's role is to demystify technology and create greater access to technical processes as empowering devices. This formulation is in some contrast to the earlier community development practice that used data as a natural and neutral force within the economic system.

A THEORY OF NETWORK DESIGN AND DEVELOPMENT. Much has been made of networks as the new interactive modalities in today's world. However, *network* is a vacuous term that requires more specific content. A theory of community network development would build on the notion of aspatial information exchanges. These information exchanges are a web of interactions that will transform images into action. The collective resources of a network are far stronger than a mere summation of the participant institutions and individuals or both.

Operationalizing network building theory suggests several elements. First, networks are formed from concerns and interests of individuals and not from geographical elements. As a result, even when people share a common geography, they need to develop or nurture specific actions that will facilitate network formation. This is a matter of invisible public policy. Second, networks must be cross-institutional alliances as well as multiple alliances of individuals and organizations to be successful. Finally, network design and development is the primary activity of the community development specialist and must take prime consideration over individual matters. Individual concerns, then, are better addressed through self-interest groups that have built their capacity to problem solve rather than through sentimental organizations. In a sense, the responsibility of the community development specialist, in this construct, is to find others who can solve or help solve problems rather than to engage himself or herself directly or indirectly in problem solving.

A THEORY OF LOCAL ACTORS. Localism remains a component of community development theory even in the changed circumstances discussed here. *Local* is now a quality of the action rather than the locus of the action; it means an interest in preservation of values, character, or environment. Localism, in this context, is intended to take local actions that not only affect the immediate environment but act as symbolic gestures for people at various levels of government. The preservation of inner-city buildings and housing units transcends the immediate geographic situation and immediately takes on a national character. Similarly, any attempt to develop, attract, or preserve local jobs becomes intertwined with the national and international economic system. In essence, moving locally influences patterns globally. It is this dimension of localism that remains a major component of community development theory.

The operational principles that are built from this construct for community development practice suggest the notion of the development of *vision* as an essential initial step in community practice. Vision or values clarification becomes the cornerstone of determining the rationale for community development intervention within the confines of the time in which it takes place.

> Efforts to run away from valuation are misdirected and foredoomed to be fruitless and damaging. The valuations are with us, even when they are driven underground and they guide our work. When kept implicit and unconscious, they allow biases to enter. The only way in which we can strive for objectivity in theoretical analysis is to lift up valuation into the full light, make them [values] conscious and explicit, and permit them to determine the viewpoints, approaches, the concepts used. (Myrdal 1957, p. 343)

This notion is based on ideas in the earlier discussion of the need for the change to meet the requirements of the situation. Each situation in a rapidly changing socioeconomic order has new sets of assumptions. Values conditioned by the immediate past may be of little relevance in dealing effectively with the institutions at hand. For example, one in four Americans now live alone and one in six children live in poverty households. As a consequence, traditional values of family and community responsibility may not provide either an adequate or accurate vision of what is or what is not possible.

Moreover, the community development specialist has to help the group move conceptually both through time and across space so that it does not stagnate and develop antisocial behavior as a vehicle of collective expression. Community development is a value-forming activity. The role of the community developer is to provide the context in which the values can be formed and the vision of alternatives can be continually developed.

Summary and Observations. Community development as a field of practice and as an arena for action is undergoing fundamental transformation. The forces that are impinging on the society are propelling the changes. While community development specialists are responding to the requirements of international, national, and local structural change, they are also—without knowing or stating it—reformulating the theoretical framework that guides the field. This new theoretical construct de-emphasizes the "community lost" paradigm of restoring the agriindustrial values of the past and

builds a new paradigm out of the conditions of the postindustrial socioeconomic system.

In community development today there is a fundamental shift away from the view of development *of* the social solidarity community toward development *in* the community in an instrumental (economic) sense. This paradigm schism provides the opportunity for a new set of theories of community development to coalesce from current practice. The new theoretical constructs articulated in this chapter are built on the reformation of professional field practice as it adapts to the changing environment. Of course, this is not the last word in a field as dynamic as community development. Currently, one of the values of community development specialists, regardless of their roles and responsibilities, is that they do contribute substantially to theory building. This chapter is intended to provide a starting point for that discussion.

References

Alinsky, S. D. 1972. *Rules for Radicals.* New York: Random House.

Bellah, R., R. Madsen, W. M. Sullivan, A. Swidler, and S. M. Tipton. 1985. *Habits of the Heart: Individualism and Commitment in American Life.* Berkeley: University of California Press.

Berger, P. L. 1974. *Pyramids of Sacrifice.* New York: Anchor Books.

Biddle, W. W., and L. J. Biddle. 1965. *Encouraging Community Development: A Training Guide for Local Workers.* New York: Holt, Rinehart and Winston.

Blakely, E. J. 1980. Building theory from practice. In *Community Development in America,* J. A. Christenson and J. W. Robinson, Jr., eds. Ames: Iowa State University Press.

_____. 1985. Community megabends. *Vanguard,* 60(Winter):8–10.

_____., ed. 1979. *Community Development Research.* New York: Human Sciences Press.

Blakely, E. J., and K. Bowman. 1986. *Taking Local Initiatives.* Canberra: Australian Institute of Urban Studies.

Blakely, E. J., and P. Shapira. 1984. Industrial restructuring: Public policies for investment in advanced industrial society. *Annals of the American Academy of Political and Social Science* 475(Sept.):96–109.

Bluestone, B., and B. Harrison. 1982. *The Deindustrialization of America.* New York: Basic Books.

Cary, L. J. 1970. *Community Development as a Process.* Columbia: University of Missouri Press.

Castells, M. 1983. *The City and the Grassroots.* Berkeley: University of California Press.

_____. 1986. The new urban crisis. In *Quality of Urban Life: Social, Psychological, and Physical Conditions,* D. Frick, ed. New York: Walter de Gruyter and Co.

Drucker, P. 1986. The changed world economy. *Foreign Affairs,* 64(4):774–91.

Edwards, A., and D. Jones. 1976. *Community and Community Development.* The Hague, Netherlands: Mouton and Co.

Galster, G. 1986. A cumulative causation model of the black underclass: Implications for urban economic development policy. Wooster College, Wooster, Mass. Unpublished paper.

Jacobs, J. 1984. *Cities and the Wealth of Nations.* New York: Random House.

Kanter, R. M. 1972. *Commitment and Community.* Cambridge, England: Cambridge University Press.

Kaufman, H. F. 1959. Toward an international conception of community. *Social Forces* 38(Oct.):8–17.

Kim, K. 1973. Toward a sociological theory of development. *Rural Sociology* 38(4):462–76.

Lackey, A. n.d. Defining development. Columbia, Mo. Mimeo.

Malizia, E. 1985. *Local Economic Development: A Guide to Practice.* New York: Praeger.

Mayer, N. 1986. Roles for planners in community development. In *Strategic Perspectives on Planning Practice,* B. Checkoway, ed. Lexington, Mass.: Lexington Books.

Myrdal, G. 1957. *Economic Theory and Under-Developed Regions.* London: Duckworth.

Oberle, W. H., K. R. Stowers, and J. P. Darby. 1974. A definition of development. *Journal of the Community Development Society* 5(1):61–71.

Pilisuk, M., and S. Hillier. 1987. *The Healing Web: Social Networks and Human Survival.* Hanover, N.H.: University Press of New England.

Poston, R. 1976. *Action Now.* Carbondale: Southern Illinois University Press.

Pulver, G. 1979. A theoretical framework for the analysis of community economic development options. In *Non Metropolitan Industrial Growth and Community Change,* G. Summers and A. Selvik, eds. Lexington, Mass.: Lexington Books.

Shaffer, R. 1985. *Community Economic Analysis.* Madison: University of Wisconsin Press.

Spaulding, I. 1987. General theory for change. *The Rural Sociologist* 7(1):69–74.

Summers, G. F. 1986. Rural community development. *American Review of Sociology* 12:347–71.

Sutton, W. A., and J. Kolaja. 1960. The concept of community. *Rural Sociology* 25(2):197–203.

Tiebout, C. M. 1962. *The Community Economic Base.* Supplementary paper no. 16. New York: Committee for Economic Development.

Warren, R. 1972. *The Community in America.* Chicago: Rand McNally.

Wellman, B. 1979. The community question: The intimate networks of East Yorkers. *American Journal of Sociology* 84(5):1201–31.

15

The Future for Community Development

KENNETH P. WILKINSON

A N understanding of the future for community development must begin with a clear idea of what the community is and how it develops. In other words, *community* and *development* can mean many different things, and to combine the two without delimiting their separate meanings would add to the potential for confusion and misunderstanding in projections about the future. This analysis begins, therefore, with crucial distinctions of these two questions in order to specify the meaning of community development.

Community Development. Two distinctions in particular serve to sharpen the focus of the discussion. The first, suggested by Sanders (1958), is between community development as a process – something ongoing in local social life – and community development as a method, program, or movement – something of interest that people use to try to influence the community. Without disparaging the usefulness of either, it is obvious that the former refers more directly to the phenomenon of central interest in the study of community development, that is, to local social interaction. The process gives substance and legitimacy to the search for ways of doing, organizing, or promoting community development. This discussion, therefore, concentrates on the process of community development and its future.

337

The second distinction, suggested by Kaufman (1959), is between development *in* the community and development *of* the community. Development *in* the community takes the community as the location or setting where various developments occur, such as job development, service development, and leadership development. Development *of* community, on the other hand, seeks to develop *community* per se as a social characteristic of the local population. Again, both are important from the standpoint of trying to understand how communities change and develop (Wilkinson 1986), and the two types of development can influence one another (Summers 1986). Still, they are different, and the future prospects for one are not necessarily the same as for the other. In this discussion, having selected the process of community development as the central object, precedence is given to development *of* community rather than to development *in* the community, although the latter cannot be ignored in assessing the future for community development. The concept of development *of* community takes precedence because it relates explicitly to the process of community development, while development *in* the community views the locality only as a setting. Community development is the process wherein community develops in a local population.

With this specified, other questions must be answered before the future can be considered. What is community? Why is its development of interest? How in fact does it develop? Answers will bear heavily on projections about the future for community development.

COMMUNITY.   Social interaction, of course, is the essential feature of the human community. Shared territory, a common life, and collective behavior—the three elements in most sociological definitions of the community (Hillery 1955, p. 118)—refer essentially to social interaction. Social interaction is what delineates an area as shared territory. A common life is a complex of interactional relationships. Collective behavior is social interaction directed toward a mutual goal. As the common thread among these defining elements of the community, social interaction is the main ingredient.

Recognizing this, it is equally important to distinguish community interaction, which is a particular kind of social interaction, from other interactions within a local population. Ignoring the differences, one might say community interaction is simply the aggregation of all the interactions that take place in a given locality. The future for this would be easy to foresee: people will continue to interact in places so long as there are people in places. Obviously, a more precise statement is needed to discern the distinctive characteristics of the community and to assess its future prospects. The three central elements of community mentioned above—a shared territory, a common life, and collective action—give criteria for making the needed distinction.

First, there is the territorial element. Community interaction has a territorial orientation and can be distinguished from other local interactions on this count. It is *community* interaction because it expresses common interests and common problems which arise more or less explicitly from the fact that people share a territory (see Sutton and Kolaja 1960). Second, community entails a common life, which in itself is a complex of social interactions. Community, however, is not simply the summation of these interactions. Rather, community interaction is the process whereby the many different interactions and associations that compose a common life are integrated as a whole. Community interaction is distinctive in this sense because it contributes to the wholeness of the local society. The third element is collective action. Community action is a special case of collective action that seeks to enhance the well-being of the whole of the local society. In community interaction, people not only live together and interact in the numerous ways that make up a common life, but they also work together in an attempt to solve problems and to unify and improve the community which they share. Thus, community interaction, unlike other interactions, relates to shared territory, contributes to the wholeness of local social life, and seeks to improve the well-being of the local society as a whole. Taken together, the community interactions in a local population make up a process, the future of which defines the future for community development.

An interactional conception of the community such as this (Kaufman 1959; Kaufman and Wilkinson 1967; Wilkinson 1970) yields a restrictive definition. Community is not a place, but it is a place-oriented process. It is not the sum of social relationships in a population, but it contributes to the wholeness of local social life. A community is a process of interrelated actions through which residents express their shared interest in the local society.

COMMUNITY INTERACTION AND SOCIAL WELL-BEING. Why is it worthwhile to examine the future for this process? Why not consider instead the futures for area development, job development, service development, and so on? What is the importance of the interactional community?

While the interactional definition is restrictive, it identifies a most important factor in human experience and well-being, especially for the future. Part of the importance is in the fact that community interaction is the locus of contact between the individual and society. As Konig (1968) explains, society is an abstraction one can experience only indirectly or symbolically. The empirical manifestation of society is interaction in specific localities. Contact with society occurs first in the family and then, comprehensively, in community interaction. This interaction process is important because it meets the needs of people — their everyday material needs as well as their needs for collective involvement and social definition of self. For these reasons, the quest for community is a central theme in human history — past, present, and future (Nisbet 1953).

DEVELOPMENT. As a process, *development* means capacity building and *community development* means building the capacity of local people to work together to address their common interests in the local society. Dunham (1960, p. 3) expresses this meaning when he writes, "For purposes of this discussion, I would define community development as organized efforts to improve the conditions of community life, and the capacity for community integration and self-direction." He places special emphasis on "efforts" in his definition. Community development takes effort. It is purposive action, not random change or natural evolution. The future for community development depends in large part on the intentional efforts of people. Community development, therefore, is purposive effort by people to articulate and maintain community as a relationship among themselves. In community development people work together with community as a goal. They consciously seek community in their collective experience.

In the abstract, community and community development, both of which are processes of social interaction, can be distinguished from one another on the basis of purpose. All social interaction involves purpose, but only in community development is the purpose explicitly that of building community. Schmalenbach (1961), elaborating Toennies' (1957) *Gemeinschaft/Gesellschaft* typology, explains this distinction. *Gemeinschaft,* or community, he notes, is a preconscious state and not a product of purpose. People in *Gemeinschaft* simply live together in a common life. The bond among them is natural and not contrived. It is not an object of thought or purpose. *Gesellschaft,* in contrast, entails a high level of consciousness. Behavior is rational and calculated as people plan their actions carefully and enter into liaisons with others selectively to reach specific goals. This is a useful distinction, but, as Schmalenbach says, the typology is incomplete because it leaves out the conscious experience of community. People can become conscious of their community relationships and they can work together purposely to build and maintain those relationships without slipping over, as it were, into *Gesellschaft.* Schmalenbach suggests the term *Bund,* or "communion," for the missing type: communion, in his framework, recognizes and celebrates community. Likewise, in community development, people try to give unity and meaning to the social life they share.

In practice, community development means that people who are engaged in efforts to reach specific goals and solve specific community problems also pay attention to the community relationships involved in their efforts. Specifically, they attempt to strengthen the community networks through which they can work together cooperatively in the future. Ironically, however, community development rarely is the manifest purpose of the action. More often this purpose is secondary to such purposes as attracting jobs to the local area or solving some particular local problem. The purpose of developing community modifies and qualifies the actions taken to achieve other purposes. In fact, if the actors declare that community development is the primary objective, there might well be cause for suspicion that they are seeking to enlist community support for actions that would serve their own private interests (see Molotch 1976). Community development emerges typically as an assertion of community interest during the course of actions addressing other more specific goals.

In examining the future for community development, therefore, the focus is on a process of community building which is always purposive. To be sure, many factors other than purpose figure in community interaction and community change, and the future for community development depends to no small extent on these other factors. Purpose, however, is the key factor, by the definition used here (see Wilkinson 1972). Without purpose, there is no community development. Moreover, the purpose is always positive in the sense that the actors seek to build and enhance community. Community development expresses a positive purpose.

It need not, however, have the intended effects. This is a most important qualification to the concept of community development as purposive action. Purpose can never be more than one among many factors in community change. As a consciously purposive and subjectively positive activity, community development will occur in the future, as it does now, in the *efforts* of people and not necessarily in the outcomes of their efforts. Trying is enough to qualify as development by this concept. Community development is simply the action taken with positive purpose.

This qualification is consistent with the concept of community development as a process. A process is never fully "developed"; it consists simply of behavior in process. The development is in the do- ing — in the working together toward a shared goal. To require success in goal achievement — even in achievement of the goal of being able to continue working together — before accepting an activity as community development would violate the process approach and would ignore the many other factors in social change. In community development, the action itself is the development.

With these distinctions in mind, the analysis of the future pros- pects for community development takes a somewhat different tack than if the focus were on, for example, change in aggregate level of living of local populations or increased efficiency in delivery of services within local service regions. Here the concern is with the future of a social process, albeit a process with the potential to influence other aspects of social well-being.

Prospects for the Future.   Three factors dominate

the future prospects for community development as a process. First, there is the matter of the future of the local society, which is a neces- sary setting if not a sufficient condition for community development as described above. The central question about this issue has two parts: What will be the significance of local territory in the community of the future? and What will be the significance of community in territorially based social life in the future? This is to say, the future for community development depends on the interplay of territory, social networks, and social interaction. Second, there are impediments to community development to be considered. Contemporary social and economic trends, particularly population distribution and patterns of inequality and exploitation, presage serious problems facing community develop- ment in the future. The future for community development depends as much on these trends as it does on the latent potential for community to emerge whenever it is not restrained by external barriers. Third, the future for community development depends also on the efforts of peo- ple to encourage and cultivate it. As a purposive activity, community development in the future, as in the past, will require conscious ef- forts — efforts in policy and efforts in practice, outside the local society and within it. These three factors – the future of local society, impediments or barriers to community interaction, and conscious efforts to build community relationships – are keys to the future for community development.

TERRITORY, NETWORKS, AND INTERACTION. Taking local territory as the base for community, a most important question about the future for community development is whether space will play a central role in social life in the future. This already has become a controversial issue in the literature, and some writers have suggested that the territorial element be dropped from the definition of community (notably Bender 1978; Gusfield 1975; see also Chapter 14 of this book).

Perhaps the strongest argument against a territorial conception of the community of the future is the fact that people will have extensive social contacts, including essential ones for meeting daily needs, outside the immediate place of residence. Contact technologies (e.g., automobiles, communications linkages) along with multisite organizations make it possible for people to participate simultaneously, as it were, in many community networks. Bender (1978) says this is the case already. Community, he says, takes many forms structurally but consists essentially of "a network of social relations marked by mutuality and emotional bonds" (p. 7). Reviewing the pattern of community development in America, he writes, "Territorially based interaction represents only one pattern of community, a pattern that becomes less and less evident over the course of American history" (p. 6). From his perspective, communities of the future should be sought not in particular places but in intimate networks wherever they might occur.

Furthermore, extending this argument, local territory can even be viewed as a constraint on the future development of community. In the future, according to Wellman (1979, p. 1227), contacts outside the locality can free people so "their ties are not encapsulated in 'decoupled' little worlds." In the same vein, Scherer (1972) heralds the collapse of "place-chains" and the growing importance of territory-free networks. These trends, she says, will lead to greater human well-being in the future. Others, taking a critical perspective on the community, argue that solidarity on a locality basis would force lower and working classes to subjugate their own interests to the interests of the elite who benefit disproportionately from locality-based actions (Bell and Newby 1976).

Taken together, these objections to the territorial concept of community raise serious questions about the potential for community development to occur on a territorial basis in the future. In response, however, there are good reasons for retaining the territorial element and for anticipating a resurgence of locality-based action and identity in the future. The best reason is that people will go on living in interaction with one another in local territories in the future as they always have in the past. As Hawley (1950, p. 177) puts it, "Organisms either live together or they don't live." If the essence of community is a process of social interaction, then the local territory, which is where people live and move and have their being in interaction with one another, is the place to begin the search for the community of the future (Kaufman 1985, p. 55). Territory-free and multilocality networks are worthy of study in their own right, but so are relationships in the locality of residence. As to mobility and freedom, Fischer (1977, p. 192) counters the "place-chains" criticism of the territorial community, arguing instead that what is declining are involuntary constraints on community attachment and not necessarily the actual strength of attachments to particular places. As people become less constrained and more mobile in the future, the freedom they experience could serve to strengthen rather than to weaken the voluntary commitments they make to the process of acting on behalf of the community of residence. This could occur because community development as a purposive activity thrives on freedom and is stifled by bondage (Wilkinson 1979). Finally, the fact that localism can be a tool for class domination and exploitation is an important challenge to community development in the future, but this fact does not rule out the possibility that community will develop on a locality basis. An important task for analysis of community changes in a setting of class divisions and exploitation is to avoid the error of mistaking pseudo-forms of community and false appeals to community solidarity for the real thing. In promoting community development, an important task is to identify and cultivate the underlying potential for community to emerge and become a factor in reducing inequality and exploitation in the local society.

The other side of the argument about the future of the territorial community is a question about whether community as an interactional phenomenon can develop in settings other than a local territory. Wellman and Leighton (1979) argue for tracing the community to networks beyond the locality, but for them the *locality* is the neighborhood, and *beyond* for them refers to the totality of the local urban settlement. The approach by Bender (1978), who argues for truly space-free communities, poses a more basic question. Can people who are not in frequent interactions on a face-to-face basis and whose lives are not organized on a daily basis by many of the same associations and networks be said to make up a community? If community requires a "common life" in the sense Toennies gave to *Gemeinschaft,* it seems doubtful that space-free networks could support community development. Individuals in the future no doubt will meet many important needs in space-free contacts, but such contacts can never suffice to meet the needs that are met in community interaction.

The idea of a common life in the local society, of course, is what actually is at issue in most arguments over the territorial element in community definition. Indeed, theories of community usually concentrate not on territory but on the organization of institutions and social networks in the social life of the local population. As MacIver (in MacIver and Page 1949, p. 9) says, "The mark of a community is that one's life *may* be lived wholly within it." The crux of the matter of how territory will relate to social networks in the future is the question of whether such complete communities will be found in the future.

MacIver's point, however, is easily misinterpreted. Community needs a complete local society but this need not be the only local society to which residents relate. It need not be the "cradle to the grave arrangement" (Redfield 1955, p. 4) of the folk village, although its structure must be complete and no important aspect of society should be missing from it. Furthermore, a local society can be an open one, a "community among communities" (Redfield 1955). It can support community even though people move constantly through its open structure as they relate to other units such as the family, the neighborhood, organizations, other local societies, and state and national structures. Multiplicity of involvements of people need not rule out the development of community in the local societies of the future.

A serious threat to community, however, is implied in the observation that the local society is becoming only a stage or arena rather than a coherent social unit. Warren (1978, pp. 408–22) comments on this by drawing a distinction between two conceptions of the community, one using the concept of system and the other using the concept of field. As a system, the community is an integral unit, a system of systems, as it were, relating to its environment and to the outside world as a single acting entity. A field, on the other hand, is a dynamic, turbulent arena in which separate acting units pursue their own interests, forming temporary alliances with one another but having no enduring solidarity as a locality-based whole. What is happening, he says, is that the community is becoming less of a system and more of a field as the various parts (or subsystems) of the community become more firmly integrated into separate systems outside the locality and less connected systemically to one another within the locality.

If the local society is no longer to be a system but instead to be a site where the separate activities of outside systems are staged, what kind of a future can there be for community development? An answer requires a critical appraisal of the observation that the community once was a system and now is a field. In contrast to this notion of a transition from system to field is the thesis that the community has been a field and not a system all along—at least throughout the history of the community in America. System and field are different conceptions of the community, not different stages in the evolution of the community (see Wilkinson 1970). System exaggerates the orderliness and cohesion of the communities of the past, and this feeds the myth that the community is now disappearing or becoming only a stage. When community, past and present, is recognized for what it actually is—an interaction field characterized by both order and disorder—a different view of the future for community development is possible.

As a field, the modern community has always been connected to the outside through multiple separate ties, and local life has always been a setting for lively and sometimes vicious confrontations among separate interest groups. Community as an interaction process copes with the turbulence of local interaction, and community development operates within it. In brief, the problem with a concept of system demise as a scenario of the future of community development is that this scenario assumes community is or has been a system. This reifies and distorts the community. When the community is viewed instead as a field of social interaction, a more hopeful perspective on the future is possible.

There is, in fact, considerable room for doubt that much change has occurred in modern times or will occur in the near future in the fundamental structure and role of community in American social life. People live together in places, no matter how fuzzy and changing might be the boundaries of those places. They encounter the larger society primarily through interactions in the local society, albeit through organizations with outside ties. And, at crucial moments, they can act together to express a common interest in the place of residence. Local social life is complex, and perhaps it is becoming more so, but complexity and turbulence do not in and of themselves rule out community and community development. Community development in the past has occurred in a milieu of turbulent change, and it can occur in such a milieu in the future. In the midst of complexity and turbulence, the latent bond of solidarity among people who share a local society can draw them together now and then in the process of community interaction.

IMPEDIMENTS TO COMMUNITY DEVELOPMENT. Taken alone, the potential for community to develop whenever neighbors interact does not assure the occurrence of community development. Other factors can suppress and distort community interaction. Population size and inequality are leading examples. In assessing the future for community development, trends on these and other potential impediments to community interaction must be taken into consideration.

The effect of local population size, of course, is the subject of one of the most longstanding and confused debates in the literature on the community. Does community tend to disappear as size increases, or does increased size contribute to community development by enhancing adaptive capacity? Between these positions stands Dewey's (1960) well-known assessment of the sociological consequences of rural-urban variation in local ecology. The consequences, he says, are "real but relatively unimportant." Dewey's judgment, however, refers explicitly to effects of rural-urban ecology on sociocultural organization, that is, on the complex of institutional patterns and values that comprise a total way of life. A quite different judgment can be defended when the focus is narrowed to consider only the immediate effects of local population size on the process of local social interaction. At this level, the effects are both real and important.

In particular, as Mayhew and Levinger (1976) argue (building on earlier observations by Durkheim and Simmel), the number of persons in interaction affects opportunities for social contacts, and these opportunities can influence both the volume and form of social interaction. This is a matter of considerable importance to community development if community development is defined as a local process of social interaction. For example, to use network concepts proposed by Granovetter (1973), population size affects opportunities for "strong ties" and for "weak ties" among people—the former being repeated, intimate contacts and the latter being passing, formal contacts. When the population is small, more of the contacts are in strong ties, simply because opportunities for weak ties are limited. In places with larger populations, opportunities are conducive to weak ties as well as to strong ties. Thus, both the volume of potential contacts and the probable mix of weak and strong ties vary by size of population.

Community development obviously depends on the presence of strong ties among local residents; without these there would be little cohesion in local interaction. But as Granovetter (1973) argues, weak ties also contribute to the unity and stability of community structure; strong ties in isolation, without weak ties to link them to the larger community, can become disruptive. Thus, rural areas, where strong ties predominate, have an advantage for community development in one sense but a disadvantage in another. Small population size encourages close contacts and these are essential for community development. But small population size discourages other contacts that also contribute to community development. Thus, a small community has a community problem.

At the other extreme, as Hoch (1976) shows, the benefits of increasing size tend to level and then recede beyond some threshold, although the threshold point can differ from place to place. The problem in this for community interaction is that beyond some point the local population becomes too large for the whole to comprise a community, even though community-like relationships (e.g., strong ties) might persist in parts of the whole. Considering both the benefits and costs of increasing size, therefore, it appears that the optimal setting for community development would be closer to the middle of the population size distribution than to either of the extremes.

With this as background, an examination of prevailing trends in population distribution uncovers a serious threat to the future for community development. In a nutshell, the trends suggest that the middle range of this distribution is disappearing. Specifically, notwithstanding a brief (though dramatic) reversal of the nonmetropolitan pattern in the early 1970s (Fuguitt 1985), the dominant population trend in modern societies is metropolitan growth. To be sure, the trend today and for the future is not simply an extension of the suburbanization movement of the 1950s and 1960s. As Hawley (1978) notes, the current trend is a new pattern of "diffuse urbanization" made possible by new developments in technology, especially in technology for long-distance communications. New cities are growing outside the old central-place hierarchy, and metropolitan influence is reaching far beyond old hinterland limits. Consequently, most people and settlements are being drawn one way or another into massive metropolitan fields, and the residual population is being reduced, in a kind of distillation, to those who are, as it were, truly rural. This polarization, with most people in large metropolitan fields and some left behind in relatively isolated and truly rural settlements, presignifies an imperiled future for community development.

Inequality is another major factor in the future for community development. As is true of population size, inequality can have direct effects on both the extent and the quality of local social interaction, and these effects can block the emergence of community among people who live together and share a common life in a local settlement. As a general effect, inequality suppresses contacts among people whose lives in fact are interrelated. That is, it impedes the free and open flow of communication and negotiation among population segments, and community development is blocked to the extent this flow is impeded. Moreover, inequality can distort the interaction which occurs. It can engender, for example, a state of hegemony wherein an elite grouping convinces other groupings to support schemes that in fact will benefit only the elite grouping (Bridger and Harp 1987). Inequality also can provoke hostility and violence, and it can disrupt community interaction in numerous and subtle ways (Wilkinson 1984). Trends in inequality, therefore, bear heavily on the future for community development.

Unquestionably, many of the traditional bases of inequality within communities have declined over the years in the face of institutional changes and increased education and levels of living. The emergence of a global political economy, however, has introduced a new basis of inequality, one likely to grow rather than to decline in importance in the future. In particular, the incorporation of local areas into a world economy is contributing to an unevenness of development among communities and regions (see Gartrell 1983), and this spatial inequality in turn is contributing to inequality within local areas.

Unevenness of development among areas is reinforced if not produced (see Browett 1984) by profit-seeking strategies in the global economy. These strategies govern the movement of capital and the uses of space. Capital mobility, augmented and expanded to world scale by modern technologies, makes possible a system whereby local areas are assigned specialized uses and thus are stratified by use-value in the larger system. Moreover, the development of a global system makes development in local areas dependent on outside investments. Freed by technology from fixed location, capital can be moved quickly from place to place in the search for profits, and profits produced in peripheral areas can be moved quickly to a center for accumulation and extraction. Thus, modern development entails and reinforces a pattern of spatial inequality in the distribution of access to socioeconomic resources for meeting the needs of people.

In modern development, inequality within local settlements generally accompanies inequality among settlements for a more or less self-evident reason. The process of stratification of places whereby local well-being comes to depend on use-value of the local society in the larger society also stratifies local groupings according to their access to outside resources. An elite class of "gatekeepers" emerges locally in this process not so much because of traditional deference patterns within the local population but because the larger system favors a selected local grouping which becomes, as it were, the agents of the larger system. Stratification within the community becomes, therefore, less a consequence of local interaction and more a consequence of interaction with the larger society.

The new technologies which facilitate the pattern of diffuse metropolitan growth in modern society also facilitate the development of a global political economy and its attendant spatial inequalities. In fact, these developments can be seen as different faces of the same process, a process that will make community development as defined here an uphill fight, to say the least, in the future.

EFFORTS TO PROMOTE COMMUNITY DEVELOPMENT. Community development is a natural, ubiquitous tendency in local social life but one impeded seriously, if not ruled out entirely, by extant trends in modern society. Assuming that a natural, ubiquitous tendency in social life has the potential to contribute to social well-being (see Wilkinson 1979), the prevailing trends pose something of a threat to human welfare as well as to community development. Potentiality and impediments to the realization of human potential, however, are only part of the story. The future for community development also depends on the volitional efforts of people, people who will promote community development in the future. Purposive effort, in fact, can be the most important factor in the future for community development.

Efforts are needed at three levels to promote community development. These include (1) efforts by local actors to build local capacity for collective action and self-help, (2) efforts to articulate and implement community development as a policy goal in the larger society, and (3) efforts in science and education to assist those who promote community development in local societies and in the larger society. If the assumptions of the interactional theory of community are correct, such efforts have the potential to overcome the constraints on community development represented by modern trends.

A call for efforts at the local level simply affirms the concept of community development as a local action process. Whatever the volume and intensity of efforts at other levels, the process of community development does not occur unless local actors make it occur. Efforts to promote community development as a national policy goal and efforts to create and implement community development strategies in science and education must keep this simple fact at the forefront: community development in the final analysis consists of purposive actions by local actors.

By the same token, however, local efforts alone are not likely to overcome the formidable barriers to community development represented by modern trends. Community actors need help in coping with forces that are organized at regional, national, and world levels. National policy is one important arena where community development can be promoted. In this arena, perhaps the most important guide to an effective policy for community development in the future would be to emphasize the role of community in the development process. As noted earlier (and see Wilkinson 1979), economic development and other forms of area development without community development can be divisive and exploitative. Where development of community is an explicit goal, on the other hand, developments in communities can be undertaken and directed in such a way as to enhance community well-being (see Ryan 1987).

This is not to say, however, that the emphasis in policy should be explicitly on the process of community development. Instead the emphasis should be on conditions which block or facilitate that process. In a sense, the process takes care of itself—as a natural disposition it occurs on its own when unimpeded. In practical terms, the emphasis in policy should be on assuring that people can meet their needs together and can participate actively and collectively in solving their common problems. People need jobs and services, for example, and the meeting of these and other such needs should be the overriding objective of a community development policy. The distinctive twist that would make a policy a community development policy rather simply a policy of job development or service development, however, would be that the policy would promote job development and service development through a process that would also encourage and involve community action.

Likewise, in science and education the focus of community development programs should be on developments *in* the community that operate through and contribute to the process of development *of* community. Community leadership development is a case in point (see Moyer, Heasley, and Tait 1986). In the past, many educational programs have emphasized individual leadership skills and technical knowledge in such problem areas as economic development, service delivery, and environmental resource management. In the future, without neglecting these important tools, it will be equally important to emphasize the community element in community leadership development. Otherwise, skills and knowledge acquired by individuals can be tools to promote private rather than public interests. In practice as in policy, community development in the future will depend on how well actors are able to attend to the needs of the process of community interaction while they work toward accomplishing specific action goals.

A Challenge for Research and Action.
Community development, a keystone of rural and urban planning in the past, is emerging again as a focus of proposals to address pressing problems in more or less developed societies. Poverty, inadequate services, and the consequences of these persist as problems of local settlements around the world, especially in rural areas; and community development – the process of building local capacity for community action and self-help – promises to be part of the solution. The revival of interest in the process of community development is part of a search for ways to transform fragmented and transitory development initiatives into comprehensive, self-sustaining programs at the local level.

Renewed interest in community development, however, also calls renewed attention to gaps in research on this topic. Theories of community development have not been as well formulated as prescriptive models have been, and much of the empirical literature on community development consists of project descriptions rather than the scientific studies needed to test and refine theories. Unanswered are such elementary questions as, Under what conditions does community development occur? What are the effects of differences among localities in ecology, history, and level of economic development? Beyond these basic issues is the crucial question for policy and practice: Assuming that community development makes a difference in social well-being, how can this process be cultivated and encouraged in the future? Closing the research gap by answering these questions is a necessary step toward ensuring a future for the interactional process of community development.

References

Bell, C., and H. Newby. 1976. Community, communion, class and community action: The social sources of the new urban politics. In *Social Areas in Cities,* Vol. 2: *Spacial Perspectives on Problems and Policies,* D. Herbert and R. Johnston, eds., pp. 189–207. London: Wiley.

Bender, T. 1978. *Community and Social Change in America.* New Brunswick, N.J.: Rutgers University Press.

Bridger, J. C., and A. J. Harp. 1987. Molotch's growth machine revisited. Paper presented to the annual meeting of the Rural Sociological Society, Madison, Wis., August.

Browett, J. 1984. On the necessity and inevitability of uneven spatial development under capitalism. *International Journal of Urban and Regional Research* 8(2):155–74.

Dewey, R. 1960. The rural-urban continuum: Real but relatively unimportant. *American Journal of Sociology* 66(1):60–66.

Dunham, A. 1960. The outlook for community development. *International Review of Community Development* 5:3–55.

Fischer, C. S. 1977. Comments on the history and study of "community." In *Networks and Places: Social Relations in the Urban Setting*, C. Fischer and associates, eds., pp. 189–204. New York: Free Press.

Fuguitt, G. V. 1985. The nonmetropolitan population turnaround. *Annual Review of Sociology* 11:259–80.

Gartrell, J. W. 1983. Agricultural technology and agrarian community organization. In *Technology and Social Change in Rural Areas*, G. F. Summers, ed., pp. 149–62. Boulder, Colo.: Westview Press.

Granovetter, M. 1973. The strength of weak ties. *American Journal of Sociology* 78(6):1360–80.

Gusfield, J. 1975. *Community: A Critical Response.* Oxford: Basil Blackwell.

Hawley, A. H. 1950. *Human Ecology: A Theory of Community Structure.* New York: Ronald Press.

_____. 1978. Urbanization as a process. In *Handbook of Contemporary Urban Life*, D. Street and associates, eds., pp. 3–26. San Francisco: Jossey-Bass.

Hillery, G. A., Jr. 1955. Definitions of community: Areas of agreement. *Rural Sociology* 20(2):111–23.

Hoch, I. 1976. City size effects, trends, and policies. *Science* 193:856–63.

Kaufman, H. F. 1959. Toward an interactional conception of community. *Social Forces* 38(1):8–17.

_____. 1985. An action approach to community development. In *Research in Rural Sociology and Development*, Vol. 2: *Focus on the Community*, F. Fear and H. Schwarzweller, eds., pp. 53–65. Greenwich, Conn.: JAI Press.

Kaufman, H. F., and K. P. Wilkinson. 1967. *Community Structure and Leadership: An Interactional Perspective in the Study of Community.* State College: Social Science Research Center, Missouri State University, Bulletin 13.

Konig, R. 1968. *The Community*, E. Fitzgerald, trans. New York: Schocken Books.

MacIver, R. M., and C. H. Page. 1949. *Society: An Introductory Analysis.* New York: Rinehart.

Mayhew, B. H., and R. L. Levinger. 1976. Size and density of interaction in human aggregates. *American Journal of Sociology* 82(1):86–110.

Molotch, H. 1976. The city as a growth machine: Toward a political economy of place. *American Journal of Sociology* 82(2):309–32.

Moyer, H., D. Heasley, and J. Tait. 1986. *Community Leadership Development: Present and Future.* University Park, Pa.: Northeast Regional Center for Rural Development.

Nisbet, R. A. 1953. *The Quest for Community: A Study in the Ethics of Order and Freedom.* New York: Oxford University Press.

Redfield, R. 1955. *The Little Community: Viewpoints for the Study of a Human Whole.* Chicago: University of Chicago Press.

Ryan, V. D. 1987. The significance of community development to rural economic development initiatives. In *Rural Economic Development in the 1980's: Preparing for the Future,* D. Brown, ed., pp. 1–15, Ch. 16. Washington, D.C.: Economic Research Service, U.S. Department of Agriculture.

Sanders, I. T. 1958. Theories of community development. *Rural Sociology* 23(1):1–12.

Scherer, J. 1972. *Contemporary Community: Sociological Illusion or Reality?* London: Tavistock.

Schmalenbach, H. 1961. The sociological category of communion. In *Theories of Society,* Vol. 1, T. Parsons, E. Shils, K. Naegele, and J. Pitts, eds., pp. 331–47. New York: Free Press.

Summers, G. F. 1986. Rural community development. *Annual Review of Sociology* 13:341–71.

Sutton, W. A., and J. Kolaja. 1960. The concept of community. *Rural Sociology* 25(2):197–203.

Toennies, F. 1957. *Community and Society,* C. Loomis, trans. East Lansing: Michigan State University Press.

Warren, R. L. 1978. *The Community in America,* 3d ed. Chicago: Rand McNally.

Wellman, B. 1979. The community question: The intimate networks of East Yorkers. *American Journal of Sociology* 84(5):1201–31.

Wellman, B., and B. Leighton. 1979. Networks, neighborhoods, and communities: Approaches to the study of the community question. *Urban Affairs Quarterly* 14(3):363–90.

Wilkinson, K. P. 1970. The community as a social field. *Social Forces* 48(3):311–22.

_____. 1972. A field-theory perspective for community development research. *Rural Sociology* 37(1):43–52.

_____. 1979. Social well-being and community. *Journal of the Community Development Society* 10(1):5–16.

_____. 1984. Rurality and patterns of social disruption. *Rural Sociology* 49(1):23–36.

_____. 1986. In search of the community in the changing countryside. *Rural Sociology* 51(1):1–17.

Learning Exercises
and Case Studies

This section was designed to provide material for class discussions, group projects, and/or test questions.

1. Community Development

1. What are the primary goals of community development?

2. How does community development impact localities?

3. There are different definitions of community mentioned in this chapter. One definition emphasized community as a network where social interaction takes place. For example, people who work together share a common bond, their work, and therefore are a community by this definition. The same can be said of people who share an interest in and play a sport together. Community development is defined in Chapter 1 as social interaction among people living within a geographical area who have psychological ties with each other and with the place where they live. Using your own experiences, give examples and defend each perspective of community before explaining which definition you accept and why.

4. The authors define community development as a group of people in a locality initiating a social action process to change their economic, social, cultural, or environmental situation. Look in today's newspaper. Can you find an example of this form of community development occurring in your locality? Can you think of examples of community development actions taken to change the economic, social, cultural, or environmental situations in your area?

5. Take each of Drucker's (1986) three worldwide changes and bring them down to the local level. Use communities you know in describing how these worldwide changes have affected local areas.

6. The section on the future mentions leadership as a critical element in successful community development. What makes a good leader? Where are the good leaders today? Do they exist? Why or why not? In other words, what promotes or impedes the development of good leadership?

7. Rural reflation emphasizes preserving towns, that is, survival instead of massive expansions. Do you think this is viable, or is it an underestimation of what can be done in communities today?

2. *Themes of Community Development*

1. Are all development efforts considered to be community development? Why or why not?

2. Can you have community development without people development? Why or why not?

3. Defend your response to each of the following questions: Is all change development? Can community development occur without change? Can change occur without community development?

4. What is the difference between development *in* the community and development *of* the community? Can the two types be separated? Should they be separated? Why or why not?

5. Compare and contrast the self-help, technical assistance, and conflict orientations of community development. Which do you prefer and why?

6. Why is citizen participation so important to community development?

7. What are some problems with community development as an area of study?

8. Describe a community development program or project which began because of a community conflict. In other words, reflect on your experience for a moment, then in a brief narrative describe how conflict stimulated change and development.

3. *The Self-Help Approach*

1. What is the relationship between a commitment to the idea of self-help and the social concept of community?

2. Why is it sometimes necessary to have an outside professional consultant to enable a community to help itself?

3. Why might it undermine a community development worker's effectiveness if he or she were perceived as an official or a gatekeeper for the needed resources?

4. Why might local community development goals differ from national development goals?

5. What does it mean to say that many contemporary communities have become dependent?

6. Is dependence on democratic participation and decision making an "efficient" way for communities to improve themselves?

7. What can communities do when they realize that many of the factors that affect community life and economy are beyond their control?

8. Can a community achieve a greater degree of self-determination while remaining partially dependent on outside resources?

9. What are some of the reasons community members fail to participate in community development efforts?

10. What difference does it make whether people participate or not, as long as community improvements are made?

11. Why might it be useful to the success of self-help efforts for communities to establish policies for themselves?

4. The Technical Assistance Approach

1. When is the technical assistance approach most appropriate for community development? Why?

2. What are the advantages and disadvantages of using the technical assistance approach in community development?

3. In what way is the technical assistance approach appropriate in developed nations and in developing countries? Why?

4. What ethical dilemma may be associated with the use of technology transfer? Why?

5. How does technical assistance contribute to community capacity building?

6. Some feel that the process by which technical assistance is carried out is as important as the content of the assistance. React to this statement. What are your opinions and why?

7. Discuss the relevance of the mnemonic "A V-I-C-T-O-R-Y" for the practice of technical assistance in community development.

8. Are the Principles of Good Practice (developed by the Community Development Society in 1985) relevant to your situation? How?

9. What is "appropriate technology" in community development, in terms of technical assistance?

10. Discuss the ideological, political, and agency-related factors that frequently inhibit the linkage of technical assistance with other approaches to community development.

5. The Conflict Approach

PART ONE: A CASE STUDY— THE DILEMMA

There is a problem among residents, landowners, and the U.S. Department of Agriculture personnel in the "One-Stop USDA Center" in Hill County, a county with limited water resources, much marginal farmland, and severe erosion problems. Hill County lies forty miles south of Central City, a very large metropolitan area. A small river divides the county, and erosion from spring flooding is frequently a problem. Summer and fall are especially dry periods.

Recently a group of developers from Central City have taken options to purchase over 5,000 acres of land along the river just north of the county seat, a town of 2,500 people. These outside entrepreneurs propose to develop a needed water resource for the county seat, but their primary objective is to provide lots for weekend retreats for Central City residents. They plan to build a 2,500-acre lake and to sell over 2,000 lots. Mobile homes will be located on the east side of the lake, while the other side will be zoned for large lots and houses of various size requirements. Also, the developers propose a public marina for boating and water skiing.

The Soil Conservation Service (SCS) of the USDA became involved when the developers sought help in certain areas. First, they want the watershed protected from soil erosion. They are willing to give free water to county-seat residents if SCS will require all landowners in the watershed to put all sloping and highly erodible land in trees and pasture within five years. No cultivation! The county zoning authority and the town council favor all of these actions, but the County Board of Supervisors (Commissioners) is divided. The chairman of the County Board is a large land owner with over 2,000 acres of row crops. All of his farm lies in the watershed, about three miles north of the proposed lake.

In brief, the developers are saying, "We will build the beautiful lake for recreational use and for a public water resource, but the SCS must persuade farmers to take all the watershed land which is really too steep for cultivation out of production." And, here is the kicker—they expect the Agricultural Stabilization and Conservation Service (ASCS) to pay the farmers for complying, even though the land is marginal. They said, "We have read about government subsidies for farmers and it's a good deal for them."

The County Board chairman has attacked these "outside city slickers who will destroy the beauty of Hill County countryside." Also, he said, "We don't need trailer courts filled with riffraff from Central City." However, many prominent local business leaders, especially those in lumber, hardware, and construction, favor the development.

The district commissioner for SCS has agreed to help conduct an environmental impact study for the developers. However, when the local Soil and Water Conservation District (SWCD) Board of Directors learned of his decision, they objected. One stated, "You ought to be working for us farmers instead of doing leg work for a bunch of money happy @#*$ from Central City!" The SWCD Board threatened SCS and ASCS with drastic action if the district conservationist didn't do all he could to stop the "raping and flooding of our beautiful countryside!"

Instructions and Discussion Questions

Respond to each of the following questions. If you are working as a team, select a team leader to record notes and report on your discussion to the entire group. If you are working alone, write a brief answer to each question.

1. What are the major sources of conflict?
2. Identify all the threats made.

3. What territories are challenged?

4. Assume you are the district conservationist. How will you manage this conflict?

5. Have you experienced any conflicts similar to this situation? If so, how did you respond? Did it work? Why or why not?

6. What benefits could result from this conflict?

7. What liabilities (negative outcomes) could result from this conflict?

8. Identify each of the following stages of the conflict cycle by listing behavior which describes it:
   a. Tension development
   b. Role dilemma
   c. Injustice collecting
   d. Confrontation

9. What adjustments would you propose?

10. Should SCS be involved? Why? Justify your position.

11. What would you do if you were
    a. the district commissioner?
    b. the chairman of the County Board?
    c. the president of the Hill County Soil and Water Conservation District?
    d. the major of the county seat?
    e. the owner of the only hardware and lumber company in town?

PART TWO: STUDY QUESTIONS

1. Review examples of roles or descriptions listed in Chapter 5 for each of the following management behavior styles. Check all the behaviors you have used in real-life situations.

Dominator

_____ Confronted actors
_____ Imposed solutions
_____ Used authority

_____ Used power
_____ Told people what to do
_____ Made threats

Manipulator

_____ Appealed for help
_____ Used guilt, pity, or duty
_____ Accepted blame

_____ Emphasized values
_____ Offered bribes or rewards
_____ Overworked

Mediator

_____ Established ground rules
_____ Confronted all actors
_____ Developed trust

_____ Used involvement
_____ Kept communications open and flowing
_____ Used questioning and listening behavior

Compromiser

_____ Argued some, but not forcefully	_____ Diverted action to other problems
_____ Avoided judging or ridiculing	_____ Gave in to others
_____ Used ego needs	_____ Used humor

Avoider

_____ Withdrew or missed work meetings	_____ Took sick leave or vacation during crisis
_____ Turned leadership over to avoid having to assume risk	_____ Assumed no responsibility for leadership during crisis
_____ Used delaying tactics to avoid having to assume risk	_____ Simply ignored the problem

2. Tabulate your totals for each style.
   a. Which style do you think you use most frequently?
   b. Which style do you use second most often, or what is your back-up style?
   c. Which style do you use least?
3. Describe situations where
   a. the dominator's style won't work.
   b. the manipulator's style won't work.
   c. the compromiser's style won't work.
   d. the avoider's style won't work.

6. Professional Community Development Roles

1. What are the tasks generally associated with a community development professional's role?

2. Describe the relationship between a community development practitioner and the community. Ideally, what should it be like?

3. Have individual traits been found to be associated with the success of community development professionals? If yes, in what ways?

4. How does the organizational affiliation of community development workers influence the way they function?

5. Discuss the pros and cons of certification and accreditation within the community development profession. How do these two concepts differ?

6. How is the community development professional's role changing?

7. The Practice of Community Development

1. Think of an agency, organization, political subdivision, or other group that might be involved in planning. What internal and external factors – social, political, technological, economic – should be analyzed as a part of the planning process?

2. Two purposes of evaluation are to measure accomplishment and to modify process. Are there other purposes for evaluation? At what times and in what ways might evaluation be done in a planning effort?

3. Imagine an agency, organization, political subdivision, or other group that is involved in planning. Discuss Friedmann's concept of mutuality in relationship to that situation. Specifically, what might a planner contribute? What would the local group contribute?

4. Assume that you are part of a group planning a neighborhood park on land reclaimed by a city in an inner-city neighborhood. Write an appropriate goal, a set of objectives, and a method for the project.

5. Frequently special populations (e.g., incarcerated persons, mentally retarded persons, children) are not consulted about their needs when services are being planned for them. Discuss how they might be consulted and the benefits and risks involved.

6. Using the examples cited in the discussion of community organizing, suggest specific ways in which a community developer can provide support but discourage dependency.

7. Can you identify additional examples in which professionals, volunteers, and other helpers work together in community development? In what ways can this cooperative relationship be enhanced?

8. What are some of the barriers to inclusiveness in community decision making? How can these barriers be removed?

9. If you were a potential donor, what criteria would you use in judging proposals for community development projects? Why?

8. Teaching Community Development

1. How would you go about designing a fieldwork experience to apply the concepts discussed in this chapter?

2. How do you relate the complex and continuous process of social change to the discrete and interventive process of community development?

3. Human relations is an important concept in community development. Give some examples of how this concept relates to community development practice.

4. An operational theory of community development should bring theory, knowledge, and practice together. What practical steps can community development professionals take to bring an operational theory into being?

5. Some authors believe community development places too much emphasis on consensus and citizen involvement. Do you agree or disagree? State your position and be prepared to support it.

6. If you were responsible for designing a master's degree program in community development, what would your major objective be, and what, in general, would you include in the curriculum?

7. How much practical internship experience should a potential community development professional have? What should be the characteristics or major ingredients in an internship? Defend your position.

9. *Community Economic Development*

PART ONE: STUDY QUESTIONS

1. What does the concept of community competition mean in the context of community economic development efforts? In what forms or dimensions of the community does it occur?

2. Are community economic development and community economic vitality short-run or long-run concepts and why?

3. An analogy of community and household/business decision making was given in the text. Do you think such an analogy is appropriate? Why?

4. Why are market signals and resource mobility so important to the supply-oriented approach to community economic development?

5. Technical change and spread (adoption) are crucial aspects of the supply-oriented approach. How does technological spread affect community economic development, and what might influence its rate of change?

6. Explain the significance of the statement that "community economic vitality requires public and private support . . . [to] insure continued availability of factors of production."

7. What might prevent local states from exceeding "national normals of equity"?

8. Since the local state cannot create financial capital, how might it influence the local supply of capital?

9. What are some characteristics associated with entrepreneurs that are particularly significant to a community adapting to change?

10. What are the elements of a comprehensive community economic development strategy? How are they interrelated?

11. What are some of the anticipated socioeconomic changes in the community after an economic development event? What might alter their magnitude?

12. What is the logic of rural industrialization as a development policy?

PART TWO: A FIELD WORK OF PRACTICUM STUDY GUIDE

The following questions are offered as examples of dimensions of a community's economy that need to be examined as a community consciously seeks to chart its own economic future. Despite the desire of many, there is no standard list of questions that is applicable to every community. The two sets of questions that follow need not all be answered and many of them lack concrete answers. However, this should not prevent individuals within a community from thinking about the implications of various responses. Consideration of them will help in developing a picture of the community and the level of its economic development.

The second portion of this exercise is a community self-survey on how prepared the community is for economic development. There are no correct answers that ensure local economic development. This survey is best used as a discussion device for a group. The group needs to make the qualitative judgments on how well they are doing at the end of each question, but unanimity is not required.

PART A: DIMENSION OF COMMUNITY ECONOMY

  I. Population
    A. Number of people by
      1. Age (by five-to-ten-year age cohorts)
      2. Immigrants last five years
      3. Education of population
        a. Median years
        b. Percent with high school diploma
        c. Percent with college diploma
      4. Occupational structure
        a. Technical
        b. Professional
        c. Operatives
  II. Income
    A. Sources of personal income
      1. Wages and salaries
      2. Proprietors' income
      3. Passive income (dividends, interest, rent, and transfer payments)
    B. Earnings
      1. Farm
      2. Nonfarm
        a. Manufacturing
        b. Trade
        c. Services
        d. Government
 III. Location
    A. Distance to major metropolitan areas
    B. Distance to next largest community (either 20,000 inhabitants or at least 1½ times the municipality's population)
      1. Miles
      2. Time

IV. Transportation/communication
    A. Access to interstate or limited-access highway
    B. Number and condition of state or federal class A highways passing through the community
    C. Access to airports
    D. Communication
        1. Telephone capacity to carry computer data
        2. Availability of fiber optics for long-distance data transmission
        3. Cable TV
    E. Availability of newspapers and radio stations
V. Employment (current, preceding five years)
    A. Full-time jobs
    B. Part-time jobs
    C. Sectors of employment
    D. Wage levels for various occupations
        1. Unskilled, semi-skilled, skilled
        2. Factory work, office work, clerical work
VI. Natural resource base
    A. Access to water
        1. Transportation (harbors, rivers)
        2. Recreation
    B. Forestry resources
    C. Mineral resources
VII. Mainstreet/commercial sector
    A. How many new retail establishments have been established in the community in the last year, two years, five years?
        1. What proportion of them have been in the central location?
        2. What proportion of them have been in a suburban location?
    B. How much of the community retail occurs in a central business district versus scattered outlying business areas?
    C. What proportion of the storefronts are vacant or deteriorated?
VIII. What are the financial resources of the community?
    A. How many financial institutions are there and what are their sizes?
    B. What has been the growth in deposits, assets, total loans, and business loans of the financial institutions?
    C. What types of business loans have the financial institutions made?
    D. What are the working relationships among financial institutions?
IX. What is the attitude/institutional arrangement of the community?
    A. What is the working relationship between the business sector and local government?
    B. What types of private and public partnerships exist?
        1. Industrial development
        2. Commercial revitalization
        3. Labor training and mobilization
        4. Financial packaging

PART B: COMMUNITY ECONOMIC PREPAREDNESS

Instructions

The purpose of the community economic preparedness index* is to help citizens analyze and plan action to improve their community's opportunity to increase employment and income. The index is a list of activities and conditions that can be controlled by the community.

To complete the form, check the *yes* or *no* blanks for each item, then rank the category as a whole. If you do not know, mark *?*. Items marked *no* and categories rated *fair* or *minimal* indicate areas in need of improvement. The index was designed for communities of between 1,000 and 20,000 people in size.

1. The community has an economics development plan.

Yes	No	?	
____	____	____	a. Prepared and reviewed by a citizens committee.
____	____	____	b. Formally adopted by the village board/city council within the past three years.
____	____	____	c. Includes a complete analysis of sources of employment.
____	____	____	d. Encourages economic development.

Circle one: Excellent - Good - Fair - Minimal

2. The community has a land use plan and zoning ordinance that delineates industrial commercial areas.

Yes	No	?	
____	____	____	a. It has been written or formally reviewed within the past three years.
____	____	____	b. Provision is made for expansion of commercial and industrial sites.

Circle one: Excellent - Good - Fair - Minimal

*Produced jointly by the Wisconsin Department of Development and the University of Wisconsin-Extension.

3. The community as an industrial development corporation.

Yes   No   ?
_____   _____   _____   a. There is an organized industrial development prospect contact team.
_____   _____   _____   b. An annual update of industrial development information has been filed with the Wisconsin Department of Development.
_____   _____   _____   c. The corporation has financed an industrial prospect search outside of the community within the past two years.
_____   _____   _____   d. Budget (amount).
_____   _____   _____   e. Membership (number).

Circle one: Excellent - Good - Fair - Minimal

4. The community as a contact system for inventorying vacant and available commercial buildings.

Yes   No   ?
_____   _____   _____   a. A list of current vacancies can be provided within two days.
_____   _____   _____   b. The list includes square footage, photographs, property description, and ownership.

Circle one: Excellent - Good - Fair - Minimal

5. The community has an industrial site (with vacancies).

Yes   No   ?
_____   _____   _____   a. It owns or has an option on a site of 1 acre or more.
_____   _____   _____   b. There is an adequate water line (10" or more) to the property line.
_____   _____   _____   c. There are heavy duty streets not through a residential area to the boundary.
_____   _____   _____   d. There is an adequate sewer line (12" or more) to the property line.
_____   _____   _____   e. A firm site price has been set.
_____   _____   _____   f. A soil test boring has been made.
_____   _____   _____   g. A copy of site covenants and restrictions is readily available.
_____   _____   _____   h. A topographical map is readily available, including site layout.

Circle one: Excellent - Good - Fair - Minimal

6. The community has a vacant shell building on an industrial site.

Yes   *No*   *?*

_____ _____ _____   a. Minimum of 10,000 sq. ft. total.
_____ _____ _____   b. Floor to ceiling clearance, 16 ft.
_____ _____ _____   c. It is expandable.
_____ _____ _____   d. Layout and photo are available.
_____ _____ _____   e. An annual update has been filed with the state department of development.

Circle one: Excellent - Good - Fair - Minimal

7. The community has done a labor survey within the past three years.

Yes   *No*   *?*

_____ _____ _____   a. It includes the number of people by employer.
_____ _____ _____   b. It includes a wage rate and fringe benefit analysis.
_____ _____ _____   c. It identifies which labor unions are present in the community.
_____ _____ _____   d. It describes the absenteeism rates.
_____ _____ _____   e. It identifies work force participation rates.
_____ _____ _____   f. It indicates the distance people will travel to work.
_____ _____ _____   g. The community is organized to do a special labor survey on request.

Circle one: Excellent - Good - Fair - Minimal

8. The community has a promotional brochure.

Yes   *No*   *?*

_____ _____ _____   a. It describes the recreational opportunities.
_____ _____ _____   b. It provides a description of services (e.g., retail, restaurants).
_____ _____ _____   c. It describes the quality of public services (e.g., schools, hospitals).
_____ _____ _____   d. It describes the private housing quality.
_____ _____ _____   e. It describes major employers (e.g., industry, commerce, government).
_____ _____ _____   f. It has been revised within the past two years.

Circle one: Excellent - Good - Fair - Minimal

9. The community has completed and distributed a Community Economic Profile within the past year. (Example: Those done by the Wisconsin Department of Development, public utilities, etc.)

Yes	No	?
___	___	___

Circle one: Excellent - Good - Fair - Minimal

10. The local government helps business acquire financing.

Yes   No   ?

___   ___   ___   a. Has passed an industrial revenue bond interest resolution.

___   ___   ___   b. Has created a tax increment financing (TIF) district.

___   ___   ___   c. Has encouraged the formation of a small business development organization.

Circle one: Excellent - Good - Fair - Minimal

11. Local banks support community economic development.

Yes   No   ?

___   ___   ___   a. Local banks have utilized a correspondent bank relationship in financing a local project within the past two years.

___   ___   ___   b. Local banks have actively solicited commercial and industrial loans within the past year.

___   ___   ___   c. Local banks have made Small Business Administration guaranteed loans within the past two years.

___   ___   ___   d. Bank officials are active in community economic development organizations.

Circle one: Excellent - Good - Fair - Minimal

12. The community has a program to encourage existing businesses (commercial and industrial).

Yes   No   ?

___   ___   ___   a. At least three adult courses in business management were taught last year.

___   ___   ___   b. The Chamber of Commerce, business organization, or industrial group makes regular visits to business managers.

___   ___   ___   c. An annual industrial and commercial recognition event (exhibit, field day) is held.

Circle one: Excellent - Good - Fair - Minimal

13. The community has a chamber of commerce or business organization working on retail sales programs and commercial development.

Yes   *No*   *?*

____   ____   ____   a. Has a paid executive (chamber of commerce, business organization) at least on a part-time basis.

____   ____   ____   b. Has a tourist promotion committee.

____   ____   ____   c. Number of members (total number).

____   ____   ____   d. Budget (figure).

Circle one: Excellent - Good - Fair - Minimal

14. The community has completed a trade area survey/analysis within the past three years.

Yes   *No*   *?*

____   ____   ____   a. The findings have been reported to local businesses.

____   ____   ____   b. The findings have been communicated to business prospects outside the community.

Circle one: Excellent - Good - Fair - Minimal

15. The community has an active downtown program.

Yes   *No*   *?*

____   ____   ____   a. It has a regular calendar of main street promotion activity (e.g., monthly trade days).

____   ____   ____   b. Has completed a downtown physical renovation within the past 10 years.

____   ____   ____   c. Merchants are following the plan when renovating.

____   ____   ____   d. Has a uniform billboard and street sign ordinance.

____   ____   ____   e. Has improved main street lighting, parking, and traffic flow within the past 10 years.

____   ____   ____   f. Number of downtown business area public parking spaces (number).

Circle one: Excellent - Good - Fair - Minimal

16. The community has a published directory.

Yes   *No*   *?*

____   ____   ____   a. Of restaurants.

____   ____   ____   b. Of motels and hotels.

____   ____   ____   c. Of recreational facilities.

Circle one: Excellent - Good - Fair - Minimal

17. The community has at least one major community event each year (one which has an impact broader than the community, attracting at minimum people from neighboring communities, e.g. pageants, festivals, contests, derbies, fairs).

List the events: _____

Circle one: Excellent - Good - Fair - Minimal

18. The public services of the community are adequate.

Yes   No   ?

____ ____ ____ a. The municipal fire service is Grade 6, 7, 8 or better (as rated in past five years).

____ ____ ____ b. Has capacity for environmentally sound solid waste management in landfill sites for at least five years.

____ ____ ____ c. Meets all Department of Natural Resources sewer discharge requirements or has initiated the facilities planning process.

____ ____ ____ d. Has excess water capacity equivalent to 5% of its current population.

____ ____ ____ e. Has an organized plan for next five years for capital improvements on streets.

____ ____ ____ f. Has an airport with a 3,900 foot paved runway or better.

Circle one: Excellent - Good - Fair - Minimal

19. The community has submitted proposals for state and/or federal funding for development programs.

Yes   No   ?

____ ____ ____ a. For housing.

____ ____ ____ b. For two of the following: sewer, water, streets, fire protection, waste management.

____ ____ ____ c. For one of the following: airport health protection, public parks, community building.

Circle one: Excellent - Good - Fair - Minimal

20. The community presents a positive living environment.

Yes	No	?	
___	___	___	a. There is an organized senior citizen transportation system.
___	___	___	b. There is a senior citizen public housing development.
___	___	___	c. There are 10 acres or more of public parks per 1,000 people.
___	___	___	d. There are fewer than 1,000 people per physician.
___	___	___	e. The percentage of low and moderate income households with housing assistance needs is below 12.5%.
___	___	___	f. All educational systems are adequate.
___	___	___	g. How many (number) youth organizations are there functioning in the community?

Circle one: Excellent - Good - Fair - Minimal

10. Local Organizations and Leadership in Community Development

PART ONE: STUDY QUESTIONS

1. Describe three major changes affecting communities today. Describe one consequence of each of these changes on how communities function.

2. Identify and briefly describe the four elements of the action approach to community analysis. Analyze how these elements produce a community action field.

3. You have been elected as the chair of the Parent-Teacher Association at your child's school and assigned the task of organizing a fund-raising program. Given your knowledge of the situational-contingency approach to leadership, what factors would you take into account as you begin preparing for your leadership role?

4. Explain how action research can be used to strengthen local organizations and leadership.

5. Describe the function of enlarging the information base of local communities in enhancing the operation of the action field of local communities.

6. Describe how the four tasks of local organizations (identified by Esman and Uphoff) would fit into the five-stage model of the community action system (proposed by Warren).

PART TWO: A CASE STUDY

Woodford County, Kentucky, is a part of the Lexington metropolitan statistical area, yet it retains a significant agricultural character. Twenty-nine cents of every personal income dollar in the county is derived from agricultural sales and services, and the number of hired farm workers increased by 1,440 or 34 percent in a five-year period. A considerable proportion of the vitality of the agricultural sector can be attributed to the presence of several very large and prominent horse farms. Indeed, about one half of the county's agricultural land is in horse farms.

Manufacturing is also an important economic sector and the five-year-old industrial park has just been filled with the addition of four new plants. The economic ties to the rest of the metropolitan area are very strong. Approximately 40 percent of Woodford countians commute to adjacent counties for employment, and approximately 68 percent of the persons working in Woodford on a daily basis are from neighboring counties.

In the last twenty years, the county has been experiencing growing pains. The county's population increased by 23 percent between 1970 and 1980 and by 23 percent again between 1980 and 1986. Residential subdivisions have been filling the urban services area of the primary city, Versailles (1980 population, 6,427), and a considerable number of five-acre residential tracts have been developed along the county roads by parcelling agricultural land. The pressures for this kind of development in the agricultural zone of the county are enormous. While agriculture is fairly strong in the county, not all farmers have weathered the recent economic crisis equally well. Agricultural land costs between $1,500 and $2,500 an acre. The same land subdivided into five-acre parcels will bring an average of $10,000 an acre. People from the central county of the SMA are attracted to the rural character of the county and the price of a five-acre parcel in Woodford is less than the cost of a residential lot in a subdivision in the central county.

There are five neighborhood organizations in the rural portion of the county, and two are actively seeking a historical district designation for their portion of the county. The county economic development association has been extremely successful, attracting five new plants to the community in the last three years. County residents have played significant roles in state government: the current governor, the lieutenant governor–elect, and a previous governor are long-term community members.

The county is currently revising its comprehensive land-use plan. At the same time, a proposal to subdivide a 134-acre farm into twenty-four 5-acre "minifarms" stimulated a strong public outcry from persons living near the affected area. Moreover, the water districts serving the rural portions of the county are seriously strained, and in some cases, water pressure drops to less than half the state recommended level for safe water. The city has proposed purchasing a farm approximately two miles from the city limits for building a new sewage treatment plant, and this too has provoked strong public protest. Finally, a bypass has been proposed that would link two four-lane highways that pass through the county. The bypass would divide nearly fifteen farms, one that has been in operation since the 1780s, and the bulk of the bypass would be outside the urban service area.

You have been asked to provide assistance to the county planning and zoning commission and the fiscal court, the governing administrative body. Given your knowledge of the importance of capacity building in community development, answer the following questions:

1. What recommendations would you give to these government bodies?
2. What strategies would you employ if the fiscal court told you to maximize citizen involvement in the development of the comprehensive land-use plan?
3. What would be your role as a community development specialist in this process? Would you use conflict? Why?

11. *Evaluation for Community Development*

PART ONE: A CASE STUDY

A bilateral international development assistance agency has provided funding for five years for a project that will set up an umbrella agency to channel funds and technical assistance to a group of private voluntary organizations (PVOs) using community development in an underdeveloped country. The umbrella agency is operated by a contractor. The host government's sponsoring agency is the ministry of agriculture. The concrete objective of the project was to change agricultural production practices – including practices to prevent soil erosion – using community development techniques. Each PVO uses a slightly different set of community development strategies. The project was detailed in a cause-effect scheme called "logical framework" at the time it was designed.

The project will be evaluated at midterm and at completion. At midterm, the evaluation will focus on assessing implementation and on potential midcourse corrections, including an early comparison of the different community development strategies being implemented. On completion, the evaluation will focus on (1) determining whether, and to what extent, the project met its goal(s); (2) whether the project should be refunded; and (3) which community development strategy was most effective. Finally, both evaluations will examine the extent to which the umbrella agency, the PVOs, and the community development strategies being pursued are viewed (and accepted) by the major stakeholders, including the small farmers who are the potential beneficiaries.

In addition, one of the project's proposed outputs is the existence and use of a method whereby participating communities evaluate their own activities in the project(s) in order to continuously improve them. The goals, purposes, inputs, and outputs of the project are given in more detail, as required in the project paper, in the logical framework matrix (logframe) below.

This project is one of a group of similar projects that a bilateral assistance agency has funded recently. The agency seeks to determine whether it was too hasty in abandoning community development twenty years ago, and hopes to determine from these projects whether community development can be used as an effective instrument for agricultural and rural development.

PART TWO: STUDY QUESTIONS

The following practice exercises may be used with this case study.

1. For both midterm and end-of-project evaluation, (*a*) identify where they fit in the logic of the logframe, and (*b*) identify specific measurements that could (should) be made and the major method to be used for each. Note that for (*b*) a number of different types might apply.

2. Focus on community development as you understand it, and use activity precedence diagrams to work out the details between the inputs and outputs of the logframe. Having done so, create mini logframes in which you identify the verifiable indicators of each task and the critical assumptions on which the task is contingent.

3. Where do the three major functions of community development evaluation (evaluation in community development, evaluation of community development programs and projects, and evaluation of the community development enterprise as a whole) fit into the evaluation tasks identified in the case study?

PARTIAL LOGFRAME FOR CASE STUDY

Goal Level

Major Goal or Goals	Verifiable Indicators	Means of Verification	Critical Assumptions
Decreased soil erosion without reducing agricultural productivity	Measures of soil erosion and agricultural production in watershed	Before/after comparisons of agricultural statistical data	1) That improved technologies can be found 2) That supporting institutions remain viable

Purpose (*Objective*) *Levels*

Purposes	Verifiable Indicators (or End-of-Project Status)	Means of Verification	Critical Assumptions
1) Develop and disseminate soil-conserving practices	10% of farmers in watershed using improved practices developed	1) Data generated by project evaluation component 2) Ministry of agriculture data	1) That time frame is adequate 2) That no crises (weather, political crises, etc.) interfere
2) Develop and disseminate more productive agricultural practices	25% of farmers in watershed improved practices developed	1) Date generated by project evaluation component	1) That time frame is adequate 2) That no crises (weather, political crises, etc.) interfere
3) Develop and put in place CD methods for achieving change in agricultural practices	1) All PVOs using a selected CD methodology 2) 50% of local communities have CD organization and program	Data generated by projected evaluation component	1) Local CD technicians can be recruited and trained 2) CD is found acceptable in local culture
4) Viable PVOs supporting CD in local communities	PVOs provide effective training and logistical support to local CD organizations	Project evaluation and evaluation of key stakeholders (e.g., ministry of agriculture)	External influences not weaken PVOs or change their commitment

Output Levels

Outputs	Verifiable Indicators (numerical goals)	Means of Verification	Critical Assumptions
1) Farmer co-operators obtained for field trials	At least 10 in each of 10 communities	Project records	
2) Soil conserving technologies identified, screened, and field tested	At least 50 different technologies	Project records	Ministry of agriculture and international centers provide information and materials promptly
3) More productive agricultural practices identified, screened, and field tested	At least 50 different technologies	Project records	(Same as above)
4) CD-based extension mechanism in place, effectively extending technology	See above under Purposes 1 and 2	Project records	(Same as above)
5) CD models developed detailed, implemented, and field tested	Four different models documented and applied in field by PVOs	Project and PVO records	1) PVOs are capable of implementing CD in the field 2) Four distinct models can be identified
6) Evaluation method designed and in use by local CD organizations	Evidence of use of explicit feedback or action research by local groups	Project and PVO records, interviews with community participants	Cultural acceptability of evaluation methods

7) Umbrella organization supporting PVOs in place, providing technical and logistical support	Existence of organization, necessary advisory bodies, etc.	Project information, interviews with major stake-holders	Local govern-ment can assign necessary staff

(Much more detail can be provided concerning project outputs.)

Input Levels

Inputs	Indicator

1) Technical Assistance:
  1 Chief-of-Party
  1 Agronomist
  1 Horticulturist
  1 CD specialist
  1 Socio-economist
  1 Accountant/mgt. specialist
	Numbers of person-months, etc.; specification of qualifications

2) Materials and equipment	Quantitative parameters, detailed by types
3) Financing of PVOs through umbrella organization	Amounts, detailed by different functions

12. An Overview of Community Development in America

1. How would you describe the community movement?

2. When did a distinctive body of community development literature begin to appear? Why?

3. Give an example of a social service project with community development overtones.

4. What has been the primary focus of settlement houses? Are they related to community development? If so, how?

5. What is Biddle's major criticism of urban development programs?

6. What was the major purpose of organizing rural area development committees in the 1960s?

7. What does *CRD* refer to and when did its usage begin?

8. What was President Lyndon Johnson's first major domestic program?

9. What was the federal government's response to demands for more local control over federal spending on community improvement programs?

10. What are the six or seven most significant events in the history of community development? Why?

13. An Overview of International Community Development

1. International community development, described as a national program with a national, hierarchical bureaucracy, is located with the executive office of the president, above the respective ministries (or secretaries of departments). Answer the following questions about this structure:

 a. What advantages does this kind of national community development structure have? Why do you think it was used?

 b. What disadvantages does it have, and why might it have failed?

2. Many less developed countries (LDCs) are single-party states. In these countries it is common to require that members of the bureaucracy (e.g., community development specialists, agricultural extension agents, public works officials) carry out certain responsibilities in mobilizing the population to follow the party's ideology. In others, which allow several or many political parties, bureaucrats are formally prevented from engaging in politics and in such mobilization. Discuss the implications that these two political structures might have for implementing community development. Consider that community development is, itself, a form of mobilization, especially in *Animation Rurale*.

3. Why is community development sometimes viewed as an especially attractive strategy in LDCs?

14. Theoretical Approaches for a Global Community

1. Describe how the changing world economy is currently affecting local communities. How might they be affected in the future?

2. We now recognize that changes in the world economy affect the economies of small communities.

    a. Does this change what can be done in small communities?

    b. Is there still room for planned, locally based change, and can local people get things done?

    c. Are there still opportunities for local entrepreneurship?

    d. Have the changes in the world economy opened up new opportunities in small communities?

3. Contrast neoclassical community theory and development theory. Discuss development *of* and *in* a community. How do they complement one another?

4. Contrast and compare systems theory with network theory. How do these theories treat people, locality, change, and social interactions?

5. What is the role of technology in relation to networks, locality, change, and local initiative?

15. *The Future for Community Development*

1. Community development might be seen as development *in* the community and/or as development *of* the community in a local population. How do these different perspectives affect our understanding of the future for community development?

2. If current trends in society seem to work against community development, what is the justification for promoting community development in the future? Exactly what does community development have to offer for social well-being?

3. Can space-free networks comprise a community? What are the implications of the development of space-free networks for the future of community development?

4. In the study of a specific community, what evidence could be gathered to determine whether the community is best understood as a social system or as a social field?

5. What are the major advantages and disadvantages of a very large population and a very small population, respectively, for community development? What strategies could be best used to promote community development in each of these settings, considering these advantages and disadvantages?

6. Give a critical appraisal of the argument that spatial inequality is encouraged by the development of a global society and has the effect of constraining community development at the local level. If this is a valid argument, what can be done – through local action, by national policy, or in sciences and education – to promote community development in the future?

7. Contrast Blakely's view of change and local development with that of Wilkenson's. Discuss *place* for each.

    a. What are the assumptions and values that form the foundation for each of their statements?

    b. What evidence do they give to support their views?

    c. Do these presentations conform to the definitions of *community* and *community development* presented in Chapter 1?

    d. How do these presentations relate to those in Chapter 9 on economic development and in Chapter 10 on local organization and leadership development?

Contributing Authors

Notes on the Editors

JAMES A. CHRISTENSON is professor and chair of the Department of Sociology at the University of Kentucky. He is former president of the Rural Sociological Society, former president of the Anthropologists and Sociologists of Kentucky, former editor of the *Rural Sociology* journal, and has received numerous other awards and recognitions. He has coauthored or edited three books, including *The Cooperative Extension Service: A National Assessment* (Westview 1984), has written over one hundred articles and reports, and has been active in national and international task forces and policy committees.

JERRY W. ROBINSON, JR., is professor of sociology and rural sociology at the University of Illinois, Urbana–Champaign, with appointments in three colleges — Agriculture, Liberal Arts, and Medicine. His primary contributions to community development have been through his writings and extension work in organization development and human relations, especially in conflict and stress management. He served as editor of the *Journal of the Community Development Society* from 1976 to 1979.

Notes on the Contributors

EDWARD J. BLAKELY is professor and chair of the Department of City and Regional Planning at the University of California-Berkeley. He is the author of over fifty scholarly articles and several books on community and economic development, including *Rural Communities in Advanced Industrial Society* (with Ted Bradshaw; Praeger 1980) and Community Development Research (Human Sciences Press 1979). He has served as an advisor to many national task forces on rural and community development and most recently (1986) as Senior Fulbright Fellow in industrial policy in Sweden.

MARCIE BREWSTER is an agricultural economist for a federally sponsored, technology-information–dissemination program for farmers and community leaders. She has an M.S. degree from the University of Arkansas-Fayetteville. She spent two years in Togo, West Africa, as a Peace Corps volunteer, teaching agriculture at the secondary school level. As a graduate student, she spent ten months researching traditional bean production and its relationship to socioeconomic characteristics of farming systems in Rwanda. Her interests include small farm systems for the United States and community development strategies for agricultural communities.

LEE J. CARY is professor emeritus of community development at the University of Missouri–Columbia. He has had considerable experience in class and field teaching in community development, extension assignments, and applied research. He is a founding member and the first president of the Community Development Society, editor and coauthor of *Community Development as a Process,* and coauthor of the training series, Community Development–FFA Style. Working with colleagues Jack Timmons and Don Littrell, he has taken major responsibility for a module on developing leadership in the national program: Working with Our Publics: In-Service Education for Extension. He continues his research activities and writing in the field of community development.

BOYD FAULKNER is professor emeritus of community development at the University of Missouri–Columbia. He served as a community development advisor in Afghanistan, Iran, and Tanzania for the U.S. Agency for International Development for thirteen years as well as an extension agent for the U.S. Bureau of Indian Affairs for thirteen years.

FRANK A. FEAR is associate professor in the Department of Resource Development at Michigan State University. He serves as the department's associate chairperson and coordinates the department's graduate program in community development. He teaches courses in community development theory and practice. Current research efforts focus on community leadership development and planned change strategies within communities and organizations. He has served on the boards of professional organizations at the state and national levels. In 1986 he was the first person to be named Person of the Year by the Michigan Community Development Society. He is a consultant for a diverse set of public and private sector organizations. Recent clients include the W. K. Kellogg Foundation, the Michigan Department of Health, and the Salvation Army.

KIM FENDLEY has an M.S. degree in rural sociology from the University of Arkansas–Fayetteville. She is currently a Ph.D. candidate at the University of Kentucky. Her work focuses on demography and community development. Her dissertation involves a panel study of social and economic development in the forty-one counties impacted by the location of the Toyota plant in central Kentucky.

MARIE ARNOT FISCHER is a professor in the Department of Community and Regional Planning at the University of Nebraska. She teaches courses in human services planning, planning with low-income persons and minorities, working effectively with groups, persons writing grants, and fund-raising. She was formerly the director of the Community Affairs Division at the Nebraska Department of Economic Development. She has had extensive experience as a trainer with groups such as the international General Federation of Women's Clubs, the PTA, the National Rural Electric Cooperatives, and HUD; and frequently is a planning consultant to state and local governmental bodies and human services agencies. Among her publications are two books, *For Better or Worse* and *The Volunteer Organization Handbook* (coauthored with Lee J. Cary and Mary Jean Houde), and numerous journal articles. She has served as secretary-treasurer and as president of the Community Development Society.

FREDERICK FISHER is president of IDIOM, a private firm involved in international development work. His professional work experiences include serving as urban management advisor to the Regional Housing and Development Office for East and Southern Africa, USAID; associate professor of community development at Pennsylvania State University; director of professional development at the International City Management Association; vice president of the National Training and Development Service; and city manager of Grove City and State College, Pennsylvania. He has consulted with a wide range of organizations in over twenty countries, including the People's Republic of China, India, Bangladesh, Syria, Japan, Chile, Brazil, Australia, Philippines, Indonesia, Malaysia, Canada, Kuwait, and twelve African countries. His publications include over eighty articles, monographs, book chapters, and position papers on management, organization, community development, and training.

LARRY GAMM is associate professor of health administration at Pennsylvania State University. He is professor-in-charge of graduate studies in health policy and administration and a member of the community systems planning and development and the policy analysis graduate programs. He has published in the areas of interorganizational relations, organizational change, intergovernmental policy, community development, voluntarism, and health and human services administration. He has consulted with national and state governmental and voluntary agencies, regional and local governmental units, public utilities, and health service organizations.

LORRAINE E. GARKOVICH is associate professor of sociology at the University of Kentucky. Her research activities focus on the relationships between population and community change, and farm families and community change. She also serves as a consultant to a wide variety of community and state organizations. She has recently written *Rural Population Change in America* (Greenwood Press 1989).

DARYL HOBBS is professor of rural sociology and director of the Office of Social and Economic Data Analysis at the University of Missouri–Columbia. He has a wide range of rural development research and project experience – both domestic and international. He is a former president of the Rural Sociological Society and coeditor of the book: *Rural Society in the U.S.: Issues for the 1980s* (Westview 1980).

E. FREDERICK LIST is associate professor and extension specialist in the Department of Community Development at the University of Missouri–Columbia. He has served as a community consultant at Southern Illinois University and is particularly concerned with group process in community development and the design and implementation of community attitude surveys.

DONALD W. LITTRELL is associate professor and state extension community development specialist in the Department of Community Development at the University of Missouri–Columbia. In 1986 he was awarded a Fulbright professorship at Prince of Songkla, University of Southern Thailand, where he was involved in designing community development courses and developing a community development extension program. He is widely known for incorporating theory and practice and has been a consultant/trainer for state, regional, national, and international groups. He is also author of *The Theory and Practice of Community Development: A Guide for Practitioners.*

BRYAN M. PHIFER is professor and extension specialist in the Department of Community Development at the University of Missouri–Columbia. He is a former director of the University Extension Community and Public Sector Programs and served as assistant director of Community Resource Development for the Extension Service at the U.S. Department of Agriculture in Washington, D.C.

RON SHAFFER is professor of agricultural economics and community development economist at the University of Wisconsin–Madison. His extension responsibilities include working with community groups to build economic development strategies and to understand local and nonlocal forces affecting community economic development. He has performed research on the local economic impacts of economic development, on the sources of employment change, on identifying types of economic development most likely to employ specific types of workers, and on the functioning of rural capital markets. He teaches a course for graduate students on community economic analysis. He has served as an advisor on economic development policies to the state of Wisconsin, the Organization for Economic and Cooperative Development (OECD), and the National Council on Urban Economic Development. From 1980 to 1981 he was a visiting professor at the Institute of Industrial Economics in Bergen, Norway.

GENE F. SUMMERS is professor of rural sociology at the University of Wisconsin–Madison. He received a Ph.D. from the University of Tennessee where he was an NDEA Fellow. He also was an NIMH postdoctoral fellow at the University of Wisconsin and was a Fulbright Senior Research Fellow at the University of Bergen, Norway, in 1978. He has held teaching appointments at the University of Tennessee, Indiana State University, Vanderbilt University, and the University of Illinois. He also has been a Distinguished Visiting Professor at the University of South Florida and Guelph University (Canada), and president of the Rural Sociological Society from 1989 to 1990. His publications include eight books and monographs, numerous book chapters, and journal articles in several academic fields (social psychology, economics, community development, and rural sociology).

DONALD E. VOTH is professor of rural sociology at the University of Arkansas–Fayetteville where he teaches and does research in rural and community development, international agricultural development and farming systems research, and project and program design and evaluation. He holds M.S. and Ph.D. degrees in rural sociology and Southeast Asian studies from Cornell University, and taught for five years in the Community Development Department at Southern Illinois University. He serves on the boards of the Community Development Society and the Arkansas chapter of the Community Development Society. He has also served as president of the latter and as secretary of the Rural Sociological Society.

PAUL D. WARNER is assistant director for community development and staff training with the Kentucky Cooperative Extension Service and professor and extension specialist in the Department of Sociology at the University of Kentucky. He is serving as president of the Community Development Society from 1989 to 1990. His work has focused on community development, leadership development and organizational management, program development and evaluation, and survey methods. He has piloted new approaches in the delivery of employment services, the use of paraprofessional community development workers, and the identification of community needs. He is coauthor of the book *The Cooperative Extension Service: A National Assessment* (Westview 1980).

KENNETH P. WILKINSON is professor of rural sociology at Pennsylvania State University. He is engaged in teaching, research, and writing on collective action and social change in small towns and rural areas. He is a graduate of Mississippi State University, where he studied community theory with Harold F. Kaufman. His work elaborates on the concept of the community as a social field. In recent years, he has concentrated on the implications of rural policy for community development and social well-being. He is a former president of the Rural Sociological Society.

Author Index

Subject Index